The Farthing Poet

The Farthing Poet

A Biography of Richard Hengist Horne
1802–84

A Lesser Literary Lion

ANN BLAINEY

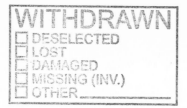

LONGMANS

LONGMANS, GREEN AND CO LTD
48 Grosvenor Street, London W1
*Associated companies, branches and representatives
throughout the world*

*Printed in Great Britain by
The Shenval Press, London, Hertford and Harlow*

Contents

1968(B-353)X

List of Illustrations

Chapter 1

Blood of Youth

That fine essayist and literary leech, Edmund Gosse, described Richard
Henry[1] Horne when an old man as 'gay, tactless and vain to a remarkable degree'. 'An amusing study,' he went on, 'to those who could be
patient with his peculiarities . . . an incredible mixture of affectation and
fierceness, humour and absurdity, enthusiasm and ignorance, with his
incoherency of appearance at once so effeminate and muscular.' He
reminded Gosse of a curly white poodle, particularly when he threw
himself on a sofa and rolled about in a most undignified way for a man
in his seventies. 'And yet he had a fine buoyant spirit, and a generous
imagination with it all. But the oddity of it, alas!'

Gosse's view was typical among Horne's younger literary friends.
He was an oddity in personal appearance and literary career; a diverting
paradoxical little Bohemian. For a mere seven years he had written with
a 'fugitive vitality' that had culminated in a brief burst of fame in his
forty-first year when he published his epic poem *Orion* and sold it for
a farthing. But for the following forty years he was no more than an
'inspired scribbler', 'a curious and pathetic literary phenomenon'.

At the time of Horne's death in 1884, his obituaries had predicted
that 'so strange and vivacious a personage will surely not lack a
biographer' but they were underestimating the waning interest in the
Victorians. Moreover there were those like Gosse who argued that to
explain the disparity in standard between *Orion* and the rubbish Horne
had poured out at the end of his life 'was beyond all skill of the literary
historian'. Horne was to be left alone for three-quarters of a century:
he was remembered as a fat little poodle reclining on a plush pre-
Raphaelite sofa and shaking his milk-white curls as he played a rib-
boned guitar.

[1] Horne was later to change his name to Hengist.

And yet how different is the picture of Horne in the year 1823 when he wrote dramatically, 'I first took to scribbling, and resolved upon literary success.' He was then a pale serious youth of twenty with sloping spaniel eyes and curling auburn hair, his face already possessing the dramatic quality that the poetess Elizabeth Browning was to describe as 'fifth act', the face of a devil or an angel. Sitting in his study in his mother's house in St James's Place, Hampstead Road, he spent day after day pondering those strange inexpressible moods he felt within himself and wondering if these were really the signs of poetic genius.

Horne was born in the small village of Edmonton, set amid green meadows on the outskirts of London, just as the bells of the square church-tower rang in the new year of 1803. He later felt he had been set apart from his fellow men from the very beginning, for although it was officially recorded as December 31, 1802, Horne was never able to make up his mind on which day or in which year he had been born. His family was middle class and financially secure, thanks to the endeavour of his grandmother. She was the least socially acceptable but the shrewdest member and undeniable head of the household: in her grandson's words, 'a most kindhearted, sensible practical sort of woman; not exactly vulgar, though somewhat coarse and of no education beyond the most ordinary. To be frank in the matter she was not a lady.' She had come as a housekeeper to Richard Horne, the poet's grandfather, who was secretary to the naval hero Sir John Jervis, later Earl St Vincent, and had risen with his master to be first clerk of the Admiralty. He, admiring his housekeeper's 'sterling domestic qualities', had married her. Lady or no, after her husband's death Sarah Horne enhanced the already adequate family fortunes by marrying a very rich merchant.

Her second marriage appears to have alienated her only child James Horne, the poet's father. Regrettably, no evidence is left of James Horne apart from a studiously impartial account written by his son, and even that has large gaps. He was 'probably at school' when his mother remarried, and 'probably the youth resented his stepfather and of a consequence he ran away to sea', but where he went none of them knew. He returned home, probably once again because he could not bear the hardships of the sea, and then followed a succession of employments and debts that his doting mother hurried to pay. Reviewing what he knew of his father Horne tried hard to be fair, but he could find little extenuating to say because, despite the efforts of friends and family, the restless adolescent grew into a dissolute adult. A half-hearted attempt at law was followed by a present from his mother of a lieutenancy in the Royal Glamorganshire Militia where, his son remarked, 'he seems to have spent a great deal of money'; and the militia steered him to his true profession – at the gaming tables of London, with a glass in his hand. Drifting, drinking, gambling, and owing so much that even his mother with her recently inherited second fortune had difficulty in paying, his story was a difficult one to excuse. And yet his son was forced to acknowledge that James Horne had personal attraction; a reprobate he might have been, but a charming one.

It was then, in the cynical words of his son, that 'one day in a temporary state of handsome reformation he saw, and fell in love with', Maria Partridge, the poet's mother. She was 'a beautiful and bright-hearted girl of eighteen', who had, in addition, a few thousand pounds' fortune. Sarah was delighted, saw it as the means of reclaiming him, and took the newly married pair to live at Edmonton where she was living with her new husband, the Reverend Samuel Tice. But James's reformation was temporary, his restlessness continued, and the brightness faded from Maria's heart.

Into this atmosphere of disillusion and uncertainty their eldest child was born; he was baptized Richard Henry after his paternal grandfather on St Valentine's Day 1803 at the Edmonton Parish Church of All Saints. In the following years there were two more sons: Frederic born on March 27, 1806, and James on March 28, 1808. Nine months before the youngest child's birth, James Horne, who had 'gone through his money too soon' and therefore was forced to enter the army, became Quartermaster in the Sixty-First Foot. He was subsequently ordered to the garrison at Guernsey, a military stronghold during the current Napoleonic wars. There his wife joined him, leaving Richard with Sarah Tice at Edmonton.

If Richard were not old enough to realize his father's shortcomings he could still sense the insecurity of his home, especially, one suspects, when in his fifth year his parents went abroad. From his account of his childhood he seems to have clung to his grandmother and his nurse; to his grandmother in particular, who seems to have undertaken his upbringing, teaching him to walk and to read and thereby opening up the physical world and the mental world of books for his exploration. Seventy years later he was able to write that 'her aged, wrinkled, snuffy finger, and sometimes a silver bodkin, are palpably before me, pointing the first steps of the way'. He was close, too, to his nurse, his 'dear Anne', the confessor to whom he confided those 'secrets of a painful and terrifying kind' that beset his early childhood. His feelings for his parents are much less apparent. It seems likely, though, that the child who in adulthood could remark that 'grown-up people should be extremely careful and circumspect with regard to certain things they do and say in our little-pitchered presence' and that he himself had 'many keen and sore recollections of maltreatment of this kind' understood more of the divisions of his family than they realized. It also seems likely, from his adult view of the situation and the evidence of the close bonds that later existed between himself and his mother, that in such conflicts his loyalties would have lain more with mother than father. His *Recollections of Childhood*, a series of vividly remembered episodes written at the end of his life, provide an even fuller emotional barometer of his childhood than their author intended, and there emerges the picture of an excitable and highly imaginative little boy, capable of 'extreme though unintelligent emotions', violent resentments, and fantasies. What a volcano lay beneath the surface of the child the adults do not seem to have recognized. 'I have been told in after years,' Horne wrote, 'that I was a good child amusing myself by myself and giving as little trouble as possible.'

One event that concerned him did, however, penetrate the adult minds around him. It occurred, according to his later recollection, around his fourth year and was the most disturbing and vividly recalled of all his early memories: 'Somewhere about the age of four I committed my first sins. The worst, and by far the most serious, painful and haunting of these shall now be narrated. It amounted to a tragedy or, at least, to the acts and emotions of one, with all the remorse and horror upon an infant scale, yet not the less real to me.' Further on he described it as 'murder'. He had been given a leather doll by a friend of his grandmother; not a suitable thing, he complained, to be given to a small boy, who does not want to be lavishing love on a doll. Soon after, a 'bad accident' had knocked out its left eye, and in attempting to mend it he made the eye-hole larger, which gave the doll's face a hideous look. Finally he decided to destroy it altogether and began to hit it with a wooden mallet, each blow producing a terrifying dull squelch. The next part of the narrative is so emotionally charged that Horne's own words must describe it:

And Oh! far worse to me, for the expression of the battered face changed from anguish to menace – from defiance and threats to tortured horror – and, at last, it had a ghastly mutilated smile! Being quite unable to endure this, with chattering teeth I wrapped it round in some old matting, and hurrying to a remote part of the garden, buried it. I felt that I had murdered my doll in the most

4

barbarous manner. Its hideous, mutilated face haunted me from day
to day. On the third day, hoping that it was not only quite dead, so
to speak – that is to say, that it had gone to pieces beneath the damp
mould, I went and dug it up. What dismay was mine! From the
rains and earth stains it was more frightful than ever! Gathering
several large stones I gashed them again and again, in frantic manner, upon the wincing leathern body, which, being hollow, vented
at each blow a sort of husky squeak that made me respond in
smothered cries. Nothing could be done but to bury it again, which
I accomplished in a state very like delirium.

After miserable and terrified days and nights his guilt forced him to
confess to his nurse. This was sin and he expected retribution, so that
when his grandfather, the Minister of God, came to his bedside with a
rushlight, he lay trembling awaiting the expected punishment. However, the old man merely murmured prayers and called him an innocent
lamb; and his grandmother had the family gardener burn the doll, and
the ashes were shown to the child. His fears were calmed and 'Richard
was himself again'. Or almost so; for the physical symptoms of illness
seem to have lasted somewhat longer and finally merged, according to
his later memory, with an attack of measles.

It is impossible to discover the circumstances surrounding the story.
The dating is vague, the comings and goings of the Horne family at
this time are vague. One does not know when Mrs Horne joined her
husband in Guernsey, whether she gave birth to her third son in
Edmonton or Guernsey, which of the other children remained behind
with Richard, or when they rejoined their parents; there are no satisfactory answers to any of the questions. The most that can be said is
that the phrase 'about the age of four' could refer to the time when his
mother was in Guernsey; significantly no reference to her appears in
the story. Or, stretching the timing a little, the phrase might cover that
notoriously distressing event in the life of any child, the birth of a
brother. In that event it was either Horne's youngest brother James,
born soon after his fifth birthday, or Frederic, born three months after
his third birthday – rivals whom a resentful small boy (to echo Horne's
narrative) may well have considered unsuitable presents and not
something to lavish love on. Whatever the causes the event seems to
have been so important that it cannot be ignored. It haunted his
imagination for almost eighty years and its images often found their
way into his work. Mutilated heroes, rotting bodies often exhumed
from the grave, blindness and maiming sadistically inflicted, the tor-

tures of murderous guilt: they were subjects popular with many Romantic writers, yet so intensely and persistently do they appear in Horne's writing that one suspects they had a personal fascination beyond the demands of mere literary influence. And never were they more forcibly expressed than in his mythological autobiography, *Orion*, whose poet-hero lies, like the doll in the Edmonton garden, helpless on the ground while his eyes are viciously put out. Whatever the connection between the doll and Horne's later poetic plots and symbols, one thing is clear: most of the qualities revealed in the child in the story were to be attributes of Horne the man. The sadistic impulses and rebelliousness he was to be aware of in himself with varying degrees of consciousness and guilt in all his adult life; and probably their emotional origins were buried at least as far back as that period of childhood.

The following period of Horne's early childhood appears equally unsettling. He left the comparative security of the Tice home and joined his parents for a time in Guernsey. Then, on April 16, 1810, his father died. Among his earliest childhood recollections is one in which, as a very small child in his nurse's arms, he watched the funeral procession of the great naval hero Nelson from a tea merchant's balcony opposite St Paul's, and became so overwrought at the plumes and muffled drums and endless trappings of death that his alarmed mother ordered his nurse to take him away. What, one wonders, must have been the reaction of an imaginative seven-year-old boy to a nearer taste of death and its trappings – the death of a father towards whom he bore feelings almost certainly equivocal. Included in his *Recollections of Childhood* is the projected title for an account of his father's death, but it was never written.

After the death of James Horne, the family settled down in Edmonton. Unfortunately James had named as guardian for his children his close friend and family physician, Dr Maule, for whom small Richard felt intense dislike, dating, he claimed, from that time shortly after the doll incident when he was ill with what was diagnosed as measles: Maule had said 'as though I had been deaf, or nobody, that sometimes pigs were afflicted with measles' and this, explained Horne, 'hurt my dignity'. The animosity was to grow considerably and to include Maule's son, slightly older than himself, who later became a judge and with whom, in childhood, Horne seems to have felt some amount of rivalry.

Young Richard grew to love Edmonton as he roamed its gentle countryside, fishing and swimming in its streams, exploring its boisterous country fairs, particularly the big fair at Edmonton: three fairs rolled into one extending from the field behind the *Bell*, characterized by its sign of a harassed John Gilpin minus hat and wig, to the field behind the *Angel* with its sign of a buxom dairymaid in a white calico shift and wings. That fair was full of bands and dancing, gingerbread and bulls' eyes, swings and waxworks and travelling theatres, to say nothing of Polito's menagerie with its scarlet-coated attendants and mangy Bengal tiger, and the side-shows concealing albinos and dwarfs. They were blissful adventures for a small boy. If he tired of them there were beggars sitting by the bridge with hair-raising tales of wounds received at Trafalgar, or gypsies in the surrounding fields in little dingy blanket tents – the women sunburned and seductive in red cloaks and suckling their babies, the men lazily smoking pipes. These memories were the credit side of childhood, long cherished.

On the credit side, too, were the games among the trees and graves of the churchyard or in the shadow of the old church walls. A medieval monk named Peter Fabel was said to have cheated the devil there and it was a story young Richard Horne loved. Indeed, he loved Edmonton passionately. His highly active imagination had begun to flow into creative channels. He responded most markedly to tales of Red Riding Hood and David and Goliath and the more sophisticated Robinson Crusoe and Don Quixote. He had watched with rapture the travelling theatres at the fairs; and his grandfather, that whimsical old clergyman and scholar, Dr Tice (who was said to have been the original of William Combe's parody of picturesque travellers, Dr Syntax), was quick to foster the interest. A theatre-lover himself, he took the child on exciting excursions to the great London theatres in post-chaise and pair with lamps for the dark homeward journey. It was a delicious experience for the small boy who sat in the theatre, 'ears, eyes and nerves' all alert, weeping unashamedly with his 'reverend grandsire' over John Philip Kemble's tragic utterances and the great clown Grimaldi's magnificent pantomime. He never forgot those early theatrical performances which did much to ignite his own dramatic ambitions; the most minute details remained so vividly in his mind that seventy years later he would be able to recall, with an extraordinary intensity, the terror he had felt watching the incomparable clown miming the dagger scene from *Macbeth*, and with what commiserating delight he had watched him as an 'Oyster Crossed in Love'. Visits to the theatre were the highlights of childhood.

School life was less absorbing. He was sent at first to nearby Enfield, to the establishment run by the Reverend John Clarke, father of the

7

future writer Charles Cowden Clarke. It was renowned alike for its distinguished pupil John Keats, its liberal atmosphere, and its ornate architecture – the façade of red brick moulded with flowers, pomegranates and cherubs now preserved by the Victoria and Albert Museum. Clarke's pupils were mostly the sons of tradesmen and his syllabus included practical subjects that may even have proved useful to a future poet, and certainly found response in Horne. He believed in encouraging the good rather than beating the devil out of his young charges. The grammar school to which young Richard was probably later transferred at Edmonton was less enlightened and, as might perhaps have been expected for so sensitive a child, was not a happy experience. His only recorded comment of schooldays was the heading in his projected autobiography: 'School miseries'.

When he was sixteen Horne's relatively peaceful Edmonton life came to an end and his family sought a career for him. There were a number of alternatives, but with the memory of James Horne behind them the family's uncertainty was understandable. He may have been intended for the church. In an article published in 1847, part fiction, part fact, he said that his 'father intended me for the church'; and with his own exalted sense of sin he may have welcomed a calling in which he had a chance of doing penance through religious service. This was more than suggested in his attitude, five years later, in choosing that other sacred vocation of poet. But the practical side of the family character came uppermost and Horne was entered for the Royal Military College at Sandhurst, with the idea that he might later enter the East India Service. The decision was inspired perhaps by his most exalted ancestor, an eighteenth-century John Horne of the East India Company, who had distinguished himself at Gamroon in Persia in 1729.

When Horne entered Sandhurst in April 1819 the institution was approaching a peak in its reputation for bullying, brutality and corruption, which subsequent reforms would later rectify. The gates he entered, however, were still those of a school much given to licensed sadism and tyranny, and therefore unlikely to soothe or tame a turbulent, sensitive adolescent whose violent instincts and capacity for feeling had already been demonstrated in the incident with the doll. And certainly there was rebellion in that year he spent at Sandhurst but, even more evidently, there were the first visible signs of Horne's capacity for suffering, a capacity which was to grow. He found satisfaction in suffering, and furthermore he believed that it was a necessity for him and that he was destined to suffer. No doubt, amid rigid, harsh and oppressive discipline, he found ample opportunities for developing such attitudes, if only as a defence and compensation for the misery of hours passed in the punishment cell – '*vulgo*, the Black Hole' – on a diet of bread and water. The emotional origins of these views, one suspects, were buried deep in childhood – witness the readiness of the murderer of the doll to suffer – but it was probably at Sandhurst that they found, for the first time, intellectual and conscious form.

Whatever their origins, these ideas appear in the earliest of his poems to survive. Composed during a spell in the Black Hole, in 'darkness with bread and water to nourish the love of slaughter', he saw that in fact such suffering nourished a flower of a different kind in him; that he was in fact different to other students who had hung their heads on that hard wooden pillow,

> *Out of this long, long darkness and solitude,*
> *This aching silence, and this audible heart –*
> *Something shall rise, therefore dull wood*
> *And vault – like walls, yet act a fostering part.*

What was to rise, what was to be fostered, he did not yet know.

But for this shaft of hope his time at Sandhurst might have been unendurable: 'objectless and interminable drudgery', according to his later description, of 'studies, drills, parades, guards, sentries, bread and water and the "black hole" '. His marks grew progressively worse, though he was by no means stupid. The comprehensive academic course included mathematics, philosophy, classics, astronomy, natural history and religion as well as military subjects, but he did well only in military drawing, where he claimed that his short eyesight helped him to draw the numerous fine lines with ease. At the end of the probationary year he was withdrawn, having in the words of the official record 'failed to pass probation'.

He returned home disgraced. Hating Sandhurst had been one thing, but being rejected by it was quite another, and for such an unexciting reason as failing his examinations. He felt it keenly, but over the following years the actual rejection came to matter much less than the reason, and when later he read how his hero, the poet Shelley, had been expelled from Oxford for professing atheism, he was able to claim with pride that 'one of the highest honours that can attend a youth's onset in life is to be expelled from college for manifesting a resistance to servile ignorance and brutal tyranny'. It was generally, he went on with his own experience obviously in mind, 'a wild escape from dull, turgid words, innumerable rules, an dry, marrowless systems, into

B   9

riotous illumination of the spirit . . . reckless defiance, exuberant folly'.

With the self-delusory ease with which inconvenient memories can be so easily forgotten, the real reasons for his withdrawal began to be submerged in more exciting ones in which there may or may not have been some truth. What mattered was that they embodied, on a school-boy scale, the spirit of Shelley's atheistic manifesto. He himself was expelled, he said, for having been 'reported to the Horse Guards three times for insubordination' – for tying a pig's tail on the mathematics master, for swimming in a lake out of bounds, and for leading a rebellion and caricaturing the Principal. In this form his Sandhurst experiences were to be recounted to numerous admiring or unwilling listeners in later years. He posed as the rebel, the adventurer, the essence of the Romantic poet.

Whatever the schoolboy pranks he might ascribe to himself, he was decidedly a schoolboy no longer. When he returned to the home his mother had now taken in St James's Place, Hampstead Road – the Hornes invariably lived on the Edmonton side of London – he was a fortnight off his eighteenth birthday, an age he once recalled 'when human emotions collect, concentrate and culminate; when the vital stream, the sap of life . . . presently finds itself meeting, coalescing, and fusing with the equally torrid glow of youthful Imagination'. He had already been in love once with a girl from the school at Edmonton, run by Shelley's feminist friend Elizabeth Hitchener. Sitting over his solitary studies he often found his mind turning from his books to 'forms and pictures of beauty and passion' – thoughts that were often 'dominant, and often overmastering'.

The studies themselves were partly to blame. Much of his reading lay among the gloomy wanderers, merciless women and satanic lovers of Byron's poetry – the combination of forbidden passion, suffering and pleasure that so preoccupied Romantic poetic taste. He was ab-sorbed in everything which 'shocks the virtuous philosopher' and 'delights the chameleon poet', as John Keats put it. Sandhurst, too, had been partly to blame. In those blessed 'suspension of studies' when the young gentleman cadets had thrown themselves into tandems and post-chaises and rushed up to town, he had learnt a taste for mild excursions into 'the all-pervading licentiousness' of pre-Victorian London. With the other cadets he had indulged in the rounds of tailors, gaming houses, fashionable hotels and theatres, while his money lasted. The first evening of their excursions they always spent in military dress of scarlet dress-coat and brass spurs, rushing through the saloons, lobbies and staircases of Covent Garden and Drury Lane in 'wild and un-speakable delight', often with never a glimpse of the stage, even the licentiousness of the scene being 'noticed more as a dazzling vision and phantasmagoria' or held 'in abeyance for some hours, so wild was the sense of joy at emancipation'.

Only briefly did he follow in the cavalier footsteps of his father. He had mapped himself out a strenuous course of study which embraced music, painting, literature, and philosophy. The Romantic movement, that amorphous and violent surging of ideas, now absorbed his desires: to know all aspects of human experience, to explore every facet of the human personality, to tear down the crumbling values and customs of artificial society and build them anew. To feel was to live; to fight and suffer for humanity and liberty one of the highest goals. It was a philosophy of the rebel, the idealist, the introvert, and as such it suited the nature and present state of mind of young Richard Horne perfectly. He felt himself endowed with so many of the Romantic writers' attributes: the 'more than mortal energy' . . . 'more passions than are commonly possessed by any *one* man . . . a nervous desire to do everything I see others do' . . . the unconscious ability to project himself into another's personality with 'fine-wrought intensity'. Even the astringency of the philosophers he studied – Descartes, Hume, Berkeley – was to be tempered by the Romantic climate, and on the first page of his notebook devoted to *Metaphysical Meditations* he amended Descartes' famous statement (*Cogito ergo sum*) to 'I had rather he had said, *Cogito et senito ergo sum* – I think and *feel*, therefore I am'.

As befitted the Byronic hero, he took a tour to study different landscapes and peoples. It was only to Wales and Ireland, the glories of a grand tour being presumably beyond the family means; yet he listened with appropriate ardour to local legends and songs and spent a night in ghostly Caernarvon Castle, among the ruins, in the true style of a student of demonology and the occult. Next day he followed the Byronic example still further by trying to swim an English Hellespont – the straits of Anglesea; no easy swim since the strong current in the centre made it a hazard for even strong swimmers and caused him to swim, he complained, 'nearly six miles before I reached the other side'. Nature had not been overkind to his physique. He was only five feet five inches tall, a fact of which he was always sensitive. He lacked the muscular grace of a hero. He was inclined to fat, but took great pride in developing his strength through exercise, especially swimming, which he had learned in Edmonton streams as a child. At twenty he presented a picture that must have been typical of many a poetic youth at a time when the Byronic legend was so potent a literary influence, and when its originator, the scandalous Lord Byron, was enhancing his poetic and amorous reputation in European exile.

Later Horne was to decide that those whom nature had most neglected in outward form – particularly in height – generally had the greatest 'inward powers of mind'. Now, however, he savoured his poetic appearance carefully: the high pale sloping forehead, the myopic, heavy-lidded, grey eyes, the long and curling auburn hair; his face full of sensitivity, and saved from weakness by its large mouth and somewhat coarse aquiline nose. In his study with its 'wasted lamp', and the pet owl and caged linnet rousing his 'rapt soul to homelier themes' as he worked through the reaches of the night, he believed he presented the correct portrait of a solitary student.

It seems likely that he was encouraged in these studies by his mother. Though the evidence is meagre, the few letters that do survive seem to indicate that Maria Horne's relationship to her eldest son was close, affectionate, and intensely sympathetic. Their tastes appear to have been similar. He could, and did, treat her as an equal in feeling and intellect as well as a parent. He was always carefully deferential to her wishes, and sympathetic to the irritating fits and starts of her 'nervous system' and the constant changes of scene her restlessness urged her to take. For her part it seems possible that she hoped, through this eldest son, to satisfy at second hand – a not uncommon hope among women – some of those artistic cravings which her sex and early marriage had given her no chance of satisfying.

At the same time he was encouraged in his literary enthusiasms by two friends of his own age: a lad named Tom Stone, a surgeon's apprentice like that other poetic lad John Keats; the other the son of a disreputable theatrical manager named William Beverly, whose talent in later life made him a well-known scenic artist. Together in 'loving emulation and friendly competition' young Horne and Stone wrote poetry, a watery mixture of Byron and Moore's *Irish Melodies*, and read philosophy from the same book. They sat on tombstones in the graveyard of St James's Chapel, Hampstead Road, on summer evenings, conducting 'chemical experiments' to an audience of pot boys, nursemaids, and William Beverly. Later, in 1824, they went together to pay homage to Byron's body and followed the funeral cortège on foot for several miles out of London. It was a loss to Horne when Stone eventually went to Edinburgh to study medicine, though their friendship was to last many years and survive even Stone's absorption with fashionable society.

The other friend of these years was Charles Jeremiah Wells. A strange youth almost three years older than Horne, short, snub-nosed, redhaired, and an embryonic poet, Horne had known him since they had been at Clarke's school. Wells had a magnetic and dominating nature, irresistible to people stronger than Horne and curious even for those eccentric circles in which he mixed. At school he had been a rebel, a truant, the school dunce whose energies had gone into fishing in Enfield streams or the imaginative world of his reading and writing. In future years he woul in turn become lawyer, poet, farmer, scholar, recluse and religious mystic who claimed to raise the dead. Now at twenty, he was lazy, vain, aggressive, neglectful of his legal profession; quite irresponsible but decidedly brilliant. Fifty years later Horne confided that Wells had 'the readiest wit and the richest fancy of any man in London. His talk was simply wonderful. He had only to see a man to make him do anything.'

It would seem that Wells could make Horne do anything. Wells had written a long dramatic poem, *Joseph and His Brethren* – his one masterpiece which would delight pre-Raphaelite poets in another fifty years – and he used Horne as transcriber and purveyor of the poem around various reluctant publishers. He also persuaded Horne to lend him money – the money was never repaid – to finance the poem's publication in 1824; the exact sum is uncertain, but was probably the two hundred pounds Horne later mentioned in his book *Exposition of the False Medium*. It was money Horne could ill afford to lose, and a measure of Wells's domination and persuasiveness. A measure too of that domination was to be found in the literary influence Wells exercised over his younger friend. Not least of Wells's accomplishments was his ability to attach himself to brilliant literary friends, whose friendship he guarded jealously, allowing Horne only tantalizing verbal glimpses. Undoubtedly he meant to impress, and certainly he succeeded. Even Wells could not have calculated the effect of these anecdotes on Horne's impressionable, adolescent mind: the worship they encouraged would grow in time to extraordinary proportions.

Wells had been at school at Clarke's with a lad named Tom Keats and through him had come to know his older brothers George and John, intense schoolboys who had admitted Charles Wells to their private literary world where they pored over poetry and myths and wrote each other Spenserian stanzas. It was a world in which Wells flourished, yet from which, despite his intellectual compatibility, he eventually alienated himself. The reasons for his expulsion were strange. He had sent Tom Keats – morbidly sensitive and dying of consumption – a string of love letters as a joke, supposedly from a lady named Amena Bellfillia. Tom had believed them, and been stricken when he discovered the truth, whereupon the brothers had angrily expelled Wells. This was not before Wells had filled his own mind with their brilliance.

One can only assume that it was through Wells that Horne acquired his early and profound veneration of John Keats. There is no evidence he knew the poet personally, though both had been at Clarke's school and Keats had for a time lived at Edmonton. John Keats was seven years older than Horne, which makes their friendship at school unlikely; and Horne himself, never backward in claiming famous friends, made no such claim on Keats. His only reminiscence was how as a small child one snowy afternoon at Edmonton he had been dared by older boys to throw a snowball at the poet, at that time an apprentice of the Edmonton surgeon, as he dozed in his master's gig outside a patient's house. Nor was Horne likely to have learned this veneration from Keats's popular reputation, which, during his short career, was scurrilously blackened by influential critics writing a series of articles called 'The Cockney School of Poetry'; a literary disgrace that brought misery to the victims and caused the death in a duel of one of the critics. The 'Cockney School' articles certainly roused Horne's anger, but it is unlikely that mere partisanship for an insulted poet could have inspired such intense and personal feelings.

It seems, too, that the same assumption must be made about another of the 'Cockney School' victims; a writer who, like Keats, was a friend in these years of Charles Wells and an object of Horne's early and lifelong devotion. In fact Horne was generally to bracket their names together as double objects of his worship. This was William Hazlitt, the critic and essayist, whom Horne could not have known personally, since his first sight of Hazlitt was in September 1830 when he lay in his coffin. Horne adored Hazlitt and it would seem that his veneration could only have come through Wells, who had approached the bitter, unapproachable critic with the excuse that he was 'also a thinker', thus rousing in Hazlitt the perception and generosity that make his work so memorable. Hazlitt took the brash young man into his circle, and Wells's enthusiasm ignited a similar torch in Horne.

Listening to Wells's incessant anecdotes, Horne must have felt like a child peering through glass at coveted sweets: he longed to taste them, and if he could not taste them with his tongue he must taste them by the vicarious means of imagination. In fantasy he tasted and consumed them and in fantasy he *became* them. Horne's overwhelming response to the writing of Wells and Keats and Hazlitt was also based on an instinctive recognition of mutual similarity. As he came to explore his own nature he came to believe that they shared common sensations, longings, energies, compulsions, that they shared a common nature – and a common destiny. This last supposition was disturbing as it was exciting, for the lives of Keats and Hazlitt told a bitter story. The writer, it would seem, could not expect the ordinary contentments of normal men. Keats's life, from the time of his high-spirited Enfield schooldays to his tragic death in Rome, a dedicated and neglected poet, mirrored a struggle inherent in Romantic aesthetics and Romantic temperament – Art versus Life. One could not serve both masters. And Art, it would seem, had to be served even at the expense of personal happiness and one's very life. John Keats had watched his mother and brother die and recognized their symptoms quickening in himself, had watched his hopes of marriage dwindle and endured the attacks of critics, yet had known he could spare neither strength nor misery in following the appointed course of genius. So, too, had Hazlitt suffered: the victim of critics and enemies, real and imagined, of violent vagaries of his nature, of the vicissitudes of two unhappy marriages. He had resigned hopes of private happiness to duty and work. Genius had its glory but above all its tragedy. It was a sacred disease, its victim an outcast and a sufferer, doomed by the laws of Fate and the peculiarities of the artistic nature. 'Few or none,' Horne would later write, 'will ever understand him, and while feeling an intense sympathy with all the best feelings of humanity he remains himself a solitary outcast from all sympathy.' It was an inevitable conclusion, and a grim conclusion; for Horne was beginning to wonder if he might not have genius.

Chapter 2

The Mission Revealed

It was at the beginning of 1823 after two years of reading and self-searching that Horne decided that fate had meant him for a poet. A few months earlier on the beach near Leghorn, surrounded by dark pine forests and the snowy Appenines and the sparkling blue Mediterranean, the funeral fires had consumed the body of Percy Shelley in 'inconceivable beauty', as though, in Leigh Hunt's words, 'it contained the glassy essence of vitality'. Later it was to seem to Horne that in some mysterious way the same Promethean flame that had burned in Shelley had been relit in his own soul; that an essence of vitality, liberated on the clear Italian morning, had travelled to cold England to inspire himself as Shelley's successor.

It was probably *Queen Mab*, the incendiary poem of Shelley's adolescence which lit up many a rebellious youth and fostered a great poet in Robert Browning, that finally ignited the poetic spark in Horne. He had read *Queen Mab*, it would seem, during 1822, when he was nineteen, and had been roused to such enthusiasm by the magnificent sight of a young man of his own age standing up to the wrongs of the world that he had gone the following year to call on the widowed Mary Shelley in London to tell her of the veneration he felt for her dead husband. As though conscious of his lag behind Shelley's precocious genius, he had pored over his books more intently than ever. In March 1823, when his resolve for literary success cannot have been more than a few months old, he felt ready to begin what he later described as his 'first notable poem'. It was his own *Queen Mab*, its theme similar to Shelley's, of death, superstititon, persecution and tyranny, its setting a ruined city, its title the subtitle of Shelley's poem – *Philosophical Poem with Notes*.

Horne's identification of himself with Shelley was to last his life and at times amount to almost an obsession. In studying Shelley he saw into a mirror that returned an image, often an unduly flattering image of himself. It may have been a result of those early years when he was so wretchedly aware of his difference to his fellows, but emotional similarity, in people of either sex, always attracted Horne, and when this was allied to similar mental interests the effect was overwhelming. It was like falling in love: immediate, exhilarating and complete. The shortcomings, the vagaries of this twin spirit, the possible separations from it, were of almost no consequence. Perhaps the most successful of such relationships were with those he never met and knew only through their work and friends. Shelley, Hazlitt, and Keats could be loved in safety from afar, without the demands and difficulties of personal association.

In that first long poem the main themes were lifelong, and too obsessive to be classed as a mere legacy from Shelley. In Shelley's work Horne believed he had found causes to which he wholeheartedly responded; strains of feeling native to them both. In Shelley's life, too, had he known it then, he glimpsed into a mirror, returning an image as frightening as it was flattering: the rebellious son of a tyrannic father, expelled from Oxford for atheism, dedicated uncompromisingly to iconoclasm and reform and a new morality, leaving in his wake through England and Italy a trail of shattered lives as well as conventions, haunted by real and imagined persecutions and weird fantasies in the months before he was drowned at the age of thirty-one. Shelley's life, in most facets except longevity, was a foretaste of Horne's own.

It was this awareness of similarity, as much as any other factor, that influenced him as he sat in his study at his mother's home in St James's Place pondering the course of his future life in that year of Shelley's death. For it was the poetic nature as much as poetic talent, according to Romantic theory, that formed the signpost to the poet and alerted him to his true vocation. As in many a religious sect, the elect bore outward signs of their inner grace. According to Wordsworth the poet had intense sensibility and 'susceptibility to passion'; according to Shelley he was more delicately organized than others and felt pleasure and pain more. Horne, after reading and thinking much on the subject, wrote in his *Philosophical Poem* that poets were more enthusiastic, and felt intenser passions and sufferings than ordinary men of '*Cooler Blood*'. They saw, moreover, what could not be seen 'with the eyes of a common man'. The poet conversed with the spiritual world; in a time of crumbling and chaotic values it was he who could present the permanent and underlying truths. Only those so specially endowed and

called by destiny were poets, and the certainty was dawning on him
that he was so specially endowed.

Sifting his past experience and probing into his own character with
the zeal of self-centred adolescence, he found incontrovertible evidence
that he neither saw nor felt as a common man. From his first self-
awareness he had been conscious of 'dissimilarity to other men' and
disconcerted by 'inexpressible things within', which yearned for expression and development. He was obviously drawing on his own
experience when he wrote, in his flowery biography of William Hazlitt,
how the adolescent genius is possessed of 'an elemental being yearning
for operation, but knowing not its mission. A powerful destiny heaves
for development in its bosom; it feels the prophetic waves surging to
and fro; but all is indistinct and vast-caverned, spellbound, aimless . . .'
Had it not been this quality, his chief source of comfort as well as
torture, that had made his time at school and Sandhurst so wretched
and cut him off from his classmates?

He devoured every experience as fuel to his own expression. The
great acting of Edmund Kean which had produced a convulsion in
Byron produced in Horne an intense excitement, though the actor was
past his prime. The tightrope walkers at the circus could produce an
equal excitement. Anything exciting or dangerous gave him the craving
'not so much to imitate as to show the same through my own medium'.
As though in answer to the claim of John Keats that poets have 'no
identity' and constantly 'fill some other body', he found himself able to
project himself into another's personality: to 'dramatise myself into the
identity of any man, and think his thoughts'. Yet he also had sense
enough to realize the dangers of such a viewpoint. Such personal
qualities were indicative but not conclusive. 'Poetical feelings,' he
owned, 'are not sufficient to constitute a poet.' It was only too easy to
be deluded into mistaking signs for talent, the fault of many another
unsuccessful poet. Not even those qualities he was later to claim as the
basis of his talent – an 'intensity of feeling and a universal sympathy,
added to a most dramatic and *truth*-like imagination' allied with a
mechanical capacity for self-expression could at first convince him.
Describing the months in which he agonized over his own fitness for
the calling he wrote in his autobiographical notes – 'the agony . . . not
the attainment, but a clear sight of the object . . . The Mission Revealed'.

Early in 1823 the mission was revealed; and once revealed there was
no turning back. A subscriber to Romantic poetic beliefs could no
more reject his mission than a novitiate in the priesthood. He had been
set apart by destiny, endowed with divine gifts, selected to pursue a

special purpose. He had committed himself – a difficult task for one who tended to shrink from initial commitments – and he must now accept all the mission entailed. Nor could he plead himself unaware of its demands. He had already learnt the first commandment in Romantic poetic theology: that the wages of genius are suffering and neglect, that the poet suffered a sacred disease that made him an outcast from normal society and happiness. Deeper sensitivity carried as corollary its deeper pain. Hypersensitive poetic nature presupposed incompetence and failure in practical matters – or so it was believed. Whatever the tangible reasons ascribed for it, the destiny of genius was martyrdom. Horne, as he very well knew, had committed himself to a probable life of suffering.

From the notes to that first *Philosophical Poem* there can be no doubt that he realized this, nor can there be much doubt of the fascination the belief had for him. Of the actual poem today only a few fragments survive with the word 'Burn' scrawled across them. Horne later admitted that on seeing *Hecatompylos*, his first poem in print, in 1828, he had burned his pathetic attempt at 'juvenile philosophy', an action not unlike that of young Robert Browning, and motivated perhaps, as was Browning's, more by a fear of self-revelation than shame for its artistic poorness. The notes survive almost complete: pretentious, juvenile, tedious and, to a biographer, clear keyholes to their author's mind.

It was not a tranquil mind. At twenty years of age he was preoccupied with haunting, ambivalent fears: he feared the poetic life and, like the small boy with the murdered doll, he feared death, suffering, and physical decay and their surrounding religious doctrines. It was 'not the act of dying that excites so terrible an apprehension, it is the . . . idea of decay and putrefaction that is so revolting to human nature. Alas! the white and livid appearance, the cold, the penetrating icy touch of the soulless form defies the language of expression.' (The themes may remind one of Shelley but their argument carries their author's own conviction and experience.)

No stoical reasonable resignation could cancel out his fear of death and it sapped his capacity for life with gloomy 'hypochondrianism' and apprehension. Nor was it comforting to know that before the thirty-ninth year, two-thirds of the population faced death, though Edmonton's wholesome air and water appeared to foster longevity. It was a fear, moreover, that religion only intensified when the true purpose should have been to calm. All religions – save those of Nature and Love – enchained man in sadistic fetters of superstition; Christianity no better than those of torturing persecuting savages. 'The voice of reason must be allowed to remonstrate with all its energy and original force.' But the voice of reason, Horne had already come to recognize, was not equal to the task: one could cast off belief intellectually perhaps but not emotionally. Belief was not an act of will nor, he had discovered, was unbelief. He had discovered that all men were prey to childhood associations and a man 'usually dies in the same belief as was instilled into his mind during the earlier hours of childhood'. The foundations of his life struggle with his fears and conscience were already indelible.

And instilled indelibly, or so it seemed, was the conviction that he was born to suffer. He dwelt on the sufferings of poets, or persecuted men, or religious martyrs, with violent but fascinated abhorrence. Examining the evidence he deduced as an incontrovertible fact that poets suffered, though when he came to examine why they should suffer the causes did not seem completely adequate. He saw the poetic personality as impractical, passionate, impatient of earning a living, adamant in protecting artistic integrity and refusing to succumb to the world's tastes. He saw too the poet's need to withdraw: 'to engage the whole force of his intellect, and draw it into focus towards the accomplishment of One Great End'. Now reason might suggest answers or alternatives; later, as with unbelief, reason was powerless against what was ingrained. Nevertheless as early as 1823 the mixture of rational and irrational which made up this conviction was already implanted, a flourishing cancerous growth. The laurel grew only from the sod; the man of 'plane [sic] good sense' was so much happier than the poet. Causes were less compelling than convictions. He must suffer and genius was concerned with suffering; he had the personal attributes, the mechanical capacity, the creative longings. He was a Poet. He must resign himself to solitary wretchedness and neglect, abandoning all pleasures and hopes of normal life.

Yet, though his mind seems to have revolved in this gloomy treadmill, it must be admitted that the martyrdom of the poet was more an abstract than an immediate notion. He had made the proviso that genius was a curse unless attended by worldly prosperity, and in 1823 he had good reason to expect worldly prosperity, for the money inherited from father and grandmother could, with a little management, give him an adequate income for life. There was in Horne, as well as the self-punishing, self-destructive strain, a self-protective instinct. If the threat of poverty in 1823 had been a real one, he might have thought about it more practically and less ardently. As it was, the picture of the starving unknown poet was sufficiently remote to be stirring, noble, self-sacrificing and extremely attractive. Shelley the reforming, fearless youth was his master; the real, misguided, exhausted, tragically un-balanced Shelley was unknown to him. He was twenty and he was now a Poet.

Chapter 3

Midshipman in Mexico

Through a fault of Horne or his teachers, neither school nor Sandhurst had given him the education that his poetic mission required. In the two and a half years after he first dedicated himself to poetry he studied Berkeley, Locke, and Hume, treatises on demonology, and Jacobean tragedies, a course of study not entirely adequate. His taste, like that of his time, veered towards the unusual and exotic, and he followed that taste. Yet he was certainly not idle. He wrote a lot: mostly verses that were slight, Shelleyan, and juvenile, rising and falling with his volatile spirits. He also wrote a melodramatic novel set in Renaissance Italy, whose hero was forever gazing out of gloomy casements. A young man also endowed with genius, the hero had a marked resemblance to an idealized version of Horne himself.

More years might have passed with desultory reading and unpublished writing but for the intervention early in 1825 of an old friend of the Horne family, a post-captain in the Royal Navy named Thurlow Smith, who was also a distant relation of that celebrated admiral of the Napoleonic wars, Sidney Smith. According to the curious version of the incident told afterwards by Horne, he and Captain Smith were playing billiards in a fashionable London hotel when Smith, in facetious mood, made a wager on his own skill. In usual circumstances his money would have been quite safe since he was an experienced player and Horne was a bad one, but a gnat landed on Smith's nose and put him off his shot and Horne managed to win. Smith pretended the bet had been a joke, but his default was on his conscience and when, a few months later, he was at last offered command of a ship he found a way of repaying the bet by offering Horne a midshipman's berth in his new command. And so it would seem, according to Horne, that an antic of fate and the intervention of destiny in the form of a gnat, gave him one of the great opportunities of his life.

Horne accepted that berth and it proved to be in no ordinary Royal Naval ship. Smith's command was the *La Libertad*, a ship loaned secretly to fight for Mexico in her war of independence against Spain. Horne was thus given a chance to fight, as Shelley had fought with his pen, for the oppressed; to take up arms for the struggling New World just as Byron had been prepared to fight and die for the Old. It was 'Fate's resistless impulse'. A chance to follow the very sea routes of Francis Drake and the Elizabethan adventurers! It was a chance no rebellious, adventurous youth of twenty-two, dedicated to Romantic ideals, could possibly have refused.

The background to the expedition was a complicated history of English diplomacy in Mexico over the preceding two years. Mexico had been fighting for independence from Spain for nearly fifteen years, and at the end of 1822 the only part still occupied by Spanish troops was the island fortress of San Jaun de Ulua at the mouth of the harbour of Vera Cruz. In the following year George Canning became British Foreign Minister, and had the foresight to see that, by helping Mexico, England might be rewarded with a large slice of Mexican trade. One way in which Britain furthered this policy was to fit out a Danish man-of-war for the Mexican service early in 1825. Officially Britain knew nothing about this; unofficially the British Government supplied the captain and crew as well as the ship.

It was command of this man-of-war that Smith now assumed. And it was to join this ship that Richard Horne, midshipman first class in the Mexican navy, now hurried to Falmouth. He had been offered three times more money than he would have received in the Royal Navy, and a uniform which was 'very elegant, expensive, and ridiculous considering what we were going to do': the Mexican officials had gaudy tastes. They sailed at the beginning of June, their destination and purpose known officially only to the captain and the Mexican officials aboard. Even Horne, who was called to act as interpreter between the Captain and his Mexican colleagues – Horne's Spanish being one of the fruits of that exotic self-education – learned few details of their mission.

One assumes Horne must have known at least the ship's purpose, and the fact that he was embarked on something he believed in must alone have made the voyage bearable. From the view of material comfort it scarcely was bearable. The privations of a midshipman's life had dismayed his father and it equally dismayed him now. Their quarters, in area no more than twelve by sixteen feet and housing sixteen 'young gentlemen', were 'hot as an oven and not half so clean'. The food was 'indescribable': beef that seemed as indestructible as mahogany, coffee made from what appeared to be burnt cork and water, salt pork with fat inches thick, pudding studded with huge gross plums and biscuits 'hard as flints'. When the midshipmen were not 'singing, capering, drinking, talking, smoking, flute blowing', they were playing practical jokes and not of the kindest type. They would have victimized him, Horne complained, had he not shown them early he was not to be baited. Instead they took it out on the captain's brother, a quiet, sensible lad. Nevertheless Horne found his hammock full of tar brushes and split peas or even broken bottles, or had it cut down while he slept.

Horne must have seemed a ripe target for baiting: this poetic youth with his auburn curls and fastidious ways, who studied a manual on tropical medicine, a parting present from Tom Stone, and took such care of himself, refusing ship's liquor and drinking only water and a little wine. The sleeping in particular disturbed him: not only the midshipman's pranks of bottles in the hammocks but the very 'sight of bodies sleeping'. 'I can scarcely separate,' he wrote in terms reminiscent of the Notes to the *Philosophical Poem*, 'the idea from death, for the eyes are glazed, the cheek and forehead marbly white, and the expression of the mouth seems fixed in the one last unutterable con-conclusion – all is over – it will speak no more.'

Yet, despite his discomfort and his lack of conformity, Horne managed to survive remarkably well. At certain times in his life Horne was to surprise observers by his ability to cope with the most out-landish situations and yet keep his poetic character unaltered. Running side by side with the poet in him was a man of toughness, vigour, and practicality. They were qualities reminiscent perhaps of his paternal grandmother, Sarah Tice, and they were qualities of which – though they were given less scope than his poetic ones – he was extremely proud.

In spite of his adaptability, the difference between himself and his companions must have been most noticeable. But for two Royal Navy officers on half pay and aboard in secret, and a former North Sea skipper of brutal efficiency, the rest were mainly mercenaries, deserters, criminals – a repulsive bunch. Sitting in the midshipman's cabin, oblivious of the noise and heat around him, Horne noted in his journal their physiognomy and life histories, elicited with a poet's zeal during the long night watches. There was the chief mate of the starboard watch, a thin, sinewy, pock-marked fellow with a hungry mouth, large earrings and moist, sensual eyes – Horne was always a keen student of physiognomy – who had fought for Spain, Venezuela and now Mexico and told 'of seas, shipwrecks and battles with indifference and naïveté worth pages of description'. There was also the chief bosun's mate, a gigantic negro named White, with the dignity and slumberous power of a classical statue, who had once quelled a mutiny single-handed and claimed to have second sight. He confided to Horne he was a deserter from a British man-of-war and had an Irish wife. In his journal Horne remarked that here were poor common fellows accepting hardship as a matter of course and with cheerfulness. A poet, he implied, could not accept his fate so stoically.

There was even wider scope for literary comment in the captain's cabin, where he met for the first time the Mexican dignitaries who accompanied the ship: the Baron, suave and intelligent, an engineer with great moustaches and tuft of hair 'below the netherlip' and steady grey eyes that 'would fire' when he spoke; the Ambassador who missed nothing, seldom spoke and, when he did, moved not a muscle; the Treasurer, Señor Castillo, who talked with great haste and had his library on board. There was also the Ambassador's French cook, most fascinating of all, a porpoise-like little man, with a fat body and red bloated face; an ex-soldier but, according to Horne, more an ex-sensualist, who over a second bottle would debate questions of free will and necessity and the comparative amatory skills of the French and English. The cook greased his feet with butter to slide them into Hessian boots, and there was 'as much expression in his stomach as in his countenance, both showing his high pursy grossness and measureless vainglory'.

Dining in that large fore cabin with the ports open on to the glittering sea, the guns slewed away, the wind on the beam and 'the keen slant of our large table, with the swinging tables overhead hanging askance, with all their fruit plates and decanters balancing themselves so admirably' was a sight 'highly piquant', and to be described with clarity ten years later. Off Puerto Rico they saw a Spanish ship which the Captain, to the crew's disgust, refused to chase. The Captain came up, instead, with the foolhardy plan of going ashore at Puerto Rico, disguised as English traders, for no better motive than to collect pineapples and cigars. For Horne the best part of the escapade was a huge black pineapple, a 'bronzed, mossy rind with ebony thorns rising from the top of every cone or joint in the shelly mail of the entire pyramid, built like a Temple of the Sun'. He had tasted none with so 'richly vinous and masculine a flavour', and he so far forgot the strictures of his medical book as to consume it all at one sitting.

At length they came to the small island of Sacrificios, a safe anchorage just outside Vera Cruz and out of range of the Spanish guns on the fort of St Juan de Ulua. Horne, however, had eyes only for the extraordinary beauty of Vera Cruz. It had been a chilly winter morning when they arrived but by midday the

> little flat sandy island of Sacrificios seemed alive with light, and the sea shot and glistened as the principle of heat was at work with it. We could see Vera Cruz, and the fort of St Juan de Ulua directly opposite it, at less than half a league across the Channel, and Mt Orizaba in the distance, its sublime head covered with snows, and towering above the clouds.

This was, in all its extraordinary beauty, perhaps a fitting object for a poet to risk his life to free. And yet a closer view revealed its true nature: a glorious façade, like a lush poisonous plant, beneath whose beauty lay death and decay. With Smith he went ashore at Sacrificios, and their visit was to be a symbol of the entire expedition. So beautiful in that first glimpse, on close view the island was barren and deserted, as though 'pestilence and death had ruled over it from time immemorial'. When they approached its guard house they found several diseased creatures in ragged clothes, asleep by rusty muskets. A little mulatto boy rolling in the sun directed them to the commandant's house, at the far end of which was a creature in a cigar, short cloak and no breeches 'who advanced with great dignity and gravity'. This was no other than the Mexican 'Admiral', Commander in Chief of the Mexican Navy, who had visited the *Libertad* the day before in a flamboyant uniform adorned with gold braid and huge gold earrings, and complete with a retinue of theatrically dressed sailors – the same sleeping scarecrows they had just encountered. And it was to be only a taste, as they were soon to discover, of the state of the Mexican navy. The squadron of warships that Horne's ship was to head was a sad collection of cast-offs: a brig with ten guns and English and Irish officers, a two-masted American schooner with rusty guns, and a de-masted brig. With this fleet they were expected to rout the Spanish from a near-impregnable fort.

Yet if the Spanish had been the only enemy, the Englishmen would not have been so concerned. The swamps of Vera Cruz swarmed with mosquitoes carrying yellow fever, and as strangers lacked the inhabitants' immunity they were especially prone to the disease. Though the cause of the infection was not understood, all were well aware that foreigners invariably caught it and usually died. The heat of the place bored into one's very soul; between it and hell, they said, lay only a sheet of paper. Its fierce northerly winds, 'Los Nortes', attacked with 'blistering and sweeping fury'. If the Spanish cannon, the sharks in the bay, and the knives of treacherous Mexican allies did not kill the invader, Vera Cruz herself, the city they had come to save, almost certainly would.

The glorious dream of adventure began degenerating into a nightmare. Word came that a Spanish expedition had left Cuba to relieve their besieged countrymen in the fort. This was the very event the *Libertad* had been brought to prevent, but no sooner had the news arrived than an incredible list of mishaps took place. The Mexican governor, ignoring Captain Smith's protests, insisted on hustling 207 native soldiers, who had never before seen the sea, into the ship to act as marines. He also insisted on sending a frisky black bull which at once went berserk 'tossing and trampling to pulp' all in its way until the ship's butcher managed to hack it to pieces with a carving knife. Then the unfortunate soldiers, having all guzzled a considerable meal of soup, peas and salt pork on a very rough day, were promptly sick. During this confusion the Spanish ships were sighted; a larger fleet than anything Mexico could muster. On board the *Libertad* the confusion increased. The scraggy Mexican colonel in charge kept shouting that they were ready 'to prostrate' themselves for their country – more likely die of seasickness, Horne thought with amusement.

His amusement was premature, for the next moment, in his capacity of translator, he had mistranslated the phrase 'to prostrate' as 'lie in bed', and both nationalities were furious. He escaped their anger by going to man the foremost guns on the port side of the main deck, for the Spanish were by now near and it seemed that the *Libertad* had no chance at all. Horne, as he later confessed, was so frightened that he stripped to his canvas trousers, intending to swim to the Spanish ship and be taken prisoner if the worst came: 'This was my first time of going into action and the silence throughout the ship had a touch of the dreadful about it.' They were now close enough to the enemy ships to hear comments shouted.

Then, suddenly, they were saved. The rusty Mexican brig came up, and the enemy hesitated, probably suspecting a trick, and that hesitation cost them their victory. The north wind freshened; the 'sea burst over our bows, and boomed and hissed along the upper deck, as though we had been boarded by huge, hissing serpents'. The deck of the *Libertad* was a shambles of water, scrambling sailors pulling in sails, frightened soldiers stabbing at sailors' feet, and the sound of praying, screaming, vomiting. They made thankfully for the sheltered lea of Sacrificios and the Spanish fleet disappeared in search of shelter. Later they heard that the Spanish flag ship had been demasted and the remnant had retreated to Havana.

Nature had been kind to them once; it was not kind again. The yellow fever raged in all ships, and strong and healthy men died within days. Horne knew the terrible anguish of watching friends die, and the equally terrible anguish of thinking he too would die. Once on the deck of the ship he bent over the covered corpse of a man who had smiled at him only a short time before; and like that child with its doll in the Edmonton garden, he could not, however much he forced himself, lift the covering and look down on that emaciated, already putrifying face. The faces of the dead – even of the sleeping, since they looked like the dead – always had the power to disturb him and now they gripped him in a morbid fascination. Pages of his sketch books were covered with drawings of them: yellow fever victims in delirium, raving eyes staring forth from ravaged, unshaven faces, a corpse with waxen eyes shut in 'that last inevitable conclusion'. One death alone gave him hope and courage: a native soldier, dying on the lower deck, his last request that his pay should go to his mother, his last words a prayer; he folded his arms 'and sinking back died in a few minutes very quiet, resigned and conscious'. Although Horne was so terrified, part of himself was observant, almost detached, and analytical. The 'most difficult task in life,' he was to note, 'is to die with quiet fortitude and resignation.'

It was futile and positively dangerous to reflect on such matters during the day when all one's wits were necessary for work. Such thoughts were pushed aside until the evening sunset tinged Orizaba's 'everlasting snows with glaring hues'; and then, alive with that painful beauty of gold and snowy crags, he would climb a coral rock and look out over the bay to the graceful ships at anchor, the mass of the enemy fort, and beyond it to the open sea. Then the questions that must be answered came into his mind. He must not die; he was not ready to die. The echoes of past beliefs and sins, too strong for Shelleyan rationalism, would give him no peace. Nor would the recollection of his poetic mission. Had he been right to risk so precious a life as his amongst these pestilential airs? He was, after all, a poet. 'Have I done well', he asked himself:

> *My home to leave – my few, though well-tried friends –*
> *My treasured Poet's words of love and power –*
> *My own strong wish for one green laurel wreath –*

To mingle with the thoughtless, and be mute,
'Midst hateful deeds, and uncongenial minds?'

They were questions to which, in 'reasoning hours', he knew the right answers: the cause was just, the tyrant must be destroyed, however unworthy the character of the oppressed; it was experience, furthermore, which would give his poetic genius the essential knowledge and maturity. And yet he could not banish the vision of his own grave.

Inevitably he caught the fever. His head shaved, his body gripped by the fearful symptoms – the bloody vomiting, the jaundice, the raging heat – he lay with eight others on the gun deck and drew on his reserves of strength and will to fight. Before he had felt powerless to escape; now it was actually upon him it was almost a relief: an enemy at last to be faced and fought. He fought relentlessly, and when a shipmate passing his hammock remarked 'What poor creatures we all are!', Horne in his agony growled back 'Speak for yourself'. He had heard it said that one in nine were the chances for recovery from yellow fever, and realizing that eight others lay with him he was determined to be that *one*. He became absorbed in a grim and not altogether rational contest for survival, his will power directed mainly against his neighbour whom he fancied was also determined to be that *one*.

The sense of competition, to which Horne was always prone, roused him as nothing else could. His sick companions died but his neighbour remained alive. Then one morning, when they both felt particularly low, Horne told the doctor as he passed that he felt strong enough to climb the main top and wished he might prove it. As he spoke his boast he watched his companion's hammock: 'I saw the man's jaw drop. He never lifted his head again; and the next morning at daybreak I saw him rolled up in his hammock like a silkworm, and full as yellow, and dragged into the jollyboat to receive a watery burial.' Later, he recorded this curious incident as an example of his own 'determinate will', which was so strong that at times it might kill – a notion which also haunts some of his work.

> I once kill'd a man [he wrote] . . . and this was merely by making him feel the contention, as we were both lying in sight of each other on our expectant deathbeds. I did this to gain the chance (one in nine is the common calculation as to recovering from the yellow fever) because I fancied he was endeavouring to do the same; otherwise I should not have thought of it, and leaving all to nature should probably have died.

As in childhood with his doll, Horne had committed what he recognized as a kind of mental murder – murder by an act of will. 'I alone,' he wrote to his mother, 'rose up like a ghost scarcely knowing if I had quitted my body or still retained any portion of earth.'

By the end of 1825 the Spanish fort was taken and Horne, recovered but weak, was able to spend his pleasantest days in Vera Cruz, exploring and hunting up the rivers, past native villages like birdcages made of reeds and thatch; or lying in the shade on hot afternoons, learning 'to twangle the guitar after the manner of the native Mexicans' and watching the lithe-bodied Mexican girls sing and dance. They were so simple with their bright dresses and naked copper legs, so innocent in their dignity and nobility, knowing 'nought of sin'. It was a state of mind that Horne, tutored in the Romantic school of noble savages, and aware perhaps too much of sin in himself, always found particularly attractive. On one visit to a native village he entered a woman's house and, at her silent invitation, began to caress her naked foot until the fancied approach of her husband brought the escapade to an abrupt end.

Such diversions, carried on in the lassitude of convalescence, could not continue. Another summer was approaching and Horne knew he must be out of Mexico before the heat began. He had decided to return home across the United States and Canada, a task that must be done in summer. There was the problem, however, of obtaining his rightful pay from the Mexican Government. Though the numbers of the volunteers were pathetically reduced 'by fever, by the waters, or by assassination' – of thirty-six American and English, only three were said to have ever reached their homes again – those who remained were refused their prize money, while bogus Mexican heroes paraded 'the gold-laced streets of Vera Cruz'. It was a cause for extreme anger but he was powerless to redress it. 'We have all been deceived and cheated,' he told his mother, ' . . . Those who remained longest with them fared the worse. Had I left the service one month or even three months sooner, I should have had nearly 40 pounds more than I have at present.'

Carrying a certificate stating his 'conduct was highly satisfactory on all occasions', with what Mexican doubloons he could manage sewn into his money belt and the rest sent off to his mother in England, he boarded a ship for New York. His fellow passengers included the Bishop of Chile, several priests and some shipmates from the *Libertad*, and it seemed as though the horrors of Vera Cruz would forever pursue them. Five days out two 'already putrid' bodies, victims of yellow fever, were committed to the sea. The weather was in a continual squall

and food in short supply; they were obliged to survive on a diet of
turtle, and Horne was surprised to find how soon such a luxury became
intolerable. They were relieved when they finally arrived at New
York and were put ashore at the quarantine station at Staten Island.

And yet during the voyage there had been one experience worth
remembering. Standing by the deck rail on a calmer day in the gulf of
Florida he had seen a small white butterfly hovering above the waves,
lonely, fragile, beautiful, extraordinarily self-confident, and suddenly
it was transformed in his mind as the symbol of the poet, doomed to
loneliness and suffering and yet assured in his mission, compensated
for wordly wretchedness by heights of experience others would never
know. The thought was translated into one of his most charming poems
copied into the back of his travelling notebook:

> The tiny soul then soar'd away,
> Seeking the clouds on fragile wings,
> Lured by the brighter, purer ray
> Which hope's ecstatic morning brings,
> Far out at sea.
>
> Away he sped with shimmering glee!
> Scarce seen — now lost — yet onward borne!
> Night comes! — with wind and rain — and he
> No more will dance before the Morn,
> Far out at sea.
>
> He died unlike his mates, I ween;
> Perhaps not sooner, or worse cross'd —
> And he hath felt, thought, known, and seen
> A larger life and hope — though lost
> Far out at sea!

Now he was at last away from Vera Cruz, Horne's spirits, which
always tended to veer to extremes, soared recklessly. He was light-
headed with relief. 'Now that I have escaped that dreadful place,' he
wrote back to his mother, 'I feel as tho' the sensation of fear would
never again visit me. I wonder how people can die in England.' He was
immune from fear, overwhelmed with this 'very self-complacent feeling of safety', and filled with enormous energy and curiosity. To his
mother's fears he wrote reassuringly that he was 'very well, getting
rather lusty and at *last* tanned by the sun' and that 'with some worldly

31

caution' he would manage excellently. Once more he was the Romantic adventurer in control of his role and his future; the bewildered, frightened lad was safely left behind in Vera Cruz. He meant to enjoy himself.

Nor were his adventures across America in any way an anticlimax. With his heavy luggage and fare home despatched to New Brunswick to await him, he packed a small tarpaulin bag with three checked shirts and a pair of canvas trousers and set out from New York. He visited the Catskill Mountains in a covered cart, went up the Erie Canal by flour barge, and through into Canada, pausing a short time at Niagara Falls on the way. He overflowed with eagerness to explore: not a monument, or waterfall, Indian tribe or new tree or plant went unexamined or a striking scene unsketched. The foaming waters of the falls on the Mohawk and at Niagara fascinated him. At Mohawk, gazing into the compelling fury of the waters he covered his notebook with disjointed phrases: ' . . . the sense reels confounded . . . ponderous falls and booming far below in the black chasm . . .' At Niagara, whose picture he had often pored over back in England, he found even his expectations far surpassed. Having explored the caves behind the falls his imagination was caught up by the savage, swirling destructive waters and he tore off his clothes and plunged into the pool below the falls in a gesture worthy of Byron. He was fished out – less gloriously – with broken ribs and sent to recover at a nearby house that had recently sheltered the actor Edmund Kean. It was there that he afterwards claimed to have lost, at the billiard table, the 'six or seven handfuls' of Mexican doubloons with which he had left Vera Cruz.

By the start of August he had covered the 600 miles up the St Lawrence to Quebec. He still enjoyed himself but not with the same wholehearted enthusiasm. He continued to enthuse over the beauties of the St Lawrence and admired French Canada, which, he told his mother, was in many ways like the Guernsey of his youth. He made friends with a group of 'young ladies and gentlemen (at least they call themselves so)' and went on picnics with them on the river among the islands. But his lodgings were necessarily cheap and infested with bedbugs, the weather already gave promise of the severity of the winter, and the sight of British uniforms brought longings to be home. The ecstatic freedom of the escape from Vera Cruz was wearing off; even he was finding he had had enough of travels.

There was also a more sinister reason for his desire to be away. He had been involved in another struggle for survival which, like his mental bout with the yellow-fever victim, would return in future years to haunt his thoughts. One day in the market place in Quebec he quarrelled with an Iroquois Indian and had been forced to 'wrestle for my life'. A few days later the Indian lay in wait and tried to stab him; and Horne, it would seem from later accounts, was forced to kill him. The circumstances are misty but the incident stayed uncomfortably in his mind.

His money was almost exhausted and it was imperative he make some decision. He therefore took ship without delay along the St Lawrence, joining the labourers at the ports where they stopped to unload cargo, earning 'two or three dollars per day, and on one occasion, four' for his work on the wharves: welcome money for his poverty was pressing, and doubly welcome in that he earned it by practical labour. His self-sufficiency amazed and delighted him. Seldom before had he felt such a sense of personal power. There was scarcely a place where, had he wanted, he 'could not have remained . . . and done very well'. He was 'proud as Lucifer', proud as 'any living man who ever wore clay'. His confidence recharged he prepared to go home, a very different man to the lad who had set out.

Chapter 4

Fallen Fruit

Horne arrived in England to a winter for body and soul. Yet the first impression was not so wintry. He had longed to be home; a hundred fresh plans surged in his mind. He had the superhuman energy and elation of one who had survived a long, difficult and exciting journey and amazed himself with his own competence and resourcefulness. He felt relief, self-congratulation, and that light-headed feeling of safety that had first possessed him on leaving Vera Cruz. The voyage home had been far from quiet. The ship he had taken down the St Lawrence from Quebec had been wrecked near the river mouth and he had been forced to travel on foot across to Saint John to collect his luggage and money. Even then his troubles had not ended. The voyage across the Atlantic in a timber ship had been enlivened by fire and mutiny. But indestructible, or so it seemed, Horne had at last come to London and the calm of his mother's house at St James's Place.

In fact, his nerves were strung to such a pitch that it was an unnatural energy that possessed him. And, as the elation faded, he found himself mentally and emotionally rudderless, adrift on a nightmarish sea of confusion and depression. That quiet security of home that he had so longed for back in Mexico was too quiet for one who had known constant excitement, challenge and danger. He longed for a chance to prove again to himself his own resourcefulness. Yet as he lapsed more into his old life he began to feel that those adventures belonged to another person; he belonged nowhere. Nothing seemed real, nothing had purpose. Recalling his adventures he had difficulty in knowing whether he was 'creating or recollecting a series of fact . . . The matter-of-fact occurrences of actual life are no food for my existence.'

Nevertheless the horrors of the journey had not faded. He was obsessed by death. Those memories of the dead and rotting bodies of his shipmates, the companion he had killed by 'determinate will', the Indian in Quebec, returned to disturb him. He admitted he had learned a 'great reverence' for death, and his thoughts, as of old, filled his notebooks: 'Let no man boast of his contempt for death . . . I do not believe it a real evil, unless it resemble *this* life . . . If we could retain our form in a petrified or crystallized state . . .' Like the child with the doll and the eager author of the *Philosophical Poem*, putrefaction played a large part in his fear and loathing, the more so now that he had memories of the yellow-fever. Those indefinable echoes – 'present though beyond recall' – had never haunted him so persistently. His thinking turned into fantasy and fruitless self-probing; his spirits fell to the blackest despondency. Fear, horror, self-disgust and reverie took control of him.

There was joy in nothing, not even writing; the hundred fresh plans were gone. The only satisfaction lay in giving 'palpable and definite form' to his 'own extreme misery'. His work suited his mood: his main effort since his return was a long poem, *Homer's Soliloquy*, its hero, old, blind and tired, its hopes – like its author's – 'dead and wither'd, like fallen fruit, that rots in greenness'. Its reception among his friends endorsed his despair. When he had expected 'ready sympathy' he found only 'doubts and denial'. (Nor can one wonder for it was turgid and pretentious.) He was supported alone by that belief which had comforted him at Sandhurst and in Mexico – that this misery was the poetic badge, inevitable and necessary to foster genius. Even this was small comfort. 'A man,' he wrote dolefully, 'may encounter every danger, and yet return safe; he may escape death a thousand times, but he can never escape from the world's ingratitude.'

Spring came and he found himself watching nature's rebirth without a shred of his usual feeling, while he waited in vain for his own rebirth. In June 1828 he saw his first poems published. *Hecatompylos*, a long Shelleyan effusion on the theme of the ruined city and the tyrant, appeared in the first number of the new literary magazine *The Athenaeum*; and *Eurus* appeared in *The Oriental Herald*, its opening lines characteristic:

> *Years roll away and hopes unrealiz'd*
> *Decay and die . . .*

Neither publication gave him the joy or even the satisfaction he might have expected.

He endured this depression for over a year, too long a time for it to leave no permanent marks. Nothing, it seemed, had the power to make him again the ardent, purposeful youth he once had been. Yet he himself had predicted the antidote the year before in a poem he had written around the Orpheus legend. Autobiographical and one of the simplest and most charming of his earlier pieces, he had called it simply *Orpheus*, its hero, like himself, the poet returning from war, death in his ears, confusion and despair in his mind, lament on his lips:

> *. . . Heavy at heart*
> *The sense of wasted toil for human praise*
> *Comes strong upon me, and the bitter pain*
> *Of genius given by God, denied by man.*
> *No more I flourish the intemperate hope*
> *Of fame, and thus shake off unworthy grief.*

In the midst of his aimless wandering Orpheus had come on his Eurydice, the embodiment of earlier hopes and fantasies; and although their love was doomed – destroyed, as it so often is with Horne, by preordained fate at the very moment of its consummation – it had given Orpheus renewal of his purpose and himself. Horne now found the same thing. Like Orpheus, he fell in love.

Probably he had never been so ripe for falling in love. He craved sympathy, he needed comfort; he needed the admiration and the excitement, the hope and energy engendered by a love affair to drive out his 'mental hypochondriacism'. He needed, above all, to get back the sense of purpose which had been lost in the upheavals and transitions of the past few years. He found all these in the girl he called 'A'.

It is possible today to make a reasonable reconstruction of this love affair by combining three different sources. At the time he wrote comments in his notebook; at least one of his poems, though undated, refers fairly certainly to the affair; and a final account he wrote in 1876 – a manuscript headed 'In Search of a Wife By a Bachelor of the Inner Temple', and marked 'Private'. This last account contains a mediocre hotch-potch of comments on love and the charming little story of Maria Dian, a story so perceptive, so vital, and so unlike the rest, that the reader instinctively feels that this has really happened to its author. Its facts seem to correspond with both poem and notebook, so it seems reasonable to assume that, though supposedly fictitious, in outline at least it is autobiographical. Its setting is 'the green lanes of Berkshire', its hero a young man educated, unsuccessfully, for the army and supported, until his succession to an expected inheritance, by his family.

The heroine is one 'destined to evoke new life', unaffected, gentle and sympathetic, her name Maria Dian – Dian presumably a reference to Diana, the chaste moon goddess, and to the frigidity lurking in her nature, and Maria apparently chosen at random. But to readers of this pyschological twentieth century, where the resemblance between a lover and a parent is a commonplace, the name of Maria is interesting, for that was Horne's mother's name. In the notebook she is simply referred to by the letter A.

Horne was now twenty-six and the girl much younger. He had fancied himself in love several times since he first experienced such feelings for the girl at Elizabeth Hitchener's school at Edmonton. His sentimental archives were littered with poems to young ladies. Yet he now confessed that

> never before had I met any girl, or any woman of whatsoever age, who so thoroughly seemed to understand me; who mentally was so intensely in sympathy, in fact so *en rapport* with me, that we anticipated each other's thoughts, and began at once to utter the same words.

Sometimes she said 'in her most innocent manner, the most admiring flattering things', so much so that he confessed to feeling most embarrassed. She was also naturally sensitive and intelligent, though uneducated, and he watched with joy as she responded to his own literary tastes. She, he believed, encompassing '*all sympathies in one*', could transform his 'self-centred and unnecessary violence . . . to wholesome power and practical wisdom'. The result was inevitable. 'By, degrees and the degrees were gone through in two or three weeks, I became deeply in love.'

For three weeks he was exhilarated, overwhelmed, bewildered. He walked with her in the woods beside her father's cottage (her father was parish clerk), or they sat

> side by side with no one else in the room on the huge old-fashioned sofa, holding each other's hands with fingers entwined as the twilight stole softly over the windows and ceiling till sometimes her head would sink on my shoulder, her lovely fair hair, of angelic tone and texture, falling down my breast – and, so placed, she would softly sigh herself to sleep, which lasted perhaps a quarter of an hour, as I scarcely allowed myself to breathe for fear of waking her.

They talked of love only indirectly, through the books they read together – with what vicarious rapture on Horne's part – including in their reading, ironically, the *Liber Amoris*, that chronicle of Hazlitt's disastrous infatuation for his landlady's deceitful daughter who dispensed breakfast and kisses to her mother's lodgers, and so obsessed Hazlitt that he divorced his wife and ruined his reputation for her. The memories of that book were to become so interchanged with his own love affair in Horne's mind that he later had difficulty separating his own reactions from Hazlitt's.

Horne had every reason to be happy, but he found his happiness mixed with uneasiness. He had discovered in her those precious factors in any relationship, mental sympathy and temperamental similarity, for the first time encountered within the intoxicating context of sexual love. It was so precious that it must be preserved: nothing must be allowed to interfere. He shrank from even the most chaste of 'personal caresses', which might, he felt, unnecessarily complicate and disturb what a little time would soon perfect. Physical manifestation of love was therefore out of the question: 'superfine' feelings and 'nervous delicacy' precluded it, together with the more formal reason that he was in no position financially to declare himself until he reached his inheritance. And yet his feelings were sufficiently aroused for him to be violently jealous of that captivating charm that seemed to emanate from her 'involuntarily and even unconsciously'. He was 'vexed' and 'disturbed' to see it directed at others. He was quick to notice that there were ways in which she could have subtly indicated her feelings – hints she could have given – but she gave none, though she was uniformly tender and gentle. He was torn by a reluctance to make love to her (he did not really understand why), a reluctance to make even the most cautious of declarations. He searched heart and mind for explanation or solution and received none. The idyllic platonism was preserved, and he kept what he later termed with exasperation as his 'overpunctillious, dogged, self-besotted, spoony silence'.

And here one arrives at a common ingredient in Horne's relationships with women. He was not wrong in noting her lack of special response to himself, to dwell so intently on her 'innocence'. That innocence a modern reader might be tempted to call sexual neutrality. She was 'winning', but devoid of obvious sexual enticement. She demanded nothing from him. It may have been a measure of his timidity, feelings of vulnerability and general unsureness; perhaps it was connected with that unconscious attitude of his towards sexual enjoyment that seemed to equate pleasure with punishment and loss; the lovers of his plays and poems were so often punished for loving and were robbed of their beloved. This was certainly in contrast to his intellectual attitude to love, which, as befitted a disciple of Shelley, was extremely liberal.

Whatever the causes, Horne's initial response to a woman was invariably more mental than physical. Physical attractions, however strong, were as much an object of doubt as gratification. It was the mental climate of love that he craved and fed on. In the light of such reasoning it was therefore easy to see why undisturbing 'innocence' was such a potent attraction: within its atmosphere he could feel nothing further was expected of him and those qualities he so prized could flourish unmolested by the complication of physical presence. Later, when those physical advances he finally felt compelled to introduce were rejected by that same 'innocence' – which at least twice in Horne's life was the sign of frigidity – it would become also the bitterest of qualities. Then all his earlier doubts and fears would be confirmed in agony of self-reproaches.

On an ecstatic wave of feeling with uneasy undertones he passed those weeks until his holiday ended and he returned to London. He was still harassed by doubts, still buoyed up with elation. He would give his feelings time; she was very young and he could not afford to marry for the moment. So he convinced himself though he later admitted such reasons were mere excuses for deeper motives which he dimly apprehended but did not understand. Such 'equivocal' conduct was beyond self-explanation.

Working at his writing with renewed zest, transformed from the miserable creature he had been, he might have gone on hugging his undeclared love to himself indefinitely had not something happened. According to the later version it was the rumour of her engagement. In a state of tumult he heard the news and on impulse arranged to go to Berkshire and confront her. Arriving at the nearest village he took a room at the inn and sent her a note to meet him at the outskirts of the wood. The meeting took place just before dusk, and to his joy she confessed that the engagement was not yet finally settled. Thereupon putting his arm around her, he expressed his true feelings:

> alluding to the great sympathy and affection between us – the great love I had felt for her from the first week I had seen her, and which she must have known, though I had never directly spoken of it before – what was my confusion and dismay when she informed me she had no feeling of that kind towards me! And never had.

She was only 'mentally fascinated', nothing more. She felt only reverence, admiration, and 'a sisterly or daughterly affection'.

Horne was dumbfounded. Then without the 'slightest feeling of shame, or the least effort at self-command' he burst into tears. Meanwhile she kept on with her incoherent explanations: he was like a character from a poem, she could never love him as he would want or deserve, she never wanted to marry and had only agreed to the engagement because of her family. Walking, or as he later put it, swaying, 'up and down a sort of grassy wood-path, both of us weeping bitterly', he reproached her, then overcome with tenderness, forgave her and kissed her; she covered her madonna-like face with her hands and the tears trickled through her fingers, and down her pretty wrists. He called her Hazlitt's Sarah, the deceitful heroine of *Liber Amoris*, and then, seeing her misery, apologized. Finally they embraced and parted forever. 'I do not know,' he wrote reviewing it much later, 'if I come very well out of it, my conduct . . . having been equivocal, if not reprehensible.'

There can be no doubt that Horne was deeply hurt, even though he would persist in using Hazlitt's phrases to express it. In fact it was prophetic the way *Liber Amoris* had been drawn into the relationship at the start and now so repeatedly echoed his own feelings. He bitterly blamed himself, as Hazlitt had done: 'Pride, vanity, and a certain incredible humour for refining upon the heart till its passions are confounded with the intellect, have ruined my happiness forever.' Breaking into verse he wrote *Forget Me Not*:

> *Why was I lured by the sweet voice,*
> *The mellow glance, the heaving breast?*
> *Why did I seem thy bird-like choice*
> *If thou prefer'd an empty nest?*
> *Thy words were rapturous! – could I know*
> *The secret ice, the fatal snow.*

The question kept haunting him that if he had been more forward with her, attempted to make love to her, and shown more ardour and less 'delicacy, respect and adoration', the outcome might have been different. Thus Hazlitt also had thought on hearing of his Sarah's lack of moral scruples with others, working himself into a fury because he himself had not seduced her. The analogy was not exactly apposite, but Horne began to have the same regrets. Had he

. . . plucked the ripe peach on the wall.
I could have gather'd it and made
Delicious rapture o'er its fall –
A wild delirium in the shade.

With less bravado and more disillusion he wrote in his notebook: 'Women like to have all the *reserve* and delicacy to themselves; let a man try them with it, act upon it, put them to the test, and he is admired in the abstract. Passion is seldom the result.'

As the poet and analyst of character he searched for other reasons to render his failure less depressing, although it was to be another thirty years before he found a reason he could accept. With the experience of a broken marriage, so similar to that early love affair that even he could see the likeness, he wrote an explanation that could have applied to either relationship: 'Some women (many more than the world at all suspects) should never marry anybody – nature had secretly forbidden it. They seldom know this fact themselves until too late.' She, he believed, had known this of herself instinctively.

In July 1829 he looked for more obvious reasons, and turning consciously or unconsciously to that current bible of his passions, *Liber Amoris*, he agreed with Hazlitt's first explanation of his Sarah's coldness attributing it to a previous unhappy attachment.

I sought [wrote Horne] for admiration as the groundwork of passion – I gained it to excess, but the rest was pre-engaged – all had *been* felt, and I was too late . . . the premature drawing off of the vital sluices has made A almost insensible to any passion but her own . . . Love has indeed *stolen* her heart and therefore she is rendered heartless.

It was only after his own marriage that he concluded that A, like his wife, was one of those unhappy women isolated by their sexual frigidity.

The damage to his spirits was devastating. The depression returned a hundred times stronger. He feared – and again the attention strays, perhaps unfairly, to love-crazed Hazlitt – for his very sanity. Certainly there was something in his fears. Thoughts and sensations, 'eccentric from overnervousness', flew from his brain without bidding; introspection, self-pity and disgust took control.

The sight of a girl bearing the remotest resemblance to A was enough to start 'unceasing nervous associations of sensibility'. 'The physical is deserting me,' he wrote wearily, 'because I am become, as it were, all thought; I grow sick and annoyed from looking too deeply into myself and human nature; I am agonized and disgusted at finding the best of my heart's core thrown away and rejected, like a worthless blank, or something to be admired at a distance.'

His writing suffered after the gloomy end to the affair. Once again the plots suited his mood: a novel *Albert Westley* subtitled *The Grave of Passion*, and another novel *Guardia or The Moral Martyr*, described as a tale of the 'strongest passions of the noblest kind' and 'Creative power building over and upon the heart's ruins'. He wrote without vigour; the 'vanity, the glory, the enthusiasm of hope' had gone out of literary creation. He tried instead solid reading – 'with amusing touches' – but the effect was still depressing. 'I wander through a wilderness of words, but my heart still accompanies me with all its wounds.'

He was engaged in his introspective tunnel-raking and peering 'out of bounds' on the twentieth day of July 1829, dashing off maxims which were 'not mere feathers of my brain' but the products of his 'whole life'. He wrote as Hazlitt had done after his unhappy love affair, after the manner of Rochefoucauld, and like Hazlitt he found a 'peculiar *stimulus*, and at the same time a freedom from all anxiety in this mode of writing'. Maxims flew from his pen 'with a kind of knack' at the rate of at least six to the hour. In this relaxed temper he suddenly began self-analysis more searching and serious than any he had yet undertaken, and for the next eight pages he hunted himself 'down to the bottom' as sincerely and faithfully as he knew, hoping that perhaps by self-knowledge he might find a remedy to his mental predicament. The resulting *Miscellaneous Thoughts* are a boon to the biographer: self-conscious, rather pretentious, reminiscent of Hazlitt's *Characteristics* in their frequent references to blighted love but nevertheless distinctively Horne's own thoughts. Conveying his fears of death and decay, shot through with fleeting allusions to indirect murder, haunted by memories of Mexico and North America, they laid bare the prominent strains in his nature as eloquently as they depicted his current state of mind.

Horne, in his self-analysis, was looking for a positive, reassuring sense of his own identity. He did not find it. Instead he found a poet who dramatized himself into another's thoughts unconsciously. His own real character was virtually impossible to discover, his motives equally equivocal. He became a prey to emotional violence that startled, appalled, and exhausted him. He might have been an actor 'of fine-wrought intensity, scarcely equalled', he wrote, had it not been for the fear of 'personal exposure' and the fear that on stage, through an assumed character, he might 'kill somebody outright'. He was a prey to imagination to the extent that the imagined was often more real for him than reality. 'Romance is real, and reality romance.' He was a prey above all to anxiety, self-disgust, and a desire for self-probing that was unhealthy and compulsive, a probing done not to set himself aright but 'to please myself with a view of unpleasant things – which is part of my complaint'. In all, he was a prey to those very qualities that proclaimed him a poet: the chameleonic self-projection, the intense moods and passions, the truth-like imagination, and capacity for analysis of character, the ability to turn 'sensation into thought', and to 'resolve or analyse thought again into sensation'. 'My mind,' he concluded, 'is not in so healthy a state as I could wish: it never has been: and why? – because the heart "the most central of all things", has always been running over to *waste*. The last grand gush has just passed – it has fallen into a dreary void of high and refined abstractions.'

Horne apparently believed that some outside influence – he had hoped it might have been A – was necessary to transform his extravagant emotions to wholesome power. In fact, only self-knowledge and self-management were more likely to transform him. Unfortunately the type of management needed was not the type Horne was likely to employ. Unwittingly he had begun to uncover one of the tragedies of the Romantic view of the poet, a view that put such a premium on personal characteristics as to confuse them with genius itself. The Romantic poets, intensely aware of self and absorbed by their own psychology, had looked into themselves for the answer to what is genius and had found personal qualities that seemed common to most poets and which they had then assumed were part of genius. In fact, as Horne had recognized, those qualities could exist independently of genius just as, though he may have doubted it, genius could exist independently of them. In practice a would-be poet who saw these personal qualities in himself fastened on them, identifying them with the poetic faculty, fostering and developing them as part of his poetic duty – and that task was often easier than developing actual creative skills. Not only did this delude many a mediocre writer into thinking himself a genius; those qualities, nourished to excess, also made normal life impossible. Similarly it was feared that the encouragement of vigour and resourcefulness and other practical qualities might interfere with the poetic side, since they presupposed self-control rather than the releasing of feeling or imagination. Practical qualities must be held in abeyance – if not denied – even though they might be capable of keeping the poetic ones in healthy balance. The two sides of his nature must be in continual tension: compromise was seldom adequate. It meant either war or the complete sacrifice of the one to the other; and since the sacred gift of genius allowed no rivals, it was generally the sacrifice of reason, discipline and practicality to the poetic nature.

Shelley was one of the few who found a solution in theory. With his inspirational theory of poetry, he had been able to see the poet and the man as two separate natures occupying the same person in peaceful coexistence, the poet in command during those periods of inspiration, the man in control during the intervals. It should be pointed out that Shelley's own life did not match this theory, for in few others did the extravagant poetic qualities run greater or more constant riot. Horne never discovered a solution: and his striving to serve both gods was to cause him much anxiety and introspection.

Chapter 5

The False Medium

Horne's depression was passing: almost despite himself he had begun
to feel more cheerful. His rising spirits put some of the old vigour
back into his writing but his career was still clouded by 'doubts and
denials'. They were brought unhappily home to him in the piles of unpublished manuscripts which lay in his tin trunk: plays into which above
all other literary forms he put his 'Heart's best blood', massive novels
copied painstakingly in triplicate, and underscored with careful cor-
rections in the attempt to make them perfect. The unpalatable fact
remained that at the age of twenty-seven, after seven years of dogged
effort, his only publications were ephemeral verses in ephemeral
magazines. Though he had had 'many a grievous fit of despondency
and indulged in many a savage mood at the delays and disappointments', he was devoted as ever to his mission. That urgency he had felt
from the start to develop his poetic capacities now amounted, he confessed, to 'a passion'. He was sustained by 'cold solid will'.

As his energy returned he threw himself back into rigorous and,
as ever, spasmodic self-education. He read diligently with special attention to art and music; he went constantly to the theatre; he visited his
old friends Charles Wells and, more frequently, Tom Stone who had
now finished his studies in Edinburgh and was practising in London as
a physician. As the year 1830 ended there was one incident that excited
and unnerved him, awakening a welter of emotions, and conjuring up
echoes of those childhood fears that never quite deserted him. It
happened one afternoon when he had gone to dine with Charles Wells.
They were about to sit down to dinner when a message came for
Wells, telling him William Hazlitt was dying and urging to him to come
and make his peace before it was too late. Wells, blaming himself for
the recent estrangement between himself and Hazlitt, prepared to go

at once to Hazlitt's lodgings. Then, seeing Horne's distress and possibly feeling the need for support, he invited Horne to come with him. Naturally, Horne accepted.

Wells, his wife and Horne then went through Soho's dingy streets to an address in Frith Street, up two flights of 'dusky stairs' and into a meagre room filled with a 'close and earthy' smell and lit only by thin shafts of light which filtered through broken blinds. No details of that room went unrecorded in Horne's mind. In the gloom they saw that it had been tidied: it was again 'to let' for Hazlitt was dead. Beside the neatly made bed and the bookcase filled with Hazlitt's books stood the coffin set on trestles, covered by a tablecloth. They called the char-woman, who kept up a commentary on Hazlitt's last hours – how he had laughed and joked, unafraid, though he was suffering the tortures of cancer of the stomach – she removed the coffin's lid, and Horne looked down for the first time on the face of his god. It was a 'fixed, unfathom-able face', with a slight Sphinx-like smile. He stood 'in silence, for a considerable time' looking down. Then he kissed the cold hand and with Wells took a strand of the thick iron-grey hair which he always treasured. Before leaving he noticed Hazlitt's hat and gloves – apart from the books the one personal symbol of Hazlitt's occupancy of that impersonal room – and the sight moved him unbearably. A long time later he translated his memories of that afternoon into a sadly mediocre poem which he dedicated to Thomas Carlyle.

Wells was overcome with remorse and, being Wells, with the de-sire to perform some service that would link him with Hazlitt in the eyes of posterity. Horne was equally eager in some way to serve the Master he had never been bold enough to serve in life. Together they took it on themselves to arrange the burial and have a death mask taken of the body. Horne sent to Sardis, the Italian statue makers, for a craftsman to make the mask and watched while the unfathomable face was swathed in plaster. It was a grisly custom, but an accepted custom nonetheless, and it was obviously not it alone that now caused him such disturbance. Some of the left eyebrow came away with the plaster and he was much put out. Then, soon after, when he and Wells went to St Anne's, Soho, to arrange for the burial, he issued the Sexton with curious instructions. Giving him extra money, he ordered that the grave be five feet deeper than customary, and that it be filled in with trusses of straw as well as earth, making any later attempt at exhuma-tion difficult. The rotting remains of William Hazlitt must never again be shown to the world. The reason he gave for such anxiety was that a grave-robbing phrenologist might covet the skull. And yet, so close are the details to the episode in his childhood of the murdered doll – the damaged eye, the horror he felt at its exhumation – that one wonders if his reactions were not unconsciously governed by this memory more than by any rational motive.

He left Wells to compose the cumbersome epitaph that originally appeared on Hazlitt's headstone. He himself wrote his epitaph in verse, in an elegiac ode, for this man he had worshipped from afar for ten years, with whose beliefs and emotions he had so closely identified himself, and never more closely than in this past eighteen months. He dedicated the poem to Hazlitt and also to those two others he worshipped: Keats and Shelley. (An odd combination if one remembers Hazlitt's tepid opinion of Keats and particularly of that 'philosophic fanatic', Shelley.) The theme of his poem was predictably the one that preoccupied him, refuelled by the sight of that cheap coffin and meagre room. It was the neglect of the poet and the poverty and suffering all poets must endure.

> *With him a pulse of truth and power is gone,*
> *And the world feels it not; because its brain,*
> *To all except self's proper gain,*
> *Like gold upon dead eyes, is folly cold.*

Original genius, he had written the year before, 'is a wretched state for the individual, in private life; since few or none will ever understand him, and while feeling an intense sympathy with all the best feelings of humanity, himself a solitary outcast from all sympathy!' How exactly now those words must have seemed to fit William Hazlitt.

Horne had recently come face to face with another solitary outcast who had genius of a kind though it was not precisely original, and this meeting too had reinforced his latent fears. One day rummaging in a bookseller's near Hampstead Heath he had struck up acquaintance with a dark military-looking man in his early fifties. The man whom Horne took at first glance for a 'sunbrowned general officer' turned out to be William Henry Ireland, who thirty years before had duped literary society with his Shakespeare forgeries. The despised son of an ardent and gullible collector of old manuscripts, William Ireland had decided to surprise his father by 'discovering' Shakespearian relics. As apprentice to a lawyer he had access to old parchments; with the aid of an unscrupulous bookbinder he had forged letters, poems, a lock of hair, even a new play of Shakespeare's, which every expert pronounced genuine. His delighted father held an exhibition to which Boswell and the learned Dr Parr had come to pay homage. Meanwhile a few experts were growing dubious about the literary and historical errors; the play *Vortigern and Rowena*, put on at Drury Lane, was laughed off the stage. Finding himself about to be exposed Ireland saved his opponents the trouble, confessed, and made off to France.

In fact Ireland was, as Horne was to discover, an innocent dupe – 'the dupe of his own ungoverned fancies'. He had believed he had seen Shakespeare's ghost watching benignly over him as he made his forgeries, and that gave them somehow a pseudo-genuineness. Now rejected by society as cruelly as he had been rejected by his father, his present fantasies were similarly endorsed by his imagination. He lived in a world of make-believe which flamboyantly compensated for the poverty of his cottage in Camden Town and drew to him a collection of odd admirers: French and Spanish refugees, musical young ladies and guitar-playing Napoleonic sympathizers. His family was large, his means meagre and dependent on spasmodic bursts of journalism, but his hospitality was whole and unapologetic. Horne remembered there was often only salad and baked apples for dinner and the plates were cracked but it was served with an air. No neglect or poverty or fantasy could disallow Ireland that air. He had it himself as he stamped about the room, grasping his long grey hair on both sides in a characteristic gesture and holding forth with great energy, articulation and high spirits on whatever topic took his fancy.

Though he recognized that Ireland lacked genius, Horne was nevertheless considerably influenced by the forger. Time after time he would go alone or with Tom Stone to Camden Town to soak in the impoverished 'French elegance' of Ireland's curious little court and to listen to their incessant reminiscences of Napoleon. Horne, as the son of a soldier, had grown up under the shadow of the old bogeyman Boney, but later he had conscientiously discarded such family prejudices and taken on the equally fervent bias in favour of Bonaparte held by William Hazlitt, who had gone about dishevelled, drunk, and almost demented for days after Waterloo. At William Ireland's, Horne found a fanatical devotion that outshone Hazlitt's, for Ireland, recently returned from France, was an ardent supporter of the Napoleonic régime and loved to gather French *emigrés* around him. Amongst them was the Comte de Dure, whose face with its huge forehead and the appearance of the wear and tear of antiquity reminded Horne of the Elgin marbles. The old count had a prodigious memory, quite appalling to Horne in its tenacity and immense sweep. Here, too, he met the Marquis de Maubreuil, one of the Emperor's former favourites, whose sinister, quiescent looks convinced Horne of Napoleon's wisdom in sacking him. Finally there was the most interesting of all, Baron Las Casas, the son of one of Napoleon's companions on St Helena, a small delicate man obsessed by a plan of revenge against Sir Hudson Lowe, Napoleon's gaoler on the island. He had come to the right ally for not only was Ireland devoted to the memory of 'the greatest patron of genius and art in every possible class that ever lived' – as he was fond of describing the Emperor – but abrim with enthusiasm for any hairbrained scheme. In no time he had concocted a plan as farfetched as his forgeries, to confront and horsewhip Sir Hudson outside his London home with all the friends from Camden Town involved in cloak and dagger machinations in the background. Even Horne was to play a part. To Horne's evident relief Sir Hudson, however, refused to play his part and hurried indoors when he saw the fanatical little Frenchman approaching with a whip in hand. Like all Ireland's schemes it came to nothing, and like the others too it was transformed by his devious imagination into an undoubted triumph.

Between that first meeting in the bookseller's soon after his return home, and the first years of the new decade, when he was a frequent visitor to Ireland's home, Horne came to study Ireland with the sympathy of a friend and at the same time the detached curiosity of the poet. He saw in him qualities that undoubtedly called forth affection: generosity, good nature and modesty, and the gift of being a 'most entertaining companion'. He saw that 'half his sins were his own defence', and that 'he deceived others, having first deceived himself'. What must have been more disquieting in his present state of mind, he saw as he analysed further that Ireland had mistaken in himself 'extravagance for originality, and wild absurdity for genius', that his imagination was 'unbalanced by a sufficient weight of other powers', and that ungoverned fancies ruled him. Uncomfortably close to those self-doubts and anxieties Horne had expressed in *Miscellaneous Thoughts* were these traits he was now observing in Ireland. There was a terrifying example of the fate to which the poetic life and poetic temperament could reduce a man. Once in the fading twilight of a summer's evening Horne had come on Ireland, his usual boisterousness evaporated, holding a tumbler of sugar and water and thinking about suicide. He was sick of life, he said: 'The more I struggle, the further I am pushed back.'

Before, with Keats and Shelley, the poetic sufferings had been remote, perhaps even glamorous; now that he had witnessed them first hand with Hazlitt and Ireland their pain was brought disquietingly home. In some ways Ireland's sufferings were the worst. He lacked real genius – except perhaps as a forger – but outwardly he had the signs of genius, he 'suffered poverty and persecution all his life', he was a prey to the corrupting poetic nature, as much as any genius. His nature, his sufferings, his ambitions were like those of genius. Who could blame him for deluding himself? He would pay the penalties, yet have none of the rewards; no future generations would applaud William Ireland. This was the fate of deluded mediocrity. His life had nothing to redeem it. What if Horne's life, too, was to be like this?

While Ireland's society, though entertaining, was not particularly consoling, Horne was finding both consolation and entertainment in another kind of literary society. He had managed to find casual work on a newspaper, a compromise perhaps with his admission the year before that he had 'been a mind to do some stupid work for the kitchen' while taking breath for a 'fresh attack' on poetry. If this was only a breather or diversion, it was nevertheless extraordinarily productive. The newspaper was the new *True Sun* and in its offices he met a group of young men, his own age or even younger; men who were to dominate literary society in ten years time. The paper's offices were indeed more like the midshipman's cabin aboard the *Libertad* than those of a progressive paper. They were full of high spirits and practical jokes and it was not unusual to see one of the contributors, an ugly little fellow named Douglas Jerrold, whose previous career had included like Horne's a spell as a midshipman, implant in an inkwell the pug nose of his tall dignified companion, John Forster. Later there was likely to be a water fight down the stairs with Jerrold, who was quicker than the more cumbersome Forster, and generally splashed water over Forster and onlookers alike. Horne struck up a firm acquaintanceship with John Forster, an ardent and likeable young man some years younger than himself, little knowing then how closely their lives would be connected in future years. He met there, too, the older journalists, Robert Bell and Laman Blanchard, who watched indulgently their younger colleagues' antics; he may also have seen if not met another casual reporter named Charles Dickens.

The devotion of these young men to their profession – one less exalted than his own poetic destiny – was surprising to him. They were ambitious: despite their fun they took journalism and literature seriously, writing biographies or plays or novels in their leisure. They were energetic, and none was content to sit down and bewail his poverty or neglect or lack of social standing. They were prepared to fight, determined to raise their status and improve their prospects as men of letters. They viewed their situation calmly, good-humouredly and, above all, rationally.

In the summer of 1832 such rational influences were valuable. Hitherto Horne's consideration of the fate of men of letters had been comfortingly conditioned by his own wealth. Most writers were dependent on the miserable living their literary work could earn them, and improvident, too, probably because of their artistic natures. This Horne believed would never entirely be his fate: the money left him by his father ought, with management, be enough to keep him in comfort for life. Now, in the summer of 1832, that insulation was removed and Horne was frighteningly confronted with a personal prospect of that wretched life.

The inheritance bequeathed him by his father had been left in a trust, the guardian being his father's friend, the family physician, Dr Maule. Maule's death early in 1832 revealed the trust to be in a state of distressing confusion, despite, or perhaps because of, the fact that Maule's son Henry was a rising lawyer. Horne had hated both father and son since childhood and had no great opinion of the son's honesty. He now felt his distrust had been overwhelmingly confirmed. The immediate cause of annoyance was a debt of £760, incurred by Maule as trustee, for which Horne now found himself liable. A bitter legal battle followed, waged at first unofficially through Horne's appeals to Henry Maule 'as a son, as a gentleman, as a decent human being', and as one who owned a debt of patronage and friendship to the Horne and Tice families, and then officially in the court of Chancery in a case that ended in July 1832 with an order for Horne to pay both debt and costs.

Horne was furious; at least he was rid of the Maules but at a terrible cost. He had had to stand by for twenty years 'while a selfish old man, no actual relation of mine, dissipated in sensuality and folly what properly belonged to me'. He had had to stand by and see his security as a poet vanish. How much was actually dissipated is not kown. It was enough, however, to disturb him seriously and to indulge those rooted anxieties concerning the poverty of poets. At a blow he seemed reduced to the ranks of those who starved because they wrote. For the first time his devotion to his poetic duty began to waver.

The practical side of his nature came up to tempt him with recollections of those days in Canada when he had earned four dollars a day working on the wharves and the thought then that he might have stayed on there and done well. Any existence was surely better than the starving writer's; he was a fool to starve when he might earn a living quietly and write his masterpieces in his leisure time. He was thirty now, his youth virtually gone, nothing published, and no prospect of a more hopeful future. In another ten years he might well be dead. Not for another twenty years would Horne come again so near turning his back on the poetic vocation.

Spring found him in the mood for action; it was either fight or let the anxieties overwhelm him and he was determined to fight. His change of mood was also due to a magazine which was then exercising a considerable influence. He had taken to reading *The New Monthly Magazine*, an advanced and liberal magazine, edited by Lytton Bulwer, a young man of his own age who had been William Godwin's last disciple and was currently a radical politician and fashionable novelist. Bulwer was also the disciple, as was Horne, of Isaac D'Israeli, father of the future prime minister, Benjamin Disraeli, the revered friend of Byron and Walter Scott, and himself a writer who devoted his life to the cause of the downtrodden professional author in books like *The Calamities of Authors* and *The Despair of Young Poets*, whose pages Horne knew by heart. With such common idols it was perhaps no wonder that Horne read *The New Monthly Magazine* so assiduously.

Two articles keenly moved him. The first was the story of Shelley's early life, and his sense of separateness always from his fellows, which made Horne feel surer than ever of his own genius. Inevitably too it raised the question of Shelley's suffering. 'Shelley,' Horne wrote significantly, 'would have received the meed of other Martyrs, if he had not chanced to possess means independent of the world.' The second was an article by Bulwer himself, writing as the disciple of Isaac D'Israeli. Bulwer argued that professional authors were among the most abused sections of society and that the causes of this abuse were apparent. If the authors banded together, he maintained that they could better their condition: he suggested some type of co-operative society, common then in industrial England. Bulwer's ideas were not new and for a generation similar and futile remedies had been suggested, notably by Bulwer's predecessor on *The New Monthly*, Thomas Campbell, and by Isaac D'Israeli himself. The Royal Literary Fund had been such an attempt. None had worked, perhaps because the authors themselves, though assuredly downtrodden, had shown so little interest in them. Now reform in all spheres of English life was in the air; the new decade would see a change in the attitudes and activities of the authors themselves.

Previously Horne had accepted his fate tamely as a type of immutable law, pursuing the writers 'through life, like a graduated rack to the grave', from poor blind Homer to poor consumptive John Keats, and likely to include all future generations. Now it came to him that fate was no more than the personification of ordinary forces; it could be analysed and fought by reason. By May 1833 he had formulated his thoughts into writing and, once begun, the work flowed swiftly into a volume of 330 printed pages which he opened with a dedication to Lytton Bulwer, a 'Patriot and Man of Genius'.

Believing [he wrote later in a letter] it was *not* a necessary condition, most especially when the worth of the individual was known, and that instead of resigning ourselves in hopeless fatality to so disastrous and disgraceful a system of things, some attempt should at least be made to rouse the world to a full perception of the melancholy history of its greatest benefactors, with a view to turn the knowledge to some use, and prevent it in future, or, at least, adopt some systematic means of superseding such results as far as possible, I wrote and published 'The Exposition of the False Medium'.

He called the book by the meandering title of *The Exposition of the False Medium and Barriers excluding Men of Genius from the Public*. Every drop of his despair at those 'doubts and denials' over the past ten years, every drop of his hatred for those formerly unknown enemies, went into his words. At times there was a sadistic vigour that at least one critic called 'an ornate cruelty' and found profoundly shocking. All his research on that topic that had become for him an obsession, all the problems and arguments he had been rehearsing to himself and his friends for years were to be found in its pages. He might have described it, as he had described *Miscellaneous Thoughts*, as the sum of his whole life. It opened with accounts of the sad histories of numerous men of genius drawn from the books of Isaac D'Israeli, from his own experience, from the lives of his friends Ireland, Tom Stone, and Charles Wells, and inevitably from his heroes, Shelley, Keats, Hazlitt. It went on to discuss those suddenly analysable reasons why such men should be persecuted. The answer, he proclaimed, was prejudice, wisdom and the 'heart's nobility'. It was also people and institutions: the stuffy, tyrannical Royal Academy, the monopolist systems of the two great theatres, Covent Garden and Drury Lane, the ignorant, tasteless theatrical managers. Above all, and here the long arrears of personal disappointments were let loose, it was the publisher's reader, 'the author's

unknown and unsuspected enemy'. For fifty-one pages, too absorbed
in his task to think of quitting in the interests of literary balance, Horne
worried that unsuspected enemy, like a terrier worrying a rat. 'He is
incorrigible', Horne wrote in his 'psychological anatomy' of the unfortunate Reader, 'incorrigible in his mistaken studies.'

> He pores over the gospel according to St Criticism, and we, who
> are living men, with all our feeling about us, are to be crippled,
> bound hand and foot, hamstrung, broken upon the wheel, pared
> down, and melted to make candles for him to read by! Upon this
> heretic lore he gazes 'with fervency'; . . . Oh, men of genius, to
> what would he reduce you!

After such violence the solution – over-involved and naïve like most of
Horne's business propositions – was disappointingly tame. No existing
institution for the relief of impoverished genius was adequate. Therefore, wrote Horne, a new one must be devised to encourage talent and
provide pensions; its cost no more, he calculated, than a sum of fifteen
thousand pounds a year. Such a 'Society of English Literature' was the
only hope for the man of letters. Until then he could offer only the cold
comfort of personal experience. Take heart and, if necessary, take other
work. Beware – and no more eloquent testimony could he have given
of those past experiences and new influences that had brought him to
it – beware emotion and imagination. Confine them to their place; and
let reason and sober judgment be the 'severe examiner and stern
artificer' of the writer's life and work.

He wrote with no more expectation of having it published than
anything else in the past ten years, though at least it had the doubtful
merit of being the least poetic of any of those other rejected efforts. It
was also affected in style, pretentious in its author's parade of learning
and omniscience, tiresomely long and hopelessly redundant. Its intensity and conviction made up, however, for a lot of its faults and
those were the qualities that undoubtedly caught the eye of Effingham
Wilson, a radical publisher who had published for Hazlitt and did not
mind taking chances with an unknown and unconventional author.
(It was to Effingham Wilson that the world owed the first published
collections of the poems of Robert Browning and Alfred Tennyson.)
To Horne's incredulous joy, before the end of the year he held in his
hands his first book, published anonymously it was true, but still
published: the persecuting, frustrating false mediums and barriers for
once defeated.

His joy was shortlived. Before the year was over he also held in his hands a copy of *Blackwood's Magazine*, that same magazine which had persecuted Keats and Hazlitt, and in it an article by their arch persecutor, the critic Christopher North. North, in real life John Wilson, the Professor of Moral Philosophy at Edinburgh University, had mellowed in the fifteen years since he had begun his attacks against Horne's heroes of the 'Cockney School' of literature, but his ageing wit still carried its sting. And that sting was inflated to full venom by Horne's pamphlet fulminating at the neglect of those very men whom North had made it his business to see neglected over those past fifteen years. In general Christopher North did not believe men of genius should be coddled; in particular he could not allow these 'Cockney' men of genius to be vindicated. On all accounts the book was meat for his skewer. Consequently he pricked Horne's weakest points: the book's crudity, its obsession, its pretentiousness, its redundance; and inspired by the 'ornate cruelty' of the tirade against the publisher's reader, he hurled it back to its author with interest, in precisely the same style. This anonymous author − this defender of Keats and Hazlitt − must, he declared, have 'all the worst attributes of human character most formidable in a Cockney'.

> . . . he is a monomaniac! − a stark-staring martyr! − the Glasgow gander! − proud as Pharaoh! − like Jack Scroggins! − his worship! − Jack Ketch! − the prophet! − an atheist! − the man of Plato! − a cannibal! − an inspired idiot! − an unfeathered biped! − monomaniacal necromancer! − Achilles in the Shades! − the great Founder! − the Frosty-faced Fogo! − the Gentleman in Black! − our friend!

It was clever, wickedly funny and viciously hurtful, nor, by the end of fifty columns, much less monomaniacal than what it set out to attack. Horne and his book were in tatters.

A worse reception for a first book − indeed any book − could scarcely be imagined. Reading it, Horne alternated between fury and despair, torn with conflicting reactions. Part of him wanted to fight back at any cost, part had already given up, another part was rejoicing with a grim satisfaction at having joined the glorious martyrdom of the Cockney writers. He was published and he was ruined. Yet should he consider himself more ruined than Hazlitt and Keats: might this not be proof he was indeed one of that glorious company?

His mind was billowing with despondency, anger and confusion when he picked up another review in a modest radical minor magazine, *The Monthly Repository*: 'An original, startling, and eloquent book; disproportionate in its parts, defective in its details, but full of vital energy.' It seemed like the sign for which he had been waiting. Emboldened he wrote with gratitude to its editor who invited him to call and bring his work. Though he could not know it, his poetic integrity had been saved. He had passed that perilous 'probationary trial' that he knew so often was fatal to young authors. The point where he might have turned away discouraged was, for the time being, gone and he was once more on the straight, and – for a stretch – easier path, of the poetic mission.

Chapter 6

Craven Hill

Number 5 Craven Hill, Bayswater: a cottage overlooking Kensington Gardens, covered with honeysuckle and roses, overgrown with cherries and apples and acacias, surrounded by cool green meadows spotted with grazing cows. 'How beautiful it all was!' sighed the authoress Mary Howitt remembering it many years later. 'There was a poetry, a grace, a beauty, and a life about it that remained its own to the last.' Today the site of the Craven Hill cottage is swallowed up in the rows of lodging houses and small hotels of Lancaster Gate; but in 1835 it was a matchless out-of-the-world corner to a dozen people who, in the eyes of some visitors, appeared almost as matchless as their surroundings. To this idyllic cottage Horne very often came in those years following the publication of *The False Medium*.

The cottage was the home of William Johnson Fox, the editor and owner of *The Monthly Repository*, who had praised *The False Medium* and was the 'literary father' of Robert Browning and 'the first public advocate of the then neglected poet Alfred Tennyson'. 'He used to say,' Horne wrote gratefully many years later, 'that he regarded me as his son.' And indeed it was one of Fox's most admirable qualities that as well as pursuing his own work actively and ably, he devoted himself with such pains and patience to his young protegés. In 1834 Fox was a 'little thick-set bushy-locked man of five and forty' with, according to his friend Thomas Carlyle, 'bright sympathetic-thoughtful eyes', a 'tendency to pot-belly and *snuffiness*' and a broad, flat face, according to another view, like a 'thinking orange'. Horne remembered his beautiful voice, his red-brown complexion and glowing hazel eyes, and his ungainly body, so short that it was a full head shorter than Horne's. He recalled too how Fox would 'amuse his circle of friends by placing himself in the attitude of a weaver at the loom and throwing an imaginary shuttle'.

He had been a poor weaver's boy whose ability had led to the pulpit of the Unitarian Chapel at South Place, Finsbury Square, to fame as an orator, and the friendship of the leading disciples of Jeremy Bentham, whose doctrines of social and political reform – popularized in the slogan 'the greatest good for the greatest number' – penetrated so much of Victorian Society. But fame had not brought Fox happiness: his feelings were torn between loyalty to his resentful, shrewish wife and love for his thirty-year-old ward, the devoted and sympathetic Eliza Flower, who lived with her sister in Fox's house. It was soon after Horne first met him in 1834 that Fox, unable to bear his intolerable home, made the step that almost ruined his career. Taking his deaf and dumb son and small daughter Tottie, he left his wife and eldest child and moved with Eliza Flower to Craven Hill.

After the vitriol of the attack in *Blackwood's*, Fox's generous review of *The False Medium* was emotionally received by Horne. Quick to follow up his advantage Horne sent off a formal note of thanks to *The Monthly Repository*, presenting his compliments and enclosing an article for the magazine. The publishing of the article, a fictitious emotional dialogue between a bishop and a clergyman whose son had committed suicide, provoked such a response from the radical, dissenting readers that Fox was amused to pass on to Horne numerous offers of money for the unfortunate clergyman. Encouraged, Horne now sought Fox's opinion of the play that he had been completing over the past months. Called *Alsargis*, it was set in Palmyra, the city whose ruins were the setting for Shelley's *Queen Mab*. It was also dedicated in *False Medium* style to Shelley, who with Keats and Charles Wells 'never during their whole lives received public recognition'. Fox was delighted with it, and from this beginning Horne became a regular contributor to the *Repository* and a regular visitor to Fox's home.

At Craven Hill Horne was introduced into the most important literary circle he had yet encountered. Fox's decision to live with Eliza Flower had cut him off from the Unitarian Church – though not from his own loyal South Place congregation – and had cut him off also from society in general. He and Eliza had countered by setting up their own society: one so intelligent and serene that they had no need of the world in their 'snug out-of-the-world corner' as Eliza called it. All who visited its quiet rooms or sat in its charming garden were infected with the peace and security of Craven Hill and the vitality of Fox himself; relieved of the strain of the past years, he seemed endowed now with second youth.

The young men who wrote for the *Repository* and visited

Craven Hill are for the most part forgotten names today. There was Egerton Webbe, a poet and musician who was to die young in tragic circumstances; Thomas Wade, another poet; his future brother-in-law, William James Linton, a poet and wood engraver who was to become a well-known Chartist. Two of Fox's young visitors were to become famous: young Robert Browning, the intense, Italian-looking lad, and John Stuart Mill, the precocious young philosopher whose Benthamite father had also known Fox. Benthamites were well in prominence and chief older visitor to the group was Thomas Southwood Smith, medical reformer and friend and physician to Jeremy Bentham. He had dissected the philosopher's body on a thunderous June afternoon on 1832 in the presence of his friends and kept the remains embalmed and fully dressed in a glass case in his rooms, an anecdote that – possibly because it contained the familiar ingredients of mutilation and decay – always fascinated Horne. Southwood Smith's gentle manner and absentmindedness endeared him to the women of Craven Hill in particular; years later Horne was to remember how Smith rode an old horse which incessantly bobbed its nose and how Smith was likely to knock into trees, being too deep in conversation to notice where he was going.

While those traditional enemies Bentham and Shelley were united as household gods at Craven Hill there was a third deity of equal importance: Mary Wollstonecraft, the eighteenth-century feminist who had married William Godwin, written *Rights for Women*, and died giving birth to the girl who became Shelley's wife. Her female disciples at Craven Hill were headed by Eliza Flower. Beautiful, sensitive, adored by Fox's young men – two of them at least, John Stuart Mill and Robert Browning, had been in love with her – Eliza was as unconventional as she was talented. Her musical gifts were, according to her friends, considerable, and her unconventionality was attested by an old friend of her family, Harriet Martineau, the political philosopher, who remarked that Eliza was 'ignorant of many of the important proprieties of life'. She gathered around her a group of women as unconventional and talented as herself. There was her sister Sarah, a more flamboyant, unstable version of herself, who aspired to be an actress and was the author of plays and devotional poetry, amongst which is still remembered her 'Nearer my God to thee'. When Eliza had gone with Fox, Sarah had married the former son-in-law of the political radical Francis Place, a man much older than herself and much disliked at Craven Hill, named William Bridges Adams. In Eliza's group there was also that dark-haired poetess of mediocre talents, Harriet Taylor, the wife of a wealthy manufacturer who betwitched John Stuart Mill and provided one of the most ambiguous and celebrated of Victorian romances. There was also Caroline Hill, daughter of Southwood Smith, an ardent feminist and educationist, and her two close friends, Scottish sisters Mary and Margaret Gillies, the one a writer, the other a successful portrait painter. The impact of such intellectual women on Horne was considerable: after a year in their society he wished that the convinced antifeminist Hazlitt could have known them.

Life at Craven Hill was leisurely. On summer's afternoons the friends would gather in the overgrown garden under the huge cherry tree on which Fox had hung the placard 'Blackbirds May Eat Cherries Here'. The family pet was a tame blackbird and Horne would recline beneath the branches and whistle to it or play his guitar. The children would play games, and novels would be read aloud, novels unfit, Horne complained with fatherly concern, for little Tottie Fox's ears, being 'full of domestic passions, described with all the minute literal finish of a Dutch picture, or a lecture on anatomy, but in as homely language as Robinson Crusoe'. In the evening in Eliza's lamplit drawing room there would be more reading; Eliza might play the piano, possibly one of her own compositions, or perhaps one of Horne's poems set by her to music. Or her sister would act dramatic tableaux or scenes from some of her friend's plays.

And always there would be talk: a mixture of politics, literature and art delivered with the intellectual and radical ardour that was typical of Craven Hill. It might be on Bulwer's latest play, Margaret Gillies's latest exhibition at the Suffolk Street Galleries, the corn laws, or divorce reform, or any of the swarm of causes that enlisted their radical sympathies; but it was always ardent and intelligent. And if Horne's mind wandered, his eyes could alway seek the low ivy-covered wall of the neighbouring house. If Craven Hill needed anything to make it more perfect for him, the ivy wall provided that touch. For behind the walls lived the musician Vincent Novello, the devoted friend of Keats, Shelley and Hazlitt and so a link with Horne's imaginative poetic roots.

Having enjoyed a literary circle only at secondhand through Charles Wells or in the second rate with William Ireland, the entry to a circle such as Fox's was like the fulfilment of a dream. To discover the faith and encouragement of Fox and his friends was an emotional windfall. Entry to Fox's home moreover meant entry into literary society in general, for so concentrated was London literary society, and group so overlapped group, that even in Eliza Flower's socially dubious drawing-room one was likely to make friends who would later take one farther afield. Fifteen years later, there was scarcely a friendship of Horne's – and of Robert Browning's too – that did not have its roots in that Bayswater cottage.

The society of Fox's home produced in Horne an intellectual and emotional ferment only to be compared with that first reading of Shelley. Presumably he had already met the ideas of Bentham; certainly he had admired the radicalism of Hazlitt and his own rebellious temperament had responded to Shelley, the most radical and socially conscious of all the Romantic poets. Infected by Craven Hill's bitterness following the disappointments of the 1832 Reform Bill, Horne's reforming zeal, which had previously directed itself towards the fate of genius, was suddenly redirected. Abruptly his object became the common man, his opponents a new set of persecutors. Within a few months of his first visit to Fox he had another book at press with Effingham Wilson, a 'dramatic burlesque' entitled *The Spirit of Peers and People*, a vicious attack on church, king and parliament. Demanding for every man those undoubted rights given to all by nature this new disciple almost equalled his master in fervour.

Fortunately Horne at this time felt none of the tension between the functions of reformer and poet that he was later to feel. His ardour inflamed, he felt both functions were necessary and compatible; he, like a Renaissance Universal Man, would emcompass all aspects of reform within his genius. He did not yet have fears and guilts that the energy spent on practical causes was energy lost to the poetic mission: and his peace of mind must, partly at least, be attributed to that unusual intellectual climate of Craven Hill. Though elsewhere the ideas of Shelley and Bentham might be at war, at Craven Hill all visitors were expected to discuss poetry and Utilitarian reform in the same breath. Only such a circle, perhaps, could have produced the alliance between John Stuart Mill and Harriet Taylor; possibly one of the most curious and genuine marriages of reason and imagination in the nineteenth century.

We glimpse Horne, in the three years that he spent as a regular visitor to the Craven Hill cottage, rushing importantly about his business dressed in his flowered waistcoat and swirling cape-cloak. His hair is long and already balding on top, his recently grown moustache droops dramatically about his mouth. He is to be seen hurrying down Bayswater Road to Craven Hill, bustling off to his publishers at the Royal Exchange or to *The Monthly Repository* offices in Paternoster Row, or at night in the audience at Covent Garden and afterwards at parties in the actors' dressing rooms. Or we glimpse him at breakfast at the lodgings he had taken at the end of 1834 in Charlotte Street by Rathbone Place, a poor and shabby Soho street inhabited mostly by Italian artists and gloomy warehouses. Much of his time is still devoted to his mother whose nervous system, as he was accustomed to complain, is still liable to sudden fits of change, so his luggage is likely to be packed for a few days at the sea while he is dashing off a parting note to Fox about the *Repository's* business. His energies are recharged, his anxieties temporarily forgotten, he is absorbed in new enthusiasms.

His impetuous letters to Fox betray him, at thirty-three, as still liable to enthusiasms and antagonisms more typical of an adolescent. He is brash, over-eager, over-facetious, and often over-grateful. Yet as the months of 1835 pass there comes a gradual change of tone in the correspondence: more confidence, more maturity, and an even larger measure of his old ambition. Where he was timid and over-effusive he becomes authoritative, possessive and demanding, until Fox must be wondering if this protégé that he has nursed with such kindness and tact might not prove a nuisance.

Horne's confidence grew extraordinarily. In part, this was due to his rising reputation as the author of two published books and to the encouragement of his Craven Hill friends. In particular it was due to the sympathy and encouragement of one of those new friends, one of Eliza Flower's quiet feminists, the Scottish authoress Mary Gillies. Little is left of Mary Gillies today. Her artist sister Margaret has left more behind her and her portraits look out from the walls of the National Portrait Gallery and from a dozen literary biographies, displaying the 'soul' for which they were praised in their time. Of Mary, however, there only remain a few children's stories, outdated and never read, a few letters and fleeting sentences in nineteenth-century memoirs. It would seem that she had been introduced to Fox's home and the pages of *The Monthly Repository* by Thomas Southwood Smith; for Smith was her nearest neighbour at Highgate, where the Gillies sisters lived together with their ageing father in a rambling old house called 'Hillside'.

From acquaintance with Smith and Fox and Eliza Flower, Mary had become a regular contributor to the *Repository* and an impressionable visitor to Craven Hill. When Horne first met her she was nearly three years older than he: a quiet woman with an unassuming manner and a noticeable Scottish accent. She had been born in London in 1800, the eldest child of William Gillies, a Scottish merchant, and his Welsh wife Charlotte. Her father had gone bankrupt, and her mother had died when she was eleven, and she had been packed off with her younger sister, Margaret, to Edinburgh to live with her aunts and an uncle, a Scottish judge. The girls had disappointed their aristocratic guardians by turning their backs on Edinburgh society and developing with determination their artistic and literary talents. Mary at least had the precedent of literary kinsmen, for another uncle, Rev. John Gillies, had been a classical scholar and historian, and a cousin, Robert Pearse Gillies, had written for *Blackwood's Magazine*. That a young lady of Margaret Gillies's upbringing should aspire to be a professional artist was unthinkable, but Margaret, the more open and forceful of the sisters, had had her way and both had gone to London to study. Margaret was the more talented and with little formal training became a successful portraitist and miniaturist – and later a well-known water colourist – and the records of those who sat to her bear tribute not only to her skill but also to her endearing nature: both the actor William Charles Macready and the poet William Wordsworth, men not noted for their sociability, were softened by her charm.

Mary's manner was more severe. Flamboyant Harriet Taylor stood in awe of her. Mary Howitt, the Quaker authoress who met her often at Craven Hill, wrote eloquently that she was 'the embodiment of peace and an admirable writer', but that her talent 'like the violet, was left in the shade'. Lady Lindsay in 1877 remembered her as a restrained woman, taller and quieter than her more impulsive sister, and of 'douce appearance', courteous ways, and that delicate Scottish speech that 'is now never more heard'. Horne's only recorded comment of this woman who for thirty-five years was his devoted friend and amanuensis was simply: 'My oldest, truest friend . . . an angelic nature.'

Regrettably there is no way now of discovering the details of his relationship with this oldest, truest friend. Amanuensis and confidante she certainly was, correcting his proofs, often answering his letters, taking charge of the historical research for his biographies. It was to her tact in later years that he was to entrust his overtures to his estranged wife, and it was to her compassionate ears that he was to release his grief at his illegitimate son's death. She was the guardian of his domestic comfort, planning him suppers of strawberries, sewing flannel in his waistcoat to keep him warm, taking him to live in her house for over a year in 1846, though in what capacity the biographer is left to wonder. Those maternal qualities that Horne was to demand time and time again were never more apparent than in Mary. Even her age reinforced them: and those actual three years of difference between them may have seemed more because of her restrained manner and delicate health – though like so many Victorian invalids she lived to be over seventy.

Denied children of her own, Mary worked for the better education of English children and lavished care and love on the children of her brother and of her friend Caroline Hill, whose daughter Gertrude she virtually adopted and raised. It would seem that mothering may have been the essence of her bond with Horne. But not the only bond: for Horne was more to her than either son, lover or friend. He was her duty. No one reading her letters can doubt her emotional strength, a strength that found expression so often in vicarious ways. Like many Victorian women her feminist soul craved an independent career but found her ambitions thwarted by her meagre education, unsuitable upbringing, the pressures of society, and above all by her lack of outstanding talent. She was also intensely if unorthodoxly religious. She believed it her sacred obligation to serve mankind. From that first day she met Horne at Craven Hill, his became a life through which she might live and earn, if not the reward of an independent literary career, at least the satisfaction of fostering his genius.

Mary was unrelenting in her efforts to inspire him. The backs of her letters were sometimes scrawled with quotations from Shelley's *Defence of Poetry* proclaiming the poet to be the unacknowledged legislator of the age. The contents of those letters were likely to be a mixture of concern for his health and comfort and intense spiritual urging. Pages of her handwriting, determined and sloping and sharp on paper that is today creased and crumbling, found their way to his sentimental archives to be carefully preserved. 'Oh,' she would write, 'to see you out of the hard world and working to change it.' She longed 'to see the world influenced by high poetic feeling and purity'.

How quickly she identified herself wholeheartedly and intensely with the poetic mission may be seen in an incident as early as October 1835. Mary was at Peterborough and she had with her the manuscript of Horne's new poetic tragedy *Cosmo de' Medici*. It was the story of Cosmo's wild passionate son, Garcia, who accidently killing his detested brother suffers the guilts of a murderer until his father takes his life in recompense: a plot which fascinated Horne and may well have contained more of his own self than he realized. On a clear autumn afternoon, sitting out of doors, Mary read the manuscript. She was overwhelmed, so filled with the sense of its author's nearness, that it was as though Horne was beside and 'truly my companion'. She sat on, oblivious of the cold of the waning day. She watched 'the bright colours fade from the sky in a sort of dreamy enjoyment of what I had felt and occasionally of delight at the thought that fame must come to the author of such a tragedy'; later she was to recall that the day was 'hallowed . . . as one of the happiest of my life'. The new moon was in the sky before she felt calm enough to comment. 'I can *feel* it,' she wrote, 'but I shall never be able to say *how* or *why* I feel it.' That evening she was able to cover page upon page of an exercise book with analysis which ended with the sentence: 'It is a truly original work of genius. That I may see it worthily brought out and *soon* has become one of my best and brightest hopes.' She signed it 'Py', the affectionte shorthand by which Horne seems to have sometimes called her. No one reading those pages can doubt the intensity of a devotion that illuminates all her surviving letters to Horne with an unearthly light.

For unearthly they are: though the pages throb with her ardour, they contain not one endearment, not even one conventional 'dear' by his Christian name, though she signed the letters 'Mary'. Why should she attempt to conceal feelings when there was no apparent reason for concealing them? Was she, one wonders, trying to conceal the feelings from herself or was this merely a trait of this enigmatic woman's nature? Repeatedly a biographer comes back to the question of whether she was friend or mistress; or why, given their mutual sympathy and affection, they did not marry. No obvious obstacles barred it; her aged father who might have opposed a marriage himself took a third wife, a friend of his daughters named Mary Leman Grimstone who wrote for *The Monthly Repository*. There is one possible explanation. Did Mary, who showed such marked restraint in outwardly affections, share with those other women who overwhelmingly attracted him – A. in his past, his wife in his future – that fatal quality of 'innocence': his name for what was presumably these women's distaste for physical love? It seems possible. For though there are many straws of evidence which the wind blows many ways, it seems likely that this relationship, lasting for thirty-five years, was a platonic one. The charm, the comforts of love – free of the emotional responsibilities of a sexual relationship – were more than sufficient to him, it would seem, for the time being.

By the end of 1835 Horne's relationship with Mary was firmly established and his relationship with Fox was changing. The most considerable of these changes centred around *The Monthly Repository*. Now that Fox had cut himself off from the main Unitarian Church by living with Eliza Flower, he knew that his days as a Unitarian minister, even at the loyal South Place Chapel, were likely to be limited.

Journalism had always interested him; he had, one recalls, been one of the earliest contributors to *The Westminster Review*, and he now turned his full attention to it as a possible career. For a time *The Monthly Repository* had fully absorbed his energies as he transformed it from a purely Unitarian paper, which he had bought from the Unitarian church in 1831, into a gospel of Bentham and the arts with a circulation which was, as he could proudly claim, small but influential and select. But to a restless and ambitious man, and one who further-more was enjoying a second youth, the little *Repository* was not enough. During 1835 he had joined Horne's old paper *The True Sun*, under its radical new owner, Daniel Whittle Harvey, to become its chief leader writer. Taken up in this new work, Fox began unloading the tasks of the *Repository* on to his colleagues, and most of all on to Horne. Not that Horne was unwilling. He was more than willing for anything that might give him greater status in Craven Hill society, and that society had centred almost as much around the *Repository* as it had around Fox's personality. It was their voice to the world for their causes and enthusiasms. To take over the responsibilities of the *Repository* was like taking over their unofficial leadership.

It is therefore not surprising to find, by late 1835, that Horne re-garded the magazine as much – or indeed more – his personal property than its actual owners; and that he was in a state of anger and panic when he discovered that Fox, disgruntled with its chores and waning circulation, was prepared to sell it. Horne would not hear of such a surrender. Nowhere, he told Fox, was the truth so 'broadly or philo-sophically spoken': the journal could not be allowed to die or pass into other hands. For months Horne and Mary considered rescuing the *Repository* and together making it once more the outspoken journal dedicated to literature and reform. They believed they could, and after months of discussion, misgivings, false starts, and doubts and apathy on Fox's part, Horne finally proposed early in 1836 a triple partnership with himself as editor and Mary and Fox assisting. He would fight for Fox's policies against 'the standing army of hereditary legislators', against the Protestant church of Ireland 'propped in bayonets and blood', and the protectionist Corn Laws which 'bake . . . our bones to make our bread'. He would carry on the policy of educating the people to expect those rights that only ignorance prevented them from demanding. It was the author of *The Spirit of Peers and People* who pledged himself to *The Monthly Repository*.

Since his policies and ideals were already so clear to him it remained only to draw up the agreement with Fox. He devised a complicated set of terms that were the forerunner of many similar business transactions he was to devise during his lifetime: so naïve and tortuous in finance and drawn up with such ill-placed confidence in his own shrewdness that he never realized how impracticable they would be. On these terms he could not, he calculated, make a loss. 'If,' he said, 'if it be granted by Providence that we should make a profit, then every pound up to £20 a month will go to the editors.' If Providence should be even more kind, then Horne himself would be more kind also and allow Fox (still the owner) all profits below £30 a month and above £20. If there were still undivided profits, the three would share them. Fox was expected to supply half a sheet of copy for each issue. Mary had promised her undivided efforts 'Think it over well,' he told Fox, 'and I will draw up the Shylockian bond.' Fox did think it over well and, not unnaturally, had qualms.

By July 1836 Horne was installed as official editor with Mary and Fox as unpublicized partners. After one month Horne sensed he was trapped in the legal maze of his own shrewd document, and he had to rush down to Southwood Smith's country cottage near Loughton in the Epping Forest for a breath of fresh air and 'leafy shade'. After one year he needed more than a breath of air, for not even artificial respiration could revive the gasping *Repository*. The year of his editorship had been a ceaseless struggle against falling sales which had become hopeless after six months. Horne had grown a worry to himself, a worry to Fox whom he was forever cajoling or cursing for copy, and a worry to Mary and Eliza Flower who tried to keep the peace. Deserted by most of the *Repository's* old contributors – and no wonder if he treated them as he treated Fox – he and Mary were forced to churn out three quarters of the magazine themselves. He found himself filling the pages with his own unsigned literary articles and reviews instead of politics. Some of these were, in fact, remarkably good: one careful modern historian has attributed no less than three of his unsigned *Repository* articles to no lesser figures than Hazlitt, Charles Lamb, and Thomas Peacock. Yet he was worried to distraction that the political columns were thinning, and he knew that Fox alone could restore them. He knew too that Fox was unwilling to do so. 'Once,' he wrote to Eliza, begging her to intercede with Fox, 'Once the *Repository* was quoted as an authority for its political articles. This character is now on its last legs. I am not able to support it.' But by Christmas 1836 Fox had begged out of the agreement altogether and Horne and Mary were left to battle alone.

The Repository degenerated to a second-rate literary magazine with dwindling circulation. Horne could not bear to admit that his lack of ability, experience, or temperament might have been responsible for the failure. Yet it is so obvious from those letters that sped anxiously between Charlotte Street and Craven Hill that Horne was totally unsuited to this type of responsibility. He fussed constantly over trifles: one week he would be urging Fox to make his articles more radical, the next he would bemoan that they were too radical and would frighten new readers. Perpetually anxious, he squabbled with the printer, kept changing his mind, forever imagined crises which did not exist. By July 1837 even he must admit defeat and he wearily told Fox to look for a buyer. Yet to the last he protested it was not his fault and made excuses: a sectarian 'stigma' was still attached to the magazine from its Unitarian days, he claimed; or his dwindling personal finances – for his foolproof scheme for profit had, of course, backfired – prevented him persevering any longer when with a little more perseverance the *Repository* might still succeed. Fox understood his need to save his pride and did not contradict him; and with mutual relief they began to look for a new owner.

It was an unlikely task. And then, to their surprise, they found a buyer. It was Leigh Hunt, the former editor of many a radical journal, who had first won fame and a two-year term in prison in his *Examiner* twenty-five years previously for calling the Prince Regent a fat, dishonest, disreputable libertine. Hunt had an optimism that was nearer to foolhardiness; it alone had sustained him through the fifteen years of relentless misfortune that had come to him after Shelley's death. Since that golden day on the Italian beach when he had watched the body of his friend and patron perish in its funeral flames, he had known nothing but poverty, ill-health, domestic troubles and a succession of journalistic failures which included his recent *London Journal*, to which Horne himself had contributed a sonnet on snowdrops and a letter praising Keats. Without this knowledge of Hunt's character, his readiness to take over the run-down *Repository* is incomprehensible. Hunt accepted it cheerfully and its two old editors, glad to be rid of their white elephant, watched with uneasy heartiness.

As Fox and Horne had anticipated Hunt made intensive use of his literary friends. As they might also have anticipated, too, they were of little use. Though the poet dramatist Walter Savage Landor canvassed on the *Repository's* behalf, and though the noted literary hostess Lady Blessington gave her support, and though Hunt, in reply to queries, said the magazine grew 'imperceptibly, almost as a flower growing', it was dead within a year. And Horne, who two years before had said he could not bear to see the *Repository* go, looked on with undoubted satisfaction, observing complacently that Hunt had done no better than he in fighting the sectarian stigma.

Chapter 7

An Unacted Dramatist

Horne fell into a mood of dejection. Harassing and humiliating as the *Repository* had proved for him, now that it was gone his life seemed empty. For the past year there had been little time for anything else. Moreover, for the past three years its pages had been the recipients for all his enthusiasms and hatreds: his philosophy of the poet's mission, his indignation at the neglect suffered by genius, his reforming zeal and his memories of the past. Articles from his pen had covered a bewildering range of topics from recollections of the forger, Ireland, to trade policies in China. It was testimony to the challenges of editorship that never before or after did his journalism have more wit and vitality or such an urgent sense of communication. Without its challenge he felt exhausted, self-disgusted, and forlorn.

He had other losses, too, to disturb him. He was forced to confess to Fox that because of the money he had lost on the *Repository* his income was barely enough to keep him going. There was an emotional loss as well: his friendship with Fox did not really recover from the strain of those months of anxiety and bad temper over the magazine's affairs. It seemed as though the literary son had grown into adolescence, at odds with Fox's fatherhood. Nor did it seem that Fox could ever again regard that son with the same amused tenderness and concern he once had done. Besides, Fox's interests had also changed and he was absorbed in new journals preparing for his famous role as a leader of the Anti-Corn Law League in the next decade. The matchless security of Craven Hill was lost to Horne for ever, and these days he confronted Eliza and Fox with irritation and impatience.

Bereft, but for Mary Gillies, of the outside forces that had comforted and guided him since he emerged as a published author, he sensibly busied himself with new friends and work. Chief among these friends was the *Repository's* new owner, Leigh Hunt. On that first meeting when Horne handed over the magazine, his gaze must often have searched Hunt's long, sad face, with its grizzled dark hair parted in the middle, and seen not the pathetic, middle-aged journalist but the youth of twenty-eight – five years younger than Horne's own age – who had defied the Regent and the Government and turned his years in Surrey gaol to triumph, painting his prison walls with roses, his ceiling in a likeness of the sky; installing his family, his piano, his busts and vases and books, and holding court to sympathixers from Byron and Lord Brougham to Jeremy Bentham. And behind Hunt's figure he must have seen the ghosts of his three beloved masters – Shelley, Keats, and Hazlitt – whose friend and champion Hunt had been. To know Hunt, the guardian of their memories, was almost to know them: better perhaps, for in this way there was no fear of his worship being shattered by the vagaries of a direct relationship.

In the following months a quick intimacy grew up between the two men, based on Horne's hero worship, Hunt's need of an admiring audience, and their mutual sympathies and similarities. Hunt's faults are better remembered today than his virtues: the irrespressible poetaster who with his family at Pisa drove Byron to distraction, the over-effusive man with petty pretensions and class snobbery; the egotistical friend who had at times so irritated Hazlitt and Keats, reducing, as Keats remarked in disgust, everything to the level of his second-rate mind.

The years had mellowed Hunt's radicalism, atheism, and sinister reputation. Though a reactionary spinster like the authoress Miss Mitford might hint darkly that no woman should ever praise Leigh Hunt, the adulterer, athiest, and bogeyman had long been released from the pillory, even by Christopher North, who had led the vituperative Cockney school attacks on him and Hazlitt. In the suburban settings of Craven Hill and Chelsea, looked up to by quieter and unexceptional, radical, middle-class writers, Hunt seemed at last to have found a background that did not detract from him. His generosity shone out; so did this sincerity, his honesty, his enthusiasm and wholehearted devotion to literature. His faults seemed simply endearing eccentricities: the celebrated effusiveness became, to one as unsure of himself as Horne, a manifestation of charm and flattering and reassuring.

A few months after Hunt had taken over the *Repository* Horne had contributed the manuscript of a play called *The Death of Marlowe*, and Hunt, in publishing it in the magazine, took the liberty of correcting a faulty passage. 'For your sake', he wrote to Horne, 'I was chiefly moved to venture on the officiousness; having conceived for you, during our short acquaintance if you will permit me to say so, the regard of a friend.' To be accounted, on short acquaintance, a friend of one of the closest friends of Shelley was an overwhelming honour; and when *The Death of Marlowe* was published as a book the following year, Horne tried to show his gratitude by dedicating it to Leigh Hunt who had 'long assisted largely and most successfully to educate the hearts and heads of both old and young'.

He had already visited Hunt at home. One Tuesday evening in August 1837 he had walked along the river in the spring dusk, past the home of Thomas Carlyle in Cheyne Row and round the corner to lift the knocker of number 4 Upper Cheyne Row (now No. 22). The scene that must have met his eyes as the door opened has already been described with gusto by Hunt's near neighbours, the Carlyles: 'an indescribable dream-like household', indeed 'a poetical tinkerdom without parallel even in literature'. Beautiful, wild children ran about like gypsies while their mother dozed amid a sordid mess of broken chairs, ragged carpet, and the crusts and eggshells of their last meal; while, in the midst of it all, Hunt floated about in a muslin wrapper, oblivious to the disorder, ready to whisk his guest upstairs to his vases and books where, perched on the window seat of his study, he would proceed to impress his temperament on a wide range of topics. Though beset by a nagging, hypochondriac wife, a dishonest, spendthrift son, squabbling offspring and dunning tradesmen, Hunt was still able to sit serenely in his study, immersed in Chaucer or speculating cheerfully on the dignity of Man, or to retire with equal serenity to his bleak backyard to contemplate the wonders of Nature in a blade of grass.

To most, Hunt was either pathetic, revolting, or amusing. To Horne, though he quailed before the collective chaos of the Hunt family, Hunt's eccentricities were part of the temperament of genius, or, at the very least, quaint, lovable vagaries allowed to the talented. Horne was used to Romantic lovers of nature like Mary Gillies, who sent him pages of pastoral descriptions and would forget her delicate health to go out on frosty December nights to contemplate the sky. He was not therefore surprised to be taken out by Hunt to the backyard cabbage patch to observe the diamonds of dew on the green leaves, and he similarly saved his protests as he watched Hunt play his piano close to a raging fire because – though he knew it would ruin the piano, which he could ill afford – the sensation was delicious. His ardour was engaging; his honesty, courage and sincerity were admirable; his generosity and humility equally remarkable if somewhat mis-

Richard Hengist Horne in the Craven Hill days

Charles Wells

Leigh Hunt, a portrait by Margaret Gillies

William Johnson Fox, a portrait by his daughter

placed at times. Horne was to confess that he could scarcely stand by and watch Hunt apologise to his voracious family for spending a few pence on books he needed in his work. What had begun for Horne as a veneration for the past friend of the Romantic Masters became a genuine veneration for 'one of the most amiable and widely-sympathizing men that ever lived', possessed of 'boundless charity', a 'religious passion in his soul' and the integrity to proclaim uncompromisingly his political and religious creeds regardless of danger to himself. Horne was uncomfortably aware that Hunt was much braver than himself.

They had not known one another long when they realized they shared another considerable bond. Nothing moved Horne more than to discover a nature like his own: it had drawn him to Shelley and now it drew him to Hunt. Disciples of *Shelleyan* atheism, both were troubled with spiritual struggles for which rebellion and atheism provided no complete solution. Horne had long held the irrational conviction that he was one who merited Divine wrath, though intellectually he rejected the very notion of its existence. In his Anglican childhood he had learned all men were miserable offenders and his particular conscience was prone to tell him so. As a child he had lain in bed, the murdered doll on his conscience, waiting in vain for God's punishment to breathe through the mouth of his clergyman grandfather. Nor was the Shelleyan adolescent, so notably preoccupied with divine punishment in his first long poem, totally calmed by either reason or rebellion. Shelley's religious iconoclasm was to colour his thinking deeply: he would never again subscribe to the doctrines he had 'adopted with the family name'. On the other hand he could never find some tranquillity by wholly rejecting them.

His mental depression and those 'midnights of the mind' that followed his return from Mexico convinced him more than ever that suffering was his destiny. The belief that he must suffer – as a purification for guilt or as a necessary part of the poetic destiny – was by now ingrained into the very core of his nature. Later, in the quiet reasonable atmosphere of Craven Hill among people of intense but intellectual and unconventional piety, the religious doubts and fears in Horne's mind came once more into the open. The people of Craven Hill were radical Unitarians: progressive thinkers of that denomination which so many nineteenth-century intellectuals preferred and which put emphasis on the rational and intellectual rather than the irrational, on Love rather than Wrath. Talking with Southwood Smith – a fervent convert to Unitarianism whose treatise on Death attracted Unitarians, poets, and physicians alike – Horne found comfort. He found sympathy and comfort too in the reassuring creed of Fox, who rejected Old Testament ideas of retribution, and in the creed of Mary Gillies, that other twin – but more secure – spirit to his own. But these people were, for the most part, spiritually reconciled, and Horne was far from reconciliation.

It was in Hunt that Horne found someone much nearer to his own spiritual mood. Hunt had suffered as Horne was suffering, and it had been precisely for this reason that he had privately published and circulated among his friends a pamphlet called *Christianism or Belief and Unbelief Reconciled* in which he set out his unorthodox faith and the spiritual exercises which, having helped him, might also help his friends. It was far from theologically profound, but it contained the very words Horne longed to believe. 'The world,' cried Hunt, 'has outgrown the terrors of its childhood'; nor could Hunt subscribe to 'one single dogma which the reason that God had put into our heads, or the heart He has put into our bosoms, revolts at'. If an angel, Hunt went on, were to tell him to believe in eternal punishment he would refuse to do it, for 'it would be better to believe the angel a delusion, than God monstrous'. How profoundly Horne was moved by Hunt's theology can be guessed by the note he scrawled, with evident emotion, at the end of his presentation copy of Hunt's autobiography, whose last pages summarized the author's creed:

And if you, brave and tender-hearted Leigh Hunt, had never written anything but the concluding pages of this book, you would nevertheless deserve to rank among the greatest benefactors of mankind.

R. H. Horne

Had it not been for disappointments that came crowning on him with the reviews of his play *Cosmo de' Medici*, Horne might have managed to stay the drift to deep despair. *Cosmo de' Medici*, his first published play, had appeared early in 1837, almost sixteen months after that October day at Peterborough when Mary had known such exultation reading it. Many of those sixteen months Horne had spent on revision, heeding the generous advice of Fox, who was now drama critic on *The Morning Chronicle* as well as a political journalist, and the advice also of John Forster who as drama critic on the influential *Examiner* was one of the most powerful reviewers in journalism. And yet, in spite of Mary's faith and Fox's and Forster's advice and encouragement, the critics were hostile or unimpressed. *The Literary Gazette* was the most hostile, calling the play melodramatic, lurid, unlofty, sensation-seeking: citing such devices as the killing on stage of a son by his father, a brother by his brother, and the confronting of the guilty Garcia, again on stage, with the decaying corpse of the brother he has stabbed. That scene with the decaying corpse had been inspired ostensibly by the seventeenth-century dramatist, John Webster, a writer much admired by Horne, but one wonders if it did not also have other inspiration of more personal nature. In fact the entire play, with its analysis of hate and guilt in the characters of Cosmo and his son Garcia, its theme of murderous rivalry between two brothers, its vivid depiction of the persecution and punishment of Garcia by his royal father, may have been fraught with personal significance. For the play is a study in the unconscious wish to kill and in the disproportionate remorse which follows when that wish is translated accidentally into fact. The guilt-ridden Garcia's plea for sympathy and understanding raises echoes of the child with the mutilated doll in the Edmonton garden. If he is guilty, cries despairing Garcia, then 'all the world' bears some guilt of murder, for

> . . . those who ne'er have done a deed of death,
> Have oft in private thoughts imagined it
> From trivial causes that have stirr'd their passions:
> Even the child who strikes intends to kill!

The Literary Gazette particularly renewed that old grudge against reviewers which had been ignited so fiercely by Christopher North. Always he longed to fight back at his critics and this time, armed with the convenient facts that the review had misquoted him and contradicted itself, he counterattacked through the *Repository*; a course that reflected little credit on him. Indeed his use of the *Repository* – which he was then still editing – to gain free publicity for his play was unscrupulous. No less than three long articles on his play appeared in its pages; the second of the three, and the abandoned preface refuting the historian Sismondi's interpretation of Cosmo's character, was published later as a pamphlet by Saunders and Ottley; the third, a glowing but unsigned review which appeared during Hunt's editorship, was almost certainly written by Horne himself since the paragraphs poking fun at German Shakespearian criticism, appeared later under Horne's name in *Fraser's Magazine*.

Horne was now established in literary life and one vexing set of reviews should not have had so devastating an effect. In his present state of nervousness, however, few things could have been more disturbing; it was only the first of what was to seem like a slow landslide of disappointments and frustrations. So many of them, indeed too many of them, concerned his plays; and towards his plays in the past few years he had developed an attitude of particular intensity, coming to believe that through them alone he would fulfil his mission. He had undertaken, with enthusiasm and under the tutelage of Fox and John Forster, an intensive study of the greatest English and German dramatic critics until, he modestly told Forster, 'I have never met anyone who had more studied than myself, nor anyone who I thought understood them better.'

What he synthesized from their writings was a theory of drama peculiarly Horne's own, emphasizing the dramatist's immense psychological power over his audience. He had come to believe that the dramatist could be the supreme educator of his age. He himself responded, he knew, to acted drama more than to any other art; so aware was he of his extraordinary capacity for involvement and self-identification with stage characters that it had prompted his confession in 1829 that, as an actor on a stage, he would be capable of murder. He concluded that in the dramatist's hands rested the precious power of 'teaching the human heart, through its sympathies and antipathies, the knowledge of itself'. In a theatre, 'thrown completely off his guard and all his social restraints', giving way to 'unrestrained impulses', identifying himself with the characters and with their experience, Horne believed that a man was capable of feeling 'emotions more generous, more just, and less selfish than under any other circumstances'.

Such a theory presupposed that a play be acted as well as read—and on this point Horne was to suffer more distress than with any reviews. For whereas it was comparatively easy to publish a play in London in the late eighteen-thirties, it was extremely difficult to have a play accepted for acting. For this Horne and his unacted fellow playwrights blamed, with some justice, the patent monopoly, which since the time of Charles I had given the theatres of Covent Garden and Drury Lane the sole right to perform legitimate drama. If a five-act comedy or tragedy were to be performed in any other theatres it had to have music – a ditty, as Horne said contemptuously, for Ophelia and a jig for the ghost of Hamlet's father. For decades the dramatists had been trying to abolish the monopoly. A Royal Commission on which Bulwer had sat in 1832 had actually recommended its abolition, and

Horne also had minutely pricked the dragon in *False Medium*. The dragon, however, was not to be slain until 1843.

Obviously the monopoly was degrading to the life of the theatre. Contemporary legitimate drama lacked incentive and opportunity: extravaganza, crude burlesque and animal shows which, as Horne complained dismally, the public seemed to prefer anyway, dominated the theatrical scene. In fact, Horne and the dramatists who blamed the monopoly solely for their ills brought much of their own misfortune on themselves by persisting in writing that strange hybrid, the Romantic, pseudo-Elizabethan poetic drama. Their plays might contain page upon page of poetic felicities and violent passions (a modern literary-dramatic critic, Allardyce Nicoll, has remarked on the scene after scene of poetic beauty in *Cosmo de' Medici*); but those same plays were invariably unactable, without drastic cutting and alteration. They were also totally unrelated to contemporary life and their authors were contemptuous of demands to make them otherwise. 'Universal truths', they appeared to argue, could only be conveyed through forms and subjects of the past: the present was degraded and degrading. When plays did appear before audiences at Covent Garden or Drury Lane Theatres, some like Bulwer's *Lady of Lyons* were a huge success: others, like Browning's *Strafford*, or plays by Thomas Talfourd and Leigh Hunt, were not. The authors, however, refused to learn from their mistakes; they persisted in their Elizabethan forms and themes and concentrated their hopes for success instead in the person of one man, the actor-producer William Charles Macready, 'the finest living tragedian', in Horne's estimation, 'since the death of Kean'.

Macready was an imposing man, square-jawed, pug-nosed, with heavy grey hair clubbed over his ears. He was also intelligent, sensitive and loyal as a friend, affectionate and generous as a husband and father, with a domestic life made tragic by illness and death. But in the theatre he was a tyrant, tortured by uncontrollable bursts of temper, ruthless and ambitious, though not without remorse, for he was said to spend his evenings going guiltily over the quarrels of the day. Theatrical history of the eighteen-thirties reads like a chronicle of his quarrels and rivalries: quarrels with the American actor Edwin Forrest, with the English actor Charles Kean (son of the actor Edmund Kean), with the proprietor of Drury Lane Theatre, and with the unscrupulous showman Alfred Bunn, who threatened legal action after Macready had displayed physical violence.

Saddest of all were his quarrels with those unfortunate friends whose plays he was persuaded to stage and act. In fact his friendship with the poet-dramatist was a contradiction. Though he did more than anyone of his time to raise acting in art and respectability, he despised his profession and wished he had been a lawyer. He was said, with some truth, to oppose the monopoly's abolition because he craved the power the manager of a monopolist theatre could control, power he actually achieved in 1837 at Covent Garden. He was opposed therefore to the political aims of the poet-dramatists and unsympathetic to many of their beliefs, and yet he courted their friendship and, when possible, put on their plays.

Like the others, Horne turned to Macready in the hope that his new play would be acted. Horne had first met him through John Forster at the end of 1834, not long after Forster's own first meeting with Macready at Edmund Kean's funeral; and Horne had introduced the two of them to Craven Hill. These newcomers had developed with Fox a closer friendship than with Horne, so that when Horne tried to launch his play on the stage he asked Fox to intercede for him rather than go himself to Macready with his acting copy of *Cosmo de' Medici*. Horne was almost desperate that *Cosmo* be performed, and Macready via Fox seemed his best chance of achieving it. At first that chance seemed good. Macready's letters after reading the play seemed, as Horne remarked, 'very kind, gentlemanly, and have every appearance of sincerity'. The actor considered, Horne learnt from Fox, that 'the poetry, the deep insight into the human heart and the terrific situation of characters are evidence of no common mind'. Horne was so elated by this judgment that he informed Macready, using Fox as his courier, that it was his 'earnest wish' that the actor put *Cosmo* on, not in London 'prostrate with raree-shows, got up by the scene shifter and tailor', but perhaps in Bath. He would not 'be fastidious' about any changes Macready might want to make but, he added contradictingly, he 'wanted to retain the liberty of doing as I please with the tragedy'. Then, confident of a reply, he waited. And that, according to Horne, was all he ever heard from Macready on the play and the last he saw of 'the only copy of *Cosmo* that I thought fit for acting'.

Horne was extremely and understandably bitter. And yet it seems likely that much of what happened had been his own unwitting fault. He had misinterpreted Macready's character, attributing to him the same poetic ideals and dramatic creed as he himself held. Even worse, he had insisted on keeping control of the play, and it was this type of playwright – the dedicated poet determined to see his unactable tragedy acted successfully yet kept intact – that Macready was learning to loathe. Young Robert Browning had driven Macready almost to distraction over his *Strafford* in 1837 and had pursued him even to his bath with the unactable *Return of the Druses*. And if he was difficult what would Horne have been: a poet so religiously devoted to ideals which Macready did not share; a man whose very appearance with his bohemian 'horrid moustachios' and flowing cloaks could provoke exasperated remarks in Macready's diary. There is no reason, however, to doubt that Macready was sincere in his praise of Horne's play – as a manuscript.

At first Horne accepted Macready's silence hopefully; when the silence lengthened into seven years and embraced other acting copies of other plays he saw the *Cosmo* incident as the first instance of the 'odd behaviour, and neglect' and 'continued and systematic delusion of tragic authors' by his 'very faithful friend Mr Macready'. Macready's behaviour was another proof that the world conspired against him and all genius.

He could still, however, find some causes for optimism. *Cosmo* at least had been published and within a few months another play was to join it. He had written a couple of published pamphlets – one *A Russian Catechism* parodying the Anglican catechism to attack Russian despotism. He had written, too, with much pleasure an introduction to a new edition of Hazlitt's *Characteristics*, the book by Hazlitt that he probably loved best, yet not even that was free from vexations and disillusion.

It had been seven years since he had looked down on that calm, dead face in the dingy Soho lodging-house and in that time Hazlitt's reputation had been largely forgotten by all but a few admirers. Then, in 1835, at Charlotte Street, Horne had discovered his neighbour to be none other than Hazlitt's only surviving child, William, the unfortunate son whose childhood had been troubled by his father's wild infatuation for the landlady's daughter and the father's subsequent divorce and unhappy remarriage. Caught in quarrels, scandal, and bitterness, his loyalty given to his mother, his feelings for his father were understandably equivocal. Nevertheless the young man – seven years younger than Horne himself – had seemed to Horne unequivocally proud of his father's genius and so anxious to perpetuate his literary memory that he had already urged Saunders and Ottley to reprint Hazlitt's work.

Dining with young Hazlitt, sitting afterwards at Charlotte Street, not far from that very house where Horne had seen the father's body, they discussed books, politics and, of course, the father: one imagines how immensely satisfying this relationship must have been for Horne. Soon to this satisfaction was added the intoxicating experience, known to all biographers, of looking into the private mind of a person with whom he had identified himself with intense emotion and intellect. For during those evenings he learned that the youth stored his father's papers in a hamper and that he intended bringing out a volume of literary remains with a memoir. The task of the memoir was intended for a family friend or perhaps Lytton Bulwer. Nevertheless within a few months it was clear that Horne's friendship with young Hazlitt had achieved for him the cherished honour of being Hazlitt's official biographer: the memoir had 'devolved on one who would not otherwise have presumed himself equal to the undertaking'.

So he began his intellectual and emotional pilgrimage. Who, it might have been argued, was better fitted for the task than Horne, a promising writer already deeply committed to Hazlitt's life and work? 'A biographer,' he was to write later, 'must know the man as well as the circumstances.' He must even, he considered, be like him in character and nature, and feelings. It had been, after all, that very bond of recognized likeness that had committed him to Hazlitt from the first. Now he came to know the excitement of seeing Hazlitt through the scrawled writing; of seeing him revealed as he had been revealed to few – perhaps to none – of those who had known him living; of feeling himself in Hazlitt and Hazlitt in himself in that curious interchange that seems inevitably to take place between biographer and subject. As he wrote of Hazlitt's childhood it became also his own childhood: eventually it became the childhood of all genius. In those parts of the biography that he published in the *Repository*, the only parts that survive today, it is often difficult to tell which is Horne and which Hazlitt, so close and emotional is the bond.

And yet within a few months he quarrelled with young Hazlitt and the biography was abandoned. Later, Hazlitt's grandson said that the family resented Horne's opening sentence 'Man is a common stone' – and that Horne had got no further. In fact, as the *Repository* articles suggest, Horne had got a great deal further. At all events, patron and biographer quarrelled, and Horne's version of the affair, confided to Fox with indignation, was that young Hazlitt's vagaries had been responsible. 'God help the young man,' wrote Horne, 'his self-interest is driving him out of his senses. . . . He is one of those curious fellows who fancy that everything advantageous to himself should be immediately effected by anyone who can do so, under any circumstances. . . . But I am not to be used in this way.' Lytton Bulwer, to whom reverted the task of biographer, was less touchy, and his version with the *Literary Remains* appeared in 1836. The following year *Characteristics* was published, independently of the Hazlitt family, with a preface written by Horne in order to 'supersede some erroneous impressions that might result from hasty glances'. True to himself he made it not only an indictment of the neglect of Hazlitt but of the neglect of all genius, adding a prophecy that in fifty years the Master's reputation would be immeasurably greater. At least he had done something to perpetuate Hazlitt's memory and increase his literary fame; he had not altogether failed his literary master.

Chapter 8

The Pit of Talent

The New Year of 1838 brought no comfort: another year and another birthday, his thirty-fifth. Only five years off official middle age, he felt he had achieved so little. Physically he already seemed middle-aged: his face had acquired that ageless-aged look it was to keep for another twenty years. Bald on the top of his head, his auburn curls falling to his collar, the trained moustachios drooping elegantly, the heavy-lidded blue eyes more sadly spaniel-like than ever: the effect was calculatedly Shakespearian, he looked a poet. His small body, inclined to paunchy fat, was still lithe, invigorated by regular exercise and by frequent holidays with his mother, at the sea where he swam almost regardless of the weather, and at Loughton where he walked long distances in Epping Forest. His health was good, his vitality enormous. Mentally and intellectually the picture was less pleasing.

Only five years of literary recognition lay behind him, and that only partial: and behind that again stretched wasted years of literary disappointment, personal depression, and disordered nerves. At thirty-five he had to his credit two published plays, a short book, several pamphlets, an ephemeral collection of articles in monthly magazines, and a tin trunk crammed with manuscripts that would never see the light of a publisher. His youth was almost gone and he had virtually nothing to show for it, for at his back were always the shadows of his literary masters, Shelley and Keats, who had crammed lifetimes of work and experience into their short lives. Though they lacked public recognition no one could say they had failed to develop their gifts. The same could not be said of their disciple.

Even the relative success of Horne's new play could not soften his sense of failure. This new play was *The Death of Marlowe*, printed by the *Repository's* printer and part owner, Reynell, and dedicated to

Leigh Hunt. Clad in pale grey paper wrappers it was sent with the author's compliments to appreciative friends: Fox, Southwood Smith, Thomas Talfourd, and of course to that dearest of friends, Mary Gillies, inscribed 'from her friend R. H. Horne'. The reviews that followed were almost all that its author could have wanted; and justly so for *The Death of Marlowe* – the only one of his tragedies he ever saw acted, and possibly the only one actable – contains his writing at its best: swift, clear and vigorous.

As with *Cosmo*, he had chosen a theme vibrant with personal implications. Marlowe was the poet destroyed by an ignorant and resentful public, victimized for that sensitivity of feeling and unconventionality of vision that is part of the poetic temperament and from which all poets must suffer. Horne's Marlowe is made to die at the hands of a tavern scoundrel embodying all the qualities of an unsympathetic public; contemptuous of the poet's genius, resentful of his power, playing on his vulnerable poetic sensibility. Horne's Marlowe is made also the victim of love, slain for loving a woman forbidden to him by society. Even so exalted a love as Marlowe's for the prostitute Cecilia is haunted by punishment and death.

Leigh Hunt reviewed *The Death of Marlowe* in the *Repository*, responding to the dedication with words of praise, and congratulating its author for daring to present a prostitute with a 'heart in her bosom'. 'It is a masterly specimen,' he wrote, 'of the concentration of a world of life, passion and sympathy,' and he went on to pay his fellow disciple of the Elizabethan dramatists the compliment of declaring it would have delighted Marlowe's contemporaries 'to the content of their stout and truly refined souls'. Another poet-dramatist with an Elizabethan soul, the ageing Walter Savage Landor, added his praises to Hunt's, exclaiming it had given him 'more delight than any other dramatic or poetical work in the last twenty years'. (Horne had saved Landor's *Examination of William Shakespeare* from neglect with a glowing review in the *Repository* the previous year, so he may have felt he was returning the favour.) Congratulations came from all sides; *Marlowe* was Horne's unequivocal success. Yet in the midst of it all he was apologising to the experienced playwright Thomas Talfourd that he was afraid 'the roughness of the execution would have subjected me to your censure'. This may have been more than polite modesty, for *Marlowe* is the simplest of his plays and Horne always tended to confuse simplicity with ineptness and complexity with polish.

Yet praise from friends, however sincere, was not enough to balance the malevolent fates. Nor could he cast depression forcibly from the mind; he believed no peace ever came from arbitrarily shutting out painful emotions. In February 1838, dark and wintry, he sat in his shabby room overlooking the narrow, dreary cobbles of Charlotte Street, and felt the burdens of the poetic life engulf him. He had seldom felt more wretched – probably not since those devastating depressions after his return from Mexico and after his love affair with A. And it was in this state that he sought help from a writer he had long admired: Thomas Carlyle, author of *Sartor Resartus* and the newly published *History of the French Revolution.*

Nothing was more precious to Horne than a sympathy shared with a nature and intelligence he believed similar to his own. He believed he had found it now in this dour Scottish genius whose 'incomprehensible' *Sartor Resartus* had appeared the same year as *The False Medium* and with a similarly depressing reception. Carlyle was seven years older than Horne, the son of a poor Scottish farmer, and had known, for most of his life, poverty, illness, melancholia, and religious doubts. He had abandoned his study for the ministry, been unhappy as a schoolteacher and earned little success so far as a writer. Beset by nameless fears, he could accept neither conventional Christianity nor atheism and had no peace of mind until, walking in Edinburgh's Leith Walk in the midsummer of 1822 after weeks of sleeplessness and depression, he had a curious spiritual experience that led to a view of life holding many of the elements of Horne's own.

Carlyle's literary guides were the German Romantics – Horne's were the English – and their doctrines on the role of genius were remarkably similar. Both believed in suffering, self-renunciation, and devotion to duty. Life owed no man happiness, according to Carlyle; man's only hope of peace lay, not in logic or speculation, but in acceptance of misfortune, rejection of self-interest, and dedication to work. Unconventionally religious, he believed that all things in the universe were symbols of God, whose divine spirit successively revealed itself in those men of genius whom he named the Heroes: a 'perpetual Priesthood from age to age' which governed the progress of mankind and revealed anew the eternal truths to man. It was a priesthood, moreover, which would welcome martyrdom as the common fate of Heroes. Nevertheless the Hero, in Carlyle's eyes, was by no means necessarily equatable with the poet: indeed of the Poet he was decidedly dubious. As Carlyle grew older he was prone, as Horne would note with dismay, to 'utter his anathema against poetry'. He despised Keats and Shelley, loathed Hazlitt, was to be called the prophet of the anti-Romantics for his stand against extravagant flights of poetry into a private emotion and fantasy that was totally divorced from reality. Despite this Horne was quick to see that there was nothing basically uncongenial in Carlyle's doctrines. They were, in essentials, the same as his own.

He had already met Carlyle. It happened that Carlyle had read in the *Repository*, early in 1837, Horne's poem *Delora* and had remarked to his neighbour Leigh Hunt that the author had 'a fierce nature. . . . May the gods grant him strength and patience to work it into firm metal and cast it into a shape that shall be perenniel'. He had admired also Horne's *Thought for Michael Angelo*, also appearing in the *Repository*, which had treated the subject of artistic genius, transposing the Eternal and Divine to finite human terms with (in Carlyle's opinion) 'fervid conception' and 'fine sentiment'. Hunt had passed the praise on to Horne who, conscious of their shared sympathies, had returned the compliment by quoting, on the title page of *The Death of Marlowe*, lines from the *French Revolution* which summed up their mutual belief in the divine essence of genius: 'He was a Man, fiery – real, from the great fire – bosom of Nature herself.' Thereafter, with Hunt as intermediary, a meeting between the two writers had been arranged and, a few months after his first visit to Hunt's home, Horne had walked once more along the Thames to meet a writer whose sympathies matched his own. He had gone first to Hunt's house and, at a 'trifle before six' on a dark December evening, had been escorted around the corner into number 5 Cheyne Row and the precise domestic world of Thomas and Jane Carlyle. There Hunt had introduced him to his hosts and to a fellow guest, a motherly, brown-haired little woman with an ear trumpet, that formidable authoress and political economist, Harriet Martineau.

The Carlyles being people of strict domestic habits, it is not difficult to reconstruct Horne's visit. Visitors for tea ate bread-and-butter and biscuits and jam laid out on a table before the fire in the charming sitting-room looking into the street. Honoured guests, 'capable of communion', were invited to fill their pipes from the tobacco jar on the mantelpiece and smoke with their host beside the fire. (It is not recorded if Horne were so honoured, though he was addicted to smoking and at the age of fifty is said to have won a marathon smoking match which almost finished his opponent.) What fascinated Harriet Martineau about the evening was the contrasting appearance and personalities of the host and male guests: the 'homely manliness' of Leigh Hunt, with his smooth grizzled hair, fine countenance and rapid conversation; the rugged face of Carlyle 'steeped in genius'; and Horne, the contrived eccentric in the presence of two natural ones, with his 'perfectly white complexion, and somewhat coxcombical curling whiskers and determined picturesqueness'.

In Horne's eyes Hunt was the philosopher of Hope, Carlyle the Philosopher of the Unhopeful. While the impossible optimist chirped among his books and cabbages, the ingrained pessimist fought dark life-struggles further down the street – two men seemingly so opposed yet with considerable affection and respect for one another. Horne, caught in a type of emotional and intellectual tug-of-war between them, sharing great but different sympathies with each, venerated them both, though at times this tug-of-war made him uncomfortable. He was always to remember an evening spent watching them arguing with 'that mixture of pleasantry and profundity . . . and that perfect ease and good nature, which distinguishes each of these men'. Then they had left 'the close room, candles and arguments' and gone out into the starry night. 'There,' Hunt had shouted, 'look up there! Look at that glorious harmony, that sings with infinite voices an eternal song of hope in the soul of man.' Carlyle had looked up and replied in his Scottish accent, 'Eh! it's a *sad* sight.' Horne, faced with a choice between the two opinions, was drawn reluctantly toward Carlyle: to the 'sad sight' – 'infinite worlds, each full of struggling and suffering beings – of beings who had to die . . . knowing not whence it came or whither it goeth'. He would rather have believed with Hunt, but the compulsions in his nature drew him inevitably to Carlyle.

In his gloom, in February 1838, Horne did not hesitate to set his miseries before Carlyle and beg for advice. The prompt reply was a forerunner of that celebrated advice Carlyle was to give in his lectures – and later his book – on the Hero. It was both comforting and elating:

I think that those bitter experiences you allude to are more or less, especially in these times, the lot of all men whatsoever that have any true talent to yet unfold. They are hard to bear; but useful, nay perhaps merciful and indispensible. The *infernal* pride that is in all of us needs to be trained into a *celestial*, into a silent, patient, blessed one – like what Christian people call humility, the beginning of all good, as I take it, in Art and Creation for us sons of Adam. Let us consider it as schooling; let us learn our lesson! For a true man, to whom talent *is* the great and sacred object, not the mere reputation of his talent, there can ultimately be no evil in these things. For such a man, considering what criticism is in our time, criticism can do

nothing so kind as misconstrue him, abuse him, neglect him . . .
Forward, therefore, and fear nothing. The way will be smooth or
rough; but the step being stout, the progress is not doubtful.

To Horne, sunk in depression at Charlotte Street, the way was
decidely rough; yet reading Carlyle's letter he felt it grow the smoother.
Longing to share his feelings with one he knew would feel them similarly, he sent the letter to Mary Gillies. He was not disappointed. She
reacted as strongly as he had hoped, and though it was late at night
she sent him a reply that he came to treasure almost as much as Carlyle's
letter. She too had been profoundly affected by Carlyle's advice:

I feel it quite refreshing to heart and soul [she told him] . . . these
are things to help one on one's way, and the appreciation of men
such as he is all one wants, as earnest of the appreciation of all
afterwards. They are like the mountain tops, as someone or other
said, that catch the light first, which is afterwards spread over all.

Yet she could not condone all Carlyle said. True to her femininity, she
could not look forward to the prospect of his martyrdom with the same
equanimity. It might be weak of her but 'Oh to see you out of the
hard world and working to change it.' Horne was grateful for her female concern, but, as usual, he knew Carlyle was right. The hard world
was by no by means finished with him yet. His only hope lay in trying
to come once more to terms with his destiny.

Literary frustration and disappointment were losing their edge with
time. He was coming partially to accept once more that neglect and
suffering were the normal life of the poet and, with that perverse
pleasure that was never far distant with him, to find a positive satisfaction in this sign of his genius. For the next three years, fortunately,
some of the sense of his own calamities was to be submerged in coping
with those of his friends: chief among them was Leigh Hunt, chroni-
cally poor and a financial nuisance to his friends for years. In the past
people had been amazingly generous to Hunt, and Shelley alone was
reputed to have given him huge sums of money – gifts which prompted
John Trelawny's celebrated quip that Hunt certainly had been Shelley's *dearest* friend. To help Hunt was a thankless task: it was like trying to rescue a drowning man, according to Byron, who persisted in
throwing himself back into the water. Hunt had no time, he told
thrifty Thomas Carlyle, for that mean virtue of thrift, consequently
he had no compunction in squandering gifts. All he asked was that,

when he had the means, he should be allowed to help his friends as they helped him; since he seldom had the means, and it was usually his friends' money anyway, this was scarcely a reciprocal arrangement. Certainly, though, it must be allowed that he did fulfil this obligation and when Horne was financially troubled in 1840 Hunt was the first to offer help.

Hunt, as Horne biblically put it, was a lily of the field, who accepted 'poverty as the normal condition' and sat at home 'in an easy chair under the cheerful belief that he should always ride over his troubles somehow!' And much as Horne might sympathize with this attitude, for he himself was a muddler, he could not help but be as exasperated as those others in the past who had also tried to help Hunt. It was a testimony to his affection for the man, and to the growth of his own tact and patience, that their friendship survived so well during those years in which he helped to manage Hunt's finances.

Horne had become concerned in Hunt's poverty partly because of his flourishing friendship and admiration for the ageing writer, partly because of his devotion to the cause of writers, and partly because he already knew two others who were patient patrons of Hunt. In recent years Thomas Talfourd and John Forster had been amongst Hunt's financial backers, these two being by now among Horne's close friends. Thomas Noon Talfourd was forty-three years old, amiable and intelligent and determined: an orator of note, a well-known dramatist and a successful barrister, who had come as a shy lad from a poor country family to study law at Inner Temple Lane, not far from Charles Lamb's rooms, and become the essayist's close friend and first biographer. Like Southwood Smith, the family physician to numerous literary people, Talfourd, the family lawyer, could have written the most fascinating of memoirs had he been prepared to violate professional secrecy. Like Smith, however, he was a man of unquestionable integrity who went on serving his friends, his profession, and the cause of writers, loyally and discreetly until in his sixtieth year, while sitting in his scarlet judge's robes addressing a jury, death claimed him.

Forster was a less attractive figure. The 'tall, ardent, noticeable young fellow' – as Fox had described him when Horne first brought him to Craven Hill – had advanced phenomenally since those *True Sun* days. At twenty-six, without money or genius, but with talent, ambition and colossal self-confidence, matched by almost total insensitivity, he had become literary and drama critic on the prominent *Examiner* and invaluable friend to numerous literary people. This large, pug-nosed young man with his mane of dark hair, intense eyes, and slight stoop –

The author of *Orion*, a portrait by Margaret Gillies

Southwood Smith, 'Physician of Mankind', a bust by J. Hart

Horne at about the time of his marriage

said to be copied from his friend and idol, the actor Macready – cultivated friends as professionally as he pursued his journalism. He had learned the knack of making himself indispensable and the 'knack', so one friend, Harrison Ainsworth, put it, 'of making people do as he liked whether they liked it or not'. Alert, energetic, a great organizer, he nevertheless owed his rapid rise as much to these carefully acquired friends as to his own merits. Horne described it as 'an opossum-like, bough-by-bough ascent', the friends, like rungs on a ladder, each used as a means to reach the next, yet none relinquished unless his celebrated tactlessness did it for him. For Forster, rather surprisingly for one so dependent on friendships, was notoriously arrogant and insensitive; and it was not without reason that he had been nick-named 'arbitrary gent' and 'beadle of the world' by the literary wits. His behaviour to Hunt, however, was much in his favour and one of his greatest virtues in Horne's eyes, and Forster gladly acknowledged his debt to Hunt, the first distinguished writer he had ever known, for introducing him to literary circles.

At first Bulwer, Talfourd and Forster had helped Hunt for private reasons: out of friendship, pity and admiration for his past, rather than out of cold principles or concern for a larger cause. But as the decade ended they were infected by the change – a change they had in part helped bring about – in the Professional Authors' crusade. What in 1830 had been a voice or two in a wilderness of scorn or indifference was now a crowd of voices. The idea of authors by profession had taken fire. Its old leaders still led it: Bulwer, Forster and even Horne, his right established by *The False Medium* and by his propaganda in the *Repository* on behalf of neglected genius.

Various reasons are given for this sudden burst of interest among writers concerning their status. The social climate may have been favourable, and writers and wage-workers alike combined in efforts to throw off their oppression by means of collective effort. Cheaper printing may have helped their status, as the larger stream of books from faster and cheaper presses brought them before a greater public. There were ambitious young men, too, among their ranks, risen from humble backgrounds, determined to make something of themselves and conscious that to achieve this they in turn must first make something of their profession; young men like Forster and those other young journalists Horne had known on *The True Sun*. Parliament, since the 1832 reforms, was also opened now to the writer. Bulwer, Talfourd and Benjamin Disraeli, the celebrated son of the great champion of Professional Authors, were literary parliamentarians who put in action the writers' demands for copyright laws and the abolition of the theatrical monopoly. They, for their part, were eager to raise the writers' social rank so as not to disgrace their parliamentary standing. These causes combined to produce an unconscious sporadic movement that within the next ten years would become conscious and organized, led by its early leaders, Horne included, and by those ambitious, obscurely born young writers like Charles Dickens and Forster.

A life devoted to humanity's welfare through the medium of of literature (the authors believed) also deserved humanity's recognition and protection. Hunt had given such a life and humanity's response had been, predictably, neglect. Consciously or unconsciously – probably the latter – Talfourd and Forster were looking for a guinea-pig through which to press the writers' general claim on society. And Hunt was perfect for this purpose. His genius went unquestioned in a time that was not producing geniuses, his reputation was nowadays respectable, and no tamer unrewarded genius existed. He was perfectly content to see his present poverty and past renown paraded as his friends thought fit; if anything, he delighted in it. From private pity Forster's and Talfourd's efforts grew into the Leigh Hunt Private List, its aim to give a weekly allowance of £3 – a lump sum being clearly fatal to one of Hunt's proclivities – and in time 'to get such names and feelings implicated in it, as may help to obtain L. H. his rightful renumeration "for labour performed" from the Government'. In 1838 Horne joined Talfourd as the Private List's third trustee.

Horne's motives in joining were undoubtedly sincere, though it would have been hypocritical if he had claimed that the notice it brought him was unwelcome. Enlisting subscribers he met people he might otherwise never have met: some fashionable, like the literary dandy Abraham Hayward, some politically famous, like Lord Holland, presumably approached because of his connections with Hunt's political past. The Private List ought to have been a pleasure for Horne; he had reckoned, however, without Hunt's wife. Marianne Hunt would seem to have been the least attractive of females: among Hunt's male contemporaries there is scarcely a favourable remark about her. She was reputed to be slovenly, dishonest, nagging, complaining and improvident, snobbish, malicious, a hypochondriac and possibly an alcoholic. Yet to give the poor woman her due, she had managed – somewhat haphazardly it must be admitted – to rear numerous children through a gypsy existence of constant poverty and uncertainty; she had steered them through the term in Surrey gaol, uneasy communal living with Shelley and Byron, and a nightmare voyage to Italy when, thought to be dying, she was huddled into tiny quarters with children, husband, and the family belongings. Life with Hunt would have been trying for any woman and to one of her limited nature and mentality very much so; she no doubt coped the only way she could.

This seems partly to explain, even if it does not excuse, her behaviour over the Private List. At first she appeared to welcome Horne as one of the few of her husband's friends not hostile to her. She would send him coy little letters about her concern for Hunt's health, her hopes for the fund, or invitations to call and discuss it even though her husband would not be home. Horne was undoubtedly flattered. But as time passed the discreetly coy tone of the letters changed. Horne began to think her calculating and provoking. He discovered she was not keeping proper accounts or receipts. Most disquieting of all, she began to accuse him and his fellow trustees behind their backs of cheating her and keeping back the weekly allowance. He repeatedly found himself forced to reprimand her, and rebukes such as this became typical: 'I received a letter from a Subscriber to the "Private List" *some weeks ago*, who asked if it were true you had received nothing from the "Private List" fund for the *last eight months* . . . the little memorandum of payment you sent me will not answer . . . you omitted to say *what* had been received.' Marianne Hunt was not to be trusted and Horne felt himself forced to be continually on guard in an extremely trying situation.

The Private List was not properly under way until early in 1839, though its organization had begun earlier. In the meantime Horne had been occupying himself with his usual journalism and his usual amusements. He researched into the history of copyright for Talfourd whose campaign for adequate copyright law earned him – as Charles Dickens put it, dedicating his *Pickwick Papers* to him – the gratitude of all 'who devote themselves to the most precarious of all pursuits'. He went often to the theatre, which was enjoying a burst of vitality with Macready's appointment as new manager of Covent Garden theatre. There, taking breath after his violent quarrel with Alfred Bunn, his former employer and the proprietor of Drury Lane theatre, Macready indulged his remarkable talent for imaginative and visually beautiful productions of Shakespeare. Horne joined those who thronged to see Macready's *Henry V*, *King Lear*, and *The Tempest*, and showered the stage with flowers. John Forster had been so moved by his idol's reception he had burst into tears, and Hunt too had been moved to tears by the exquisite settings of the plays. Sitting beside him in a box at *The Tempest* Horne had watched the tears on his cheeks as he exclaimed it was all too beautiful. Afterwards, with Hunt, Talfourd, and Forster, Horne had frequented the actors' green-rooms and dressing-rooms, often with the desire of talking to Macready, for the actor was still the main hope for his plays. The desire to be an acted dramatist had never been stronger, especially as he watched plays by Talfourd or Browning or other acquaintances put on by Macready and joined parties of congratulatory friends in the dressing-rooms after. If they could be acted why could not he!

Elsewhere the theatrical scene was causing annoyance to all who, like Horne, felt concerned by the state of English drama. At Drury Lane Alfred Bunn had imported the renowned American lion-tamer, Van Amburgh, who played to crowded houses and to the new Queen herself. Horne and his fellow dramatists were furious at the American's popularity, seeing in it a further sign of the decadence of public taste, and Horne was responsible for a sly and malicious, tongue-in-cheek biography of Van Amburgh supposedly by an admirer named Ephraim Watts. Published anonymously, it was highly praised by the more radical literary journals.

Most of Horne's theatrical energies were going into his latest play, *Gregory VII*. Never had his attitude to a play been more intense. He was determined that *Gregory* – as he told Fox – would be perfect 'this side of the Ideal'. When he sent the finished manuscript to Fox in 1838 he had put months of careful work into it, and Fox's reaction was consequently all the more irritating. Fox considered the play wrong in principle and philosophy. Horne was never happy with outspoken criticism, and on this occason least of all. He dashed off a reply full of unconcealed annoyance – the tone of many of his more recent letters to Fox – snapping that he had no intention of bringing out a tragedy wrong in principle and would he and Eliza kindly keep their views to themselves and not influence John Forster who admired the play. Fortunately a short stay by the sea at Margate calmed his nerves. He returned with a reconstructed last act and a more equable frame of mind, ready in a rather shamefaced manner to patch up relations with Eliza and Fox once more. It was noticeable, however, when the play was finally published in 1840 that Fox – unlike Carlyle, Hunt, Forster and the actor Charles Kemble – received no editorial acknowledgement or complimentary copy. Horne merely sent him an over-hearty letter explaining that, as he could barely afford to pay the printer, no free copies were available.

It was not surprising that Fox, the confirmed opponent of despots, found *Gregory VII* ambiguous. Horne wrote as a disciple of both Carlyle and Shelley, trapped in that Romantic ambiguity which allowed its adherents at the same time to glorify the tyrant and condemn tyranny. The result was a hero of disquieting morality. For it cannot be doubted Horne saw Gregory VII as a hero, excusing his ruthlessness to Hunt as a product of barbaric times, and even asking Carlyle to include him in his public lectures on the Hero in 1840. He had taken his plot, as usual, partly from history, partly from his own invention. (He claimed always that his plays were the essence of the best histories, an audience being more likely to accept from fact those 'universal truths' which they might not believe in fiction.) His play told the story of Gregory, risen from a poor monk to become an eleventh-century pope, unifying and strengthening his Church by violent, unscrupulous means justified as the working of divine will. Obsessed and destroyed by the monomania of belief in his divine destiny, supported by the devotion of a noble, idealistic woman, the echoes of Mary Gillies and of Horne himself are unmistakable. When Gregory is afire

> *. . . with all – exterminating wrath,*
> *And armed invulnerably 'gainst man and fiend*
> *By this high mission, acted in God's eye,*
> *And with His nostrils' breath impelled . . .*

he is Horne, releasing those energies and ambitions frustrated by real life, vicariously exploiting that violent sadistic side to his nature. Power preoccupied him, the tyrant fascinated him: it was a vision of himself that would not be banished.

He had shifted meanwhile from dingy Soho to more comfortable lodgings in the fashionable area of Gloucester Place, Portman Square: a narrow street with its pleasant three-storeyed houses, their first floors decked with iron balustrades. Horne lived in number seventy-four, near a house occupied by a family whose eldest daughter, an invalid who night after night bent her dark ringlets over Greek translations and Romantic poets, would soon exercise such influence over his own life and English literature. The family was named Moulton Barrett, the daughter the celebrated Elizabeth Barrett, Robert Browning's future wife.

Gregory VII continued to be polished, but by the end of 1838 another tyrant ruled Horne's desk. Significantly, it was Napoleon, the bogeyman of his youth and the hero of his early manhood – thanks to those fanatical Napoleonic supporters Ireland and Hazlitt. Horne's life seemed to have been lived under the shadow of Napoleon, either sinister or glorious, and now at the mature age of thirty-six he prepared to examine him intellectually. He began a biography of Napoleon, turning to use those views on biographical method he had laid down years before in the *Repository*. They are views worth repeating, not only for what light they throw on Horne's work, but because they could profitably be heeded by biographers today.

To collect, arrange, and studiously, perhaps elegantly, elaborate all the facts, dates, anecdotes and other materials, many a man can do this; . . . A fine biography can only be written by one who enters into the private as well as the public character of the object of his work. He must know the man as well as the circumstances. He can only do this by identifying himself with the thoughts, feelings, and actions, of the individual in question. He must actually resemble him in some points of character; must deeply appreciate all the chief qualities for which he was eminent, and possess sufficient imagination to comprehend and combine, where the broken or insecure chain of facts leaves shadows and shortcomings beyond the grasp of the analytical mind. In short, when he has carefully collected all the raw material of facts, he must see the truth shining clear through the contradictory evidence, through the real as well as the apparent contradictions of character; must be able to separate principles from acts, as well as trace them into each other, and have the manhood to write down in plain words the full result of his investigations.

They are admirable rules; and as Horne *seemed* capable of obeying them, what a superb biography he might have written! His sensibility enabled him to project himself into another personality. The ways in which he believed he resembled Napoleon were many: their mutual belief that the old must be destroyed to clear the way for the new, their awareness of their heroic mission, their boundless ambition, even the physical fact of their short stature – a point on which Horne was so sensitive in himself, and which he shared with his other hero, Gregory. There could be doubt, in theory, that he had sympathy, imagination, and an instinctive understanding of a being he believed was so like himself.

He was scrupulously careful over the collection of the facts. He wrote for help on sources to young William Hazlitt – that synonym of 'self-interest' – who, as a student of Napoleon like his father, was able to make a list of books. He wrote also to Carlyle, who sent an equally long list with pungent critical comments, remarking that Scott's Napoleon was what 'an English Tory Justice of the Peace might form over his nuts and wine' and Hazlitt's adoring biography was much too 'speculative and didactic' and gave 'little image of the man and his environment'. Mary Gillies's help was further enlisted and she spent many hours in the British Museum working on the sources.

In theory Horne ought to have seen the biographical truth shining abundantly clear. In fact he did not. The book was ruined by mediocrity and a fanatical devotion to Hazlitt's prejudiced biography, written in agony of mind and body not long before its author's death. Horne worshipped Hazlitt and Hazlitt worshipped Napoleon: it seemed to follow with emotional logic that he too must worship Napoleon in the same way that Hazlitt had done, and this proved his undoing. Nor did he appear to value objectivity as a biographical quality: significantly, it was not mentioned in the list of biographer's prerequisites and possibly he would have considered it too near to lack of sympathy. Competently put together, but unoriginal, hopelessly biased, evasive of moral implications, his book presented Napoleon, like Gregory, as the divinely-inspired iconoclast whose wars 'have ministered/Unto the health of nations'. Its lasting interest is rather as a mirror of Horne's mind, in which the tyrant and the tyrant-hater wrought conflicting havoc with his emotions.

Chapter 9

The Cry Within

Horne's desk was crowded and in its usual confusion during the last week of 1838. Not only was he writing character sketches for a series to be called *Heads of the People*, but also *The History of Napoleon* was appearing in a succession of monthly parts, imposing a forbidding row of deadlines that would occupy most of the following year. That became a year of minor crises. The Hunt Private List drained his nerves, Marianne Hunt still complained and bickered, small journalistic tasks absorbed his time – reviews, articles for monthlies – none large enough to be properly rewarding, all large enough to be demanding and irritating. In July came another, more serious, strain. Old Mr Gillies, that perennial bankrupt, speculated in corn and lost his money again. This time he ruined his children as well as himself, and Mary's brother Robert, also his father's partner, was forced to sell his house. The girls were equally affected. Their uncle, the Scottish judge, at the same time withdrew his usual allowance to his nieces: their ruin was 'entire and immediate'. Horne was frantic with worry for Mary and searched anxiously among his friends for possible lodgers for Hillside – 'any nice people who wanted the greater part of a furnished house'. Very much on edge, he found himself rebuking Mrs Hunt, in one of their incessant Private List wrangles, for her selfishness in view of the Gillies's misfortunes.

Fortunately his blossoming social life provided a counterbalance. Not even at Craven Hill had Horne's natural gregariousness found better outlets and he was accepted now by a gratifyingly large and diverse collection of literary people. There were still occasional visits to Craven Hill and, after November 1839, to Fox's new home in Westminster; a move much regretted by his household but made necessary by Fox's growing role as 'golden orator of untax'd bread' for the Anti-Corn-Law League. There were visits also to Leigh Hunt's new home in Edwardes Square, Kensington, where the family made fresh domestic chaos. In this odd household Horne met literary celebrities, ranging from Byron's friend, the Irish poet Tom Moore, to William Wordsworth, the grand old man of the Romantic Movement long venerated by Horne and a friend of the Gillies sisters since Margaret had painted his portrait many years before. Horne was impressed by Wordsworth, in spite of his antipathy to the old man's conservatism: he was less impressed by plausible Tom Moore.

There was another meeting place that not even Hunt's home could outrival, for here, he believed, he had found something to equal Craven Hill. This was the home of Robert Bell, a 'fine old-fashioned house, with a large garden, some six miles out of London', where Bell gave a standing invitation to his friends to dine on Sundays. Bell was an Irish journalist whom Horne had probably first met in the offices of *The True Sun*, where he had met so many of his later friends. A well-known radical, Bell had edited *Atlas* – the paper for which Hazlitt had written exclusively in his last years – and had been convicted of libelling the Lord Chancellor. Politically and aesthetically Bell's opinions coincided with Horne's. Moreover his magazine *The Monthly Chronicle*, which he had taken over in 1839, became for Horne something of what the *Repository* had once been for him; a market for his creative work, a voice for his opinions, and a place for his books to be favourably reviewed. Before its failure in August 1841, the *Monthly Chronicle* had published almost a score of his articles and poems, including that old poem *Orpheus* written after his return from Mexico, and had reviewed glowingly *Cosmo de' Medici*, *The Death of Marlowe*, *Gregory VII*, and various of his pamphlets. Bell's circle of friends, too, was equally reminiscent of Craven Hill. At those Sunday dinners he was likely to meet Hunt, Southwood Smith, William and Mary Howitt, Douglas Jerrold, the ubiquitous John Forster, all of whom had been visitors to Fox's house. He also made new acquaintances: the feminist authoress Anna Jameson, the artist Frank Stone, Dion Boucicault at the beginning of his career as playwright, the disorderly former Jesuit turned journalist, Father Prout, the distinguished physiologist Dr Mayo, and William Makepeace Thackeray. There, too, he heard the composer Felix Mendelssohn play on one of his visits to England.

Recalling those Sundays with nostalgia many years later, it was Thackeray that Horne remembered most vividly of all. Thackeray was then twenty-nine, a London journalist for two years after unsettled attempts at law and art, his personal life a nightmare with his wife's insanity; yet, as a novelist and critic, he was approaching the heights of his power. Horne had first met him briefly at the editorial offices of *The Court Journal* a few years earlier, when calling on the editor, Laman Blanchard. He remembered Thackeray's huge form seated behind the editor's desk, the 'great round-glass spectacles', the 'large camus nose'. Thackeray was, as he said, 'squirting a little warm water down the page' to help his friend. Now at Bell's, often in the company of his friend Laman Blanchard, Thackeray would sit for hours 'talking and making sketches in an album . . . richly humorous, and accompanied by scraps of verse and prose', at the same time bemoaning to Bell, who had no such difficulty, his inability to churn out copy at will. Horne remembered him standing with their host before the fireplace in the large drawing-room, lit only by the light of the fire. 'Huge figures – one upward of six foot two, and bulky in proportion – the other [Bell] being at least six foot four, stalwart and gaunt – with the large log-fire at steady red heat in front of them, and their great shoulders and backs in dark shade' – figures from Scandinavian Saga: or so Horne remembered them. It was an understandable analogy; particularly when one remembers the conspicuous shortness of Jerrold, Southwood Smith, the Howitts, Fox, and Horne himself.

The pattern of crisis and conviviality lasted into the following year. The Private List was once more a centre of troubles. During 1839 Hunt had written a play – his first – called *A Legend of Florence*, inspired by his poetic friends and quite unsuitable for the stage. After much negotiation it was accepted for performance at Covent Garden and throughout December and January Hunt had protested and argued as the manager, Madame Vestris, had attempted to put it into actable and conventionally moral form. In February it was put on, at a first night as memorable as the Professional Authors could manage, attended by literary and social elite, old friends and enemies of Hunt, anyone to give it publicity. At the end Hunt himself, pale and modest, appeared on stage to acknowledge the feverish applause. Up at Rydal Mount the great Wordsworth himself sent messages through Margaret Gillies, his guest at the time, to be passed on to Hunt through Mary and Horne, that he longed to be in London to make his 'hands burn welcoming Hunt's new play'.

The first night was an undoubted success but the play itself was not; nor was the foolhardy hope of the trustees of the Private List to make Hunt self-supporting through dramatic genius. Though the Queen attended it the play ran only a few nights. Hunt meanwhile, like the drowning man in Byron's apt description of him, slipped happily back into the water.

Nor were Hunt's the only finances of concern during those months. Horne himself now faced the first and least serious of a series of monetary troubles that were to punctuate the next ten years. Details of this first crisis are obscure but it was enough to cause him anxiety, to which quixotic Leigh Hunt, true to his code of helping friends in distress whether capable or not, rushed with offers of aid. Fortunately the embarrassment passed, and Horne truthfully was able to decline Hunt's offer.

In the meantime he consoled himself with a new and brilliant group of friends. In November 1839 he had moved from Gloucester Place to rooms at the top of number 4 Gray's Inn Square. It was a charming place, his rooms looking on one side over the delightful square with its archway into the street, on the other over the incomparable Gray's Inn gardens. Horne once more found companions to match his surroundings, for Gray's Inn was traditionally the home of lawyers – though occupied, too, by other professions – and three doors from his own rooms were those of the noted barrister Bryan Waller Proctor, also a successful playwright under the name of Barry Cornwall. He had also the further distinction, for Horne, of having been a close friend of William Hazlitt.

Proctor was as notable a literary host as his wife was a literary hostess, and if in Mrs Proctor's drawing room one found current literary lions, one found equally absorbing though less formal company at her husband's evening parties in his rooms. The guests were usually men younger than their host. Mostly they were writers or artists just coming to fame: the newly elected R.A., Daniel Maclise, the humorous artist ex-medical student John Leech, Horne's old friends Jerrold and Forster, and a rising novelist Horne had met a year before in Macready's dressing room with heavy dark hair and a quiet shrewd face, Charles Dickens. There would be older men too: Talfourd, Laman Blanchard, sometimes Macready. Horne remembered the scene with clarity and affection. On hot summer nights the scent of roses would waft through the windows from the gardens with the sound of music from the nearby Olympic theatre. The guests would serve themselves with cold ham and venison, French bread and red currant jelly; sometimes they cooked their food in butter on a silver pan over a spirit lamp. Conversation was serious, interspersed by the horseplay Horne had first met on *The True Sun* and which a further ten years had done nothing to dull in that literary set. Forster as of old was generally the butt of their jokes. One evening he and Horne were locked in the gardens and forced to climb the high spiked railing; another time when they had been discussing guillotining, and Forster had declared himself in favour of it, the window was clamped down on his neck as he leant out to look into the garden below, and he was left struggling until blue in the face. Sometimes Forster was a willing participant. Horne remembered him impersonating Cupid, dancing with a tin tube for a quiver, his bulky movements arousing jeers and applause. All their lives this group would indulge in this sort of clowning, as if in need of this type of release from the frustrations and seriousness of real life.

One evening when Forster had been reading Shakespeare aloud to them with his usual skill, Macready and Horne began discussing the place of art and reality in drama. The argument became heated and personal. Horne's latent animosity rose to the surface, and Blanchard, supposedly to make a point – and as much, one suspects, to divert them – seized a ham bone off the table and began to imitate the famous clown Grimaldi's miming of the dagger scene from *Macbeth*. The trick had its effect and they dissolved into uproarious amusement, hissing, shouting, joking – even dour Macready. Horne alone was unamused: he was too aroused to be so diverted, and unlikely to be moved in any case by Blanchard's parody, since the sight of Grimaldi miming the dagger scene was one of the most compelling and disturbing of his childhood memories.

At Gray's Inn, Horne was in the centre of literary London. John Forster brought Walter Savage Landor to call, the vigorous old poet having temporarily deserted his famous apartments at Bath. Horne, who had felt grateful to Landor ever since he spoke so well of *The Death of Marlowe*, was long to remember the 'breadth and ease' of white-haired Landor contrasting with the 'swelling and blowing' of Forster. One evening Alfred Tennyson called and sat up most of the night talking. Little known as yet, a recluse of a poet, prone to melancholia, yet so 'restful, brotherly, solid-hearted', Horne had met him first at Loughton when Tennyson was living at nearby Epping, and thereafter saw him sometimes walking in Epping Forest.

Horne was gratified, too, by the development of his friendship with Forster. Almost every morning he walked the short distance to Lincoln's Inn Fields, where Forster had his house. There sitting on high stools at opposite ends of Forster's sitting-room which looked out on the garden of the square they would play battledore, talk, and joke. Though it was an uneasy friendship, ultimately to turn sour, both men at the moment were intent on pleasing, and capable under such circumstances of being most pleasant. Horne had good reason for this since Forster, as dramatic critic on the *Examiner* and a close friend of Macready, wielded much power. In a time of faction reviewing, Forster's power as a critic was remarkable: his friendship could make a dramatist, his enmity ruin one. Bulwer and Macready were already profiting from it: the 'Macready clique' as it was called – Bulwer, Macready and Forster, the first to write the plays, the second to stage and act them, and the last to review them – was already a byword among the unacted dramatists. Horne in principle despised such barefaced complicity but he could not afford to despise it in practice when there was still a hope he might profit from it. He met Bulwer from time to time at Forster's. The gawky, dandified figure with sad protuberant eyes held little resemblance for him to that idealized patriot and man of genius to whom he had dedicated *The False Medium*.

Considering his inward despair, Horne, outwardly, in these early months of 1840, presented a surprisingly tranquil picture. He was so convivial, so absorbed in his small tasks, so taken up with cultivating important friends, managing the Private List, creating new plays and reconstructing old ones. His hours were accounted for in such a round of activities that he fortunately had little time to brood. He had discovered, as long ago as Mexico, that when he was idle his mental state grew out of hand.

Yet as always there were times when friends and activities could not crowd out the fears and depression. Usually at night, the tentacles, so familiar and so possessive, would rise to the surface and once more take hold of him. On such a night in November 1839, soon after he had moved to Gray's Inn, he wrote a letter to Thomas Carlyle that betrayed the force of his misery. His worship of Carlyle was then unabated. Earlier in the year his interest had been caught, as Hazlitt's had been, in the writings of the great German Romantic critic, August von Schlegel, and he had written an introduction for an English translation of *The Lectures on Dramatic Art*. In it he had deplored the current fashion for analysis in criticism and begged instead for synthesis. He had sent a copy of this book to Carlyle in November, sure that as a lover of German literature and opponent of analysis he of all people would sympathize. Nor had he been mistaken. Carlyle, while disparaging Schlegel the man as 'at bottom . . . a very poor creature . . . wears a flaxen wig; paints himself, tho' upwards of seventy, *aspires* indeed in a very hopeless manner after many things', had fully sympathized with Horne's opposition to critical analysis. 'It is your way,' he wrote, 'from your different point of right, of stating an emphatic truth, the beginning of endless truths, little imagined and dolefully needed in these times of ours. I bid you good speed in prosecuting that.' Had he not, he told Horne, got 'rid of that cursed malady you call by the name of "analysis", I think I literally should not be alive now. Logic is glass-spectacles; may be very useful if there be an *eye* behind it. God help them that think it a bare eyeless death's head, and pretend to see with that!' Horne must learn German; there was 'no instruction at all to be had for the like of you for pursuits like yours, in any other literature but the German'. He must also come to visit him at Cheyne Row.

Horne had been most moved by Carlyle's letter. Sitting by his 'solitary lanthorn' at the top of Gray's Inn Square, he drafted and corrected his reply and no more than a sentence of thanks was out before the deluge of misery escaped from him. 'Oh how much' had he responded to Carlyle's words, and with what 'intuitive sympathy'. He would certainly explore German literature – he had ceased to read English 'except for Mammon, because I gain nothing else but world's gold from my dealings with the beef-headed books of our own modern literature'. It was the same with writing. In describing the present situation for a writer he felt impelled to begin with 'a loud shriek – not as a spirit in torment – but confined'. No analysis, no 'accounting for it' philosophically, could afford him anything but 'an abstract and imaginary toleration'. Yet he knew what he 'could be at: not distinctly as to the forms and details; but the vital, forward-looking creation': the outline if not 'the shape and colour of the externals'.

> Will you help me? [he begged]. You of all men can do so. I have long known this – but I have waited also to know whether you thought my field worth digging to the centre. And now you seem to infer that 'it is so'. I must freely and thankfully accept any assistance of any kind you will give me, in my search through the broad depths of German literature for an answer to the cry within.

He wrote self-consciously and rather affectedly, hoping to impress Carlyle. What he said was still true. His ambitions, duties, creative longings were never more insistent, nor more confined cries. That they had found some measure of success in the past only made their present incarceration the more intolerable. But they were also paralleled by open doubts that had troubled him intermittently since his decision to be a poet. Might he not have been mistaken; might fate have never intended him for a poet? Was he not a failure? Might this be the fault of himself –

his lack of talent – as much as, if not more than, circumstance? How did one differentiate between the neglect which the mediocre poet deserved and the tragic neglect which was the inevitable fate of true genius? Might he not be confusing the one for the other? Ought he not reject this fruitless struggle and destiny of suffering in favour of the normal contented life that his practical characteristics could surely bring him?

At this stage of his life, however, the choice was not quite a real one. Later, when bitter circumstances lent more weight to the subversive voices, the choice would be real and he would be forced to the most painful of all self-confrontations and decisions. Now the voice of the poet in him was still strong enough to push them away. As he knew instinctively, to deny his poetic mission was to deny the basis of his identity: a mental and emotional suicide, no more, no less. And so, still 'exactly the man I was . . . in all essential thoughts and feelings' as when writing *The False Medium*, he followed the dangerous course of brooding over slights to himself and his profession, to the point, as his friends began to note, of obsession. A fellow contributor to *The Monthly Chronicle* named Thomas Powell who knew Horne well in these years wrote later (with insight but possibly also with some malice since by then they were no longer friends) that he had 'a tremendous self-will, which leads him to consider ten thousand acts of kindness and obligation cancelled should any word or deed come to light derogatory of his own sense of importance'. He predicted for Horne a lonely and bitter old age.

Powell was wrong in insisting that Horne was concerned only with his own personal importance. He was equally and possibly more concerned with the importance of the poetic vocation; attacks on it he felt as keenly as any attacks on himself. Unfortunately as the year progressed, attacks on it came almost as fast as in the days of Christopher North. Horne and a group of unacted dramatists, like their parent and inspiration, the Professional Authors, had taken collective action and formed an association which they called the Syncretics. This was a reference, one supposes, to the ancient Cretans of the same title who forgot their differences to unite in a common aim, the unacted dramatists presumably deciding to do the same. Today their association and the names of its leading members J. A. Heraud and Westland Marston are virtually forgotten, except perhaps for the fact that the twenty-year-old Marston's play, *The Patrician's Daughter* – performed unsuccessfully in 1842 by Macready at Drury Lane – had a verse prologue written by Charles Dickens. In 1840 they were a highly active group with a programme to abolish the theatrical monopoly, reform the theatre – too weak they considered to reform itself – and educate public taste and theatrical managers to their own type of plays.

Horne, as befitted the author of published but unacted dramas, took a leading part in their work and was to be heard as one of their chief speakers at the Suffolk Street Galleries lecturing on the 'Indestructible Legitimate Drama'. He worked zealously, also, calling on those whom he had lately solicited for contributions to the Leigh Hunt Private List to sign their names to a petition for the abolition of the patent monopoly. He had considerable success though many had the good sense, however, to warn him at the same time that this would do the Syncretics little good, the chief cause of their neglect being in themselves and not their stars. Horne called too on Benjamin Disraeli, novelist and son of that most devoted worker for Professional Authors, Isaac D'Israeli, whose books had been the inspiration for his own *The False Medium*, to beg his aid as a Member of Parliament to sponsor their petition: a request to which he was more than agreeable.

In all, his tasks kept him cheerfully busy, yet he had the suspicion that his uncompromising devotion to the Syncretics was also increasing his unpopularity. This became far too clear with the publication of *Gregory VII*. He had polished the play for two years and now in 1840 when it finally appeared it was prefaced with an 'Essay on Tragic Influence' – one of the best things he had ever written according to Leigh Hunt – in which he set out his psychological theory of drama and attacked those old False Mediums of the patent monopoly on theatres, neglectful public, theatrical managers and star actors. It was, as Leigh Hunt said, a perceptive and moving analysis of drama: it was also highly Syncretic. What was worse, he had started out by ironically dedicating it to Christopher North, thus satisfying the craving for revenge that had haunted him since North's review of *The False Medium*.

Then he had been in no position to exact revenge; now he believed he was. He intended to strike not only for himself but for Hunt and that beloved trio of dead heroes, Shelley, Keats and Hazlitt, who had suffered even more from North than he. And so he had composed a long, and in his eyes an exceptionally fair, dedication, writing, it must be admitted, with dignity and feeling. He had not, he told his public, been destroyed by North's 'memorable vituperations' but had gone on to pursue 'his appointed course with strength, with cheerfulness, and with security'; and of those 'memorable vituperations', he quoted large portions to show their author's underhand cruelty – an effect which somewhat backfired since North's 'unprincipled ribaldry' and 'slaughterous pleasantry' were so much more entertaining than Horne's own prose.

Its literary virtues were undoubted yet the dedication still showed too clearly those contrary traits in Horne's nature which invited and rejected suffering; Leigh Hunt was appalled when he read the proofs. The 'Cockney school' quarrel was buried and Hunt, who more than any man alive had reason to be bitter, could see only danger in stirring it up once more. He begged Horne to remember North's 'murderous rages' and how the 'very virtues' of an 'unconventional man' could lay himself and his friends open to attack: could he not exercise the 'serene superiority' of 'superior genius' and withdraw it? Robert Bell agreed with this suggestion. Horne, faced with the insistent advice of these two trusted friends, reluctantly obeyed but could not resist one last blow. He sent the proofs to North's private home in Edinburgh – a no 'far less dignified course' he later admitted – but fortunately received reply. As far as North was concerned the 'Cockney' cry was finished.

Horne had escaped attacks over the dedication but there was still the Essay on Tragic Influence which appeared as planned as a foreword to *Gregory VII*. The response to this among critics was almost as pronounced as that which Horne's friends had feared for the dedication. Horne was about to discover that though North might be silenced, another – if lesser – personal demon had come to take his place. The reincarnation was named Henry Chorley: a red-headed, ailing, neurotic reviewer for the prominent literary journal *The Athenaeum*, bigotad, competent, and the Syncretic's chief enemy. Chorley, called 'one of the most complete specimens of literary adventurer' of his time, renowned for his devotion to the literary hostess, Lady Blessington, and for his biting reviews, took up the cause against the Syncretics: and in September 1840 began it with a review of *Gregory VII*; for he saw Horne as their most dedicated spokesman:

> Mr Horne is a clever man; but cleverness may run into conceit . . . thought into mysticism and poetry mistake its way: and there is nothing so conducive to these undesirable conclusions as brooding over the neglect and injustice of the world, whether real or imaginary – whether personal to the man, or general to the art he professes.

Chorley was perceptive. Except perhaps for those years after his return from Mexico, Horne's mind had not contained more symptoms of disturbance. There is small doubt that he found satisfaction in playing the literary martyr; yet equally small doubt that he felt the attacks on himself and his profession keenly. His self-will and his poetic pride alone were keeping him going, and hand in hand with these went dangerous conceit and brooding. The man was being sacrificed entirely to the persecuted poet.

Chapter 10

Smoky Symbols

A change came over England as the eighteen-thirties gave way to the 'forties, not the dreaded revolution but a wave of social reform by which 'the aristocratic fabric was quietly permeated with radical ideas'. It was the very goal for which the inhabitants of Craven Hill had worked and yet, ironically, it did not bring them the satisfaction they had expected. Committed to creative literary expression as much as to the welfare of their fellows, they found the quiet revolution had also changed the literary climate. The desire for facts, figures and blue books which possessed the public appeared to have brought a corresponding taste for facts in literature. The socially realistic novel grew popular while poetry suffered a parallel decline. Facts took precedence over fantasy, reason over imagination, the reformer over the poet. The new literary leaders were novelists, journalists, historians – self-made, ambitious young men – the very leaders of the Professional Authors' movement in the next ten years. Dickens, Forster, Jerrold, Carlyle: the new rational temper had given them a status impossible fifty years before and they in turn fostered that temper in their work.

And yet the poets had only themselves to blame. Isolated in their pride and self-suffering satisfaction, obsessed with their worn-out forms, unaware or purposely blind to the demands of the mid-century, they refused, not unnaturally perhaps, to recognize their obsolescence. Their leaders had died young or were, like Wordsworth, old and past their genius, and no new titan had come yet to take their places and lead them to regeneration. Alfred Tennyson, shut up with his poems and melancholia, wrote in obscurity; Robert Browning brooded rebelliously over the failure of that poetic experiment *Sordello* which in 1840 had made him the laughing stock of literary circles. Hampered by mediocrity, the poets of the eighteen-forties went doggedly on, or wasted their talents, equally fruitlessly, on neo-Elizabethan drama or self-pitying harangues. Under attack they attempted to strengthen those threatened qualities in their work by exaggeration. The Romantic aestheticians had always put a heavy premium on emotion and imagination and these late Romantics took it to further extremes. In 1840 a young Nottingham poet named Philip Bailey published an epic, a plethora of private emotion and extravagant imagination called *Festus*, a starting point for a new school of decadent Romantic poetry in which those vital ideals which inspired Shelley and Keats found a last feverish flickering. The school came to be called the Spasmodic of Spasmodist movement. Ignoring the lack of discipline, the naïveties and crudities, the poets saw Bailey's verse as a beacon in an imaginative desert of reason and reform. They hailed it as a masterpiece.

Such an analysis is possible, of course, only in retrospect. Horne, living through the events, aware of the changes more by intuition, was implicated as deeply as any in the struggle. Poet against Man, Irrationality against Rationality, the two forever in irreconcilable tension: so personal a struggle for him could not possibly have left him uninvolved. There was an event too in 1840 which threw the entire issue into even stronger light. Shelley's name at last having grown respectable, the first complete edition of his works was published by his wife and with it the hitherto unpublished *Defence of Poetry*. It must have seemed as though leadership had come for the faltering poets from beyond the grave, for no more fiery manifesto of the Romantic poetic ideals could possibly have been forthcoming. With passionate, unphilosophical conviction Shelley had answered his friend Thomas Peacock's claim in *The Four Ages of Poetry* that as civilization advances poetry becomes increasingly expendable. Peacock had written rather facetiously: Shelley wrote with Romantic earnestness and ardour, and, for an article written in 1820, with extraordinary relevance for 1840 (though the tension between reason and imagination is as old as literary history and inherent in artistic creation). Poetry he called

something divine. It is at once the centre and circumference of knowledge; it is that which comprehends all sciences, and that to which all science must be referred. It is at the same time the root and blossom of all other systems of thought; it is that from which all spring, and that which adorns all; and that which, if blighted, denies the fruit and the seed, and withholds from the barren world the nourishment and successions of the tree of life.

Poets were the great teachers of humanity, who reveal the ideal world in the dress of their own time: they were 'the mirrors of the gigantic shadows which futurity casts upon the present . . . the unacknowledged legislators of the world'. Their superiority to the reformer was unchallengeable, for they were possessed by genius that 'arises from within, like the colour of a flower that fades and changes as it develops' – that precious faculty which, unconnected with reason, consciousness or will, visits at unpredictable intervals. The reformer follows the footsteps of poets and copies 'the sketches of their creation into the book of common life'.

The *Defence* said little Horne had not already absorbed, but the circumstances and intensity of its statement made it highly significant and even unnerving. Weighed down by the inward and outward pressures against imaginative literature, Horne had, a few months before, indulged his interest in practical affairs and taken steps to go for the first time into purely practical reform. Now faced by his revered Shelley's passionate eloquence, reading those scraps of the *Defence* which Mary Gillies wrote across the back of a letter to him to give him strength, he must have felt the veriest coward deserting to the enemy. Yet the plans were made and they were not altogether unrelated to literature. In November of 1839 Horne had approached Talfourd asking that, as a Member of Parliament, he should put forward Horne's name as a candidate for sub-commissioner on a new Royal Commission to investigate the physical and mental conditions of children in mines and factories. It was not a haphazard request. His interest had been aroused by his Craven Hill friends, by Southwood Smith who was one of the Commissioners, and by Mary Gillies in particular. To Mary it had a special interest, for so much of her energies, like those of her friend, Southwood Smith's daughter Caroline Hill, went into working for the reform of children's education, and that was one of the new Commission's concerns. This indeed was the main excuse Horne gave in writing to Talfourd: 'important objects of *National Education are involved*'. For the poet, concerned with the mind's welfare over the body's, education was presumably the most proper field of reform.

Horne's friendship with Southwood Smith had progressed quietly but firmly, and to him he would owe a lifelong concern with problems of social medicine – Smith the 'physician of mankind', as Leigh Hunt called him, whom 'ages shall honour, in their hearts enshrined' – had begun his work with a dedication to men's souls. He was a poor Somersetshire lad whom William Blake, the poet-mystic, had encouraged to become an evangelical preacher. His wife's tragic death and the teachings of rationalism had changed his mind and he had compromised by adopting Unitarianism, going in 1812 as minister to a Unitarian congregation in Edinburgh where he had shortly after begun to study medicine. From there his interest had taken him to the Utilitarians whose leader, Jeremy Bentham, had become his patient and friend, and whose philosophy had caused him to abandon his quiet Somerset medical practice for the London Fever Hospital. By nature quiet and contemplative, an academic rather than a practical reformer – years later Horne could remember how on tours of the slums absent-minded Smith was constantly having his pocket picked and forever short of silk handkerchiefs – this gentle Utilitarian had exchanged his ivory tower for the hovels of Lambs-fields and Camden Gardens, unable passively to watch epidemics carry off twenty to thirty thousand poor a year. Twice, tending feverish emaciated bodies, he himself had almost died of fever. In the early eighteen-thirties he had joined the great Benthamite administrator of public health, Edmund Chadwick, and he had sat as public health adviser on several Royal Commissions including the predecessor to the one that Horne now proposed to join.

It was March 1841 before Horne left London for Wolverhampton as one of Her Majesty's sub-commissioners on the Royal Commission for the Investigation of the Employment of Children in Mines and Factories. Cleanshaven – for in assuming the Utilitarian reformers' mantle of disinterested intelligence he had removed his moustachios for fear of antagonizing children or employers – he set off. Suddenly he left behind a countryside awakening in the spring and entered a winter's world: a world of tall chimneys, streets covered with cinder ash, and nearly forty thousand people huddled in nameless squalid courts and alleys like colonies 'of beavers, but wanting the green banks and fresh air'. Spring never came to that black town on the sandstone hill. To thousands of children working in backyards and small factories, making nails and locks and japanned trays, a green field or a primrose was unknown or exotic. Nor, he found, could minds unused to beauty have grasped its significance; to one small boy he saw, a visit to the country had no more meaning than to be stung by a nettle. Cruel masters, long hours, disease and malnutrition stunted and mutilated small bodies; ignorance, ugliness and exhaustion stunted and mutilated small minds. It was an abjectness, as he later wrote, 'which will never struggle to emancipate itself but *will* struggle, if emancipated, to return to darkness and its chain'. Few more harrowing sections of Victorian industrial

England existed than this corner of South Staffordshire, transformed by
its mines of coal and iron to a hive of small metal industries, and few
places were more calculated to awaken a poet's compassion and ardour.
While Horne thought himself unprejudiced – the disinterested reformer with his outward symbols of poethood temporarily gone – no
one of his temperament could have stayed unaffected by what he saw.

And yet he was also exhilarated. For the first time since America
that practical side of his nature, long held in abeyance in favour of the
poet, was liberated and exercised. He found it rewarding. The horror
of America conveniently forgotten, the excitement now alone remained with the vision of himself – recalled with nostalgia to bolster
his dwindling poetic pride – as the resourceful, dashing adventurer
who had faced danger to fight for another's freedom. Now, curiously,
ingredients of those American adventures were to be found again in
Wolverhampton; there was even some danger. The Commissioners
were not popular, and a few years before the poor law Commissioners
had been rescued by cavalry from a rioting mob. Horne was in fact
offered protection, which he refused.

He began visiting schools and Sunday schools and factories, col-
lecting depositions from teachers, factory owners, clerics, and local
officials, and interviewing and observing children. He had visited his
first factory on March 6 – a Wolverhampton nail factory – a 'frightful
place, turn which way you will', where the slightest mis-step meant
mutilation or death and where, among exhausted children, mis-steps
were frequent. Yet it was not nearly as frightful, he was soon to discover, as other sights he was to see.

There, too, on that first day, interviewing the children, he discovered the pattern his reports were to follow: Anna Beddoes, aged
twelve, 'stunted and anxious', Enah Sidebottom, aged thirteen, 'ex-
cessively stupid and unconcerned', John Barnesley, fifteen, who had
never heard of Nelson or Napoleon, and a grubby little urchin of six
who attended the Wesleyan Sunday School, had never heard of Christ
or Heaven, begged money from Horne for his drunken mother and
little brothers, and replied, when asked if he knew who made him, with
disconcerting biological certainty that it was his mother. Wherever
he went in those three months the children's replies were almost always
the same. They could not read or write, they had never heard of the
Biblical heroes or nursery favourites that had delighted Horne's childhood; they had no general knowledge, they could not add simple
sums. God, Christ, Queen Victoria were as unknown to them as a
common violet or the answer to two plus two.

And yet sometimes he found intelligence and was so moved by it that he copied the child's exact quaint phrases in his report. One May afternoon, walking in Cradely wood, he had met an engaging little boy who had shown him the way, chattering all the time that his nickname was Drummer, that he could write *and* read his own writing . . . 'Wish I could write as fast as you' . . . that he felt so tired at night . . . 'I been but a little 'un'. It was a most noticeable point in Horne's nature, and one not previously touched on, that Horne adored small children. It stemmed partly from a nostalgia for those happier memories of his own childhood, partly from his understanding and sympathy with their fantasies; it was possibly influenced too by Mary Gillies's love of them, and his affection for the tribe of small Hills – Southwood Smith's grandchildren – who were forever in Mary's house. Never did his affection and delight in their company come across better than the description in his Commissioner's report of little Drummer.

Elsewhere there was little delight to be found, only anger and compassion. One incident in particular aroused him. He found it was common for the children to say the words 'Our Father' before going to sleep, the only part of the Lord's Prayer that they had managed to grasp from their teachers. As an opponent of conventional religion, and an opponent of tyranny, those words had to him an 'inexpressibly affecting' ring: 'those poor children', oppressed by harsh masters and hard parents, 'lying down to sleep with this simple appeal'. To Horne it was unbearably ironical; to the pious sentimental public who read his report, it was unbearably pathetic, and probably did more than any single statement in the report to move them to awareness and tears.

On a Saturday night he would walk down the Wolverhampton streets to watch the street market crowded like avenues in a fair with pipers and fiddlers. Italian organ grinders, ballad singers, quack doctors, butchers showing gleaming sides of painted, tainted meat and chemists' shops with enormous jugs of Godfrey's cordial, a haphazard mixture of treacle and opium used indiscriminately to quieten – and sometimes to kill – noisy babies. It was exhilarating if grim: a display of animal spirits conspicuously lacking elsewhere in the town and it recalled for him the grotesque attraction of the fairs of his childhood.

On Sundays he walked the poorer lanes past the reeking cesspools outside every door, 'the colour of dead porter' and 'a disgusting mixture of soapsuds and gruel'. He saw tired, bored children 'like a row of sparrows and very much the same colour, all chirruping away' and playing on dunghills. Interviewing a lock and key maker he had heard the first of the tales of sadistic masters mutilating and even murdering apprentices. The interview was in a dilapidated hovel in which thirteen children had died and was orchestrated by hideous cackles from the lock maker's crippled wife lying on sacking on the floor, 'full of animal spirits and utterly destitute'. At the Sunday school he found the visible evidence of the stories: almost every child scarred, and pitiful accounts of whipping, kicking, branding, cutting holes in eyelids: all from the mouths of children too stupefied by weakness and fear to complain. It was the same at Sedgely. On a bright May morning he had entered this wretched little town, past the clothes prop privies – a plank across the edge of every hedge or yard – and down sludgy little lanes awash with sewerage to hear apprentices tell how they were bought and sold like animals, nailed through the ears, strung to the ceiling by their heels, or showered with red hot particles popularly called a flash of lightning. Walsall, Wednesfield, Stourbridge and Swinnerton: the stories which filled his report were almost monotonous with cruelty and neglect.

He returned to London at the end of May with that sense of unreality that generally follows a long journey to a foreign country. Mutilation, murder, oppression and tyranny had never been sights, or even ideas, he could view with equanimity, and certainly not with impartiality. In Mexico the yellow fever victims had obsessed his dreams; now the victims of Victorian industrial England were to prove scarcely less obsessing. He was wracked, moreover, by the remains of whooping cough, caught from a child in some unventilated church hall and passed on, one imagines, to many more. His chest was physically one of his weak points and he was to be bothered by the cough for months to come. Unsettled, depressed, he returned to London, to new rooms in New Broad Street, and to the literary life.

Unluckily there was little in London to alleviate his depression. His work on the Commission was received with reservations. Though Lord Ashley thanked him personally, from the industrial areas came a multitude of complaints. His pathetic little sketches of deformed apprentices were denounced by the more squeamish members of parliament as 'offensive'. The reforming legislation, shorn of its educational power, limped through parliament to a combined opposition of manufacturers and dissenters. Horne's reward lay in the public reaction to the reports of the Commissioners when they were published. The invalid poetess Elizabeth Barrett wept when she read his descriptions and inspired to poetic expression wrote *A Cry of Factory Children*, 'a long sob' (as one critic called it), 'veiled and stifled as it ascends through the hoarse voices of the poor beings themselves' to 'a nation's heart'.

There was satisfaction at least in this: the poet had perhaps, as Shelley might have predicted, won a victory denied the practical reformer.

Horne's awakening interest in educational reform was reflected in his literary ventures. He was caught up in the trend for popular educational books. Not content with contributing several articles to the *Penny Cyclopoedia*, he had involved himself in a modernization of Chaucer's *Canterbury Tales*. The project's originator was a mediocre poet and dramatist named Thomas Powell, one of the most curious of minor writers of the eighteen-forties. According to Robert Browning he had first entered literary circles by 'obtaining credit with Talfourd who introduced him to various friends and myself on the grounds of contributing to the necessity of poor Leigh Hunt'. Once in, he made sure that he stayed. He was an able flatterer, a lavish entertainer: Horne always maintained that this 'consummate scoundrel' courted William Wordsworth with 'edible presents' of kippered salmon, pressed tongue and jellies and pickles, as well as 'private letters of admiration'. In time Powell was to become the trusted friend of many a literary celebrity – Hunt, Southwood Smith, Browning, Charles Dickens – and to be one of the closest of Horne's friends until, in 1849, his friendship suddenly evaporated. Then his lavish entertaining was discovered to have been financed by embezzlement and forging cheques. His distressed family summoned Southwood Smith, the invariable answer to insanity and criminality in literary families, and Smith certified him insane. (And no wonder, if Horne's version can be believed for, according to Horne, Smith arrived to find Powell in a suicidal fit – faked with laudanum and pepper – foaming at the mouth, his clothes disordered and face swollen, 'standing on his head in one corner of the drawing-room, singing snatches of obscene songs'.) Escaping imprisonment because of his supposed insanity, he fled to New York where he posed as a leading London author and published a book of revealing memoirs about former friends until Charles Dickens threatened legal action.

But in 1840 Powell was still at the beginning of his career and seeking a patron for his Chaucer enterprise. He had cunningly chosen William Wordsworth, remote in his ivory tower at Rydal Mount and a known admirer of Chaucer. Along with those edible presents and admiring letters, Powell had sent in June 1840 a translation of Chaucer's *Knight's Tale* by Horne. Wordsworth had accepted the bait, praised Horne's translation, and promised his help. Powell then persuaded Horne, by now dedicated to the public service of making Chaucer easy and refined for modern readers, to round up more contributors.

They went to Savage Landor, and the forthright old poet told them he loved Chaucer, 'even his *language*', and would not touch it. In the end it was agreed that Powell, Wordsworth, Hunt, Robert Bell, Horne and a little-known poetess, Elizabeth Barrett, with whom Horne had begun to correspond the year before, would do the first volume and that Tennyson, Bulwer, Browning and Talfourd might conceivably do a second. With Horne appointed editor (and one wonders why Powell did not grab this for himself) they spent the rest of the year in 'countless vexations' of translation. These were due, according to Horne's account written nearly forty years later, to Leigh Hunt who insisted on translating too freely and was 'not at all like Chaucer', and not of the same calibre as a great translator like Shelley. In fact, Hunt was fairly described by a modern Chaucer critic as 'the most constant and enthusiastic lover of Chaucer in the early nineteenth century', and it seems that he, and Wordsworth, were the only members of the party capable of modernizing Chaucer skilfully. The vexations were due mostly to the other's ignorance, Horne's in particular.

Frantic messages sped between Horne's rooms at Gray's Inn and Hunt's Kensington home; penned in Horne's vigorous handwriting to be answered painstakingly by Hunt's spindly script. 'I have adopted your masterly and matchless rendering,' Horne would write. '... What were gaudies? ... Also will you help me with the line about the gelding and the mare. I cannot let the original stand. . . .' Hunt patiently answered the queries, reduced the equine difficulty to the realms of Victorian nicety, and kept his temper though he begged Horne not to apologize any more. Together they collated the other's work, and received from Mrs Bell the assurance that Horne's emasculated version of the bawdy *Reeves Tale* contained nothing to offend her. By January 1841 it was published and by February it was reviewed.

'Chaucer,' snapped Henry Chorley, in *The Athenaeum*, 'brought down to Cockney comprehension.' As he read that word 'Cockney' it must have seemed to Horne as though there would be no end to the evil Christopher North had started. And ironically, it was the greatest 'Cockney' alive, Leigh Hunt, who alone of the translators received Chorley's praise – he had an easy colloquial air while Mr Horne stumbled in every line and tampered obsessively with the original. It was strange, wrote Chorley, how men could be found to embark on such a hapless task. Horne, reading the second batch of damaging reviews in five months may have echoed his words.

Almost as soon as Horne returned from Wolverhampton he began with his usual misguided eagerness to throw himself into the latest foolhardy scheme of the Syncretics. As the public regarded the Syncretics with increasing lack of sympathy and theatres refused their plays, the unacted dramatists had decided to engage for themselves the English Opera House – the old Lyceum theatre which had become famous when the architect remodelling it had forgotten to supply a gallery staircase. Renamed 'The Dramatic Authors' Theatre', they planned it should become 'a rallying point for neglected genius and a stage for representation of unacted dramas; and with a view to redress and grievances of dramatists, and to break up the monopoly of the patent theatres'. They had arranged for their first production to take place in the last week of August of 1841, a 'high tragic composition', called *Martinuzzi or the Hungarian's Daughter*, a play with 'songs and music according to the act of Parliament', performed by well-known actors including Macready's protégé Samuel Phelps. Even their old enemy *The Athenaeum* wished them success.

Horne and his fellow Syncretics were in a state of high hope and excitement. The first performance, however – as so many might have prophesied – was a shambles of jeers and laughter. Horne (as Elizabeth Barrett told a friend) 'sate side by side with the author, they two together in a conspicuous box, the only two in the theatre with grave faces . . .', and was so upset he refused a supper invitation, 'saying he could not stir or speak the whole night long'. 'He has resolute energies in all things,' concluded Elizabeth, 'and what is rare can suffer bravely as well as act.' To add to his own suffering, and to increase the delight of the literary gossips, his old friend Tom Stone next day began circulating 'a transcript of the manuscript of the first night' marked at appropriate places with comments such as 'peals of laughter'. The wits were jubilant, the theatre closed, and the Syncretics lost heavily – twelve thousand pounds it was rumoured, and amongst it Horne's money. His finances over the past few years had been no more than adequate and to add to his troubles those barely stifled financial fears returned to haunt him with thoughts of starving and despairing writers. In all, the last months of 1841 were not a happy time.

This latest failure of the Syncretics brought a loss in prestige he could ill afford. His faith in their aims and undertakings began to waver, his common sense to reassert itself. He began to recognize that they would never help, and might only hinder, his chances of seeing his own play performed. So, despite his dedication to all projects of the unacted and neglected writer, his instinct now was to dissociate himself from them. Correspondingly, he suddenly decided that he must try to undo the harm his association with their bitter attacks on the theatre had done him, and ingratiate himself with the theatrical managers. A few months after the catastrophe of *Martinuzzi*, he wrote to that curious theatrical manager of Covent Garden, James Planché – who was also antiquarian, dramatist, and later in life the Somerset Herald – denying his connection with extreme Syncretics, and all attacks on theatrical personages except Macready. It was 'hardly fair', he told him, to connect him thus, simply because 'they paid me sundry compliments by dedication in their works and publications'. He sent Planché a copy of *Gregory VII* for himself and another to pass on to the actor manager Charles Kemble. Unfortunately Horne was not clever enough to play turncoat and his attempts were clumsy and only served to alienate both sides. In the public eye he was still a Syncretic – one of the bitterest of all. In his own eyes he was little better than a traitor: once more he was miserably torn between dedication and common sense, the poet and the man.

Chapter 11

Flowers in a Greenhouse

The Syncretics showed Horne in his worst light: complaining, self-deluding, uncompromising. On the reverse side, through that autumn of 1841, he was conducting a correspondence that showed him at his best: affectionate, generous, enthusiastic. Two years before, in the autumn of 1839, a Mrs Orme, a former governess with literary interests, had brought him poems of a former pupil of hers, a Miss Elizabeth Barrett, a frail young lady of thirty-three whose recently published book on verse had been slated by reviewers. She had hoped that some encouraging criticism from an established writer like Horne might raise the poor young lady's spirits, weighed down by reviewers' carping and the rigours of a disease – thought to be a spinal condition – that had confined her to the sickroom since adolescence.

Mrs Orme had not been disappointed. Horne had been genuinely impressed by the poems and moved to compassion by the condition of their author. He had written at once to Miss Barrett, praising her work and offering to amuse her 'to the end of the cold weather by sending anything amusable that might pass through his hands or thoughts'. He had also offered his influence in seeing her poems placed in *The Monthly Chronicle*, and had himself published a poem there, dedicated to her genius and beginning with the words 'Flower of the Soul! Emblem of sentient Thoughts'. Elizabeth Barrett had been so overcome that she described herself as in 'a fit of gratitude'.

From this beginning their relationship by way of letters flourished rapidly. He discovered she was the eldest of a large family, born in Devonshire, and that she had been his neighbour, unknown to either of them, for a few weeks in Gloucester Place in 1838 before the family moved to that house in Wimpole Street which her clandestine courtship by Robert Browning five years later would make famous. Dominated by her fanatically possessive father, devoted to her brother Edward, the parental favourite and her nursery rival, she had spent nearly twenty years in an atmosphere of stifling invalidism and ingrown family emotions. Mysterious 'bodily troubles', suspiciously psychosomatic to modern eyes, forced her to remain, as she told Horne, 'either in bed, or lying on a sofa all the days – all the nights'. It was easy, in such a life, to lose all sense of reality and proportion. 'Do you know,' she asked him, 'what it is like to be shut up into a room by oneself, to multiply one's thoughts by one's thoughts – how hard it is to know what one's thought is like – how it grows and grows, spreads and spreads and ends in taking some supernatural colour – just like mustard and cress sown on flannel in a dark closet?' Shy of strangers, with few visitors outside her household, shut up in a room from which clocks, strong light and fresh air were carefully excluded for the sake of her health, she lived in an extraordinary close twilight timeless world, overcast by the shadow of death. Once beautiful, her early looks of brown curls, dark eyes and cheeks of china-rose degenerated to the pallid careworn face of a woman years older than her actual age. Her one compensation, her lifeline with reality, were her letters; through them she lived with extreme vitality.

Few sensitive plants have ever bloomed more enticingly for the poet than that 'exotic plant in a greenhouse', as Horne called her. She embodied so many of the Romantic traditions of the chivalrous and the morbid; the frail, imprisoned beauty. Horne was by no means unsusceptible. She was, as he told W. J. Fox a few weeks after they had begun their correspondence, 'an *Arabian Nights* lady, shut up in a crystal rock afar'. And, indeed, that crystal rock was not the least of her attractions. Remote and mysterious, forever pristinely innocent in that insulating crystal rock of a sickroom, she had that one attraction Horne found so fatal in a woman. She made no obvious sexual demands. She gave him gratitude and admiration; she praised his kindness, his poetic genius, his generosity, to all her friends and most of all to Horne himself. She demanded in return only those qualities it flattered Horne to give: his tenderness and his protection. Her intelligence far surpassed that of Mary Gillies – far surpassed Horne's own as he was eventually to admit; her sensitivity was undoubted. Nor was there even any fear that so perfect a platonic relationship would ever be spoiled by the complications of their physical presence: for Elizabeth, believed by Horne to be 'in the last stages of consumption', was unable to leave her room and was too obsessed by her fear of meeting strangers to permit them to visit her. Nor did he really want to visit. Instinctively they both appeared to know that letters were the perfect – in fact the only – medium for such a friendship. Once more he had managed to enter into that delightful climate of love bereft of love's usual demands and difficulties – the safe remote love (as he would soon write in *Orion*) that dwells 'ever at peace'.

And yet even he did not manage to keep out all the difficulties. In the spring of 1840, Elizabeth's beloved brother Edward had been drowned while staying with her at Torquay, and she, being responsible for his presence there, had blamed herself. Her grief and guilt were annihilating. She had always been fiercely attached to Edward and felt, it would seem, a rivalry with him. (As modern biographers have pointed out, her history of 'bodily troubles' had begun about the time when he had gone masculinely off to school, his father's favoured son and heir, while she, an ardent little tomboy and disciple since the age of twelve of Mary Wollstonecraft, had stayed femininely at home.) Now the unconscious echoes of those old resentments may have added the terrible edge to her grief. Whatever its components the grief was indeed terrible; her sanity was feared for and never after could she bear to hear the mention of her brother's name.

That spring at Torquay she had been deeply in need of comfort and unusually receptive. Horne had written as soon as he had heard of the drowning and she was so moved by his consideration that she had replied with equal tenderness. 'Kindness and sympathy are not such common things . . . a friend is proved by remaining one in adversity'; he could no longer be for her in the 'class of ordinary friends . . . it is easier for you to forget this, than for me'.

Now a year later, Elizabeth was proving the truth of her words. With little else to do but write voluminously she inundated him with letters that revealed, beneath her tremulous feminine shyness and her wonder at his kindness, one of the most forceful female intellects of the nineteenth century. She argued and flattered, cossetted and confided, soothed and flirted gently with her 'dear Mr Horne', in letters that, if they are over effusive for modern taste, are seldom dull. Though she admired him extravagantly, she was never intellectually subservient; she demanded they speak the truth to one another, and she also demanded he treat her as an intellect in its own right, not merely as a woman.

Towards the end of 1840 Horne had proposed, as a remedy for her grief, that they work on a play together. At first she had been overcome at the thought of working with the author of *Cosmo*. Then, with the proviso that he did not let her prove a nuisance, she had accepted, working enthusiastically through the following spring and summer, until by autumn she had fixed on the plot and begun to draft the choruses, leaving the dialogue to the more practised hand of Horne. Two themes in particular fascinated her: that of the soul being awakened and purified by suffering, by means of 'a casualty relating to the body'; and that of man's fear at confronting his own identity symbolized by a phantom of himself. She had no way of knowing then how both themes, not uncommon in Romantic literature, had exercised an equal fascination on Horne. She chose the second; a choice suggested, one supposes, by her own guilt. Knowing how deeply her feelings were implicated in her work, she suddenly recalled with shock that Horne himself had three years before used the same theme in a dramatic sketch called *Death Fetches* published in one of *Finden's Annuals*. His hero in *Death Fetches* had addressed his self-image in words that she herself might have written:

> *O what art thou?*
> *Thou ghastly and accursed mockery,*
> *Which I have seen e'en now with passing awe,*
> *From fitful and night shadowed glass stare on me*
> *Confusing consciousness – turning self-love*
> *To a revolting shudder? O what are we?*

The knowledge overwhelmed her. 'Oh yes,' she wrote at the end of her letter to him, crowding the words on the flap of the envelope before she sealed it, ' – of course you must often have *seen* Psyche, "in visions of the night when deep *thoughts* fall on men". Good night now dear Mr Horne.' With Elizabeth as with Horne the knowledge of their likeness was half way to loving. And by autumn 1841 it had begun to grow clear that she was in love with him. One uses the term with hesitation, but nothing else would seem to do justice to her feelings.

Within the dreamlike confines of that one room at Wimpole Street it was easy for Elizabeth to fall in love with someone she had never seen. For Horne, caught up with the pressing immediacies of the real world, it was less possible. What he felt undoubtedly lacked her intensity and preoccupation; yet in quality it was not so very different. He responded to her sympathy and admiration and her scarcely concealed ardour with tenderness. He teased her, reassured her, protected and praised her. He laughed indulgently – and sometimes a little smugly – at her intense effusions and dealt with the constant demand for answers (for she was thrown into panic if he did not reply at once to her letters) with much the same loving exasperation one imagines he reserved for his mother's vagaries. He was touched by her solicitude: by the little presents she sent him – the pot of Devonshire cream, and the jar of West Indian tamarinds to soothe his cough, delivered with the warning that just such 'a common cough, striking upon an insubstantial frame' had signalled the start of her own illness. There were times, too, when he was startled by her instinctive perception. Seeing himself as her mentor, Horne was careful never to contradict that picture of himself as the established, polished poet; it was surprising to him how often Elizabeth seemed to see through to the despair and uncertainties. He began to rely on her opinions, to turn to her for comfort, almost as much as she to him.

This reliance was demonstrated in that lyrical drama they had undertaken together in 1841 and on which they worked diligently through the early months of the following year, before dwindling interest and other demands prevented its finish. *Psyche Apocalypte* – the Soul Revealed – and a better title Elizabeth could scarcely have found since it did reveal so much of its authors' souls – provided a melting pot for their mutual preoccupations. While it did not result in a play of much merit it led on, for them both, to greater poetic work. Using the ideas of spiritual purification arising from 'a casualty relating to the body' and the superiority of emotion and imagination over utility and reason, ideas that had been incorporated in *Psyche*, Elizabeth went on to write fourteen years later *Aurora Leigh*, her greatest poetic success. Horne would use the same material much sooner in two epics, the first begun the following year. In *Orion* and *Ancient Idols*, he dealt with the same themes as Elizabeth, and his poems, like Elizabeth's also, were, on his own admission, intensely personal documents. Into *Pysche* they had put that essential part of themselves that was so extraordinarily the same, and from this mutual mixing had come the groundwork of some of their finest writing.

Satisfying as his relationship with Elizabeth was, it could not assuage the inevitable self-reproaches. As the Authors' Theatre failed and his reports on the Royal Commission were greeted with criticism, it began to seem that whatever he touched, whether practical or poetical, was bound to fail. Even his health, in the past so reliable, appeared to be failing, for the bronchial troubles, brought on by whooping-cough, were scracely dispelled by the warmer weather. Time and age nothing at all could dispel.

At the start of 1842 Horne entered his fortieth year, not only the official eve of middle age but that mark in life-expectancy he had discussed so long before in his *Philosophical Poem*. He looked every month of those thirty-nine years. As he complained, the troubles of the last years had flown to his face and worn him out inwardly and outwardly. Not that, despite the loss of the moustaches, his actual appearance had changed so. It was rather that the man behind them had changed and the signs showed in the eyes and the droop of the mouth. He had only to look in the glass or, better, at the two portraits Margaret Gillies had done of him. The first showed him in 1837 with the glow of Craven Hill still on him, resplendent with flowing moustachios, a gay exotic figure: the other, painted in the early eighteen-forties – today in the National Portrait Gallery, London – showed a delicate face, intense with melancholy. A well-known daguerreotype, taken a few years further on, showed suffering in the sloping eyes and a hint of petulance in the mouth. The signs of the bitter old age Thomas Powell had predicted were beginning to show. He sent the earlier portrait to Elizabeth who opened it with the embarrassed excitement of love and 'started back'. No more avid or careful analysis was ever made of Horne's features, and for that reason alone her reactions are worth quoting. 'Imagine,' she wrote to her great friend and gossip, the authoress Mary Mitford:

Imagine a high-browed and broad-browed head, absolutely bald, appearing to the fancy as if all the glistening auburn ringlets belonging to it had fallen down to the base of the head and expended themselves in whiskers and moustachios! The features are very handsome – the nose delicate and acquiline, the eyes a clear blue, serene and elevated – the mouth strikingly expressive of resolution – the complexion quite colorless almost to ghastliness – with a Rembrandt light full on it. I assure you I started back. What Papa meant by 'no pecularity' I can't conceive. He says it is very like indeed – and very peculiar it assuredly is – very peculiar and very expressive. Somebody cried out 'It's like an assassin', and somebody else 'It's like a saint'. A very fine head certainly! – with a fifth Act in the very look of it! But I deprecate the moustache, and half believe and hope that it has been cut away since the picture was painted. He has a noble generous nature, in spite of all the moustachios in the world, to match his poetic genius.

Elizabeth was right in supposing the moustaches were gone. Gone too was the serenity and some of the resolution. It was difficult to be serene, difficult even to be resolute, when the insistent inner cry was

demanding poetic translation, and the phantom of that great work –
the message to the world that he alone could give – was always before
him, reproaching. The cry had grown to a scream but at least as the
year of 1842 dawned the phantom began to take on a more solid shape.
With that thirty-ninth birthday something happened to Horne that
no biographical reasoning can really make intelligible. Abruptly, for
the space of eighteen months, he developed a poetic faculty he never
displayed before or after. In that brief Indian summer of youth, before
middle age finally claimed him, he managed to grab every particle of
genius he possessed and put it to creative use. In a mental vision,
paralleled only by that other revelation nineteen years earlier when he
saw he was a poet, the phantom became tangible, the message revealed,
the mission fulfilled. Suddenly, in a burst of mental and emotional
power, reminiscent of a religious experience, Horne, the poet, found
himself able to utter 'in clearest tones'

> . . . *all the truth that burnt within*
> *His heart from childhood, and will ever burn*
> *As now, and when his ashes light the grave.*

Horne's attitude to the poetic destiny, and his attitude to God, had
the same emotional basis; both were dominated by his ambivalent
feelings toward personal sufferings inflicted by a remorseless Persecutor. Religion and poetry had always been allied in his mind, and his
search for religious truths was a search for poetic truth. The poet's role
and talents were, by Romantic definition, 'divine', and his values and
teaching sacred and eternal. These predilections had been crystallized
ever since that first explosive contact with Shelley and the English
eighteenth-century rationalists. Then going to that extraordinary
ménage in Kensington where the rationalist-optimist Leigh Hunt
held court with his son Thornton, and some of Thornton's friends, in
particular with the critic George Henry Lewes, Horne had joined in
discussions he later recalled 'the problems of religion and philosophy,
with or without the burden of real or imagined persecution'. It was
those same problems that had concerned him with the intensely and
unorthodoxly religious Elizabeth Barrett as they explored them together in *Psyche Apocalypte*, managing to convince her of the importance of a religious epic poem. And it was the same combination of
themes he also explored now with a new friend, Leonhard Schmitz, a
former factory boy who had lost an arm in a factory accident at Aix la
Chapelle, who had gained a doctorate of philosophy at Bonn Univer-

sity, married an English wife and come to England to edit a classical magazine. With Schmitz he explored his themes back into classical literature and mythology and, possibly, also in the writings of the German philosopher Hegel, and in the work of German rationalist scholars.

Yet, formidable as these influences were on his thinking, none came near to that of Mary Gillies. If anyone was the inspiration of the poems he produced in that extraordinary eighteen months, it was she. She had never ceased to encourage him in his poetic and religious searching – for they were also her searchings – and she never failed to offer help and comfort. With Mary, and possibly through Mary's Unitarian friends of Craven Hill, Horne absorbed the teachings of the liberal Unitarians, a small group, often unnoticed by historians today, the heirs of Godwin, Paine, and Shelley and the English Rationalists. In 1838 one of these English liberal Unitarians, Charles Christian Hennell, had written *An Enquiry Concerning the Origin of Christianity*, analysing the gospels as history, explaining their miracles as 'exaggeration or invention of the narrator'. The book caused much excitement in radical Unitarian circles which, like Hennell and most English circles, were then unacquainted with German rationalist scholarship. It converted at least one brilliant mind, Marian Evans, the obscure Coventry girl who became the great woman novelist George Eliot, and appears also to have converted Mary and Horne himself; for that epic which he composed in the early months of 1842 contained many of its ideas.

Just how dedicated Mary had been in encouragement and sympathy can be seen from one of her few surviving letters, treasured by Horne in his sentimental archives, written about this time, filled with her intense devotion and concern. Beginning, as usual, without the conventional preamble of 'Dear . . .', she set the scene. It was spring, a Sunday afternoon and she was at her aunt's house at Hermanstoun recovering from an illness. Her aunt's household was out riding and she sat alone below the garden by the grassy bank of a stream. She was enchanted with the peace and naturalness of the scene: the spreading trees, the grazing cows, the pigeon house of the green meadow opposite and the pigeons coming to drink beside her in the stream, stretching their small necks upwards. How she wished she could transport him here to her for an hour while the others were away. Then, as usual with Mary, the scene gave rise to graver thoughts. Beside her, the branch of a tree hung over the water, its lower leaves in the stream moved continually by the current, its higher leaves quite still: 'They might be saying,' she told him, 'to their troubled brothers (just as we hear some preachers of calm quietism) why are you not peaceful like us?' To Mary the lesson was clear; she and Horne could climb from the stream, being 'more fortunate than the poor leaves who must go on and never rest till they die'. It was a moral that poor Mary, with her female concern for him, never tired of pointing. There was another moral.

I went to Church, or rather to Chapel with my aunt this morning – what a strange jumble the worship is — sometimes addressed to the 'Great Hebrew Idol', sometimes to the Great Spirit Infinite in love revealed by Christ, sometimes to a mystic compromise, Paganism, Platonism, and Indian. . . . How very strange and unaccountable it was to look around and wonder when the division will cease – but indeed it is not a feeling of superiority I have – don't accuse me of that – I am and feel I am only an atom nearer the true worship of the Infinite – I feel my ignorance and see the mists all around me more than they do – they all think they have a creed and an establishment way ready made.

There, since it was dinner time, she broke off with 'Goodbye again, Yr. Mary'. It was the struggle between that 'Great Hebrew Idol' and his fellow idols, and the Spirit Infinite revealed by Christ, a struggle of such personal significance to him, that constituted the theme of the religious epic he wrote in the late winter and spring of 1842 and called *Ancient Idols or the Fall of the Gods*.

The strongest impression one gains from *Ancient Idols* is violence and hate: a damaging impression when one considers that the poem is vowed to Infinite Love, Nature, Forgiveness, and celebrates a religion based on these and man's best reason and passions as revealed by Christ. Horne saw it as a 'Revelation' of Divine Truth, but in fact it is more a revelation of a mind tortured by those forces that had troubled it since childhood and which America and the vicissitudes of the past few years had deepened. As in *Gregory VII* he is fascinated by tyranny, relishing it even when he is trying to condemn it. As in *The False Medium* he is ornately cruel, parading in sadistic delight a long array of heathen cruelties with the meticulous detail of an essay on comparative religion. Theologically, it is a hotchpotch. Artistically it is the most uneven of poems, its verse soaring in flights of intense emotion, then sinking to pedestrian measures that are nearer to bad prose. Though he considered it a serious literary sin for a poet to preach, much of the poem is preaching. Excitement is mistaken for inspiration, zeal swallows up literary judgment and intellectual balance, redundancy ruins it, but one can never doubt for a moment how deeply it is felt.

From the opening with the flight of the poet's soul through forest and desert to the Shelleyan ruined city, where the gods of humanity are assembled in a vast cavern to be judged by their victims, the epic embodies a struggle so personal and engrossing to its author that he is unable to abandon or resolve it. In the centre of the cavern Horne has placed a funeral urn also functioning as a womb and as an hour glass through which run the sighing ashes of oppressed humanity. Then the urn suddenly breaks apart at the appointed hour of judgment to reveal in its pregnant depths the Child, a whitewinged figure identified with Christ, the Son, Nature, and the Spirit of Humanity. From there, through nearly five more books, the violent struggle for survival proceeds, the Child against the Idols, no action but their interminable impassioned arguments. Rebel fights avenging Tyrant, Son fights Father, Love proclaims against Hate and Punishment, Christ and Jehovah repudiate one another, vigorously denying the existence of a third member of the Trinity who might interfere with the contest. Finally, declaring the True God to be no Father, but 'Almighty in Supreme Maternity', the Son hurls the idols into the abyss – none spared – with evident enjoyment: and from the ashes of Humanity the New Religion rises.

And here one comes to a not uncommon dilemma amongst those who, like Horne, were heirs jointly to rationalism, Romantic iconoclasm, and Romantic imagination. Having revolted at the orthodox mysteries of original sin, atonement, grace, eternal punishment and miracles (Horne recounted Christ's life after the manner of Charles Hennell, going so far as to rationalize the virgin birth into illegitimacy) they found reason not enough. Reason could assuage the inherent sense of guilt that seems to have inclined many searchers to unbelief; reason could argue that eternal punishment was useless since punishment is essentially corrective – though reason could never banish Horne's own ingrained need for purificatory suffering. But reason could not supply the emotional and aesthetic elements these people also craved. Just as young Marian Evans, translating – and believing – the German scholar Strauss's *Life of Jesus*, with its challenge to the Christian myth, found herself looking at an image of Christ in quest of the endurance to go on, finding in it a beauty and symbolism as relevant to her as reason, Horne found himself searching the same way for symbolism and wisdom. Having destroyed the orthodox mysteries with reason, Horne's emotions demanded he should institute his own.

The Romantic poets had always seen the poet's mission and his talents as sacred. They had seen, as Shelley so notably portrayed in *Prometheus Unbound*, the poet-benefactor as a Christlike figure, condemned to suffering, persecution and martyrdom in order to bring spiritual life to the world. The men of genius, Horne now proclaimed, were the true prophets, saints and martyrs, their divine truths doomed to be rejected by ignorant man. They were the true mystery, they the proper objects of veneration. From those ashes of oppressed humanity it was the glorious company of martyred genius he now caused to rise. Socrates, John the Baptist, Francis, Joan of Arc, Savonarola, Confucius, – poet-benefactors from all races, faiths, times, callings, led by Christ their 'Divinest Type', with last, Shelley

> *Shelley, brighter winged*
> *Than all the rest.*

And Horne, his 'hour of following not yet come', watched on, his heart strong and content

> *to know its Mission here,*
> *And work, assured of the appointed end*
> *Man's higher, happier destiny on earth.*

It was his masterpiece; he had not one doubt as to that. So great was his exaltation, reinforced by Mary's enthusiasm, that nothing else mattered to him,

Mary felt the 'highest admiration'; it touched her spirit with 'corresponding sympathy and is elevating as well as touching'; she found it in a 'grand humility worthy of a great soul'. To Horne it was an incredible relief. While in a sense he was not satisfied with it and never would be, revising and adding to it for another forty years, making its fatal redundancy even more deadly in the process, he found that by expressing what had haunted him for years he had gained a peace he had never known before. Age, time, the troubles of the past years, did not seem to matter in the face of such strength and contentment. It was mid-July, and relaxed and triumphant, he enjoyed his mood and the summer weather. But he was not quite at peace, and the mood did not last. Before long he was possessed of the fear that this masterpiece would be stillborn. No publisher, he persuaded himself, would ever dare to publish such blasphemy. Only the year before the well-known publisher Edward Moxon and two others had been prosecuted and convicted for publishing an unemasculated version of *Queen Mab*. Though that case had been in part trumped up – an attempt by a radical group headed by the poet and wood engraver William James Linton, Horne's old friend of Craven Hill days, to challenge censorship laws and try to prevent the imprisonment of one of its leaders, a publisher of revolutionary literature named Henry Hetherington – the case had been lost. Despite Thomas Talfourd's magnificent defence, *Queen Mab* had continued banned. Such a consideration cannot have failed to influence Horne's thinking now. Even if he could find a publisher willing to take the risk with *Ancient Idols*, could he bear to see this poem so personal and revealing a part of himself publicly condemned?

His sense of exposure was too acute; his feelings too vulnerable. He had not, he found, the courage to give it to the world; he could not even try. Here he was, a self-confessed member of the band of poet martyrs, without the resignation and strength to accept his public martyrdom. While in some ways this might have been taken, in one as determinedly masochistic as Horne, as a healthy sign, Horne could view his own timidity only with shame and self-disgust. Shelley at the age of eighteen was not frightened to stand up to the wrongs of the world; Horne realized that he had failed this literary master. He put the manuscript in his trunk and prepared to wait until the world was better disposed to receive his message – *Ancient Idols* was never published. As usual, the persecutors had won; and the inevitable, cruel fate of poets together with the weakness of his nature, had prevented him from fulfilling his desires and duties.

Chapter 12

The Farthing Epic

A year later Horne would feel exhausted and written out; for the present
that unusual poetic facility which had produced his religious epic continued undimmed. If anything, it glowed more brightly. He had finished
Ancient Idols on the twentieth day of July 1842, a day he felt sufficiently important to record exactly for posterity; and for four months
thereafter he picked at desultory literary tasks – petty journalism, the
reconstruction of some Jacobean plays, the revision of educational
tales Mary was writing for children. In November, however, his aimless scribblings began to form themselves into order, and produce the
plan of another poem; an epic like the last and concerned with a struggle
hardly less important and personal.

Like its predecessor, its most likely sources were those absorbing
conversations with the Hunts and Leonhard Schmitz on poetry, philosophy and persecution. For his new epic was almost certainly based on
ideas from the German philosopher Hegel, and one assumes that it
must have been through Schmitz, or possibly Thornton Hunt's
friend George Henry Lewes, a German scholar and amateur philosopher, that Horne first encountered Hegel's work. It would seem to
have been Hegel's celebrated theory of history – the Hegelian dialectic
– involving two contradictory stages reacting against one another,
followed by a third reconciling the best in both – that ignited the poetic
spark in Horne that November. Suddenly he saw anew those contradictory energies that had plagued him since he knew he was a poet, and
never more than in the fact-ridden eighteen-forties. In the light of the
Hegelian interpretation, the divided forces in his nature and in the
society around him – the poet against the man, imagination and
thought against action and the senses – were not, as he had always
presumed, engaged in a destructive and perpetual struggle but part of a

process of human development. Their reconcilement was inevitable and essential: a law of human progress. He need no longer deny the man within himself: the man was as necessary as the poet. The effect of such a discovery on one as deeply implicated in that struggle as Horne can be imagined. It was a revelation comparable with that other religious revelation which had inspired *Ancient Idols*, its inspiration, if anything, more effective. Many times in the next ten years he would write on the dialectical unity of art and life, but never as well as in that winter and spring of 1843.

He used as vehicle for his complicated theme the old Greek star myth of Orion, a choice inspired by a vision which had haunted him for years, first come upon in Hazlitt's description of a painting by Nicolas Poussin, the seventeenth-century French painter beloved of the Cockney Romantics. Hazlitt had called it 'Blind Orion hungering for the Dawn'. Horne's reaction to the painting had been no less enthusiastic than Hazlitt's, his fascination with mutilation and his adoration for Hazlitt reinforcing his aesthetic appreciation. The giant hunter, beloved of the Moon, blinded for loving a mortal and now in search of sight, his great arms outstretched and groping, remained a vivid impression in his memory for almost twenty years, to be mentioned several times in his writings. Now combining and altering the fragments of myth concerning Orion in Homer and Ovid, he and Schmitz produced a coherent tale containing the symbolic machinery to express his message and one, in addition, impregnated with personal feeling.

Few of Horne's poems are so unrestrainedly or consciously autobiographical. His hero is so clearly a self-portrait: the 'physical man', awakened to the 'noble dreams' of genius, and dedicated 'to be and to do . . . feeling and acting nobly for the service of the world'; a man, moreover, torn by his 'duality of nature', and the perpetual 'struggle between the intellect and the senses when both energies are powerfully balanced'. His hero's experiences, too, are so clearly their author's own: Orion's first love for cold chaste Artemis, deriving, one cannot doubt, from Horne's own love for A., even to its destructive aftermath; and his last love with Eos, the goddess of the Dawn – the 'perfect' and 'intense sympathy' that resolves his inner contradictions – springing almost certainly from the relationship with Mary Gillies.

Horne believed his new epic was a hopeful poem, dedicated to that idea that conflict and eventual reconciliation led to progress, that a life balanced between thought and action and between the spirit and the senses was desirable and possible. Certainly *Orion* is more serene than the previous epic. The tone is less tortured: the verse soars with ease and grace. Nevertheless, though he advocated the right of all men to normal happiness, he could not dispel the belief that genius must suffer. (And curiously, just as in Hegel he found the intellectual justification for developing the man as well as the poet, he also found in Hegel a theory similar to his own, of the poet's inevitable martyrdom.) So Orion must be punished: rejected sexually by his first lover and blinded (in a scene recalling the mutilated doll of Horne's childhood) for daring to love his second. Through blindness and pain he must find purification and truth. But even then he cannot be left in peace. Restored to sight and insight by his last, reconciling love, he must still be snatched from happiness to martyrdom. Only when dead and raised to the stars can Orion enjoy either happiness or reward: the reward of inspiring mankind to progress. The conclusion is not comforting. The only consolation of Genius is fame after death:

> *Yet lives he not in vain; for if his soul*
> *Hath entered others, though imperfectly,*
> *That circle widens as the world spins round –*
> *His soul works on while he sleeps 'neath the grass.*

By April 1843 he had produced a draft of the poem. Then came troubles that might have dampened energy and creative powers less inflamed than his. He fell ill with a liver complaint which persisted for months, inflicting weakness and vexation in the midst of his greatest triumph. Suffering miserably, he took off for Brighton to join his mother on one of her frequent seaside holidays in the hope that the sea air might invigorate his body and his poetic skill. Early in May he wrote to Leigh Hunt from Brighton, telling him that he had almost forgotten his ill health in 'the pleasant toils of paternity'. He had adopted, he went on, almost all Hunt's suggestions for revision of the new poem, and he hoped to publish it within a few weeks. To Elizabeth Barrett he wrote from New Broad Street on May 26 to apologize for his silence: he had been so busy and wretchedly unwell. She must watch the literary advertisements next day for advice of his new poem, adding she might be in for a surprise and would think him mad.

Horne had returned from Brighton with a plan which he believed would set literary London by its ears. He had always had definite and unorthodox ideas on literary publicity; often in those months when he edited *The Monthly Repository* he had delivered attacks on the bad publicising of a recent book. His own personal publicity of late also caused him much disquiet. He was becoming, he suddenly realized, universally unpopular. He must adopt a new public role, stand aloof no longer in self-satisfied isolation and complaint, assume forbearance and hopeful attitudes and cultivate influential friends. He must make 'a personal impression on contemporaries'. He determined to act drastically. At first he considered giving his poem away, but he was reluctant to see his beloved poem end as waste paper. At last, revealing a surprisingly shrewd sense of the exotic and its effect on mass psychology, he drew up a set of most unusual conditions of sale. It would be, he argued, 'an experiment on the mind of a nation', as well as a most satisfying way of placing himself in the public eye and at the same time affirming his contempt of public response. He proposed to sell the poem at a farthing a copy, selling no more than one copy to each buyer, and selling no copy to anyone mispronouncing its title. His plan he justified excitedly and with rather self conscious satisfaction:

36 New Broad St.
June 3/43

My dear Hunt,

I am greatly pleased at receiving your cordial note 'to the tune of' Orion. I *thought* the price would amuse you, and it has. You are aware that it is no hoax, no joke? Anybody who *ought* to have the poem can buy it for a farthing. The proof that he 'ought', which I have directed the Publisher to require, is that the applicant should have a good face and proper accent. A man with a horse-nose and boar's mouth who asked for 'Horion' would certainly not obtain it. And very rightly *not*, I think. The book is refused, in numbers, to the 'trade' and to 'unlikely' messengers; and no friend can obtain two copies for his halfpenny. Other things I have 'ordained' as check to rapacity. You see, this was necessary, for as the poem is published at less than the price of waste paper I had to protect myself from people sending five shillings and a sack, with an eye to trunks and pie-bottom. But, as I said, any proper person can have a copy for a farthing.*

I am, dear Hunt,
Yours truly,
R. H. Horne.

* A peculiar mode of expressing my idea of public taste.

He was right when he believed it would shake literary society to its foundations. Even Horne was unprepared for the furore that followed.

Everyone he knew – and many, he complained, he did not – seemed to be affected strongly by the release of the poem. The sales were phenomenal. The poem appeared at the beginning of June: by the start of the third week the first two editions of 500 copies each were sold and a third edition was coming from the presses. Miller, the bookseller and publisher, was nearly torn to pieces and inundated with written orders which Horne now agreed to sanction. The price went up and still the sales went on as extraordinarily as ever. By the fourth edition in July it was a shilling, with ninepence for postage, and Miller was still selling, by Horne's estimation, between twenty-five and thirty copies a day. By the sixth edition at the end of the year the price was half a crown and still it sold. It had become a fashionable rage. References to it in conversation needed no explanation. Apocryphal stories circulated about it; the favourite one of W. J. Fox told of the small boy who went into Miller's to ask for 'a pennorth' of epics.

Down at the bookshop, a journalist Horne would later know in Australia, James Hingston, recorded the confusion and excitement and the figure of Horne, taking notes on the customers – short, be-ringletted, every inch the poet, 'romantic, restless, adventurous'. Horne's friends were incredulous, doubtful, alternately admiring. Elizabeth Barrett had been rather disapproving, telling him how Papa had asked was he planning to shoot the Queen? Hunt, on the other hand, 'laughed immensely – Not at you, of course, but *with* you'. There was, Hunt noted approvingly, 'a grand epic unsordiness in the pettiness of the sum'. He only hoped Horne had not been too rash and 'overwrought the very object' at which he aimed. Of its poetry, he rejoiced 'in the thick of its words and the loftiness of its mountain tops'. Carlyle, opponent of most poetry, placed it in a different class to most poetry, and considered it great: certainly many Carlylean beliefs burned in it. Elizabeth Barrett praised it extravagantly. She had been distressed at finding herself unable to obtain a copy in the rush so Horne had presented her with his own copy of the first edition. The very first copy of that first edition he had already presented to the poem's most devoted admirer, Mary Gillies; a fitting tribute to the woman who had almost certainly inspired the Goddess of the Dawn and had given him the nearest to normal happiness allowed the doomed Poet. Mary herself was enchanted by the poem and relieved and enchanted by its success: so often she had had to comfort him in his disappointments. There were few lines more beautiful, in her estimation, than that one line of Horne's – taken aptly from his description of Eos – that has stood the tests of quotability and proved immortal:

'Tis always morning somewhere in the world

Later, with quaint appropriateness, this line would be inscribed on a sundial on the pier at Brighton, the town in which the poem had been partially written. *Orion* was a sensation. Horne was famous.

It was a success, which, though he might often in fantasy have anticipated, in real life was unbelievable, exhilarating and disturbing. Even the reviews, when they began to appear, were scarcely less rapturous than the opinions of the author's friends. In the most immoderate terms the critics praised its beauty, its power, its philosophy. It was an 'enchanted web of forms and colours, exquisite in symmetry and harmony'; it had more 'imagination, passion, and ethical philosophy, than can be found in any other production of the present age'. *The Westminster Review* found it 'classic in its own way as Keats's *Endymion*, burning with a Shakespearian wealth of imagery, full of clear cut-scenes from nature, and idealized with lofty thoughts'.

In *The Athenaeum*, Elizabeth Barrett reviewed it – unknown even to Horne – anonymously and with as much impartiality as she could manage, spending much of her time anticipating and answering objections that might be made. She admitted it had faults: 'The personal may trench too closely on the allegorical, and fades too closely away into the more symbolical, and the action becomes contemplation, the *epos* a vision, the reader a riddle guesser unstartled by meeting Father Time upon the sands.' The answer to such criticism, she contended, was that Horne had written a 'spiritual epic' suited to such concerns. One must not look in the mouth a gift horse of the 'Divine Breed of Pegasus'. In contrast, in *The Illuminated Magazine*, Douglas Jerrold was delighted to find that Horne had written a social epic, charged with concern for social justice and progress. He commended the thinly veiled attack on the Corn Laws and episodes suggesting the struggle of man to rise over barriers of class and abject poverty, views inspired no doubt by Horne's Wolverhampton experiences. Horne was as much pleased with Jerrold's review as he was displeased by *The Athenaeum*'s, an opinion he unwarily passed on to Elizabeth Barrett. That *The Athenaeum* should have seen only the spiritual implications, when he believed he had shown quite as clearly the social implications of his message, infuriated him. That their contradictory impressions were the result of his own mental ambivalence he could not recognize.

In America, in *Graham's Magazine*, its brilliant, unbalanced editor, Edgar Allan Poe, himself the devoted disciple of late Romanticism and, on his own admission, 'among the earliest readers of Mr Horne – among the most earnest admirers of his genius', apologised for his 'imperfect and cursory' treatment and went on to give it five eulogistic pages, vowing that its beauties were never excelled and indeed never equalled in English poetry. He regretted that Horne had been so misguided as to attempt to impart to the simple fable a deeper, intellectual meaning (much of which he misinterpreted, as Horne would later try to point out to him), but he still proclaimed it to be 'one of the noblest, if not the very noblest poetical works of the age'. Its defects were 'trivial and *conventional* – its beauties intrinsic and *supreme*'. Critics were everywhere unanimous: Horne had written a masterpiece.

And why, one is tempted to wonder, is a poem once so praised forgotten today? Were all critics literary fools? To find the answer it must be remembered what doldrums poetry was then in, awaiting still the mid-century messiahs of Browning and Tennyson. Lovers of poetry were liable to seize hopefully on anything they thought might resemble genuine poetry. Their aesthetic tenets put great value on beauty and emotion and *Orion* had those in abundance. It also had recognizably more intellectual control than that other praised Spasmodic masterpriece *Festus*, which had appeared several years before. Critics were right in realizing that of the Spasmodic poetry then appearing, *Orion* was amongst the best. Where they most erred was in the value they gave to that Spasmodic type of poetry. The poetic desert in which they lived had warped their judgment. The emergence of Spasmodism in a truer perspective has rendered them foolish in a way that is not fair to them, and has held *Orion* also up to a contempt that is not entirely fair to it. One suspects that in its reassessment the twentieth century may have gone a little too far in the opposite direction.

For six months Horne was a literary wonder, thanks to the publicity of his farthing and, to a lesser extent, the praises of the critics. Six months' praise set against twenty years of neglect and self-doubts! The habits of twenty years are not easily sloughed off and by now for Horne a sense of failure had become a habit. Even he who, despite his penchant for suffering, had always longed for success and loved and craved publicity could not grasp success quickly. At first it was a prank: he was incredulous, amused, candidly self-delighted, ingenuously excited – like a child at a treat. He found himself savouring every drop of attention. He shamelessly indulged his vanity, his affectation, his long-standing love of being centre of the stage. It was exhilarating to go to Miller's bookshop and watch the bustling customers and hear the praising comments, leaf through the enormous pile of written orders, and then go home and write exuberantly to Elizabeth Barrett that the publisher was being torn apart and forced to store spare copies of *Orion* under his bed. Yet it must be admitted that he clung to it from the start as a sign that he had not been mistaken in himself; that he did in fact have genius. And as such it was a considerable comfort, for the fear of self-delusion was never far absent. Too often he found himself recalling how many people laboured their whole lives under 'a delusion – a false estimate of their own powers'. Underneath, fame had not yet substantially changed him. It was play-acting, ephemeral excitement, passing intoxication: an interval in poetic suffering. It had not yet acquired that dangerous and false sense of permanence one would see in him in a few months.

The dreamlike sensation was possibly heightened by his illness, which eventually began to reduce his exuberance and which continued, despite a temporary easing, into August. He longed to rejoin his mother by the sea and effect a permanent cure through sea air, rest and exercise, but he did not dare to leave London until August. Smith, Elder, the publishers, were demanding a new book and he was too seriously worried by the state of his finances to refuse. The money he had lost in the Author's Theatre had been a blow from which he had never recovered and, to make his anxiety worse, at the start of August the copper-mining company in which so much of his money was invested unexpectedly reduced dividends. Despite the fantastic sales, he was getting very little money from *Orion*. It was ironic, but perhaps only to be expected of the poetic destiny, that in the very moment of triumph he should be plagued by that old, terrifying fear of poverty.

Meanwhile to restore his health and spirits, he definitely decided on a holiday. Combining his new fame with his need for convalescence, he accepted the invitation of the authoress Miss Mitford to visit her home near Reading. Mary Russell Mitford was fifty-four, a starchy, snobbish spinster, the author of rural sketches called *Our Village* and poetic dramas of twenty years before, her literary success well behind her. She was the close friend, by correspondence, of Elizabeth Barrett with whom she regularly exchanged literary opinions and cosy gossip, and was familiar with the radiant feelings Horne excited in the heart of her dear Miss Barrett. Though known to be generous and affectionate, she was also finicky and querulous, worn out with the strain of supporting a profligate and demanding father who had recently died, leaving her a pile of debts that a subscription raised by literary friends, including Horne, had helped to pay.

Horne never met her personally but had been in communication with her at various times since 1839 over contributions to magazines, and numerous messages had passed between them through the letters of their mutual friend Elizabeth. Horne had even, out of kindness, allowed her twenty-five copies of *Orion*, waiving the rule of one copy per person, at which Elizabeth had been slightly jealous. It would seem to have been this kindness over *Orion*, together with his new literary fame and Elizabeth's enthusiasm, which prompted Miss Mitford to issue the invitation. Elizabeth hoped keenly for friendship at first sight between these two dearest of her correspondents. In fact Elizabeth should have shown sounder judgment. Anticipating the visit with intense excitement, as her letters so touchingly reveal, she should, knowing Miss Mitford's temperament, have also anticipated the disaster.

Horne was nervous. He was cast in a role which, though he had played it often enough in imagination, he was still unused to in real life: he was a literary lion. Ill-at-ease, still unwell, he travelled in warm autumn weather down to the small Berkshire village of Three Mile Cross where Miss Mitford had her tiny cottage to be greeted by what he would later describe as 'a venerable little gentlewoman in a garden bonnet and shawl, with silver hair, very bright hazel eyes and a rose-red smiling countenance', whose chief pleasures were country rambles, her garden and the society of the country gentry whom she regarded as 'the best class' in the world. Poetic affectation she could not abide. Professional writers she regarded with suspicion; years later it would be a great sadness to Elizabeth that her dear friend regarded Robert Browning with extreme distaste, pronouncing him affected and effeminate. Her thoughts as she set eyes on the determinedly poetic appearance and manner of the author of *Orion* can well be imagined.

Horne, for his part, turned himself inside out to be agreeable. He sat in the tiny garden ablaze with honeysuckle and geraniums and graciously consented to having a geranium named after him, 'Horned Orion'. He went on country rambles and rode in a pony cart; he played his guitar sitting beneath the huge apricot tree in the garden and took part in outdoor poetry readings, hearing for the first time Elizabeth Barrett's *House of Clouds*. He did what he felt was expected of him to the extent of neglecting the pressing literary work he had taken down with him, and though one imagines he was often ill-at-ease, one also imagines he probably did enjoy himself. He loved, after all, to be the centre of attention.

Elizabeth, meanwhile, immured at Wimpole Street, waited tremblingly for Miss Mitford's impressions. Never having seen Horne herself, except in Margaret Gillies's miniature, she was both eager and vulnerable in her determination to see him through Miss Mitford's eyes. The report that came back threw her into confusion. As soon as he arrived, Horne had put the frugal little household at Three Mile Cross into chaos. He wantonly set out, complained Miss Mitford, to be a nuisance. He was 'self-engrossed, and indifferent to all talents but his'; he was uneducated, unpolished, lacking wit, and conversation and breeding. He outstayed his welcome, ignored hints to go home, and disrupted domestic arrangements by demanding 'a bath three times a day'. In all, in his hostess's estimation, that week spent under her roof was a great mistake.

Horne was unconcerned. Oblivious to the hubbub he had caused, he wrote to tell Elizabeth now much he had enjoyed himself, and went on to Brighton, and then to Shoreham with his mother where his health became much better. Elizabeth, however, was aghast. She rushed to Horne's defence, prepared to attack even dear Miss Mitford rather than accept that her own feelings had been so misplaced. Desperately she produced examples of his generosity, sensitivity, learning, shyness – his diffidence, for example, in approaching her – her father's opinion that he might not be a polished but he was certainly not a '*pushing man* – that is certain!' 'And that *is* certain,' she added '*as far as our experience goes.*' Even Miss Mitford's grudging allowance that despite his faults she liked him and that he sang and played the guitar and double-flute exquisitely could not mollify Elizabeth, who retorted: 'we do not look to Orions for cachuchas . . . but for a high-sphere music. . . .' Indeed her unhappiness was so extreme that she could not leave the subject alone, and from Horne himself, indirectly and rather transparently, she began to try to discover how Miss Mitford could be so mistaken. Poor Elizabeth! But her tentative explorations did elicit one explanation. He told her that he detested a display of poetic learning and was unable to discuss poetic views with any but the closest or most sympathetic. Since Miss Mitford was obviously neither, Elizabeth was reassured.

A biographer would like to be similarly reassured. But even allowing for Miss Mitford's incompatibility and prejudices, her criticism rings true. In years to come Horne's behaviour would too often follow similar patterns. Yet there was truth also in what Elizabeth said in his defence. However much they had been overlaid by experience or usage, the origins of Horne's arrogance and insensitivity lay deeply in his shyness and that persistent feeling that had been with him since childhood that he did not belong. More easily recognizable perhaps in an adolescent, or even in the brash young man of thirty who had gone to Craven Hill, than in the forty-year-old author of *Orion*, the traits resisted his attempts to combat them. Invariably when he wanted desperately to be successful and was ill-at-ease – as he clearly was at Three Mile Cross – he overplayed his part. He tried too hard to be witty and only succeeded in being ponderous; he tried to be eccentric and only made himself objectionable; he tried to appear self-confident and only managed to be bumptious. Had he been simply over-eager he would have been pathetic, or even endearing, and therefore forgivable. Unfortunately Horne adored being taken notice of, so that in his determination to be the centre of the stage his natural sensitivity was swallowed up. On these occasions, once he was warmed to his role, he was often very happy and usually managed to convince himself he had been a huge success. He lacked any sense of the impression he was making on other people. This, allied to his bitterness – to which, since they were both facets of his insecurity, it was related – would earn Horne many enemies in years to come.

He had changed, too, in another way within those few weeks preceding his visit to Three Mile Cross. *Orion* had ceased to be a prank. Whereas previously his sense of perspective had prevented him losing his head at the acclaim and ensured an amused and relatively detached enjoyment, the perspective seemed to have receded. In June he had been master of his success, but by his behaviour at Three Mile Cross he proclaimed it had become master of him. Mismanaged as his play-acting was, one cannot doubt it was in earnest. He had convinced himself that he was a literary lion. The publicity, the phenomenal sales, the attention he was receiving were his not by right of a farthing prank but by right of his talents; his rightful reward from destiny. This would not have mattered if, when the furore was over and the literary lion was no longer at large, he had been able to go back to his old cage of neglect. Tragically, however, Horne would not go back. He would continue to be 'Orion' Horne – the title by which he was now increasingly called – long after it had ceased to have meaning to anyone but himself.

Chapter 13

The Disastrous Menagerie

Shoreham had restored Horne's health, his spirits were high, and the excitement over *Orion* still simmered. Theoretically no riper nor more satisying season for literary creation could have existed. For the first time in his entire literary career he had reason to hope; and yet despair rather than hope had perhaps become for him a necessary ingredient of the literary process.

He prepared late in 1843 to move from Finsbury Square to Kentish Town, his home for the following year, and in so doing to enter a new mental environment. Since his success the urge had grown to stand out in society – the urge which had helped inspire the farthing price for *Orion*. Now he believed he had again the offer of that chance, and the opportunity to comment on the role of the genius in contemporary society. In July he hinted to friends that he was to be engaged on an important literary project, and three months later the literary journals revealed the details: a collection of biographical and critical sketches of leading literary figures of the day, to be written by anonymous authors and to be edited by the author of *Orion*. Horne alluded to these details with a mixture of self-importance and nervousness. He was to edit, and contribute to, an ambitious and potentially important book, and editorship of such a book would be a visiting card that many notable people could hardly ignore. On the other hand, the book's ambitious design was a legitimate cause for nervousness. To relinquish now his dearly won success would be insupportable, leading to suffering and despair. And at the back of his mind he may have realized that such a setback was not unlikely.

Editing had never been one of Horne's particular talents, as his experiences with *The Monthly Repository* and *Chaucer Modernized* had shown. He was not a lazy editor but he was an over-anxious one, with a fussiness that bordered on indecision; he could scarcely pick up one of his own published works without wanting to rewrite it. This quality, applied to the essays of contributors as touchy as himself, could not help but make trouble. Furthermore, as the editor of and a contributor to the proposed book, he would be criticising the living, a risky task for anyone, but especially for one whose criticisms had never been well received. His reputation for Syncretic bitterness meant his criticism would be suspect even before the book was published. Lastly, in proclaiming himself editor of *A New Spirit of the Age* (for the book was to be named in memory of Hazlitt's similar book of essays of twenty years before, *The Spirit of the Age*), Horne took responsibility for the opinions given by the anonymous contributors. If the book were fiercely criticized all the blows would fall on his head. Even Hazlitt, who had written all his book himself, had shrunk from printing his own name on the title page. Yet here was Horne preparing to do it, and to appear responsible for opinions that might not even be his own. On examination the omens were against the embryonic *New Spirit of the Age* and even more against its editor.

He was flustered from the start. In his letters to Elizabeth Barrett, he dithered and postured, over-confident one moment, over-anxious the next. Elizabeth bore his humours with her usual loyalty and agreed not only to being the subject of one of the sketches but also to being one of his anonymous co-authors. At the same time he may have approached Mary Gillies and Robert Bell with similar requests for help, and perhaps also Thomas Powell. Certainly Powell made the claim, both at the time and later, after his flight to America, of being one of the authors; he claimed in fact, to have been the book's true first projector, his plans being 'altered, corrected, and *edited* by R. H. H., who barbarously expunged all extracts illustrating opinions expressed in the work'. Why Powell, even if this were true, should so consistently lay claim to a book so universally condemned as *A New Spirit* is a mystery. And yet Horne as consistently denied Powell had any part in the authorship, long before Powell's disgrace would have made a false denial on Horne's part intelligible. Powell, Horne told Elizabeth, had merely lent portraits for engraving and money for publication.

It is unfortunately on Powell's suspect word that the authorship of the various sketches rests today. According to his evidence, Horne allotted to Mary the subjects of Harriet Martineau, and her friends Southwood Smith and William and Mary Howitt. To Bell he is purported to have given the novelists and Macready, though his letters to Elizabeth make clear that he himself did most of the Macready essay.

To Elizabeth, as her surviving letters attest, he allotted Tennyson, Landor, Wordsworth, Carlyle and the poet-parliamentarian Monckton Milnes. 'You work in honourable footsteps following Hazlitt,' Elizabeth told him, and certainly this was one of the chief attractions of his task. To follow that literary master was an honour and an emotional compensation for the difficulties that within a few weeks began to appear.

In November Elizabeth, as usual hypersensitive about her privacy, was thrown into a flurry of reproaches when it seemed that her part as his helper had been revealed. Fortunately he was able to calm her with the assurance that the names of the contributors remained a secret. Work resumed nervously and, on Horne's part, inefficiently. The history of the *Repository* and *Chaucer Modernized* was repeating itself: a treadmill of altering, adding, collating, bickering, and neglected deadlines, with Horne badgering his colleagues and blaming them for his own faults. Neither Horne nor his helpers were adequate for their task, with the exception perhaps of Elizabeth Barrett. Otherwise the tedious work now nearing completion was lit only by an occasional flash of precision or perception, and was too often marred by Horne's fanatical devotion to the Syncretics and the violence of his mental traits. Against Macready and against Richard Barham, the author of the *Ingoldsby Legends*, Horne made impassioned attacks: with personal rancour he blamed Macready for deluding dramatists, and he blamed Barham for his 'sick humour' (as the twentieth century might call it) in depicting murder and mutilation. Horne 'worried' (a critic later wrote) Barham's 'light-hearted and harmless fantasies . . . as though they were the gravest and deepest crimes'. A biographer must add that, to one of Horne's mental makeup, they undoubtedly were crimes. The attack, so vicious in tone, puzzled and disturbed his friends; Leigh Hunt begged Horne to delete it.

By the original publication date at the start of February 1844, Horne had not finished, and the strain on his health and nerves was so considerable that he left his rooms at Fortress Terrace, Kentish Town, and rushed to Brighton in search of quiet for the final revisions. This time even Brighton failed to perform its therapeutic miracle, and at the end of February he was still working until the early morning over his manuscripts. It was March, over a month later than planned, when the 'menagerie of modern lions and lionesses' was ready: twenty-five essays on more than forty contemporary figures, mostly writers, with some scientists and philanthropists: people of rising rather than established reputations.

It was so close an amalgam of the work of Horne and his helpers that few essays were the work of one person; but certainly every essay contained Horne's own spirit. The necessity of suffering, the dedication of the poetic mission, the cruel neglect of genius, the struggles of the authors by profession – above all the conflict of poetry and practicality – cried out from its pages. That bitter struggle between imagination and reason, the scientific reformer and the poet, he saw as a vital sympton of the time. On the one side men of reason like Southwood Smith personified that 'energy which is now put forth to make the doctrines of science known and to teach the masses how to apply them to their advantage'. On the other side the power of the soul and the imagination were personified in the passionate imagination of the poets and the genius of Thomas Carlyle. As in *Orion*, Horne prophesied their reconciliation.

By the time *The New Spirit of the Age* appeared in the booksellers Horne was worn out. On the eve of publication, one incident showed how disastrous to his nerves the whole project had been. He had gone to the printer to read over some final page proofs and found that through a printer's miscalculation he must now cut either a large part of his Syncretic attack on Macready or a large part of his essay in praise of Elizabeth. It was a difficult decision: to betray either his beloved friend, or his beloved cause. He afterwards confessed that his head had spun with dismay and anxiety. Finally, Syncretic principles had won and he had taken the pen and scored out the praise of Elizabeth. He knew he had betrayed her for the essay now did her far less than justice. A week later he wrote to her confessing, begging forgiveness.

He took himself off to the sea to join his mother before the reviews appeared, in the hope that the rest might quiet his nerves and prepare him for the expected critical onslaught. There, however, he began to succumb to nervous headaches and a heavy cold. His letters to Elizabeth were, as usual, a revealing barometer of his moods. He attempted for her sake, to appear resonably calm, but nothing could hide the undercurrent of apprehension. She, for her part, was quick to reassure, telling him that he imagined 'more harm than really exists', scolding him for 'over-depressing views' and 'over-extreme sensitiveness'. Yet once the reviews began to appear her comfort faltered. There seemed so little she could say. For his worst fears were justified. Critics, subjects, readers alike: everyone was out of temper with *A New Spirit*. W. S. Landor 'laughed aloud' when he read the description of his wit; Charles Dickens disliked the Syncretic tone and declared the engraved portrait of himself looked like the 'man in the iron mask'. Macready was enraged and demanded a public apology. Thomas Carlyle growled the question, what had he to do with spirits of the age or that 'goose goddess they call fame. Ach Gott!'

The Athenaeum, The Westminster Review, Ainsworth Magazine, The New Monthly, The Morning Chronicle, the Church of England Quarterly: the reviews appeared in abusive succession through April, May and June, until scarcely an influential paper was unrepresented. They damned everything from the book's name to the editor's face. 'A New Gull's Horne Book, Poor Tom, thy horn is dry' punned the maligned Harrison Ainsworth in his own magazine. A 'manifest misnomer of unphilosophic construction' thundered Sarah Flower's husband in The Westminster Review. The work of a vicious Syncretic clique, said Henry Chorley in The Athenaeum. For many it was the moment they had long waited to gloat over the downfall of the author of False Medium and the leader of the Syncretics. On Horne thundered down the sum of all those old enmities he had earned over the past eleven years in his uncompromising devotion to the cause of neglected genius. He quailed alike at the cries of the book's victims and those of their defending friends. He was the target for fair criticism, faction bitterness, political backbiting, disinterested disapproval, personal grudge, and almost every contempt of which reviewers were capable.

Today, of all those condemnations, one stands out in vigour, subtlety and justice though at the time to Horne it was little more than another episode in the long-drawn ordeal. It appeared on April 4, 1844, in the influential Morning Chronicle from the pen of one of its newest reviewers, Michael Angelo Titmarsh: in reality William Makepeace Thackeray, whom Horne had met on those evenings spent at Robert Bell's. No critic has ever more accurately laid bare Horne's critical faults and virtues: the 'generous' sympathies, the 'easy candour', the 'well placed' admiration, and the devastating mediocrity. Words, wrote Thackeray, 'words – such a cornucopia of them as the world has few examples of; but the thoughts are scarce in the midst of all this plentifulness, the opinions for the most part irreproachable, and the ennui caused by their utterance profound'. That such a circumscribed writer should presume to follow in Hazlitt's footsteps he could not allow. He could not believe that Mr Horne 'had inherited any portion of the stained, travel-worn old mantle which Hazlitt left behind him'; Horne – with an ironic allusion to the Cockney School controversy – was 'enveloped in a good stout suit of undeniable Bow-Bell cut'. It was a brilliant and a fair review, and hurt Horne deeply. He could not bear to be told he was unworthy to follow Hazlitt.

The attacks, once begun, momentarily calmed Horne's nerves, the reality perhaps being less perturbing than the fears his mind had conjured up. At the start of April 1844 he was able to reassure Elizabeth that his health was good and his spirits were steady. Elizabeth, for her part, could admit only to 'pain and indignation' and guilt, as she saw her own work condemned and Horne as editor blamed for it. 'The book,' she told him urgently, 'is but an accident in your literary life . . . not worthy of being the subject of one over-anxious or painful thought.' A month later, however, those anxious and painful thoughts abounded, and never before in his entire career had they been so firmly based. Never before had his feelings of persecution been so reasonably justified. It was not surprising that in the following weeks such thoughts multiplied, and sadder still that most were valid. A malicious faction, as he told Elizabeth, was indeed at work against him; many of his friends – among them Dickens, Bulwer, Talfourd, possibly Tennyson – had turned against him.

Yet at least, Horne also noted, not all were against him. Calculating those subjects who stood by him and declared themsevlves satisfied, he listed Southwood Smith, Monckton Milnes, 'Festus' Bailey, Robert Browning, Thomas Hood, Mary Shelley (the novelist widow of his beloved poet) and Miss Martineau and Miss Mitford. It was, in all, a gratifying list; and Leigh Hunt, as ever, had come to his support with comprehensive notes and the conviction that the book's virtues would override the storm of vituperation. Elizabeth, too, had hidden her true feelings, which she confided in letters to other friends, and hastened to assure him of her delight.

Despite such loyalty there was still decidedly more on the debit side than the credit. His enemies were widespread, forceful, and vocal, and as the weeks passed and their antagonism showed no sign of abating he grew increasingly depressed. His acquaintances, it seemed, took malicious pleasure in bringing him face to face with his enemies and watching the results. At the start of June Miss Mitford, who had so far forgiven his boorish behaviour as to reinvite him to visit Three Mile Cross the following July, came to town and was at a party where he was introduced for the first time to his antagonist Henry Chorley. On this occasion Horne's self-control was so admirable that Miss Mitford, observing the calm introductions, was quite oblivious that the two men were enemies; it had taken an incredulous Elizabeth Barrett later to enlighten her. The next such incident, however, Horne carried less well. At a dinner party the host deliberately left him alone with one of the book's main victims, the poet Robert Montgomery. Horne was extremely embarrassed and it was Montgomery's tact, as Horne later admitted, that saved them both. But it was Horne's meeting with Thackeray at the Royal Society Rooms at the end of July that was the most unnerving.

Thackeray's review had both infuriated and amazed Horne. The subtlety and much of the sense of the review had entirely escaped him and he interpreted and replied to it in the preface to the second edition of the book – which appeared in booksellers in June – with a pathetic literalness. That Thackeray with his great 'camus nose, and great round-glassed spectacles' dared 'to venture upon fanciful personalities', dared to preach Hazlitt's genius to himself who had 'endured abundant odium for asserting [it] ten years ago', and dared to accuse a former Mexican revolutionary of being Cockney-bound, was unthinkable. Horne ended his muddled, misguided reply with an ironic challenge for Thackeray to shake hands with him; and now in the rooms of the Royal Society they met for the first time since Horne's ironic challenge, with a group of onlookers agog with interest. Thackeray, looking at the defiant and embarrassed small figure before him, so dogged, so sincere and so hurt, must have felt remorse. Ignoring the irony of the printed challenge he extended his hand and begged Horne to take it. It was the act, Horne would later write, 'of a true gentleman'.

Not all were so gentlemanly; nor did Horne's replies to his critics in the second edition, betraying that ingrained instinct in him to have back at his enemies blow for blow, make them more so. Elizabeth had begged him to be moderate and cautious but the published preface showed scant sign of either quality. Least forgiving were the magazines to which Horne sent his work. Here certainly his feelings of persecution were justified and, afraid to defend himself in an article under his own name, he was forced to the humiliating dodge of having Elizabeth submit them for him as the work of a nameless friend. ('You will not mention this of course,' she cautioned as she later confided it to Robert Browning.) To Edgar Allan Poe, the American poet journalist with whom he corresponded following his praising of *Orion*, he was forced to apologize when asked by Poe to place some stories in an English magazine. His own reputation was too low to allow him to thus help a friend; thanks to the 'attacks and jeers' of public and critics he 'was not likely to have the power'. 'If you have seen the "New Spirit of the Age" you will readily understand that a great many critics here and some authors are far from pleased with me.' However, once the storm had passed he might be able to help, since 'those trees that are not blown down nor injured look all the fresher among the wrecks'.

How he longed to leave London! He thought of visiting Spain. Such thoughts brought memories of Mexico: of lithe dancing bodies under hot sun and the twanging of guitars, and the poetry of Calderon, so admired by Shelley. His other dream was of Germany, his intellectual home since his friendships with Carlyle and Leonhard Schmitz had engendered a love of its writers and philosophers.

The desire to escape became more insistent: a temporary escape until the attacks and injuries were forgotten and he could reassemble his shattered identity. What made the criticism so unbearable was that it followed *Orion's* success which in turn had followed so many years of neglect. London buzzed with rumours about *A New Spirit* and its repercussions, and how different were these rumours to those that had concerned him twelve months before. Then he had been the hero, now he was the laughing stock. Flung back into the familiar pit of despondency – a despondency that provided him now with neither perverse satisfaction nor fuel for the next effort – it was as though he could foresee the future: the end of the creative Indian summer, and the downward descent into tedious scribbling. Within a few months he had grown old, tired and written out.

He knew he must escape. Once more the active adventurous part of his nature saw its chance. He must go back to that role of romantic adventurer which had proved so satisfying in America and sustained him in memory through the intervening years. He would indulge the active side of himself, and quit England until he was sufficiently strong for the next attempt on the literary life, or until the outcry of *A New Spirit* was forgotten. The cracks that had begun to appear in the wall of his literary faith he did not dare examine; the following years would reveal how greatly his belief in his poetic mission was altering, and what compromises, unthinkable a few years before, he would be prepared to make.

Providentially his friend Leonhard Schmitz, born at Aix la Chapelle, a graduate of Bonn University, was preparing to revisit his old home and university. He was, furthermore, prepared to take Horne with him. It was a readymade solution, and through the weeks of August 1844 Horne excitedly made preparations, obviously relieved to have something besides the scandals of *A New Spirit* to occupy him.

One of his first thoughts, once the decision was made, was of Elizabeth Barrett. If *A New Spirit* had done nothing else, it had reestablished and recharged their intimacy, which after four years of a relationship dependent solely on letters had, not surprisingly, shown signs of dwindling. During the months of the book's compilation he felt his fondness for Elizabeth growing. His letters grew longer, more lively, more affectionate; he ceased to be irritated by her impulsiveness. It was a joy to work with her and see her vigorous intelligence, her critical honesty, her surprising business sense. Even her female vagaries became endearing and even admirable; her unreasonable demands to include a portrait of Miss Mitford in the book produced in Horne the gentlest of admonitions. (That she herself would not sit while Margaret Gillies drew her portrait for *A New Spirit* made him much more angry.) He had never loved Elizabeth more: there was nothing, he declared, that he would not do for her.

It was not so surprising, therefore, when he requested permission to call on her at the end of July. Possibly he would have requested anyway, but the prospect of leaving England 'indefinitely' added urgency. Part of his old feelings clamoured to see Elizabeth; part, as of old, were reluctant. The former proved the stronger. He confessed his imagination was unable to keep pace with the thought; he saw himself approaching her couch – his *Arabian Nights'* lady – only to find her vanished and in her place an empty Indian shawl. It was a presentiment, as Elizabeth later remorsefully admitted, he should have heeded. For the situation acted out in reality at the end of July had the tone of a tantalizing dream. Horne began by proposing to call at a definite time. Elizabeth's reply was panic-stricken. She was terrified – 'like a Wild Indian', she told Robert Browning the following year. She downright refused. She sent off a long, apologetic and defensive letter, full of excuses: she was too tired, she must not be over-excited, she was not well. She said she was also put out by the fact that, even before he had asked her permission to call, he had already announced to a female friend – who had in turn passed it on to her – that he was about to call at Wimpole Street: he was over-presumptuous. Then, relenting, she begged him to understand she was not a normal person. She ended by asking forgiveness and urging him to write and reassure her.

One thing must here be said to explain the violence of Elizabeth's reactions. In June or July Horne had paid another visit to Three Mile Cross and, once again, back to Elizabeth's unhappy ears had come a string of complaints, among them the disquieting news that Horne had paid brash – to Miss Mitford's mind, ungentlemanly – attentions to several rich young ladies. Elizabeth was horrified. Her own relationship with Horne suddenly seemed tainted; she had so loved and trusted him in these past months, so enjoyed their correspondence, believing always, as she now confessed, in the 'lofty' and 'pure love of a man of genius'. She managed to joke of it to Miss Mitford. 'The baldheartedness,' she wrote, 'is ten times worse than the baldheadedness'; but underneath it was not for joking. She felt betrayed; she could not bear to see him and perhaps be betrayed still further.

It was a time for mutual wounding. Horne, too, was deeply hurt by her reply – how hurt can be seen from Elizabeth's next letter (for his reply is unfortunately missing) in which she regretted his 'vexation and mortification'. Overcome by shame, fearing she had alienated him – for though her new insight disturbed her she could still not bear to lose him – she wrote again, apologizing for her morbid hypersensitiveness, promising to try to see him if he called. Horne replied formally that he doubted he would have the time; then added, softening, that he would try, and if he did not come it would not be because he did not want. And so, for afternoon after afternoon, Elizabeth waited tremblingly for Horne to come. 'Well!' she wrote later to Browning with a combination of anger, remorse, relief and disappointment, ' – he never came. Either too overcome by work or engagements of various sorts that he had not a moment.' More likely, she should have said, he was overcome by pain and prudence. Horne's original reluctance had found endorsement. Their intimacy, established in the last year so firmly, had been damaged too far to be repaired.

A few months later Horne would be superseded for Elizabeth by another. Then, Robert Browning, that other young poetic protégé of W. J. Fox, reading Elizabeth's latest poems, would discover 'fresh strange music'. He would write to their secluded authoress that he loved her poems and that he loved her too; he would force his way into the sealed twilight room and, under the unknowing gaze of her possessive father, he would carry her off to Italy as his wife. Only as Browning's wife would she meet Horne. If he had had hopes of achieving with Elizabeth that earthly happiness he now believed the poet's right, he hoped in vain. At least he now had no time to pine over Elizabeth's rejection, for in September 1844 he and Schmitz left for Germany.

Chapter 14

Man as Man

In the late autumn of 1844 the travellers reached Cologne, the ancient city renowned alike for its dirt and smells, its famous Cathedral and its autumn street carnival. Horne, so enamoured of English fairs, was eager to attend the carnival, a 'gorgeous and peculiar exhibition of national fancies, both of the poetical and grotesque'. Never having lost his childish delight in such entertainment he entered into this with characteristic exuberance, and on an intensely cold morning stood in a frost-covered street to watch the procession of heroes and charioted goddesses shivering in their tinsel costumes. In the afternoon he sat with the revellers at a public dinner in a tall dunce's cap trimmed with bells and became rather drunk, yet not so drunk that he could not notice that here was no drunkenness such as one saw in England.

Outwardly gay, absorbed in his travels, inwardly Horne found it less easy to shake off low spirits. His relief at leaving England was enormous, but at this distance the memories of *A New Spirit* continued to haunt him, and always hanging over him was the dreaded thought of his return. His despondency found its way into his letters to Elizabeth Barrett; and she, believing her behaviour before his departure might have contributed, was conscience-stricken. In November she wrote him more than ten pages, profuse with apologies. She was like a child in her need for reassurance and her eagerness to make up their quarrel. She owned contritely to being too impulsive altogether; she begged him to put out of his mind any fears that he himself had been remiss. She was distressed that he seemed so wretched: would he not confide in her the full cause? One wonders if Elizabeth did not guiltily suspect that he was a blighted lover and her impulsive rejection was the cause.

By December the cold was so intense that the Rhine was frozen from

Cologne to Koblenz, and one could drive a horse and cart on the ice, avoiding the thin flowing stream in mid-river. At Bonn, where the travellers now arrived, the cold was bitter. Horne would recall years later the slippery streets along which he hobbled on his way from his rooms in the house of Herr Herman Kaufmann, in the Münsterplaz, to the town gates. Clad in his dreadnought jacket and red woollen comforter – the accepted garb of English visitors in Bonn – he would take the frozen road out of the town in the morning to the nearby village of Poppelsdorf where the university professors had rooms in the old castle. With an introduction from Schmitz, Horne spent much of his time talking with professors or skating on the frozen castle moat among the students. He met Gottfried Kinkel, twenty-nine-year-old poet, a former theologian and a dedicated opponent of tyranny, and sat in his rooms overlooking the slates and steeples of Poppelsdorf and vine-covered ridges of the plains below to the shining surface of the Rhine. He was fascinated by the talk on music, history, literature and politics. From political theorists and revolutionaries (in the 1848 revolution Kinkel himself would be sentenced to life imprisonment for fighting in the insurgent's army) he heard arguments which inflamed not only his sympathies for the oppressed but formed opinions which he would later preach in England. Above all he was drawn to Kinkel the man, and would long remember with affection that first dramatic sight of him, skating down the icy road to Bonn, dressed in his old frock-coat and broad-brimmed hat, a bundle of books under his arm and his long black hair streaming after him in the wind: a figure from a fairy tale.

At Bonn both sides of Horne's nature found employment, talking with his friends, or skating on the river and climbing the Drachenfels. There, he told Elizabeth, but for the presence of a vine, he might have fallen to his death; as it was he dislocated his shoulder in another fall on the ice. The character of the Romantic adventurer brushing with danger and death had begun to re-emerge. Even his intellectual discussions were flavoured by his preoccupation with activity: the poet's active place in society, and his role in politics and even revolt. Every step on the mountains seemed to impress upon him that the poet must leave his metaphorical mountain top and descend into the turbulent world of men.

At Bonn, too, he had begun once more to work. Inspired by his own work on the Royal Commission and the work of Southwood Smith, Caroline Hill and Mary Gillies, he had agreed in the middle of the previous year to be co-worker in a series of educational stories for children. The originator of the scheme was Mary Gillies. For years she had agitated for reform in children's literature, decrying the old type of nursery tale as didactic, puritanical and often sadistic. In this Horne, with his love of children and the memories of his own childhood, could not help but applaud her. Those so-called 'harmless fantasies' of childhood literature had always seemed to him the 'gravest crimes'. His own terror at first hearing *Red Riding Hood* stood out in his mind, along with the cruelties of *Hush-a-bye-Baby*, *Cock Robin* and scores of others. They had never seemed to him objects of enchantment – and certainly not of instruction – but rather uncensored sadism: 'materials for dreams at night' – 'excellent fun – a smashed baby! – well done . . .!' He believed with Mary that parents, publishers, and critics must be educated against this insidious nursery poison and converted to tales that would awaken the child's imagination, curiosity, and sense of wonder. To this purpose he and Mary had planned their series, to be called the Myrtle books and to be published by John Crundall of Old Bond Street.

Horne had written some of his portion straight away; then as the attacks on *A New Spirit* proved unsettling, he had temporarily abandoned his task. Now in Bonn, enlivened by his new surroundings and stimulated by his new friends, he began once more to fulfil his obligations to Mary and Crundall. By Christmas he had written half of a charming story, set in Bonn, describing the adventures of a German family with a bear. Entitled *The Good Natured Bear*, it would always be the favourite among his children's tales.

Never had he found writing more therapeutic. Through December into April, enthusiasm and confidence flowed back into his letters, the shadows of *A New Spirit* banished for the moment. He confessed to 'a childish delight in reading the story' and, with disarming over-confidence, claimed that it belonged to the company of *Gulliver's Travels* and *Robinson Crusoe*. Finally he coyly accused Crundall of siding with Mary Gillies and making fun over his love for his Bear: 'I perceive that you and that lady have been making merry at my expense on the subject – to the effect that I am supposed to *prefer* it to *Robinson Crusoe*. Too bad of you both.' To Miss Mitford – herself the authoress of children's books – he had also proudly announced his new work: rather cunningly, for he knew that one of her 'dear friends' was 'the Queen's principal private attendant', and so had emphasized the story's setting in Bonn, Prince Albert's birthplace, hoping for the book to be installed in the royal nurseries. Such publicity, he well knew, would be incomparable.

So therapeutic indeed had it proved that he was able at last to face the prospect of returning to England. By April he had decided he must return to supervise in person the publication of *The Good Natured Bear*. He alone, he felt, could save it from the stupidities of its publisher, who throughout the previous two months had been disagreeing with Horne in a series of long-distance arguments, Horne forever decrying Crundall's caution, and Crundall despairing of Horne's blundering business ideas. At the start of April, refreshed but somewhat apprehensive, Horne left Bonn on his journey back to England.

His apprehension was not misplaced. Though the immediate hubbub had died down in the intervening nine months, few of those London doors closed to him then had reopened. The more maligned 'new spirits' were as little likely to forget as Horne. He retired now thankfully to the maternal comfortings of Mary at Hillside, not merely as before as a visitor, but as a permanent resident, occupying rooms in the large old house overlooking the heath. It was a move that may, in its implications, tease the biographers, but it was possibly made because the protagonists, at the ages of forty-two and forty-five, felt there were no longer implications. Certainly it must have been more comfortable for Horne to live permanently with the Gillies sisters. Whatever his relationship with Mary over the past decade – whether passion was suppressed or indulged – it would seem almost certain that they now enjoyed no more than a deep but routine friendship; otherwise, his marriage two years later to a much younger woman with whom he was violently in love could hardly have been made without seriously offending Mary.

He threw himself into his children's stories, following *The Good Natured Bear* with two more, *The Memoirs of a London Doll* and *King Penguin*, all written under pseudonyms and published by Crundall. He threw himself with equal zeal at John Crundall whose publication methods never pleased him. Otherwise, as the months passed, he wrote little. He lacked incentive, for what incentive could the author of *A New Spirit* have? He could publish his work only under false names or in the journals conducted by friends like Douglas Jerrold. As for being a poet, his hopes lay with *Ancient Idols* at the bottom of his tin trunk. As for cutting a dominant figure among his contemporaries, *A New Spirit* had put an end to that.

Consequently he drifted. His days were taken up increasingly with Mary's occupations, and they, like most English intellectual currents of late, led towards social reform. To Hillside that summer and autumn came old friends from Bayswater days until the rambling garden seemed another Craven Hill and recalled soothing memories. Through leisurely afternoons they sat beneath the trees and talked: W. J. Fox, Eliza Flower – a wraith of a woman in the last stages of tuberculosis – Southwood Smith and his daughter Caroline Hill, William Howitt who was a 'sturdily built but not large Quaker', and his wife Mary, 'the primitive Quakeress, a comely woman'. William James Linton came often, too, a fiercer radical than ever, and one of England's foremost wood engravers. Women's rights, popular education, Parliamentary reform and the general welfare of the working classes and, above all, abolition of the Corn Laws were still the issues that stirred them. As always they were dedicated, but they were also somewhat tired, somewhat disillusioned.

The atmosphere, now, was more domestic. The Howitt children often came with their parents, and six small Hill daughters – grandchildren of Southwood Smith – seemed to be constantly in Mary's house. They were 'wonderful children', Horne found; 'you can talk to them about anything'. They were equally enchanted with him and called him 'Ganner' – a corruption of the 'Dreadful Glasgow Gander', the name scornfully given to Horne by Christopher North in his review of the *False Medium*. On sunny afternoons Horne would pursue them through the garden disguised as a furious gander, 'with a sheet over my shoulders' (as he later recalled), 'neck extended – and a red tile in my mouth to represent my dreadful bill, which did not smother, but enhanced the half choking and lisping effect of my hisses, while the children fled with screams of terrified delight through the shrubs'. One of those children, Octavia Hill, renowned later as a social reformer, longingly recalled the 'sunny bright hours' at Hillside in those days. 'There remains in my mind a recollection, a vision of beauty connected with it, which can never be effaced.'

Drifting with the reforming tide of the 'forties, and in particular the currents of Mary's friends, Horne was reasonably content and relaxed. Yet not all ambitions for the poetic future could be stifled. *Orion* miraculously continued to sell, the sixth edition almost exhausted, and another edition soon necessary. Disgusted with Miller, from whom he claimed he had got not a penny, Horne consulted Leigh Hunt, who recommended one of his friends who was starting a new publishing house in Southgate Street. This was Charles Ollier, once a peripheral member of the Cockney School, a publisher who will always be remembered for the work and regard entrusted him by Hazlitt, Lamb and Keats. 'Your name,' Horne assured him, 'is associated with my earliest and strongest enthusiasm in poetry.' In the new year the seventh edition of *Orion* appeared under Ollier's imprint, and with it another book: a collection of seven ballads written by Horne over the previous fifteen years, most already published in magazines and admired by friends like Browning and Carlyle. Horne described the new volume, entitled *Ballad Romances*, hopefully to his publisher as 'forcible and popular – so far as such a thing can be expected of poetry at the time'. These ballads, he seemed to believe, having already appeared separately with success, were bound to succeed and keep the poetic name of Horne from extinction.

The critics, however, thought differently, and in their general opinion the new book was 'rather unfortunate' for Mr Horne's reputation. The pendulum of critical opinion had also begun to swing against *Orion*, now described as 'much overrated' and no more than a 'skilful imitation of poor Keate's [*sic*] "Endymion".' In a blow all Horne's hopes for reinstatement had gone; he was not, it seemed, even to be left with his past success.

His friends were concerned for him. While they could not wholeheartedly admire the turgid measures of *Ballad Romances*, which, as Elizabeth Barrett confided to Robert Browning, lacked both 'subtlety and elasticity in thought and style', they were concerned by the critical vendetta that so obviously flourished against him. Elizabeth, in the fastness of Wimpole Street, had not realized how considerable this was until Browning told her, warning her not to relay to Horne any hint of her dissatisfaction with his latest book. 'He has unmistakable genius,' Browning wrote, 'and is a fine, honest, enthusiastic chivalrous fellow – it is the fashion to affect to sneer at him, of late.' She responded at once. Both she and Browning sent Horne letters expressing 'thanks and admiration' for the ballads, and for *The Good Natured Bear*, in Browning's phrase, so 'furry, warm and genial'.

Other friends were less forbearing; among them Miss Mitford who in another burst of self-punishment had invited Horne to Three Mile Cross and reaped the usual reward. Once more she was beside herself with anger and accusations. His behaviour had been more than ever reprehensible: the catalogue of his offences related to Elizabeth Barrett was never ending. He had asked to be called at four in the morning but not risen till eight, he had arrived for a dinner party on Wednesday though invited for Tuesday, he had made fun of his fellow-guests' 'county' conversation. He had giggled, bounced on satin sofas, boasted of his wealth and his literary talents, and, as on his previous visit, had pestered the heiresses: he was even said to have proposed to one. This allegation Elizabeth quite refused to believe until Miss Mitford showed her a philandering letter in Horne's own hand.

Hurt and bewildered as much as before, but with sufficient detachment now – with Browning the emotional focus of her life – to consider Horne objectively, Elizabeth set about her own appraisal. Trusting Browning's word rather than that of clucking Miss Mitford, she
asked his advice. Happily she was reassured. According to Browning,
Horne had been grossly misrepresented. He had known him for ten
years and found him always remarkably generous to other writers,
free from the curious behaviour ascribed to him, sensitive and well
educated and a fascinating conversationalist, especially on his Mexican
experiences. Elizabeth, eloquent with relief, launched an attack on Miss
Mitford's 'dyspathy'; here was Horne surrounded by county families,
an artist in an alien environment,

> his ringlets and aboriginal use of the water glass classed by them as
> against Moral Law. . . . Writing in albums about the graces, dis-
> coursing meditated impromptus at picnics, playing the guitar in
> fancy dress – all these things that seemed to poor Orion as natural as
> his own stars, I dare say, and just the thing suited to the genus poet,
> and to himself specifically.

The biographer, however, cannot be reassured. Inflated as Miss
Mitford's view might have been, it was not without truth. Too often
in the future other observers would note Horne's social antics, as they
grew more frequent and more pronounced. As his legitimate success
receded he was forced to manufacture his own lionization. He would
cut a figure in society whatever the effort; people might close their
doors to him but he *would* be noticed, he *would* succeed.

Meanwhile at Hillside important plans for Horne were being made.
While he drifted aimlessly through September and October of 1845,
secure in his Highgate retreat, two important, and for him parallel,
events were taking shape in the outer world. In Ireland, the land of
eternal troubles – impoverished, overpopulated, agriculturally inept,
its people beset by evictions and hunger and unreasonable rents – the
approaching potato crop, the staple national diet, showed every sign of
abundance. At the same time in London, Charles Dickens, whom
Horne had praised – not much to Dickens's liking – in *A New Spirit*,
was about to establish his dream of a great Liberal newspaper devoted
to 'Progress and Improvement of Education, Civil and Religious
Liberty and Equal Legislation'. It was a dream of which all those at
Hillside could thoroughly approve: and it was presumably with interest
that they watched through October the fits and starts of Dickens's

organization as one backer failed, another was found, and staff were engaged. By mid-November the dream was almost fact, and the paper had money and a name, *The Daily News*. A few weeks later the Irish potato crop was dug and found to be diseased. The Irish people faced famine.

In the minds of those at Hillside the events may have seemed providentially connected. Dedicated so long and so earnestly to the abolition of the protectionist Corn Laws, they knew that the failure of the potato crop in a country too poor to buy high-priced corn could undermine the Corn Laws. Dickens's new paper, they knew too, was to be devoted to the causes of free trade and abolition of the Corn Laws. Perhaps the new alloy of famine and powerful publicity would forge a weapon fit to slash away the antiquated laws.

Dickens was determined to hand pick his staff and offered high salaries to those whose views and talents he approved. Already he was engaging W. J. Fox as his chief leader writer, and there were vacancies for similar-minded journalists of known competence. As the news came to Hillside, Horne felt his interest quicken. Though Hillside had not been able to restore him as Craven Hill once had done, he undoubtedly felt better. His aimlessness was now irksome, he was tired of drifting. Yet to acquire mastery through poetry, he realized, was a vain hope: *Ballad Romances* had too clearly shown that as a poet he was finished in the public's mind – for the present at least. The alternative was reform; and since that, according to his thinking, was now allowable – and possibly even desirable – for the man of genius, he began to consider it. The climate of reform in which he had lived over the past months at Hillside gave force to his considerations. Moreover he needed money; for he was facing another of those periodic financial crises, caused by the fluctuating dividends of the Cornish copper mines of which he was a director, and in which most of his money was invested. Whether on his own initiative, or at Dickens's or Fox's suggestion, one does not know, but in December 1845 Horne applied for a position on *The Daily News*.

His application was accepted, though it might well not have been considering Horne's reputation, Dickens's dislike of Syncretism, and the bias of Dickens's closest friend, John Forster, with whom Horne had quarrelled bitterly in 1844. W. J. Fox, however, may have pleaded for him; moreover Dickens admired his work on the Royal Commission on factory children. In December 1845 Horne and Dickens finalized their agreement: Horne to be employed as a branch editor at eight guineas a week with all travelling expenses, with the choice of working in India or Ireland. (What might have resulted had the author of *Orion* chosen the exotic climate of India is a tantalizing thought.) He had no difficulty, however, in choosing, nor Dickens in advising, Ireland. Obviously within the next months England's attention would be focused on that unhappy country. There was the recollection too that Shelley, fired with reforming zeal, had once gone to Ireland. But recollections of Shelley may not at that moment have been the most comforting; Horne had rather turned his back on the Shelleyan poet.

The Daily News began in January 1846, amid a tenser political atmosphere than had existed for years, with Parliament in turmoil and the old Corn Laws being overthrown. Horne, too ill to start for Liverpool where he was to catch the boat to Ireland, lay on the sofa at Hillside and read the news. Browning, visiting him, found him somewhat depressed.

It was almost the end of January before Horne was well enough to travel to Dublin, and he arrived in severe weather in a country heavy with hunger and misery. He threw himself into activity, going at once to the offices in Lower Sackville Street which Dickens had arranged for him. There, starting to organize his staff of reporters, he was in luck, for he discovered he could have partial use of those already engaged on the noted Irish paper, the *Freeman's Journal*. It was a saving of which he was doubly proud since Dickens had given him free rein with expenses, placing a cheque book (as Horne would later comment) 'in my uncontrolled hands'. He lost no time, either, in seeking out those influential in Irish nationalism, visiting the members of the radical nationalist Young Ireland Movement. Among the members of Young Ireland was one whom Horne would meet again in vastly different circumstances on the other side of the world – Charles Gavan Duffy.

His main concern, however, was to inspect the country and assess the misery. And as in Wolverhampton he was happily busy: the resourceful investigator, alert, disinterested, a change easily effected since that side of himself was seldom far below the surface. In February 1846 he embarked on a demanding itinerary that took him across to Limerick and up the west coast of County Clare to Galway and into Connemara. Inspecting the little holdings – a hut housing family and pig, a tiny garden planted with potatoes – and interviewing parish priests and local officials, he followed the routine of Wolverhampton, except that here was far more danger to his person. Though it was said to be safe to travel alone, all strangers were treated with caution – the curious stranger with hostile suspicion and the avowed *Times* correspondent or Government Commissioner with outright hatred. In a land so rife with violence, one had to take care. From Limerick he travelled down the Shannon to Kilrush, a little port on its wide estuary, where he heard in the Petty Sessions such lies and such evidence of violence that he quailed. Amongst the prisoners was an unrepentant murderer who had brutally killed his wife for no real motive in front of their small children. Violence, he concluded, was part of Ireland's national character. Such a supposition he carried with him on the rest of his travels.

Late February saw him in Kilrush about to travel up the coast of Clare. From the Shannon's mouth to Galway Bay stretched 100 miles of wild and beautiful coastline, a sea wall beaten by the fierce Atlantic and broken only by small sandy bays at the rivers' mouths, and the ruins of abbeys. It was awe-inspiring, overwhelming scenery; his traveller's intelligence was receptive and aroused. Yet he was also unnerved. His health perhaps was not as restored as he had thought; he had also possibly received upsetting news that his mother was ill. The loneliness of the journey was oppressive; the suspicion of the people was disturbing, and their sufferings distressing. He was forced, moreover, to travel in an open jaunting car with a hired driver, since no public conveyance existed, and he arrived most nights at his destination, exhausted, frozen, and weak for want of food. It was incredibly cold, and he long remembered how the 'hoarfrost lay upon the fields and bogs, and the wind blew with cutting force athwart the desolate broken road'.

One incident showed too clearly how strained his nerves were becoming. When he was leaving Dunbeg, a small town where the sea cut across the rocky coast with terrible might, he was warned by the parish priest that no inn existed in the next town. Accordingly the priest provided Horne with a letter to a friendly family; but on arrival Horne discovered the family could not take him; instead, after enquiries, he was sent to another house on the outskirts of town, in appearance decidedly sinister. From there the story, told later by Horne in one of his best narratives, assumed the proportions of a nightmare. He was overtired and fanciful; he also knew the dangers for the lonely traveller, especially if, as he feared, that traveller was taken for a Government agent. The reluctant landlord showed him to a room, dirty and disordered and dominated by a huge bed with crumpled filthy covers. It was like a scene from a Gothic romance and, he admitted later, he would have been quite unsurprised to find a corpse. Pulling himself together with effort he studied his hosts to find them equally sinister: the husband silent and sullen, the wife downtrodden and stupid, the hulking sons positively intimidating. Their whisperings in corners and strange comings and goings suggested a plot to him, whether about himself or not he did not know. Foolishly he called for ink and paper, realizing too late that this would confirm their suspicions of him as a Government agent. He tried geniality, he tried bluster; nothing altered their stolid hostility.

At last they brought him food that tasted foul: drugged, he decided, or possibly poisoned. He did not eat it. The whisky tasted the same and had a suspicious murky sediment. Examining his room he discovered it was eery with numerous doors and a trap-door – just the place for a murder. Then, consumed with inner panic he decided to run – to run anywhere, until reason told him that possible murder was preferable to certain death from exposure in a freezing field. So remembering his training in America, he began to prepare. They were preparations so elaborate and desperate that he could never recall them afterwards without feeling both proud and foolish. He made improvised weapons from stones, sharpened his meat knife, put jugs for warning against the shutters, barricaded the doors with furniture, and sat down to wait, conscious of curious noises in the house about him and a terrible isolation and despair within him. To die like this, not even for one's own convictions! At daylight he awoke from an exhausted sleep, 'delighted and surprised' to find himself alive on a dull rainy morning. Had his fears been justified? He never knew; he supposed not. Possibly the house was a rendezvous for a secret society, hence the whisperings and secrecy, the reluctance to admit him, and the curious noises; the rest was merely the result of overstrained nerves and imagination.

His mood was unsettled and cautious as he travelled on to Galway, with its winding medieval streets – 'like a Spanish seaport' – and its 'magnificent specimens' of men with Spanish-looking cloaks and hoods over their heads. From there his journey entered its final and, scenically, its wildest stages round Galway Bay and into the rugged mountains and inlets of Connemara. Despite its beauty to which he was, as ever, receptive, he was not sorry his travels were almost over.

By April of 1846 he was back in Dublin and feeling better. The reports he sent every few days to *The Daily News* gave him frequent contact with its leader-writer W. J. Fox and brought back happy memories of old *Repository* days. Fox's criticism of Irish policy made him pleased and proud; quite worthy, he told Fox, 'of the fine old days of the *Repository*. I sh'd not have thought so much could be mentioned in newspapers. But thank God for it. . . .' The position in Ireland, too, was improving. The potato crop due for harvesting in July was promising. Through May, June and the first weeks of July the weather smiled and the potatoes flourished. Then the rot struck. Horne saw it and never forgot it. One night the sun went down on green fields, the next sunrise the 'foul specks' of disease were on the plants, and by the following sunset the little fields and gardens were 'smeared with black despair'. A week later he saw all over Ireland the masses of putrefying vegetation; the crop no more than green stalks, black rotting leaves and below the earth the shrivelled tubers. From the plots came a smell of sickening decay, so characteristic that one soon identified it at once. By the edges of the plots sat their owners, wringing their hands and weeping. Wherever he went dreadful little faces looked out at him and starving infants-in-arms whimpered quietly. He was not asked for money; there was no begging but only quiet mistrust and staring faces – the more distressing for their silence – and inarticulate little murmurs like the lowing of cattle from the delirious and dying.

Horne, who had seen the less favourable side of the Irish character – the dishonesty and violence – saw now Ireland's fortitude and unselfishness. He saw them prepared to share, prepared to endure. As the cold weather came, cholera broke out. In the hovels living skeletons burned with fever and died, or were evicted by their landlords and wandered the roads to their graves. In some remote villages every soul died. A smell of death filled the air.

As Horne left Ireland in autumn, he did not see the horror at its height. What he did see left impressions that were never healed. So harrowing was the suffering in magnitude and intensity that one was rendered almost numb; one dared not feel, after a time, for it was too destructive. Instead he was filled with an anger, frustration and despair; despair for all Ireland and even more for the forces that had allowed its misery. His investigations had convinced him that the famine might have been averted. In his reports he searched with difficulty for detachment; within himself he pretended no detachment at all, for he could never look on tyranny and suffering unaffected, and here stood both on the most terrible scale. Later he would claim that, for his 'travels in all weathers, and descriptions of the shocking state of sufferings, not forgetting the fortitude and kindliness of the poor starving people, I received many thanks from headquarters and from public and private persons of eminence'.

One small poem probably expressed his feelings more aptly than all his news reports. Inspired by a true incident which he heard of in Galway, trivial in itself but symbolic of the people's resigned fortitude, it told how a blind man and three starving women carried the body of an Irishwoman to its grave three miles away:

> *Bare-foot ye go,*
> *Through the frost, through the snow;*
> *Unsteady and slow,*
> *Your hearts made with woe; . . .*

> *Now spake out her sister –*
> *'Can we be quite sure*
> *Of the mercy of Heaven,*
> *Or that death is Life's cure?*
> *A cure for the misery, famine, and pains,*
> *Which our cold rulers view as the end of their gains?'*

> *Heavily plod*
> *Highroad and sod,*
> *With the cold corpse clod,*
> *Whose soul is with God!*

Ireland did not provide the only despair he would feel that summer and autumn. From England came news, reviving with sudden keenness the old despairs of the poetic life and underlining his new attitudes to them. On midsummer's day, pursued by neglect, poverty and mental disorder, the noted painter Benjamin Haydon, who had been friend to Hunt and Hazlitt, cut his throat. His death, so tragic and immediate, shocked artistic and literary circles alike. Horne, though he had not known Haydon personally, was shocked: just as he must have been shocked in the previous years at news that Laman Blanchard, the friend of whom he had such affectionate memories from *True Sun* days, had committed suicide. Both men had chosen death deliberately by their own hands rather than suffer longer the trials and despair of creative life. Moved by poetic feeling stronger than any he had known for years, he produced lines to Haydon's memory that reflected this compelling inspiration. Who, after all, was better equipped to describe the lessons of the poetic life: when to obey and when to deny that ever-demanding, over-exacting Muse who forgot that man was man and so destroyed him. The new tone now audible in his poetry demanded equal rights for man and poet:

Mourne fatal Voice, whom ancients call the Muse!
Thou teachest to be strong and virtuous;
In labour, patient; clear-eyed as a star,
Self-truthful; vigilant within; and full
Of faith to be, and do, and send it forth; –
But teachest no man how to know himself,
His over measures or his fallings short,
Nor how to know when he should step aside
Into the quiet shade to wait his hour
And foil the common dragon of the earth . . .

Therefore, O voice, inscrutably divine,
Uplifting sunward, casting in the dust,
Forgetting man as man, and mindful only
Of the man – angel even while on earth –
Mourn now with all thine ancient tenderness,
Mingled with tears that fall in heavy drops,
For one who lost himself, remembering thee!

Five years before it would have been unthinkable for him to write thus. Even in *Orion* he could not have written with such conviction. In these last three years he had learned a new respect for the precious joys and qualities of humanity. Like the rest of the world, his genius not-withstanding, he had come to believe that he too had a right to normal human happiness and normal human weakness.

Chapter 15

Marriage

Horne's Irish career ceased suddenly in the autumn of 1846. His return to London could have been prompted by changes in the policy of the *Daily News*: the paper had undergone many troubles, Dickens had left after only a few weeks, and John Forster, who took his place, gave way to Charles Wentworth Dilke, the editor of *The Athenaeum*. Most likely, however, he returned because of his mother. Later he would admit that he had been shadowed in Ireland by a private source of grief; almost certainly he had heard that his mother was gravely ill.

Temperamentally and through circumstances, he was so close to his mother; as an unmarried son he had been more concerned with her than either of his brothers. He could watch no one's pain with composure, least of all his mother's. Possibly to take his mind from it, he absorbed himself in practical interests. Probably it was now that he gave a series of lectures at the Mechanics' Institutes at Liverpool and Manchester on the undeveloped character of Shakespeare's plays. The engagement had been made through W. J. Fox's friend, W. B. Hodgson, a director of the Liverpool Institute, and Horne was grateful for his sympathetic support after the Manchester performance ended in jeers and laughter. Before Horne spoke in Liverpool Hodgson wisely coached him in oratory; and to the accompaniment of a grand organ Horne mounted the platform with confidence, and addressed over 1,000 with no worse repercussion than a facetious, anonymous note that came next day.

Consolation, too, was to be found at Hillside and at the home of Mary's friends, the Howitts, whose friendship became of increasing importance to him. Accepted by them as a family friend, invited to their children's parties along with other friends of long-standing like Fox and Southwood Smith to 'give *dignity*', he felt one of the inner circle. To be one of the inner circle was no inconsiderable honour. At their large home 'The Elms' at Clapham, the Howitts ran something of a salon for radical literati, and in the evening one might find such stimulating company as Smith, Talfourd, Jerrold, Fox, Leigh Hunt, W. J. Linton and Charles Dickens. Horne was associated with these writers in practical enterprises – notably, the Whittington Club, an attempt to provide the amenities of a gentleman's club for the working classes, and also with the People's International League, begun in April 1847 to 'furnish a rallying point for democracy and nationalism throughout Europe'. Supported in particular by fiery W. J. Linton, the friend of the Italian liberator Joseph Mazzini, its chief concern was Italian freedom, and it found avid support from the radical writers whose thoughts, now the Corn Laws were gone, were increasingly on European politics.

Like Craven Hill, the 'Elms' circle had a journalistic mouthpiece, *The People's Journal of Popular Progress*, of which Howitt had become part-owner in April 1846. Dreaming of his own magazine devoted to education and reform for the working classes, Howitt had gone on to start his own journal, *Howitt's Journal of Literature and Popular Progress*, with the aim of advancing the morals, learning and status of the working man. Horne may have lent money; certainly he gave time and creative effort. Much of his work was to appear in *Howitt's Journal* in the following two years.

His heightening interest in reform was one sign of the slight waning of his intimacy with Elizabeth Barrett; she had preferred the poet to the reformer and had thought Horne was prostituting his talent in joining *The Daily News*. Now, she gave a more dramatic sign of her preference for the poet to the reformer, for it was in September 1846 that literary London had learnt with amazement of her secret marriage and elopement to Italy with Robert Browning. Perhaps Horne had not been quite so amazed. He had been aware of a strangeness in her letters for some time. To his last letter, written from Dublin, proposing once more to come to visit her on his return, he had received no answer. In fact, she confided to Robert Browning, the thought of having at last to face Horne in the flesh, and in such circumstances, filled her with annoyance and dismay. Nor had Browning's facetious remark that she had better look her best, since Horne was likely to be the last person from the outside world to see her before their marriage, comforted her. She had decided it best to ignore the letter.

Now, as Horne heard the news, his recollections of their past made it imperative to write. Yet to Elizabeth herself he could not bring himself to write a word. He wrote instead to Browning: what Browning himself would later describe as a 'good, kind, loyal letter'. Elizabeth, reading it in Pisa, knowing him so closely, and with recollections as keen as his, sensed his hurt. Her letter in reply was as gentle and tender as any she had ever written. It was a letter of apology and ex-planation; her past silence, uneasiness, rudeness in not seeing to him had all been so reprehensible – she begged his forgiveness and under-standing. He deserved so much better. She had thought at one time to confide in him, and indeed she now wished she had, but a quick change in plans had precipitated the elopement prematurely. If he should wonder at her repaying Browning's love for her by the 'questionable gift and possible burthen' of her broken health and spirits, she could only point to her husband's generosity. In fact she was now 'very well and very happy', and went on pilgrimages to the Lanfranchi palace in the footsteps of Byron, Shelley, and Leigh Hunt, while the statue of Cosmo de Medici – Horne's own Cosmo – looked down from the great piazza to remind her of Horne himself. 'Think of me,' she con-cluded, 'dear Mr Horne, as always, most truly and gratefully your friend, Elizabeth Barrett Browning.' And Browning too added his reassurances: 'One of these days we shall meet again, never fear, and then you shall see my wife, your old friend, and hear from her what I have often heard from her, and what, perhaps, this note tells you.'

He accepted her offer of friendship on married terms. Perhaps he rather envied her. At forty and in bad health she had had the courage to escape into a new life to be 'very well and very happy'. He wished he might do the same, but he realized such a chance was receding. For so long dedicated to that relentless mistress the Muse, he had put aside hopes of normal happiness. Then too there had been Mary, though perhaps it might be argued that in their mutual devotion to the poetic mission and, of late, to practical reform, they had achieved a truer marriage than most normal ones. But Mary's love was no longer the unifying flame it once had been in his life – more now a matter of routine; nor was the mission any longer the unifying purpose. He was left aimless and exhausted, vaguely searching for a new force to in-vigorate, inflame, inspire.

Those early months of 1847 were curious ones, for on the one side his mother lay dying and on the other he fell violently in love. It was not altogether surprising, for in a sense he was ripe for it. He needed the comfort of love, the escape into it, the counterbalancing of his misery with an equally powerful emotion. It was part, he said, of the balance of life: one's joy came from another's sorrow, and all life was linked with death. He needed, too, its rejuvenation. Love was, as it had been after Mexico, the necessary drug to restore vitality, identity, and purpose. Moreover, he was forty-four; this might be his last chance of passionate love.

He had fallen in love with Catherine Clare St George Foggo, a sheltered girl of half his age, called by her family Kate. She was not, as has so often been asserted in biographical notes on Horne, the daughter of the well-known artist James Foggo, though she could have been related to him. Her father, according to her marriage certificate, was a David Foggo, deceased, and her brothers, Algernon and George, according to Horne's later note were 'commercial gentlemen'. Had she been related to the artist brothers James and George Foggo, lithographers and radicals, she might perhaps have met Horne through W. J. Linton or Margaret Gillies. Her family's reaction to Horne as a suitor, however, suggests a more conventional middle-class background.

Kate presented to him an intoxicating combination of sexual and spiritual attractions. She was, in the eyes even of impartial observers, unusually beautiful. Elizabeth Barrett, seeing her four years later with the sharp gaze of almost a rival, was surprised at her beauty, finding her 'less pretty and more interesting than I expected – looking very young, her black glossy hair hanging down her back in ringlets, with deep earnest eyes and a silent listening manner'. Her mind was not creative but it was cultivated and alert. Her nature was sweet and undemanding; above all she was admiring and innocent and sympathetic. They were ingredients that had never failed to charm him in a woman, and added to such physical attraction the effect was overwhelming.

As usual it was the mental ingredients that attracted him most readily. The qualities with which he was just then endowing his fictitious character Ellen Lloyd in his novel *The Dreamer and the Worker* – begun at the start of 1847 – were obviously those he found so compelling in Kate, her real life counterpart: the devoted 'love of all things poetical', the 'fine sense of Art', the 'imagination harmoniously blending with and enhancing understanding', and the 'fascinating *naïveté*'. But in real life there was also Kate's unusual beauty. At no time in his previous life had sexual passion exerted such control over him. Kate's beauty tormented him; his desire to possess that beauty was torture. As of old the attraction of her innocence produced a strange ambivalence of feeling, which initially made his desire the more powerful. He both loved and hated that innocence, wished for it and wished against it. Under the gaze of those gentle, uncomprehending

The 'seductive shore': an Australian gold town in the 1850s

When Horne commanded the gold escort

Richard Hengist Horne of Blue Mountain Goldfield

'The Farthing Poet', a medallion of Richard Hengist Horne, circa 1860

eyes his erotic fantasies seemed impossible, cruel, shameful, and as of old there were times when he found himself wishing for the sentimental climate of love without the physical disturbance:

I would time now stood still,
And we might thus in rapture gaze,
With no new thought or will!

But even had this wish been wholehearted, it would have been futile. He was quite powerless to halt the disturbance. There were times – many times – when the echoes of that old love for A., marked his love for Kate. (Later the two women would often play interchangeable parts in his mind.)

Yet almost as wild as his love were his apprehensions, chief of which seem to have concerned Mary. He was about to hurt her terribly with perhaps one of the worst hurts he could inflict on her – abandoning her in middle age for a younger woman. If he considered marrying anyone, should it not, morally, be Mary? And yet was it right, he wondered, to remain out of duty with someone for whom not only had one's passion died but with whom one's mental sympathies were now deficient? For, of late, Mary was dedicating to social reform that intense care and sympathy she had once given to him. If likeness and mental sympathy were the essential ingredients of love – as he had always believed – then his future lay with Kate. Mary, he rationalized, had in a sense already renounced him by turning her feelings into reform.

These private thoughts, at once so exhilarating and disturbing, were impossible to confine to his own mind: and with every stroke of his pen he found them taking shape in the novel he was writing, displacing even its theme of the poet's place in society. As he watched, its main characters shaped themselves into himself and Kate and Mary, and from that pattern it is possible to reconstruct Horne's innermost thoughts. His feelings vacillated violently and guiltily between the two women. Was it essential, he asked, for two people who were contemplating a lifelong association to have 'personal sympathy of that intense kind which can absorb the feelings of self, in all its conditions'? Or might a difference in 'views of the means of human progress' effect a better balance in both? Ought a poet to marry someone practical, or someone intensely like himself. The final answer in the novel to these perplexing and personal questions was that the poet was justified in following his passion and marrying a woman of the same poetic feeling.

Archer, the poet-hero, after agonizing through nearly two volumes, finally frees himself from reasonable, practical Mary to whom he is betrothed. He is cautioned to be more confident, positive, and strong-minded; to have 'something of that reckless energy which forces a way through all obstacles and minor considerations'; to assume 'force of character' and 'stronger individuality'. He is helped, furthermore, by undeceiving Mary herself who, seeing his self-struggle and obvious passion for the poetically-souled Ellen, renounces him with tenderness and understanding and retires to the solace of reform. In fiction one could make one's own solution; unfortunately, in real life, as Horne knew, it was not so easy.

Through April and May of 1847 the curious drama of love and guilt and death was played out; Horne struggled with his decision in love, while his mother approached death. By the first week of June, when he made his last visit to his mother's bedside at Greenwich, he had almost certainly decided to marry. His mother's illness appears to have lent urgency to his decision; perhaps he was conscious that his mother, so ill that she was probably barely conscious, could no longer lean on him or demand of him, nor he on her. He determined to marry by the middle of June.

Mary took the decision well; if not with the magnanimity of her fictitious counterpart, at least with good grace and resignation. Horne left Hillside but continued to visit, bringing Kate with him. Kate's family rather than Mary proved to be the stumbling block of which he had to be wary. Her mother and brothers had viewed him with distrust from the start. He belonged to a precarious and disreputable profession; he had radical political views. Even worse his religious views, which he openly disclosed, proclaimed him no better than an atheist, and they themselves were strict and conventional Christians. He had furthermore inadequate means to support a wife in comfort—probably to support her at all. And she herself had no dowry; he must expect not a penny from them. Kate, however, loved him, and over-rode their objections. She was fired with high-souled ardour to play the companion and inspiration of the poet and believed in his religion and his sense of duty as wholeheartedly as Mary.

On June 5, Maria Horne died. Refusing to postpone the marriage, he and Kate went ahead with their plans. On June 17, 1847 – St Alban's day – with Southwood Smith beside him, Horne stood among the columns of St Pancras Church and heard Catherine Foggo proclaimed his wife.

At the start of July Horne brought his bride to a secluded house in

Finchley named Fallow Lodge. Not far from Edmonton, in that area he had so loved since childhood, it had for him the pleasantest associations in which to start a new life and was near enough to Hillside and the Finchley cottage of Caroline Hill to suit their sociability. The Hill children were their frequent visitors; and the coach from London, stopping at the Green Man by Finchley Common, near the end of their own lane, brought London visitors to visit or to stay. In July the newly married pair went to Hillside to meet the distinguished Danish author of children's stories, Hans Christian Andersen: an afternoon made memorable by the guest of honour's rudeness. The small Hill children had showed preference for another guest, an American children's writer, Henry Clarke Wright, and Andersen had sulked, defying all the efforts of Mary Howitt and Mary Gillies to win him over. In November the Hornes themselves gave a Guy Fawkes bonfire with 'the part of Guy by Mrs Horne – if she will accept' – to which they invited the Hills, the Gillies and young Eliza Fox, whose father had recently been elected to Parliament for Oldham. In December, on one of their occasional excursions to literary society at the house of the publisher George Smith, Horne met quiet 'fragile and vibrating' Charlotte Brontë and, inadvertently, and to his great delight, discovered her to be the author of *Jane Eyre*, which he had admired so greatly. Miss Brontë in turn was able to thank him in person for the 'very real, very sweet' poetry of *Orion*.

Their secluded life gave ample time for work, and Horne threw himself into it with renewed energy. The reformer dominated his work. In August he prepared with care three lectures on the Irish question, anxious to be both 'just – and also kind to poor Ireland'. He gave the lectures at the Aldersgate Literary and Scientific Institute and again at Brighton and Greenwich, and at his request some of his friends attended; Dickens, who had taken time off from the writing of *Dombey and Son* – 'relentless savage that he is!' – had declared himself greatly entertained by the lectures, though his friend Daniel Maclise had found the draughty hall none to his liking and had felt as though 'a Baker were rasping at his back'. At Aldersgate a few months later Horne lectured on Italy for the People's International League; a lecture written, he later claimed, with the help of Joseph Mazzini, and aimed at enlightening the 'British people as to the political conditions and relations of foreign countries', and to 'disseminate the principles of national freedom and progress'. The seeds of interest in European politics, sown in Germany, had taken firm root.

In those first months of marriage he was extremely happy. Not for years had he had such faith in himself, nor such tranquillity. Even the persistent sense of doom that seemed to have hung over him most of his life seemed to have lifted for the moment. And such faith, as he admitted in that curious autobiographical and 'philosophical' novel, *The Dreamer and the Worker*, he undoubtedly owed to the renewing power of love. At last he felt confident of having come to terms with that disturbing trio – his time, the poetic mission and himself.

Part of his confidence also sprang from the fact that he was ceasing to fight the pressures of his age. The Anti-Romantics were gaining strength and public favour, and for them the decade was a march to victory. Horne, disillusioned, subject continually to the active man in his nature, was an open target for their pressures. Though possibly as yet unconscious of it, he was succumbing to anti-Romanticism: yielding to realism, rationality, and the social and aesthetic forces that denied the cult of divinely inspired genius.

His new attitude was clearly shown in *The Dreamer and the Worker*. It had *Orion's* theme of the 'twofold', divided nature of genius; like *Orion* it advocated for all, including genius, a life balanced between thought and action. Unlike *Orion*, it discussed explicitly the problems and applications of genius in mid-century society. And unlike *Orion* it almost discarded the doctrines of poetic isolation and martyrdom. Mid-century readers needed a practical explanation of the poet, a practical purpose for the poetic function. And Horne was bowing to that need. His poet-hero, Archer, is consigned not to a fate of suffering but to sensible self-management and idyllic frugality in the wilds of Wales, not to nourishment and protection of his poetic integrity but to elevating his fellow man. The poet need not necessarily write great works of art. His enlightening, inspiring, informing genius is all that matters. Horne had wandered far from the views of literary prostitution in his *Essay on Tragic Influence* in 1840. He had wandered equally far from that view – so central to his thinking – of the poet as divine outcast.

Through Kate he had been reborn: as a writer, recharged; as an ordinary individual, afforded the normal pleasures of the rest of the world of a loving wife and home. And yet as his marriage entered its second year the old doom began once more to descend, and it began to seem again as though, inevitably, no happiness could last for him. The troubles, when they began to come, were deepened by the contrast with the hope that had gone before them. When he considered his state of mind twelve months before and compared it to this. . . . It did not bear thinking of! His poverty was the immediate problem.

As he sat at Fallow Lodge going over his accounts he was forced to admit that never in his life had he been so poor; and what was worse he was subjecting so trusting and tender a creature as Kate to this poverty.

At the start of 1847 the Mines Royal had cancelled their dividend; and Horne, since he had left *The Daily News*, had no adequate means of support. In such necessity he had approached his friends including Douglas Jerrold, renowned for his generosity as well as his wit, in the hope of placing some of his poems and articles. Jerrold, whose *Shilling Magazine* was devoted as much as *Howitt's* to social questions and working-class improvement, listened sympathetically to Horne's predicament and, over a chop, worked out with him a solution. The result was *The Dreamer and the Worker* which appeared throughout 1847 as a monthly serial in *The Shilling Magazine*, though it was not, as poor Jerrold confessed privately to Henry Chorley, a serial of the circulation-raising kind. But early in 1848 the twelve months' 'peace of mind' that Douglas Jerrold had effected – and on the strength of which Horne had married – expired. Once more the expected dividend from the copper mines failed to come. This time Jerrold did not, or could not, help. In March Horne went to him with manuscripts for publication and received a half-hearted reception. In October, Horne swallowed his pride and wrote the uneasiest of letters, begging Jerrold not to 'misinterpret', and assuring him that the letter came from 'one who admires your genius, applauds your public services and values your friendship'. Jerrold, however, apparently not mollified by the applause, turned down Horne's offer to write a play to which Jerrold should give his name and the 'master touches'. Nor was this reaction surprising, since Jerrold was a successful writer of acted comedies while Horne had not written one comedy fit for publication, let alone acting.

He and Kate by now were making every economy; the tradesmen's carts, Horne reported to Leigh Hunt, went past their door instead of calling, and a dunning clerk was often to be seen, a pen behind the ear, skulking at the garden gate. Dunning tradesmen were, of course, no novelty to the Hunts, and Hunt reciprocated with first-hand sympathy: not that this deterred that extraordinary family from announcing their intention of coming with a 'hamper' to 'carry away' Horne's orchard. Welcome sympathy, too, came from the Brownings in Florence – to whom Horne had written so miserably and lovingly, with a mixture of his own troubles and the latest gossip, that Browning was forced to exclaim: 'Nobody puts into every scrap they write, so much of their own self . . . as you.' Elizabeth added her 'deep sympathy' and comfort to Browning's reassurances about Horne's doleful financial future. 'The day for thinkers and writers,' she wrote, 'and only for those, is breaking fast.' It brought back the past to have Elizabeth's comfort again.

He confided to neither of these friends the other reason for his wretchedness. It concerned Kate. Already, perturbing echoes of the situation with A. (and of that chaste, frigid woman who had haunted his plays and poems) were beginning to arise in his marriage. In the past he had been confident that had he acted more decisively with A. he could have transformed her coldness to normal sexual love. Now, with Kate, in many ways so like her, he found it was not so easy. At first he had been disappointed but not alarmed. Sexual coldness was only to be expected perhaps from one whose upbringing had been so sheltered: such troubles in early married life he knew to be common. With time, with patience, they were overcome. If only she would not look so 'resigned'; that resignation – the closed eyes, the resigned and vulnerable face – brought out all his conscious and unconscious misgivings. (Such thoughts he confided with total lack of reticence in a bad but impassioned poem, *The Closed Door.*) Yet as time went on he began to wonder. He became disturbed about her health. She was 'subject to violent spasms at special periods, which left her prostrate for some hours'. Could it be, he began to wonder, that she had some 'physical indisposition to marriage'? Was she perhaps 'of cold and indifferent temperament, physically', a condition which neither time nor patience could correct? As the months passed and her attitude was unchanged his hopes began to die. Daily the familiar despondency crept back, the magnificent elation faded. In vain he assured Mary Howitt in June, in lines he had written for the dying *Howitt's Journal*:

> *We cannot countermand*
> *Our fate and suffering; but no mortal shot*
> *Reaches the heart within itself secure.*

Yet mentally he and Kate were still in such sympathy. No one could have been more affectionate, sweet-tempered, gentle or tender. He was touched by her eagerness to share his intellectual tastes, help with his work, copy neatly his manuscripts, take over his researches. Already she had begun research for him of a biography of the actor David Garrick. At night her beautiful dark head bent over the pages in the lamplight, or her beautiful, alert, young face glowed with mental ardour as he read aloud to her by the fire; sometimes they would squabble affectionately when both wanted to read the same book, she demanding 'first to finish this one page' before relinquishing it to him. Her beauty was admired on all sides. Even her poverty she bore bravely, though she had not been used to it. She was 'resigned', and he supposed he must be too. Really it was ironic; he who valued the mental qualities above the physical, and valued innocence in a woman probably above them all, was now in a position where he had these in abundance; and he was not remotely happy. Again came the old conclusion: he was not meant to be happy.

Chapter 16

'For I am Free'

His poetic reputation was, it seemed, on the way to restoration. That brief burst of creative regeneration in 1847–8 produced another composition, *Judas Iscariot*, his first complete play since *Gregory VII* which he had bitterly declared in 1840 would be his last. Optimism turned him once more to dramatic form to portray Judas as a man fired by ambition, forcing Christ to reveal His identity and powers, never dreaming He would submit to crucifixion. Horne owed this historical interpretation, which had obviously attracted his radical Unitarian mind as well as his dramatist's instinct, to the progressive Archbishop Whately of Dublin whom he had met during his Irish assignment. He owed his psychological interpretation to that part of his nature that found fascination in the character of the ruthless genius and the unconscious murderer. For Judas he portrayed as both: a genius irked by his destiny and determined to change it, and the unintentional cause of his Master's death. Though he claimed otherwise in the preface, Horne's portrayal was undoubtedly sympathetic; for he in a sense saw himself as Judas, just as, in a sense, he had been part of his other similar anti-heroes, Gregory VII and Garcia.

He called it a miracle play, rather an attempt to garnish so controversial a subject than a fair description of so sophisticated a piece of work. To his astonishment it was accepted for publication. By mid-1848 it was reviewed, and to his equal astonishment all agreed that though the subject was risky, the execution was well worthy of the author of *Orion*. But the play scarcely sold at all, and not even the later news from the court of the King of Bavaria that it had actually been performed – the first of Horne's only two plays ever to be performed – could make up for its neglect in the bookshops. What he needed more than praise was money.

Meanwhile he had two other irons in the fire. A conversation with Leigh Hunt had given him the idea of revising some of his old unfinished comedies in an attempt to have them performed. His main hope was Samuel Phelps, formerly one of Macready's chief actors, who, after the abolition of the patent monopoly had taken over co-management of the disreputable Sadler's Wells Theatre, and turned it from a 'bear garden' of 'foul language, oaths, shrieks, yells, blasphemy and obscenity' into a theatre as orderly 'as a lecture room' and filled with worthy working-class families devoted to Shakespeare. The project appealed to both Horne the dramatist and Horne the reformer.

Phelps refused the comedies, but suggested Horne should reconstruct for him, in the light of modern taste and acting techniques, some of the plays of Shakespeare's contemporaries – Webster, Beaumont and Fletcher and Ford. When he promised to pay a modest sum, Horne, in a mood to take anything, agreed. In February 1849 he wrote excitedly to Hunt that though he had 'never yet been father to an acted play' he was about to be 'god-father' to Beaumont and Fletcher's *Honest Man's Fortune*. The opening night at Sadler's Wells was 'horrid' weather, but the audience was larger for the second night and he calculated about 1,000 were in the pit alone. Critics remarked on the skill of his reconstructions: and the modest income was certainly welcome. 'So,' he told Hunt, 'I suppose I am launched. But as for the voyage. . . .'

But at least he was launched and on further consideration he had even more hopes. His reputation was, he realized, in a 'curiously balanced position'. As a poet his reputation was decaying slowly into 'utter neglect'. But in practical-literary-popular affairs he now had the greatest expectation of making a name. He foresaw a 'sudden rise to a popular position'. He told Hunt confidently that 'very little more from one or two high quarters would launch me on a far more *open* and *sunny* sea. Many circumstances – on many sides – show me this.' It was with this optimism that he prepared a curious little book called *The Poor Artist of Seven Eyesights and One Object*. Based on a well-founded interpretation of mid-century reading habits, particularly its thirst for palatable and simple scientific facts, his book also reflected both his old despair of the artistic life and his new interest in natural history. Over the past years at the home of Southwood Smith, Horne had heard enough discussion of the sciences to whet the practical side of his always inquisitive imagination; his reading and those conversations now paid dividends. His new book, which he dedicated to the celebrated biologist Professor Richard Owen ('That *one* head,' Smith had once remarked to Horne, 'contains all that is known of physiology up to the present time'), was a charming and naïve mixture of poetic imagination and scientific fact – most of the latter from Owen's own books. These diverse elements Horne wove together into a fable of a poor artist, taught by insects and animals that each species – and by analogy each human personality – sees the same object in a different way. Thus most artistic criticism is subjective; and the artist is condemned to abuse, neglect, and poverty by a foolishly subjective public taste. Adding a slender love story for interest, Horne looked around for a high place from which to launch it. He hit – with what success he could only have dreamed – on Charles Dickens.

Dickens was now thirty-seven, a prematurely ageing, weather-beaten man with the look of a 'seafarer', whose eyes showed the strain under which he lived during the ten years in which he had rocketed to eminence as a popular novelist and public figure. Possessed of the sharpest practical will as well as incomparable imagination, only part of his enormous vigour went into his writings: the rest was directed restlessly to numerous projects for popular education, general reform, and in particular the reform of the status and conditions of the professional author. The bitter experiences of his own poverty-stricken early life, and his struggle to improve his own station, gave fervour to his efforts. Moreover, as the list of god-parents to his numerous children bore evidence, there was scarcely a notable literary figure who was not his friend. That group Horne had so often (Dickens less often) dined with during those happy times at Gray's Inn was now more like a Dickens set, while dinner guests at his lavish home at Devonshire Terrace were virtually a catalogue of literary London: Carlyle, Talfourd, Proctor, Macready, Southwood Smith, Bell, Tennyson, Lewes, Bulwer Lytton, Forster, Jerrold, Landor, the artists Edwin Landseer, Clarkson Stanfield, John Leech, and Daniel Maclise.

Horne and Dickens had a formidable bond in their mutual dedication to raising the conditions and status of the author: there was also their connection on *The Daily News* which had convinced Dickens of Horne's journalistic abilities and had developed acquaintance into friendship. Since then there had been infrequent but friendly exchanges of visits and letters – an invitation of Mrs Dickens to Kate hoping for closer acquaintance – and every indication of cordiality. With such assurances of goodwill and influence, it was not surprising that Horne approached Dickens with his manuscript. Nor was he disappointed; for Dickens, charitably ignoring the slights on that popular taste which, after all, had made his own fame, declared himself 'delighted' with

Horne's fable. Understanding Horne's literary and financial predicament he proposed approaching his old publisher Chapman on Horne's behalf. After '*first carefully erasing your name and initials wherever they appeared*', Dickens would show it to Chapman as a work 'very good, very new' of an author unknown in literature. He would ask for £50 for this book by his unnamed friend.

Chapman raised objections, Dickens made suggestions, and a much-improved story was finally published anonymously by John Van Voorst, who had already published a popular science series on the natural history of England. Owen, with whom Horne dined in November, generously called it 'a pretty little Christmas book' and recommended it for 'a pleasant evening's light reading', a sentiment which reviewers endorsed. Horne had finally hit the mid-century recipe: 'Imagination and humour,' wrote one critic admiringly, 'go hand in hand with reason.'

Horne had found the popular recipe at the right moment; for once, fate seemed with and not against him. He had sent his manuscript to Dickens in July 1849; the following September Dickens's recurring dream of his own periodical for family reading came to haunt him, and by the end of the year he was organizing a weekly miscellany to be called *Household Words*, educational, reforming, and most of all interesting. A serious 'instrument of social purpose', *Household Words* was to portray the 'social wonders, good and evil,' of the 'stirring world around us'. Dickens intended to call upon his wide circle of literary acquaintances for casual contributions, but the regular staff was to be small. John Forster, his closest friend and part owner of the enterprise, was to be a regular writer; the former secretary on *The Daily News*, William Henry Wills, a thin flail of a man, zealously if uninspiredly devoted to his work and to Dickens, was to be associate editor; and for the other post of sub-editor Dickens was anxious to find the right person. The *Poor Artist* had shown that Horne was indeed capable. Dickens knew, moreover, Horne's urgent need for work. In December 1849 he offered him the job at five guineas a week, and Horne had no difficulty in accepting. At last the long stretch of poverty seemed over.

As though to signify his fresh start Horne moved with Kate to a new house, Beaumont Cottage at Chalk Farm – still sufficiently near to Hillside – leaving behind the unhappy memories and debts of Fallow Lodge. Once again he had been given a chance of making his 'identity felt in the literary world' and making a 'personal impression upon contemporaries', goals he had sought unsuccessfully with *A New Spirit* and advised for the literary man in *The Dreamer and the Worker*. After all, as he had reassured himself systematically over the years, there was no reason why he should not succeed. Was he not a 'devout reader, an earnest thinker, a careful student', the possessor of both philosophical, poetical and practical mind, a writer of clear and pungent prose? And was not Dickens, in every sense, one of these 'truly powerful spirits' he had advised his literary man in *The Dreamer and the Worker* to seek out, copy, and cultivate? If he had ever had any chance to succeed it was now.

In March he took up journalistic duties at the dingy three-storeyed brick offices in Wellington Street, where he found that the discipline Dickens imposed was as useful as the salary he paid. Dickens was a ceaseless worker and exacting supervisor of even the smallest details of his magazine. Articles must rest on first-hand knowledge, and be concise, relevant, of reforming and instructive purpose and, above all, entertaining. Plenty of sugar must coat the pill: 'Brighten it, brighten it, brighten it!' For a flabby writer like Horne no discipline could have been better. He wrote for an audience that was simple and wide – 100,000 copies were sold of the first number – and his writing was unpretentious; not since *Repository* days had his prose had such life and interest.

Every week he set forth on a new assignment: a trip to the zoo to welcome a new hippopotamus, an inspection of a gunpowder factory, a lighthouse, a dockyard, a country election, a visit to Smithfield slaughteryard to watch the brutal killing of the 'pallid-faced, patient sheep', or a ride in Mr Green's balloon, high above London in 'lustrous, majestic, incomprehensible' ease, with a rousing airborne luncheon of pigeon pie, cold beef, and brandy. It was years since his natural curiosity had been so enlivened, his natural enthusiasms more happily aroused. To popular audiences with little reading experience, and a curiosity burgeoning as never before in English history, he brought realistically and excitedly to their firesides the wonders of English achievements and the scandals and social abuses he and his editor longed to see reformed. Dickens had every reason to be pleased with Horne's work.

Horne also had every reason to be pleased. His hopes, it seemed, for once were to be justified. His spirits rose as his money troubles lightened, and under Dickens's generous patronage he entered for the first time since the disaster of *A New Spirit* into general literary society. In particular he entered into the congenial society of Dickens's own group, a group almost as vigorous as its leader. There were Jerrold and Robert Bell who had remained his friends throughout the *New Spirit* troubles, the artists Daniel Maclise, Clarkson Stanfield, Frank Stone, Augustus Egg, his colleague on *Household Words* William Henry Wills, and there was Dickens's closest friend John Forster. Even with Forster, Horne managed to keep a semblance of cordiality, though it was little more than semblance. Their former friendship had been finished for ever when Horne, in the nerve racking weeks before the appearance of *A New Spirit* in 1844, hoping either to prevent Forster's expected attack or to get in first, had sent him a furious letter of pent-up resentments, citing instances of his 'literary treachery' in previous reviews of Horne's work. Whether, or what, Forster replied is not known, but it was a measure of Dickens's influence that he could keep Forster and Horne from squabbling now that their paths had again crossed.

Dickens liked Horne. They got on well, if not closely or intensely, and Horne could be good company (for which Dickens and his friends were prepared to overlook a multitude of sins). He was purposely eccentric, but then they themselves were fairly uninhibited and far from conventional. His grumbles and pretensions they were prepared to laugh away or treat with good-humoured tolerance; his sincerity and integrity they respected. Besides, they liked someone whose foibles they could ridicule without real malice. They accepted Horne readily and he for his part was delighted and intoxicated to be accepted into one of the most dynamic, if not most intellectual, of literary groups. Instinctively, as at *The True Sun* and Gray's Inn, he adjusted himself to their animal spirits and uproarious practical jokes. But though he was more than content to enjoy his good fortune and bask in the reflected light of the 'powerful spirit' of their leader, whom he had so calculatedly set out to court, there was a certain strain in his relations with Dickens. Even for so hero-worshipping a nature as Horne's it was not entirely possible to feel unmixed admiration for a genius nine years his junior who had climbed to fame through the very public and the very society that had turned Horne down. This uneasiness, of which Dickens, too, seemed somewhat aware, ran through most of their communications.

In the sumptuous dining-room of Dickens's London home in Devonshire Terrace, by Regent's Park, a house bedecked with ornate mirrors and deep carpets which reflected its master's love of luxury in contrast to his childhood poverty, Horne and Kate as frequent diners met literary London. At Dickens's seaside home, set picturesquely amid cornfields and gardens at the charming Kentish village of Broadstairs, the Hornes met the more intimate friends and entered into the family circle with races along the 'rare good sands' of the sparkling bay, games with the children, and jokes and friendly arguments. To be near Dickens was to be drawn into the magnetic field of his energy, overbounding elation, and rebounding moroseness. Driven by inner compulsions stretching back to his unhappy youth when at twelve he saw his father marched off to Marshalsea prison for debt and found himself in a blacking factory – childhood traumas from which he never fully recovered – the compulsions were reinforced for Dickens in middle life by the disappointments of his marriage and the draining demands of his ever-increasing family. Often his only relief was in violent activity, usually with a desperate edge, and particularly so when his feelings involved slow-witted, clumsy Catherine Dickens. Recalling later to George Bernard Shaw the unhappy undertones in that household, Horne remembered how at dinner Mrs Dickens's bracelets would fall off her arms with a splash into her soup, while she, poor woman, the victim of a nervous lack of physical control, watched helplessly. To the guests' discomfort Dickens would thereupon throw himself back in his chair, his eyes streaming with uproarious laughter. Though merely an onlooker, the hysteria did not fail to convey itself to Horne; nor could it have been healthy for one of his own unstable emotions. Nor could the sight of another's disintegrating marriage have been beneficial or comfortable when his own feelings towards Kate still troubled him so persistently. In the circumstances Dickens was perhaps not the best of companions.

It was into violent Dickensian activity that Horne found himself drawn along with other of Dickens's closer friends. Dickens adored amateur theatricals, and in the past he and his friends had put on plays to raise money for Leigh Hunt, the playwright Sheridan Knowles, and the aged author John Poole. In the winter of 1850–1 Dickens had indulged this love of acting and producing plays at Knebworth, the Hertfordshire estate of Lytton Bulwer Lytton (who had adopted Lytton as his surname after his mother's death in 1850) and at Rockingham Castle in Northamptonshire. Dickens's amateurs had been highly successful and out of their fun and acclaim grew a scheme, devised by Lytton and Dickens, of using theatrical performances to finance struggling and impoverished writers on a permanent basis instead of when the theatrical whim moved them. It was a version of the old idea of a life insurance society such as Bulwer Lytton – and Horne, too – had proposed as long before as 1833, at last coming to private fruition. Lytton proposed donating a plot of land on his estate where small colonies of artists and writers would live in free cottages, presided over by a warden. Resident members, all with established names in the arts, would receive a grant of £170 a year, non-resident £200; the rising, struggling writer would have a one-year grant of £100. The sponsor of this rural brotherhood was to be called The Guild of Literature and Art.

They were ideals the author of *The False Medium* could not fail to support with enthusiasm. He supported the means as well as the ideals, for he had testimony – though admittedly not the best – for his own acting talents. Recently, in May 1850, he had performed the part of Shylock at a benefit night under the patronage of the Duke of Cambridge at Sadler's Wells theatre: a disastrous performance since he was afflicted with laryngitis and could scarcely be heard. (The best part of the evening, one observer had reported, was when Horne left the stage.) Even he himself had had to admit he was 'very bad'. Nevertheless he had acted in public, and since he was still eager, and also now a member of the set of closer Dickensian friends, he found himself welcomed into the band of devoted amateur actors.

Their aims were high. Bulwer Lytton had written them a play appropriately dramatizing the trials of a poor writer in the days of George II, entitled *Not so Bad as We Seem* ('but a great deal worse than we ought to be' according to Douglas Jerrold). Dickens then boldly and successfully approached the Duke of Devonshire, known patron of literary arts, for permission to stage it before the Queen at Devonshire House, the Duke's palatial town residence in Piccadilly; and from March 1851, when their rehearsals first began at Covent Garden, Dickens drove himself and his actors mercilessly five hours a night, two nights a week. Not even his wife's increasing nervous troubles which necessitated, on Southwood Smith's advice, her removal to medical treatment at Malvern, or the deaths, within that time, of his father and baby daughter, could stop that relentless drive.

The amateurs' amateurishness drove Dickens to distraction: Forster was 'too loud and violent', Mark Lemon 'too farcical', Horne 'between ourselves (I speak seriously) the very worst actor the world ever saw, and . . . must not on any account be entrusted with more words than he has already'. An 'ingenious theatre' had to be constructed, costumes and wigs prepared, scenery painted by his artist friends. Experts were consulted: Planché gave advice, Joseph Paxton, at the height of his fame as architect for the Great Exhibition, erected the theatre in the library and gallery of Devonshire House, careful to hammer not one nail in either walls or floor of the entire design. Horne later remembered

Dickens during this time to have been 'almost ubiquitous and sleepless'. By May they were rehearsing all day three days a week at Devonshire House itself, admitted by liveried footmen, and treated to free luncheons of 'profuse and elegant cold collation with the choicest wines'. The Duke himself, a modest man in rusty black, loitered among the scenery and exchanged friendly words with the actors, and Horne was to recall with pride arguments over what he himself should smoke in his stage pipe, the Queen being known to detest tobacco. At first Horne had tried herbs and rose leaves, then substituted imitation whorls of smoke from wire and cotton. Finally, to be safest, he was only permitted to toy with the pipe, in case Her Majesty might '*think*' she smelled smoke. Dickens took pains, Horne said not without irritation, 'worthy of the *Comédie Française*'.

The dress rehearsal was attended by friends of the Duke and the actors, Kate Horne among them, all carefully screened for fear that Lytton's estranged wife might slip in and fulfil her threat to create a disturbance. All loyally acclaimed the actors' success, and the success was endorsed on the following night, the Queen's Night, when to the strains of the Duke's private band the curtain rose and fell to tumultuous applause. The Queen sent correct royal approval backstage – 'They act very well indeed' – though Horne doubted whether it rightly applied to all performers. Dickens, he considered, was badly cast, resembling an East Indiaman rather than a fashionable dandy. Robert Bell, in his estimation, however, was 'perfection' as an Irish squire in a 'ragged-red wig', and Augustus Egg, 'naturally short and attenuated', was superb as the wretched author, 'intellectual and refined amidst his seedy clothing; resentful of his hard lot, yet saddened by disappointment and semi-starvation, his thoughts appearing to oscillate between independence of character, his political hiring and his hungry family'. Of his own performance as the irascible Colonel Flint – despite Dickens's foreboding – Horne appeared to have no doubts at all, nor did ne doubt the Queen's approval.

Afterwards a magnificent supper was arranged, where Victoria was to sit in a chair topped by a Gothic arch banked with roses, jasmine, honeysuckle and magnolias, twined with creepers and orchids, and surmounted by a night-flowering, heavily perfumed ceres, dotted with opal dewdrops. Creeping in beforehand to inspect the supper room, Horne still in his actor's costume was surprised by Her Majesty's sudden appearance, and took refuge amonst the lines of bowing footmen. But undoubtedly she recognized him, and showed her amusement and her approval of his performance, in his mind at any rate, by

Richard Hengist Horne, 'the last romantic'

Edmund Gosse as Horne knew him, a portrait by Sargent

Richard Hengist Horne in old age.   He was sometimes likened to a Polish rabbi

her charming smiles. At that moment those republican sentiments, suggested so openly in *Repository* days, were hasily forgotten.

The Duke, 'all smiles', insisted they perform again at Devonshire House that month, for which occasion Dickens and Mark Lemon composed a farce, *Mr Nightingale's Diary*. In this Dickens took no less than six parts in rapid succession, this time, according to Horne, with the greatest truth and art. In the middle of June they gave the first of their public London appearances at Hanover Square Rooms, and two others there in July and August. From London, despite remonstrances from Jerrold and Forster, Dickens took his strolling players on the first of several tours of the provinces, beginning with Bath and Bristol. Horne remembered nostalgically and minutely the daily programme for those provincial performances. Dickens always engaged the whole of the largest hotel. They dined together at two, then rested; after the performance there was supper, and after supper they played those boisterous jokes and games that had characterized this group, as Horne had noted long before on *The True Sun* and at Gray's Inn: usually it was leapfrog around the supper table, and the game was often made uproarious by portly Mark Lemon. So most of the evenings ended in 'unreserved hilarity'. It was a sad reflection, Horne remarked afterwards, that all their labours should have come to so little. For the fate predicted for the Guild by its opponents came unhappily to pass. Though they raised their goal of £500, the project ended with the unpleasant slur of patronage, providing annual pensions for a few mediocrities and widows of journalists, plus 'three doleful cottages' in a field, 'poor shadows and frail images of the fine idea of a College retreat for Literature and Art – sad yet suitable emblem of the mortal remains of nearly all the original projectors'.

In a way it was as well that Horne was so busy, even if the business was slightly hysterical and unsettling. In it he could find emotional escape, like Dickens, from troubles that were increasing with Kate. While naturally relieved to be over their depressing poverty, Kate still remained cold towards him. And yet the world considered him fortunate with a wife of such sympathy and beauty, a fact that had come home to him in London a few months before when, for the first time, and with a piercing resurgence of memories, he and his beloved Elizabeth Barrett set eyes on one another. Watching her expressive face he had seen her admiration for Kate, and how she 'rejoiced' to see him so 'blessed'. Similarly, staying at Broadstairs in August with Dickens, he had seen his admiration, too. It was an admiration that was obvious and one that also contained more devious elements than either of the

Hornes, or possibly Dickens himself, could have known. Since the sudden and tragic death in 1837 of his adored young sister-in-law, Mary Hogarth, Dickens had been haunted, in fact and in fiction, by an idealized vision of a girl, 'young, beautiful and good', with 'all the attractions of youth and beauty'. One such woman, it would seem, was Kate Horne. Nor could Dickens help but note the disparity between Kate and her husband. Watching them at Broadstairs he recorded that 'Here has been Horne (with guitar) bathing at "Dumblegap", the flesh-coloured horror of maiden ladies'; and there too, so 'full of beauty', had been Mrs Horne. Reading, perhaps, those thoughts in Dickens' admiring, sympathetic eyes, Kate's veneration for her husband and view of her role in their marriage began to falter.

As Horne confessed sadly in his poem *The Closed Door*, from the start Kate had idealized him,

> She loves – but loves her own idea,
> And not thy form, thy heart or brain, . . .

It was only natural she should overestimate the person she loved, seeing him as the glamorous and inspiring example of the great and persecuted poet, particularly when it was the role in which he tended to see himself. Such admiration had been one of her chief attractions. To serve as companion, amanuensis and, since it was required of her, as lover of such a person seemed the most ennobling of tasks. Now, however, amongst Dickens's more practical, less respectful friends she saw a different sight. Her husband was not all-masterful or purposeful, dignified or persecuted; often he was ineffectual, dithering, the author of many of his own misfortunes, ill-at-ease and blundering, and even an object of fun which he either did not see, purposely ignored, or purposely fanned so as to be laughed at. That Dickens and his friends regarded Horne with amused and tolerant affection, and respected and recognized his literary competence if not his unparalleled genius, probably did not help Kate much in her disenchantment. Her idol had fallen. Like Elizabeth Barret she found the sight of Horne, through less partial eyes, a shattering experience. And correspondingly in the same process she found herself lifted up under Dickens's gaze into the 'beautiful, young and good' woman. It was a transition few could have made with ease, let alone Kate who lacked both experience and detachment. She reacted to everything with a spritual intensity, and it was with characteristic intensity that she seemed to view the rift between them.

Horne may not have understood the cause of her disturbance but he must have sensed the disturbance itself. However, between the demanding timetables of *Household Words*, and the demanding itinerary with the strolling theatricals, he had little time to devote to her. His immediate thoughts, when not centred on Dickens and his schemes, were occupied in a scheme of his own. Though the practical side of him was undoubtedly in the ascendant, poetic ambitions were once more stirring. They had been fed over past months by the flattering admiration of the two young poets, whose work he had edited for *Household Words*, their names George Meredith and Edmund Ollier, the son of his old publisher Charles Ollier. As long before as 1848 Meredith, a nervous young solicitor's clerk in Pimlico, had written Horne a self-conscious letter, saying that he understood Horne's sympathies as 'a poet and critics' to be with the 'young poet' and begging to lay before him 'certain poems that I may have your opinion (in which I trust) as to their merit or more especially the power of Poetic Faculty'. Horne had pronounced their poetic faculty highly encouraging. Meredith had then arranged meetings, presented him with a copy of *Goethe* and later entertained him at his home in Weybridge, where Horne met also his newly married wife, the daughter of Shelley's old opponent in the *Defence of Poetry*, the satirist Thomas Love Peacock. In 1851 the first published copy of Meredith's poems bore a quotation from *Orion* on the title page in gratitude for Horne's instruction.

In the spring of 1852 it was Horne's urgent wish to systematize and express in prose his changing poetic beliefs to a changing world. It was five years since he had written *The Dreamer and the Worker*, and in those five years the influences both personal and literary, had all been toward realism, rationality, and reform. In his association with Dickens, who has been called the 'first and greatest of the anti-Romantic Victorians', he had been subjected to considerable anti-Romantic pressures. In his work on *Household Words* he had actually furthered them, and even before that, in his effort to gain popularity with *The Poor Artist*, he had voluntarily subscribed to them. Yet so far he had managed still to keep his belief in the divine elevating poetic function in a separate compartment, even though in other avenues he may have succumbed to anti-Romantic beliefs. Even in *The Dreamer and the Worker*, though it had undergone modifications, that faith was still substantially impregnable. Now this last bastion of faith had been invaded. He had abandoned entirely the Romantic doctrines of isolation, self-absorption, inspiring and elevating emotion and imagination, and came firmly into the world of facts.

In common with his mid-century contemporaries, he was infected with the sense that he lived 'in a period of time which has no parallel in history': a time of so many and such great events and discoveries, of such profound consequences, that neither he nor anyone else could see their future ramifications. In such a time, he cried, old laws – natural, political, aesthetic – must be revised; worn-out methods, beliefs and conventions must be reconstructed. English poetry, he considered, had grown stultified by decadent copying of the Romantic masters. It had grown 'pantheistical and sentimental' in bad imitation of Wordsworth, fantastic and overphilosophic through copying the 'brilliant spirituality' of Shelley, barrenly emotional after the 'gloom and passion' of Byron, and 'enervated' by unduly idolising 'the intense sense of beauty of Tennyson'. 'If ever,' he proclaimed, 'a period had arrived when some grand change in the Art was required by the institution of some new and vigorous elements which should be in accordance with the advanced and advancing spirit of the age,' it was now. Not only must they write of the 'imaginations and the passions, but of the understanding and the knowledge of actual life . . . not a devotion to Art for Art's sake, but for Nature's sake, for man's sake, and for his definite social progress', concerned not only with 'emotions of the soul' but with the 'sensations of the body, and its . . . active senses'. If Art did not 'unite itself (after its own spiritual manner) with science, it will be left behind by Science. *Learning and the past can do no more for it*'. In the past art and science had been regarded 'not without some degree of truth to be antagonistic'. If this did not end he foresaw that science would be the 'stupendous destroyer of all the graces of life, if not the soul of man', and poetry the esoteric study of anchorites and historians. The poets must open their insular minds and doggedly shut eyes to 'the majestic movements of the sciences'. What was needed was a 'new school' of 'progressive poetry'.

His poetic manifesto was wrung from him. He wrote, he confessed, in trepidation, confronted by the contradictory images of the great Romantics, in particular by Shelley. His feelings of betrayal of his Master were unbearable and he felt forced to justify them. It was his duty, he said, to say what he believed. He was, he truthfully protested, incapable of deserting or decrying tradition wantonly. Moreover Shelley, too, had been an innovator: his *Defence of Poetry* and his prefaces had in their time been radical. He only hoped that his own views would one future day seem as established as Shelley's now did. Was not he, in effect, merely saying in the context of his own age what Shelley himself had said: that poets were 'prophetic spirits and heralds of the ascending destinies of humanity'? In affirming his loyalty to Shelley's memory and in attempting to combine his new beliefs with his old venerations, he proposed calling the autobiographical collection of poems to which he proposed affixing his manifesto by a title taken from the *Defence of Poetry* – 'Trees and Seeds'.

He sent his manuscript to Dickens who liked the poems. He had, understandably, always liked that strain in Horne which allied imagination and fact and was 'connected with progress and the real spirit of the time'. He had been proud to print his 'progressive poems' bearing that same combination in *Household Words* and he particularly admired *The Great Peacemaker*, a poetic dialogue between the sea and the newly-laid telegraph from Calais to Dover, which ended with Horne's hope that mankind's material mastery would be accompanied by a corresponding spiritual self-mastery. Dickens, however, read the preface with dismay. Horne's views smacked far too much of the author of *The False Medium*: an image he must not, for his own sake, be allowed to revive. Dickens therefore advised tactfully that the preface should be cut: a poet's work should 'explain itself; rest manfully and calmly' on that self-explanation. Those passages praising Horne's other books (for he could never resist self-publicity) he insisted be cut altogether because 'they will be misunderstood'. With these provisos, to most of which Horne at first objected and then allowed, Dickens agreed to recommend the manuscript to his own publishers Bradbury and Evans. He did not, however, feel much hope.

A week later the publisher's rejection confirmed the prediction. They would not touch poetry. And to Horne's further pleas for help Dickens was deaf, though he praised the poems and promised to be 'bottle holder, umpire, referee, etc., etc.', to any arrangement Horne himself might make. Without Dickens's help Horne felt no hope at all, and no publisher would touch the poems.

Experience ought to have prepared him against disappointment, nevertheless he was disappointed. He had longed to impart a message which he believed was of such importance to the future of art and humanity, even though his idea of the mission was now more of a duty to society than a divinely sanctioned destiny. Obviously he had been naïve: he was, as he had always been, doomed to neglect. In this curious way, even his failure to publish an attack on the mission revived his own sense of it. Emotionally, he still regarded failure as the hallmark of the poet.

In company with this disappointment came worries over *Household Words*. The associate editor William Henry Wills, a zealous unimaginative man, had never liked Horne. Soon after Horne had joined the magazine, Wills had accused him of not pulling his weight, accusations for which Wills did not, or could not, produce evidence, a fact Dickens was quick to note. After confronting Horne with the accusations, Dickens wrote firmly to Wills, assuring him he had not 'in the least intention of changing Horne's engagement' and in turn accusing Wills of being 'hardly so disposed to accommodate matters with Horne (and never have been) as it would be pleasant and advantageous for all of us'. After such a reprimand the associate editor had no alternative but to keep quiet. Nevertheless the atmosphere remained uneasy and six months later Horne himself was dissatisfied. Confiding his restlessness to Dickens, he asked for a rise in salary, but in fact his mood was probably as much a symptom of his dislike for Wills and his dislike of settled employment, especially so confining and exacting employment as *Household Words*. Once again Dickens calmed him, promising higher 'remuneration . . . in your case, I pledge myself, than in any other'; assuring him, too, of 'real affection', and that it would give his editor 'inexpressible pain' were he to 'cease or slacken his connection' with the magazine. Placated but restless Horne continued until, in 1852, he felt that restlessness return a hundred-fold.

Constant tension with Kate, doubts and denials in his work, overwork and disharmony on *Household Words*: suddenly his life seemed insupportable. Again the desire to get away began to haunt him. He found himself reading the events and discoveries of the startling, expanding world about him with envy and vicarious excitement. In November 1851 he had read of the first gold discoveries in Australia – how a man might take a bag out of his pocket 'containing two pounds of gold he procured before dinner' – and felt unbearable yearnings for adventure. Dickens, too, became infected with the golden dream of the Antipodes and began to discuss it at length in *Household Words*. In April 1852 the fabulous evidence of the dream began to arrive at English shores: treasure ships laden with eight tons of gold, and at once 'Australian madness' infected the public. Imaginations were inflamed, wanderlusts aroused, artists and artisans alike affected by the gold fever. From the group of young artists and poets calling themselves the Pre-Raphaelite Brotherhood, the sculptor Thomas Woolner prepared to sail, his departure immortalized in his friend Madox Brown's painting, *The Last of England*. Among the poets Tennyson sighed that, but for Mrs Tennyson, he too would go. Among Horne's acquaintances William Howitt made preparations for the voyage; his

brother Godfrey lived in Australia and his own fortunes had lately
fallen badly.

Horne learned, inadvertently, the news of Howitt's departure from
his publisher. He felt disturbed and shaken, aware of the meaning of
those pangs the news had aroused in him. He was filled with the uncontrollable desire to go too. Escape, adventure, the role of the Romantic wanderer beckoned to him. But there was Kate; he could not leave
her. Wrestling with his conscience and his desire, it suddenly occurred
to him that this might indeed be, after all, the answer to all his problems: a voyage to the goldfields alone, a quick fortune, and back to a
life of literary and financial independence in whose relaxed atmosphere
he and Kate might finally overcome their troubles. That it might mean
more – the turning his back on his mission – even his mental suicide –
he did not dare admit. In mid-1852 he stood by the rail of the sailing
ship *Kent*, at sea on its way to Port Phillip, and tried in verse to
assemble his thoughts:

> *Plough onward earth-born creature of the deep*
> *And in thy beaming foster-mother womb*
> *Bear me away from England. Let no touch*
> *Of weak regret of things beyond my fate –*
> *Nor fruitless feelings for my native shore –*
> *Nor love for those I leave so far behind*
> *Weigh down my heart, or, weighing down, repress*
> *Its natural spring of action . . .*

> *I shake the ungenial dust*
> *From off my feet, nor caring if the wind*
> *Cast it like smouldering ashes on thy soul.*
> *Roll on, monotony of Day and Night!*
> *Moan sullen Ocean for thy homeless soul!*
> *Sing ancients Winds, o'er mine – for I am free . . .*

Chapter 17

The Seductive Shore

In the Bay of Biscay, the *Kent* struck bad weather. For three days the 800-ton ship pitched and tossed, making no progress, and Horne and most of the 200 passengers were sea-sick. He was probably even more miserable when he remembered the events of his departure.

Once he had decided to migrate, he indulged in an orgy of buying. He had bought camp beds, tents, picks, shovels, sieves and washing cradles, a wheelbarrow, a sheet iron pump, an expensive portable forge (the use of which he had learnt from the local blacksmith), bolts of cloth, boots, cabin furniture, needles and thread, ink, pens, paper, a bewildering variety of goods. He had furthermore planned to recruit his own faithful band of miners from those Cornish copper mines which had swallowed his money, and would have recruited them had not Charles Dickens, who was greatly diverted by Horne's elaborate preparations, advised against it, reminding how gold could dissolve the strongest of loyalties.

In all ways Dickens had been most kind. He had promised to retain Horne on *Household Words* as a casual Australian correspondent, and promised to remit his earnings to Kate. He had also sent out a reserve fund to Port Phillip to ensure his fare home. This had, to some degree, eased Horne's worries about his wife, for he believed he could rely on Dickens to take care of her most pressing financial needs during his absence. He intended to leave her in Mary's care at Hillside. Otherwise his feelings for Kate were all anxiety and guilt. Not unnaturally she disapproved of the entire scheme, and though she could not forbid him to go – indeed she ultimately gave a reluctant consent – she made clear her reluctance. To take her with him, he argued, was out of the question: she would never stand the hardships. Nor according to many friends would he; he was fifty years of age and accustomed to a sedentary life. Southwood Smith was more heartening, declaring that physical labour for 'twelve hours a day' would do him 'nothing but good'. Not that any such arguments moved him; neither Kate's disapproval nor gloomy predictions could deter him.

It was nevertheless with a somewhat uneasy mind that he collected his extensive luggage and went to Plymouth alone at the start of June. His distress was worsened when ten days later, with the ship at last about to sail, he had had no farewell word from Kate. While writing his last letters to newspapers, reminding them that it was twenty years of 'public indifference' that drove him to so desperate a step, he wrote also a last letter to Kate. William Howitt, installed with his two sons also as first-class passengers in the *Kent*, reported Horne's anguish to his wife Mary, who like Kate was left behind in London. He reported with malice; like so many in literary London he was tired of Horne's posturing, and furthermore furious that Horne should butt so boldly into his party.

Off Madeira the weather cleared, and like animals returning from hibernation the passengers emerged to read, promenade, and play whist. Horne seemed, Howitt noted, worn and thin, and his beard and hair which had grown long were heavily streaked with grey. Yet as the balmy days passed, Horne felt his spirits and health again blossoming. The life itself was calming, like a dream. At night the Southern Cross began to show low in the southern sky and a school of flying fish like 'white larks' sent the children in pursuit across the decks and scrambling over the figurehead of the Duchess of Kent. The tranquillity did not last long; the weeks of confinement and privation began to tell. Among the intermediate passengers, whose quarters were unspeakably squalid and insanitary, dissension and revolt were germinating. Scandals, Howitt noted with relentless eye, were common where adolescents of both sexes were kept in close confinement. Food for the entire ship was running low, water lower. Children died, there was fear of epidemic, the hospital was fit only as a 'dog kennel'. These were facts that the gaiety, the music, and the country dancing of the first-class passengers could not effectively overshadow.

Howitt himself was burdened with responsibility. He had sailed in the *Kent* because he knew that she was part owned by a Quaker family, and felt therefore that she ought be to more reliable and sober than other ships. Alas, the crew was frequently drunk with liquor obtained at black-market prices from the intermediate passengers, who in turn had bought it illegally from the captain. The captain was forever distributing religious tracts with one hand and selling liquor with the other. Howitt therefore confronted the shiftless captain – to no avail, for it achieved only his own unpopularity; henceforth his appearances on deck were booed by the intermediate passengers like 'an American election'. He relied on Horne for support, but got none; he complained that only irresponsibility could be had from Horne. Horne was indulging in schoolboy intrigues with the intermediate passengers from whom he expected to recruit his band of miners – they apparently had no intention of following him, but humoured him. He furthermore indulged in annoying and dangerous practical jokes, even releasing the ship's pigs on deck one night. He alienated all his friends, particularly the Howitts who were the bearers of all these allegations, by his boorish and irresponsible behaviour. He had 'turned out so egotistical and overbearing, so meddling and crotchety . . . that he was shunned by most of the other passengers', young Alfred Howitt reported at the end of the voyage.

The Howitts were unsympathetic observers; yet it was the same behaviour that other observers – notably Miss Mitford – had reported over the past ten years, and for that reason cannot be discounted. Once again Horne was in an unnerving position and he was reacting the only way he knew. Anxious and guilty about Kate, unsure of his life and yet determined to succeed, intoxicated by his apparent freedom and returning to a role in which he had once excelled, it was a bewildering state of mind to endure. If he stopped to consider, the prospect before him was not propitious. The life was likely to be extremely rough, and at playing the adventurer he was out of practice; it was thirty years since he had seen snowy Orizaba. He was gambling heavily on his powers of adaptation. He must give himself no chance to consider, allow no sober evaluation, for fear his courage failed.

At the end of August the ship entered the Indian ocean and met violent storms. So terrifying were they in the minds of the voyagers that Horne wrote a vivid account for Dickens's *Household Words*:

Sometime between twelve and two I awoke with a start, caused by a loud and violent booming blow, followed by a rush of water, which came dashing down the main hatchway, and flooding all the 'tween decks, every cabin inclusive. A lurch instantly followed, which sent all the water to the other side of the ship, but this seemed only to give a more vehement impulse to the counter-lurch on our side, the roll of which went to such an extent lower and lower that I thought this time at last we must go clean over, and while the result was yet suspended in the darkness, down came rushing to our low-sunken side an avalanche of all movable contents . . . cooking tins and crockery, washing things, all loose articles of every description, with boxes, jars and tubs, and kegs and cabin furniture bursting away from their fastenings, through cabin doors, and bringing many cabin doors and panels along with them, together with the heavy crashing hatchway ladders – one tremendous avalanche, cataract and chaos, like the total destruction and end of all things.

Then it was over, and from cabins reduced to 'rags and slush' the voyagers emerged. It was September and the southern spring, and with a sudden snapping of tension they sighted Cape Otway, one of the most southerly points on the Australian mainland, and smelt the delicious scents of land. Chattering, cheering, generally jubilant, they crowded round the incoming pilot at the entrance to Port Phillip Bay and sought news of the diggings. Beyond the 'seductive shore' of the gold region their gaze met a line of smooth hills running along the western horizon, broken by the wooden spurs of low mountains: through the gaps in those hills lay the paths to the fabulous goldfields. At the end of the bay was Melbourne and Horne was amazed to see the masts of so many ships.

It was almost dark on a wild wet evening when they landed at the wharves and encountered their first taste of colonial harshness. Unloaded like 'cattle' on to a chaotic wharf, at the mercy of insolent porters demanding exorbitant prices for carrying luggage, some spent the rainy night in empty drums and packing cases, while others walked through the sand and scrub, past strange trees whose leaves seemed cut from 'dingy green paper', past tents and lagoons, over the great stone bridge spanning the river Yarra, and into Melbourne: raw and vigorous, a town grown up in twenty years and turned suddenly by gold into an oversized fun-parlour.

In its rough streets even rougher hotels and lodging houses burst their seams with emigrants. Money flowed like water; flamboyant miners raced about in carriages with prostitutes in gaudy dresses; drinking dens sold French champagne; theatres packed with uncouth miners and their uncouth women bedecked with golden jewellery performed Shakespeare to delighted catcalls. On this shore set foot 'Orion' Horne, the most distinguished English poet, as he would later claim, ever to visit Australia. It was not a very distinguished claim.

Grotesquely alive, like the English fairs of his childhood, the country attracted Horne but at the same time repelled him. Moreover he was used to comfort and a certain measure of security, and neither were to be found here. Yet, as so often, those 'self-sustaining' and adaptive energies of his active practical side came triumphantly to his rescue. On the first night spent with fellow passengers in the rat-infested cellar of a grimy lodging-house, he was dismayed but not disheartened. Even the defection of his supposedly faithful company of miners recruited in the ship did not dishearten him. He unloaded his equipment and sought out one of the few people of distinction in the colony, Archibald Chisholm.

Chisholm was in his fifties, a retired captain of the East India Company's Army, for which Horne himself had been once destined. A 'thin, pale and sad-looking' man of 'retiring disposition and a great fondness for languages' and for Shakespeare, he devoted most of his time to furthering those philanthropic migration schemes devised by his wife, Caroline Chisholm, who had earned fame for her introduction of respectable females and families into the colonies. To Horne, Chisholm was almost another twin spirit. To find so rare a commodity in so alien a community was extraordinarily good fortune; and he undoubtedly must have blessed that coincidence which caused Caroline Chisholm to contribute articles on Australia to *Household Words*, thereby making it possible for him to carry a letter of introduction to Captain Chisholm. In Melbourne in 1852 Chisholm could not have been kinder – nor more disillusioning. The chances, he informed Horne, of a quick fortune at the diggings were remote. There were, however, other chances of making a moderate fortune in other pursuits, and this was perhaps his best course. He promised to look out for possible employment for him.

Horne accepted the cold counsel. Even had he felt sufficiently strong to attempt the long voyage back, there was little point in his returning. He had no desire to face once more the old troubles, along with the humiliation of returning defeated. Moreover those 'sustaining energies' and innate resourcefulness of his temperament told him that Chisholm was right and that for one of his capabilities there were obviously numerous chances of making money in so naïve and burgeoning a society. Horne had proved that his advice was sound, for had he not sold the mining equipment he had imported at an astronomical profit? His immediate future he decided lay in Australia, but what exactly he should do with that future he did not know – and indeed he did not seem to care. Throughout his adult life he had looked inward and analysed himself, a habit which the poet in him fostered, but now in his first days in Melbourne he found himself incapable of self-analysis and reluctant to take any thought of himself or of his future. His existence was so strange that the future defied speculation anyway.

Afterwards, he found it difficult to remember the day, the month, even the year he had come to Australia, let alone the dates of happenings that befell him after his arrival. He merely wanted to act, taking whatever role in which he appeared to be cast. And in action bereft of thought he found immense relief. He had come, he emphasized, not as a poet or speculator or philosopher but merely to dig for gold – merely to act. Almost with confidence he moved into the 'backroom of a two-roomed hovel', looking out on to a cesspool, and owned by an insolent widow; he had seen better among the slums of Wolverhampton but it was amongst the best Melbourne could offer for the high rent of thirty shillings a week.

Meanwhile, true to his prediction, Chisholm had found Horne work. A privately-owned gold escort, which carried gold between the Bendigo diggings and Melbourne, a distance of over a hundred miles, was wanting a commander for the troop. Chisholm eagerly recommended him, mentioning his Sandhurst background and his service in Mexico. The directors were charmed by such qualifications and reassured by the quickest of interviews. So it was, within a fortnight of his arrival in Melbourne (and haste, as he would soon discover, was a dominating feature of all colonial behaviour), Horne found himself dressed in the bizarre uniform of the Commander of the Escort, a cavalry sabre, pistols, long boots, an old frock coat, and broad-brimmed hat. In charge of three gold carts he led a handful of men up the rough road to the Bendigo diggings.

By day the escort raced at breakneck speed through broken tracks so muddy that in some places the horses sank to their girths in the slush, or so hot and dry that the riders were shrouded in dust. The weather veered between extremes of heat and rain. The Yankee drivers with their long wild hair and beards and their long bowie knives cracked their whips over the horses and navigated their gold carts. By night they camped, rolled up in blankets on open grass; and they awoke in daylight, Horne at first with aching limbs, to the curious warble of the Australian magpie. At Forest Creek, now Chewton, Horne saw his first gold diggings – white tents and yellow mounds of clay and scorched yellow grass at the foot of Mount Alexander. Thirty-five miles further on lay Bendigo, where the valley was covered with tents laid out in streets and squares, London fashion: a 'most imposing aspect'. There they usually rested two days before undertaking the journey back with their carts carrying up to two tons of gold.

It was exhausting and anxious work, and Horne was intensely nervous on the return journeys. The times and places were lawless, though with so much gold in circulation the men themselves were casual, almost indifferent. Horne was amazed at how often a parcel of nuggets was thrust into his hand for conveying to Melbourne at the last minute by a check-shirted miner without thought of receipt or even proper record of the owner's name. Yet if his customers were casual, he was not. James Hingston, the journalist who had once noted him behind the copies of *Orion* at Miller's bookshop in London, came upon him one afternoon in a distracted state, sitting on a broken cart beside the Coliban River, fussing in case a replacement from a nearby town did not arrive before dark. Never again, Horne declared, would he venture out without more adequate protection. Howitt heard rumours of his extreme caution and concern. He 'was so fidgety', Howitt reported, 'that the men could not bear him. He wanted them to cast up fortifications round inns where they stopped for the night with the gold.' Nor was Horne's caution misplaced when, insufficiently armed, they had to travel through the Black Forest, a haunt of bush-rangers and miscellaneous robbers. Once one of his gold carts capsized and scattered its precious contents. On another afternoon the troop insisted, despite Horne's protests, on stopping to shelter from a thunderstorm and point blank refused to guard the carts in pelting rain. Overcome by his sense of responsibility, Horne himself mounted watch over the gold for the night while the men enjoyed their comfortable beds. They reached Melbourne like 'hunted-down bandits in the last stage of destitution', Horne's nerves and patience exhausted. After quarrels and complaints on both sides, he thankfully resigned.

Back in Melbourne with Archibald Chisholm, Horne settled down to a slightly more orientated existence. As proof of his adjustment he scribbed a few poems, one inspired by news of the fate of the Arctic explorer Sir John Franklin, another on the less topical subject of Nero, which found its way in 1853 to *Fraser's Magazine*. Under his friend's generous patronage he was introduced to what intellectual society the colony had to offer, and made one congenial new friend in Dr Robert Bowie, 'wise and benevolent Superintendent' of the Melbourne Lunatic Asylum. Bowie may already have been known to him, by reputation if not in person. Like Southwood Smith he had worked in London on the cholera epidemic and had investigated public health, originating the scheme 'for Baths and Washhouses'. In Bowie's company Horne was able to pursue his interest, begun with Southwood Smith at Hillside, in science and medicine. Along with Chisholm and Bowie he signed petitions and entered into tortuous correspondence with the Government over the hanging of a convicted murderer named Pinkerton whom Bowie and his colleagues considered insane.

Horne's most pressing problems were his need for work and his need for lodgings. Moving from one sordid room to another, and unable to stay long with Chisholm, whose means were meagre, in desperation Horne bought two tents and two watchdogs and moved to a rough, gypsy-like settlement named Canvas Town on the south bank of the Yarra River. Reminiscent once more of the fairs of his childhood, but with no 'gilt and very little gingerbread', abounding in mosquitoes and fleas, impregnated with dust, littered with refuse, Horne found amid the multicoloured tents of Canvas Town a life more cruel, vigorous, colourful and pathetic than anything he had ever encountered. Sons of peers, graduates of Oxford, convicts and confidence men, labourers and clerks: Canvas Town housed all classes, all types, in indiscriminate discomfort. The streets were named with nostalgic or facetious bitterness after those of London – Bond Street, Regent's Street – and the tents bore similar names – the London Coffee Rooms, the Great Britain Stores. Among the seven hundred tent dwellers two doctors practised, clergymen held services, butcher, cobblers, bakers and blacksmiths carried on their trades. They were outcasts rather than colonizers, and yet to Horne there was safety and satisfaction in being an outcast. In detachment lay his safeguard against voracious, primitive colonial society. Aloof from it he was secure; but absorbed by it, identified with it, he was likely to be consumed and destroyed. Canvas Town with its honesty, vitality, and statelessness was far preferable to him than the uncivilized refinements of the true colonists.

Nevertheless, from Canvas Town he made occasional excursions into Melbourne society, joining in parties wild and lavish that ended too often in a shambles of broken chairs and bottles. It was noticeable that although he vigorously condemned the colonial traits of reckless energy and self-assertion they were distinctive parts of his own nature; and that although he condemned their horse-play, he did not hesitate often to match it. Thus in social circles he earned fame for his ability to bend a poker in one blow on his forearm – a trick he had probably learned in Mexico.

He also earned enemies, most of them antagonized by his patronizing poetic airs. Though he had avowedly come to Australia to escape from his poetic identity, he was finding it as difficult to banish the poet as it had been all those previous years to banish the man. The poet returned not only in these occasional poems he was writing, but in the less desirable garb of poetic pretension. When he decided that his best interests would be served by entering society, it was the role of literary lion, discredited in London, which he began to impose on Melbourne. Though he deplored Australian lack of literary sensibility, it might also be put to his advantage. So, for the rest of his colonial life, while for the most part he renounced his poetic mission, he lived unblushingly on its past. His hitherto basic honesty – one of the most admirable of all his traits – was listless in the face of his urge to play, if not to be, the poet. In Australia, subjected to the necessities and rigours of his new life, many apparent discrepancies would occur in his nature.

In his urgency to find work he called on the Victorian governor, Charles la Trobe, hinting for an official appointment and presenting him with a copy of *Orion*, of which La Trobe privately confessed he could not make head nor tail. Nor was the governor's sympathy enlarged when Horne began to write for *The Argus*, one of Melbourne's two newspapers, which was responsible for a 'determined and intemperate attack on the Government'. The governor, wrote William Howitt with relish, 'abominates any thing or person connected with it', and had confided personally to Howitt that he thought Horne 'not to be depended on, for one day he wrote for the Government and the next day against it'. 'There never was,' wrote Howitt, with even greater relish, 'so impossible a man.'

To England came various stories about this 'impossible man'. Some had it he was 'going up country', others that he 'was staying in Melbourne'. Dickens, reading his latest contributions on Australia for *Housewold Words*, remarked to Wills that they were not up to standard, and that he was dismayed to find that Horne, the elaborate equippage notwithstanding, had abandoned his goal of the diggings, was living on his return fare, and even seemed to believe that *Household Words* would support Kate Horne. From Horne, however, Dickens hid his irritation, and instead reported family and theatrical tidbits, noting that Kate had spent the New Year with them and was 'as well and happy as Julia has any right to be in the absence of her Falkland'. He added that he was delighted to find Horne 'so cheerful and hopeful' and that he pictured him like a 'Frontispiece' to an adventure book – 'in your uniform – on your charger (he's rearing of course) with your escort in the background, and you encouraging them with drawn sword'.

In Melbourne, Horne's spirits were falling, his inactivity breeding introspection and misgiving. He had almost exhausted his money. La Trobe seemed disinclined to help him; a request he had sent home to a distant relation of the Tice family in the Colonial Office, whom he hoped would put pressure on La Trobe, had not yet been answered. After a bare eight months in the colony, his predicament seemed bleak. Trying every avenue, he applied for the post of secretary of a hillbilly Road Board, and after dazzling the farmers who comprised the board with a display of knowledge of roadmaking from the Romans to Macadam, he learned with chagrin that the position had gone to a stonemason – 'a maker of tombstones!' He then applied for another secretaryship, but it was awarded 'to a clerk in the Audit Office, none of the applicants having been seen'. It seemed that no one wanted him.

It was June of 1853 before the longed-for appointment came, prompted apparently in the Colonial Office in London by his obscure relation-by-marriage. According to Horne, a bare two days after the letter of patronage from the Colonial Office arrived on La Trobe's desk, he was informed of his appointment. 'That literature had nothing to do with my receiving this appointment, it would be ungrateful towards literature to say: but literature had nothing to do with it here.' Despite his cynicism, however, it was noticeable that his literary reputation was proving a useful qualification for active life, and one he was not slow in exploiting.

His new post was that of Assistant Commissioner for Crown Lands at Heathcote, a fast-growing diggings on a flat plain overshadowed by wooded hills seventy miles from Melbourne. Horne and his two fellow assistant-commissioners arrived to find a well-built official camp, staffed and equipped on the grandest scale, while the diggings themselves covered three square miles of Crown land and held sixteen thousand miners. He himself was assigned to settle disputes on the diggings, before a 'pick and shovel jury' that was not backward in demonstrating its displeasure nor in intimidating officials and witnesses. Horne found himself inexperienced and lacking in legal knowledge. Relying on common sense and native wit, he cut through the long and involved accounts and accusations, and most times gave 'a summary decision "in equity" '. Once he fined both plaintiff and defendant 'because on examining the case it was clearly proved that they had each endeavoured to rob the other in the way complained of by the former'. When this tale was recounted in Melbourne, the Attorney General added wittily that it might not be British justice but was certainly poetic justice.

It was work for which Horne was neither mentally nor temperamentally equipped. Nor was he much better suited to his next task: to receive, weigh, and take charge of the gold brought to the official camp by the miners for safe-keeping in three great iron safes. Driven to acute anxiety by the huge sums entrusted to him – sometimes as much as thirty thousand pounds – Horne's fidgetiness may well have moved his superiors to transfer him. A few months after his arrival at Heathcote, a new gold rush on the far side of the wooded hills called for officials; and Horne, though not next in turn, was detailed to go. In September 1853, with drays, provisions, tents, and troopers, he had his first sight of Waranga: 'a wild and desolate district of arid bush, quartz hills, reefs and ranges, black, charred forests, long alluvial gullies, and during the winter chains of water-holes, thousands of acres of swamp and marsh, and all the year round, though very much diminished in summer, a huge and melancholy lagoon'. 'Miserable solitudes,' he described them, hitherto 'wrapped in the torpor of ages'. The year he spent at Waranga would be characterized by loneliness and melancholy. He would call it – until ten years later he found another place worthier of the name – his 'Siberia', his 'exile within an exile'.

At Waranga his duties were more responsible and more solitary. At two outstations of the far-flung diggings (to one of which Horne gave the name Rushworth, since he considered it 'worthy' of a gold rush) he was alone in charge, and on the recall of the Commissioner early in the year Horne was in charge of the entire area. He found the responsibilities burdensome. Made uncomfortable by the hordes of insects reminiscent of Vera Cruz, harassed by an eye infection that defied his cure of dipping the head with eyes open in a bucket of cold water, Horne felt too old for the physical hardships, too depressed to face the loneliness, and too exhausted and anxious for the responsibilities which Governor La Trobe assigned him:

When I tendered my services to your Excellency for some active employment I expressed myself willing to encounter any difficulties; I therefore do not offer any objection to my present position at a station which your Excellency well knows to be at this season famous for its Plague of insect life – with the 'gad-fly' in prospect; where the heat is sometimes from 103 degrees to 115 degrees in the shade; – Africa, without its fruits and flowers; – the sands of Vera Cruz, without the sea, or snow-crowned Orizaba in the distance; a district worthy of a corner in the 'Divine' Comedy of Dante. Nevertheless [he continued] I should feel no regret at being exchanged to 'another and better place'.

No better place was forthcoming; La Trobe was only too glad to leave him in isolation, and too exasperated by Horne's many suggestions for administrative improvements to give a favourable ear to any of his pleas. Nor did the new governor who arrived in mid-1854, Sir Charles Hotham, seem better disposed. As Horne sat in his lonely tent at night, sending the eerie voice of his guitar out over the lagoon, or reading from a page black with insects attracted by the flame of his candle, he could hardly justify his situation. He had left England merely to take on burdensome responsibilities and bodily and mental misery!

Whereas he had once gloried in activity without thought, and taken satisfaction from severing ties with home, he now clung to any tie with family or friends, drawing sustenance from even his relationship with Kate. From the desolate bush of Waranga he wrote by almost every mail to Kate and to Mary, sending them both what money he could spare and once sending Kate an aromatic parcel of gum leaves (and, according to the malicious Howitts, a squashed flea on a visiting card, which they later claimed – maliciously and quite erroneously – to be his only present to his wife from Australia). He wrote also to Southwood Smith, once sending him a parcel of gold nuggets in repayment of the £200 he had borrowed from him on departure. Noting the entries in his diary on the arrival or sailing of so many English ships, one senses not only his understandable precautions to see no mail went astray, but also his satisfaction at recording even so indirect a communication with England. To Southwood Smith he wrote that distance 'makes no real division where there is deeply-rooted feeling'; but in his heart he knew this was not true. At Waranga his life seemed to deny all he had previously treasured and provoke all he had previously suppressed.

He was already dejected when he received a letter from Kate, announcing in 'very affectionate terms, and even penitent language' that she wished him 'to give full consent to their permanent separation'. In explanation she said that 'the lamp had gone out on the altar' and 'that she was personally indisposed to be a wife'. She reminded him of her 'coldness and resistance' in the past; she begged him to believe it was not because of her 'personal regard for any other man'. Indeed she had come to believe that it was not 'in her nature to have that kind of feeling towards any man which she believed a wife ought to have'. Unfortunately, Kate's actual letter no longer exists, and the above quotations come from a later version recalled by Horne himself. However, as he kept the original letter from which his version was drawn, and waved it as proof in the face of anyone who disbelieved, one is reasonably reassured as to its truthfulness.

On receiving Kate's letter, Horne's tottering composure was shattered. The letter, he claimed, astonished him; and 'in anguish' he wandered 'into the solitude of the bush for hours, to escape from the confusion' of his emotion. Perhaps he ought not have been astonished. It was true that after her initial upset at his departure she appeared to have forgiven him; certainly his diary was full of the records of her letters to him, and the one surviving letter written to him by Mary from England includes affectionate remarks from Kate. Nevertheless neither had been blind to the situation that had forced him from England two years before. So much of their relationship had depended on her admiration for him and now she was no longer the immature admiring girl under the spell of the author of *Orion*. Kate was moving to emotional and intellectual independence and indeed to feminism. In April of 1853 she had left Mary's house – though the two women remained friends – and gone to live with a Mrs Lovegrove in Sussex. In 1854, refusing an invitation to live with her own family, she had taken the decisive step of going to live with Caroline Hill and her daughters at the London premises of the Ladies Guild, a female co-operative devoted to training women to earn their own living by painting glass to look like marble – an esoteric art then much in fashion and much admired by John Ruskin, who considered the table tops of young Octavia Hill particularly fine. Living at the Ladies Guild amongst the young feminists, known not as Kate but as Kitty, the possessor of a new identity and the prospect of a new life, Kate felt a strength and satisfaction she had hitherto lacked. She knew, too, that she could rely on the powerful friendship of Charles Dickens, whose concern for her welfare, though more equivocal attitudes may have underlain it, had sustained her ever since Horne's departure. His behaviour had been as irreproachable as it was tender; and he had included her in his family gatherings and family holidays, and had offered to find her employment. He, unlike her husband, could be relied on; her own skill and intelligence could do the rest. With the friendship of fellow feminists an active intellectual life at the Ladies Guild, and the capacity to earn her own living, she had what she wanted and needed. She neither wanted nor needed Horne. And in the circumstances, to a woman of integrity, to continue as his wife in the eyes of the world was hypocritical. Besides she still had sufficient affection for him to feel he deserved an official statement of freedom as much as she. In the light of such thinking her actions were understandable.

Horne did not understand. Though he knew that few things tied them together, he shrank from a final break, partly because it would proclaim before the world yet another of his failures, partly because all feeling for her was not dead. He was haunted by the memories of what he and Kate had once felt for one another. Above all, in this raw strange land he clung to her as the cord that tied him with security and home.

It seems likely that Kate's letter arrived in March of 1854. At the end of March Horne applied for one month's leave on 'urgent private affairs', which was reluctantly granted. In Melbourne, staying with Captain Chisholm, he wrote to Kate tenderly and forbearingly, accepting her decision since there was nothing he 'could *do* . . . in the matter', but begging her at least to keep her 'determination a secret' because, he added dramatically, he 'might never live to return, and thus painful discussions and comments of relations and friends could be spared'. He also sent her £50. Returning to Waranga at the end of May he awaited her reply. When her letter eventually came it reiterated the same intention 'with much contrition, almost [wrote Horne later] amounting to remorse'. His letter had been noble, deeply affecting; she herself was 'heartless' and blameworthy, but she could not help how she felt. Her decision to 'separate herself' was 'unaltered and unalterable'. Rather than keep it a secret, it was important to her that the world should know of it; she begged no further correspondence with him.

Had he really wished, Horne could have returned to England. And had he really wanted her, it might be argued that he would have returned. In the later quarrels on whether he had or had not deserted Kate, this moment would seem to be the crucial one, but, in fact, Horne ignored it and rested his defences on why he had decided to come without her to Australia in the first place. For it seemed now not to enter his mind that he might return and attempt in person to patch up his broken marriage. At twelve thousand miles distance he merely told himself there was little he could do, and he went back in great distress of mind, but no practical determination, to his lonely marshes and lagoons.

Ill fortune seemed to haunt him. At Waranga there was incessant trouble, and most of it his own fault. At the best of times he was an over-anxious administrator, veering between extremes of caution and recklessness – the very traits that had made him so inefficient an editor. In reflective moments even he doubted his capabilities. He had already been badly shaken when the miners in his area had threatened to riot as a result of an increase in the licence fees every digger was obliged to pay. A crowd of miners armed with guns and clubs had marched on the camp; and only the extreme presence of mind of the senior commissioner, appeasing them yet retaining some 'shadow of authority', saved them all from bloodshed. (Horne's fears were well founded, for later, in a rebellion over licence fees at Ballarat, over thirty lives were lost.) Horne doubted if he could have coped, and certainly a biographer cannot question those doubts.

Now, on his return to Waranga, incidents less serious grew quite as unmanageable. He considered his position unbearable; he was forced by the tyrannical and capricious commands of his superiors in Melbourne to behave unreasonably and inhumanely; he was answerable for everybody's faults. He was the victim of an 'odious system'. He had also entered into a continuous quarrel with the local police whom he accused, with some justice, of 'excess and misconduct'. In vain he hoped to be moved to the more equable climate of Ballarat, nearly a hundred miles away. Nagged by personal and official worries, nervous at acting as a magistrate – 'without books to guide me . . . without previous experience, or study' – he was unable to collect his thoughts or divest himself of his emotions as he mounted the Bench to judge the domestic quarrels and mining disputes that made up most of his work.

While his 'poetic justice' had always been suspect by standards of conventional justice, it now grew incoherent. He became involved in a sequence of happenings in which his behaviour, though understandable, was decidedly unwise. At the start of June he refused to convict two men charged with selling sly-grog, mainly because the constable laying evidence was to Horne's mind a perjurer and drunkard. In his own mind, however, he thought one of the men was guilty, and so he privately confided to the authorities that the man's application for a licence to sell alcohol should be refused; this was rather irregular by the light of British justice. Towards the end of June the police, particularly infuriated by his behaviour, appear to have made a plan. They laid a charge of selling illegal liquor against a Mrs McMulligan, at whose tent Horne was known to be a customer, though whether for liquor is not clear. Horne took the bait; he opposed the charges. The police sprang: nine constables and three sergeants laid a formal complaint against Horne for failing to uphold them in his duty, and the complaint was endorsed and despatched to Melbourne by their officer in charge. In Melbourne, Sir Charles Hotham, the new governor, attempting to enforce quarterdeck discipline on lawless miners and to suppress the sale of alcohol on the goldfields, was at once in sympathy with the police and called for an inquiry.

Once news of Horne's possible disgrace was rumoured in Waranga, a flurry of complaints from those he had disciplined poured into Melbourne. Among the charges was the quite unfounded one that he was trading on the side and selling Government property. In fact he had guarded in the official camp some goods which Archibald Chisholm's sons, unsuccessful merchants in Melbourne, had consigned to the Rushworth store of Horne's friend, Ludovic Marie. It was perhaps unwise of Horne, but it was not illegal.

None of these later complaints was responsible for his dismissal. The events of June on the magistrate's Bench had already made up the governor's mind. In August the Attorney General concluded that Horne had 'little acquaintance with the ordinary rules of justice and the principles on which it ought to be administered'. The Colonial Secretary concluded that Horne was unfit to be either Gold Commissioner or magistrate. The problem was how to dismiss him since the present cases seemed too trivial. The governor, to whom the bulging file was passed in September, however, had no such falterings. 'That Mr Horne,' he wrote, 'is unfit for a Justice of the Peace is clear – but if unfit for that duty he is still more unfit for the charge of Gold Commissioner where judgment, tact and discretion are required.' A sad verdict, it was undoubtedly true; but it must also be said that, from the governor down to the lowliest sly-grogging policeman, it was true of a large part of the Government. If no better, Horne was probably no worse than the rest. He was perhaps a little more honest and, therefore, unpredictable by normal standards, and that as much as anything proved his undoing.

At the start of November Horne received a 'brutal' official letter dismissing him. He had his release from Waranga, though not exactly as he had wanted it.

Chapter 18

Adrift

Horne was adrift. At no time had he so lacked roots and purpose. He was cast out in an alien community which had no place for a poet, and in which he, as a man, had failed. At the same time he had no incentive to return to England. The one stabilizing thought in his mind was the hope, fast receding, of making a small colonial fortune. But since, thanks to the incidents at Waranga, the governor was reluctant to employ him further (though as concession he provided Horne with a letter of exoneration), Horne did not even have the prospect of a salaried position. He returned to Melbourne, to the comfort of Chisholm's friendship, a frenzied search for work, and intellectual idleness.

And it is here that the biographer becomes uneasy at a problem that persists throughout Horne's colonial career. Among the surviving mass of snippets that attest to his actions in Australia, there are few intimate letters and almost none that show the inner workings of his mind. He is seen almost entirely through a public vision, undoubtedly true, but just as undoubtedly one-sided. He is perpetually that affected little figure with the corkscrew curls first so feelingly described by Miss Mitford – strutting and strumming his beribboned guitar, dressed in outlandish clothes at Melbourne theatres and parties, holding forth uninvited, forever craving and claiming publicity. Confronted at all turns by these poses, the biographer can only partially construct the whole man and hazard some guesses to explain the constant play-acting. Lacking valid identity, Horne's one solution, it seems, was to revert to the identity of 'Orion' and make it forcible enough to compensate for present fears and failures.

Though Horne might bewail Victoria's lack of culture and would continue to do so throughout his stay, in fact the colony was emerging from its golden picture of rumbustious vulgarity. The theatres, previously the boisterous haunts of diggers with an eye for burlesque, were growing not only more respectable and sober but also more discerning artistically. Literature, too, was germinating slowly. The journalists writing for the Melbourne daily papers and for the new periodials were by no means incompetent, and some of the colony's prominent men were sympathetic to literature. Horne had decided to stay just as the cultural life of Melbourne was emerging from the morass of gold fever, and he would both assist its rise and in turn be assisted by it.

That Melbourne was culturally rising was visible in that first attempt of Horne to set down colonial roots. Wisely he had decided to make firm that reputation as Poet on which paradoxically so many of his chances as colonial man now rested. In 1855, in that very leave of absence begged to deal with the problem of Kate, he had begun to negotiate for a colonial edition of *Orion* – claimed later to be the idea of an enterprising Melbourne publisher. It was a clever move on Horne's part and was accomplished by subscription. Though Chisholm had difficulty in raising the necessary subscribers, it was significant that there were sufficient eager, or at least willing, subscribers for such a publication. Dedicated suitably to so notable a worker and builder as Southwood Smith, the Australian *Orion* appeared in 1854, its preface written from the wilds of Waranga, proudly but spuriously sporting the additional title of first poetic work to appear in the 'gold trading' colony.

In the educated professional men who had been his subscribers Horne found new friends, some of whom he owned to be brilliant; Archibald Michie, a leading barrister and proprietor of the Melbourne *Herald*, a superb orator who was adjudged to be almost worthy of Disraeli; Butler Cole Aspinall, only twenty-three, handsome, witty, radical, and a lawyer and a former friend of G. H. Lewes in England, though he carried, like so many of Horne's Australian friends, the seeds of mental disturbance. Even more distinguished was Charles Gavan Duffy, whom Horne had met in the Ireland of those days he recalled now so nostalgically: editor of the journal for Young Ireland, former Member of the House of Commons, and friend of the Carlyles, Duffy arrived sensationally in Victoria in 1855, to be welcomed by Horne with a poem in his honour, a copy of *The History of Napoleon* and friendly letters. Less exalted but at the centre of Melbourne's cultural life were James Edward Neild, a suave, intellectual physician and journalist and sharer of Horne's theatrical enthusiasms, James Smith who once worked with Jerrold and was now the leading Melbourne dramatic critic, and J. J. Shillinglaw, eccentric and pompous, civil servant and journalist.

While the society may not have been precisely what he was used to, it was not to be scorned; and unlike England, few doors of Australian society were shut to him. Moreover there were the theatres and actors. The arrival in Melbourne in 1855 of Gustavus Vaughan Brooke, said by some to be the greatest English actor since the elder Kean, was a landmark for colonial theatre, for the actor was at his peak during his six years in the colony and not yet a dissipated man. Brooke was soon in Horne's circle of acquaintances. And Horne himself was soon to be among those raising the theatre to new colonial heights; he and James Smith were founders of the Garrick Club of Melbourne in 1856, devoted to study, encourage, and perform the dramatic arts, to whose first meeting he wore, to the amusement of the press, Elizabethan costume.

His amateur performances, his fancy dresses, his 'Shakespearian face' were often seen in theatres, green rooms and halls in Melbourne during the following years. On the arrival in Melbourne in 1855 of the notorious ex-mistress of Franz Lizst and Ludwig of Bavaria, the Irish-born Spanish dancer, Lola Montez, Horne was among the first to greet her with a bouquet of flowers, and was a sincere admirer of her show-manship. Looking into her magnetic eyes, the deepest blue he had ever seen and circled by the darkest lashes, he felt his blood stir. She knew, he discovered, those half-remembered songs and dances he had learned at Vera Cruz, reviving memories of lithe, seductive Mexican girls dancing in the shade. In gratitude he wrote her a dramatic sketch, *The Fair Chameleon* – never published or performed – set in Vera Cruz; he gave her books and flowers. At a supper party at her hotel he saved her – or so he later claimed – from stabbing her current lover with a pair of scissors. Lola's tempestuous image remained a long time in his mind.

Gregarious, garrulous, an oddity in appearance, his greying hair curled in negligent, contrived ringlets, a figure of fun to young observers, and more often than not in some flamboyant costume, he was now at the centre of Melbourne's cultural functions as a matter of course. He was not as successful, however, in finding employment. His repeated applications to the Government and private employers yielded nothing. So prone to feelings of persecution, those feelings had ample nourishment, and the certificate of moral exoneration wrung from Hotham over his dismissal could certainly not soothe them. On the last day of 1855 Hotham died, unmourned by the colony he had governed and unmourned by Horne, but his death failed to alter Horne's chances of employment. In the end it was his friend Archibald Michie who saved him, bravely ignoring his reputation for 'poetic justice' and taking him to work in his chambers as his counsel clerk. It was pleasant work, for Michie's rooms were a hive of conviviality and gave Horne scope for his absorbing interest in criminology, showed him the inner workings of Melbourne government, and provided more of that social life that was now his chief colonial solace. The ubiquitous James Hingston would later recall seeing Horne there, holding his own court, and making a sketch from memory of Sandhurst Military College; his thoughts in these months often turned back to his early life.

Michie's was but a stopgap; more serious work appeared to offer itself in 1856. More than culturally, Victoria was maturing politically from backwardness and the 1856 elections to the recently reorganized Victorian Parliament were to be conducted more democratically than any elections ever held in England; one novelty in the election was the secret ballot, unused as yet in any other country. Michie, a secular liberal and popular speaker, was a candidate. Horne, now familiar with the workings of Victorian government, politically trained at Craven Hill, and in search of a prominent – though unfortunately unrenumerative – position, was open equally to political temptations when approached by friends from Waranga. In a flurry of excitement, in September 1856, he decided to stand for the Victorian electorate of Rodney.

In his naïvety Horne believed he would have an easy victory; in his bumbling overconfidence he believed his natural wit would outmatch his opponents. At the start of October he arrived at Heathcote to find the election fever rising and nearly every tree and post festooned with slogans. On nomination day outside the local hotel he found himself with two adversaries: the 'Government man', and a surprise candidate, an illiterate Welshman named Baragwanath, who was the local storekeeper.

On a show of hands, Hellicar, the Government candidate, was declared first. Horne, whose policy was nationalist, secular and democratic, was called a close second, far ahead of Baragwanath who received only three votes. Horne immediately called, as he was entitled to, for a ballot, and within the next few days there followed an 'election steeplechase' of hard riding and hard drinking to near and distant townships. Horne found his former position of Gold Commissioner a double handicap, for though his 'poetic justice' had befriended a few voters it had confused more; and he was still taken for a Government

man though now against the Government. His dismissal was the seed of
many rumours already circulating and many more quickly started by
his enemies; in his opponents' hands it was a key weapon. He found it
impossible to keep his temper at some meetings:

> to stand fire singly against a mixed mass of educated minds and
> grossly ignorant minds – shrewd men, coached-up by my oppo-
> nents, or drunken brutes sent to prevent me from being heard, or to
> torment me with some offensive and insulting question, turning
> upon personalities, or a local reminiscence monstered or made
> ridiculous; not to mention some outrageous accusation invented by
> some ingenious fabricator. Talk of 'eating dirt!' [he complained]
> that seems to me only one portion of what you have to swallow at an
> election; and the most exasperating part of the business is the
> necessity of keeping your temper; once get into a rage, the whole
> body of electors, friends, and opponents fall into convulsions of
> laughter, and it is over with you for that day; probably you lose
> your election in consequence, since a man in a passion cannot
> suppress his scorn.

His generalizations came from experience. He could neither suppress his own scorn nor the elector's laughter. At his main election
meeting at Rushworth, the obsessive issue of his dismissal arose.
The usual insinuations came from the audience, so Horne promptly
produced his certificate signed by Hotham and declaring his integrity.
At once a wily interjector cried out that he would never trust a man
who had to carry proof of his character in his pocket. Horne lost his
temper. The meeting became a shambles. Horne went on with his
campaigning, dejected and angry. And when one morning, after a
particularly riotous meeting on the previous night, he found himself
clambering over the drunken, snoring bodies of potential electors, he
exclaimed dramatically: 'And these are the men who are to elect me! –
these are the men I am to represent!'

The electors spared him that indignity. At the poll Baragwanath
swept the day. Horne was last, a vote behind Hellicar. It was 'incredible'
– in his opinion a complete reversal of what would have happened in
England and in any 'civilized' country. But no amount of 'yells,
shouts and hisses' of disgruntled electors could change it. The author
of *Orion* was beaten by an illiterate Welsh storekeeper, the poorest, in
money and education, of all successful candidates at the 1856 Victorian
election.

One gesture mitigated Horne's disgrace. His supporters honoured him with a dinner at Heathcote, decorating the wall of the dining room with a huge Orion's Belt made from wild violets gathered from the slopes of the nearby mountains: 'a graceful compliment', wrote Horne greatly touched, 'from the corny hands of men in red flannel-shirts and blue jumpers'. They gave him a rousing farewell also, escorting him in gigs, drays and carts on a royal progress through the town, drinking toasts, shouting imprecations at his rivals, with many a parting glass and protracted handshake before they 'chaired' him on to his horse. The journey back to Melbourne, like the election itself, was anti-climatic. With a late start, on a frisky horse, he was lost by nightfall and spent the darkness in drizzling rain holding his horse and waiting for sunrise. Huddled into a sodden cape, his thoughts were nostalgic, disillusioned, and disconnected, indicative in so many ways of the life he was now leading:

What a motley farce a parliamentary election is! What a mockery of politics, intellect, independence, and conscience, in the majority! In the mother country it used to be a high comedy, alloyed with vulgar farce – with bribery and corruption, equally gross and un-disguised. Perhaps a taint of this yet remains at home; but here, local influences, indifference, or drunkenness prevail . . . How the little mare enjoys the wet grass! She's first-rate for the bush. The moon will rise at two o'clock . . . To whom did I lend my copy of *The Stars and the Earth*? Lola Montes borrowed my Mrs Crowe's *Night Side* – never see *that* again . . . How strange to find in D's smoky little hut [at Murchison] . . . John Mill's *Essay on Liberty*: leaves uncut, though; that explains it: left, no doubt, by some travel-ler whose swag was too heavy . . . I wish I had a pair of worsted socks! So chilly and wet, these cotton things . . . I wish I had never stood . . . I was to walk over the course, was I? No expense – cost nothing. Won't it though! I shall have to pay for being defeated by a bullock-driver.

The life of action was proving tedious; and so too was the freedom from personal ties, at first so intoxicating. His freedom was now even dispiriting: he missed the comfort and security and female concern which his mother, Mary and finally Kate had provided. Moreover, if he was to make a new life in the colony, there were few surer ways of laying foundations for a new life than through a domestic relationship.

He had become friendly – indeed more than friendly – with Jessie

Taylor, an eighteen-year-old Scottish girl born in Aberdeen and now living with her father, a carpenter, in the Melbourne suburb of Fitzroy, less than a mile from Chisholm's home. Jessie Taylor lacked that intense mental sympathy he had hitherto demanded in a woman, but since Kate's retreat he had perhaps felt distrust of intellectual women: certainly he had decided that one both 'lady-like and loving' was a rare combination – perhaps too rare for uncultivated Melbourne. Jessie undoubtedly had considerable powers of attraction, not least her youth. As he had once seemed to feel that in Kate lay perhaps his last chance of sexual love with a young desirable woman, the coming of this second chance a decade later was not easy to reject. Morally, he had little hesitation in living with Jessie. To ignore and deny the 'proudest branch of the instinct for self preservation' had always seemed to him, theoretically at any rate, a sin against humanity; and now it provided the necessary moral justification. He argued vehemently that if the separation of two people was by mutual agreement, and 'for reasons of the strongest kind' – if the partners were now, to all intents 'dead' to one another – it was morally right for either of them to honourably form another attachment. Nevertheless it gave him little pleasure to defy convention, particularly when in mid-year of 1856 Jessie became pregnant. Though only eighteen months before he had clung tenaciously to his marriage he longed now desperately to end a meaningless relationship.

His son (as Horne confided proudly to his diary) was born on Tuesday, February 3, 1857, at '$\frac{1}{2}$ past 5 p.m.' at the mother's home at Moor Street, Fitzroy. He was named Percy Hazlitt Horne, after his father's spiritual ancestors Percy Shelley and William Hazlitt. The birth was officially registered seventeen days later by Jessie herself. Either nervously or brazenly (since the registrar lived in her own street and probably knew her) Jessie gave her name as 'Jessie Horn', affirming that she had married the previous year the child's father, 'Richard Henry Horn', who was by occupation a storekeeper. Poor Jessie, knowing as little of English literature as spelling, said that her son's name was 'Percy Hazlet'. In fact one wonders what Jessie did know about her child's father. However, by her perjury she had managed to appear respectable and make her child appear legitimate. Horne himself only wished there was some way he might make these fictions true.

At least he had found means to support his new dependants. In April 1857, through the kindness of Charles Gavan Duffy, now influential in the Victorian Government, Horne was informed of his appointment as Commissioner for Water and Sewerage, carrying a salary of £400 a year. But the appointment carried also considerable burdens for which he was not really fitted, and it seemed that his colonial formula for failure was again to be enacted. The Water Commission, formed to pipe, drain and sewer the growing town of Melbourne, due to the incompetence of early advisers had been in a constant muddle since its inception in 1853; Horne and his Commissioners had to clear up the muddle. On the last day of 1857, at the grand opening of the town water supply piped from the reservoir at Yan Yean, to enthusiastic cheers from the crowd, a stream of brown mud trickled sluggishly from the ceremonial tap, and from that moment Horne and his colleagues were the butt of constant criticisms as pipes burst, taps ran dry, and citizens died with symptoms that pointed to lead-poisoning. In England, Southwood Smith was privately beseeched by Horne for help. In Melbourne, determined to admit no mistakes, Horne stood up for his policies in public with a vehemence that betrayed his doubts, and drank publicly and proudly a gallon of Yan Yean water in answer to a challenge from Melbourne's leading scientist and the Commission's chief opponent, Dr John Macadam. The uproarious antics and squabbles at the Commissioners' Thursday meetings became popular copy with Melbourne journalists, and Horne indulged his opportunities for publicity with the glee of a born buffoon.

So he was seen outwardly. Inwardly the troubles over Kate, Jessie Taylor, and his purposeless existence continued to sap his spirits. For a few months it had seemed as though there might be a solution to some of the tangles. A few months after Percy Hazlitt's birth Horne had heard first reports of the new English divorce laws, intended to simplify the cumbersome and costly machinery which had hitherto made divorce impossible for the average citizen. At once his hopes had risen, and he began to seek a divorce. Communications with Kate now went on through Mary, or Kate's elder brother, George Foggo, always somewhat hostile to Horne, and now decidedly so. Nevertheless, through difficult and indirect channels he had reached an agreement. At George Foggo's insistence Horne agreed to pay Kate £100 annually, despite her objections that morally she was not entitled to the money. It was not an agreement Horne particularly enjoyed; as he also sent money regularly to Mary, he would now be virtually supporting three households – Kate's, Jessie's and Mary's. However, the price was not too high, for Kate promised to sign any divorce papers he might send.

As soon as he entered the legalities of divorce procedure, his spirits ceased to soar. To obtain divorce under the new laws he found himself obliged publicly to proclaim himself both a deserter and adulterer.

Nevertheless he was presumably prepared to do this, for on September 15, 1857, he parcelled up the divorce papers and posted them to England for Kate to sign. In the same month, however, little Percy Hazlitt had begun to ail; a nurse was engaged for him; and on Tuesday, September 29, at the Melbourne suburb of Emerald Hill, the child died. That Horne was overcome by the death of his seven-months-old son cannot be doubted. The lines he wrote not long after on the death of a friend's child betrayed his own parental grief with unmistakable intensity:

> *He was the idol of my sight!*
> *His soul was its own altar-light!*
> *And now the shrine is dark – the image lost in night.*

Three days after his death Percy Hazlitt's little body was buried in a common paupers' grave, today swathed with grass and shaded by peppercorn trees. Horne could well have afforded a decent burial, and why he allowed such ignomy for his only son can only be attributed to his reluctance to claim the child publicly as his own.

With Percy Hazlitt gone, his plans for divorce, presumably, were pointless. The child alone had held all hopes of the normal future that Horne longed for. The completed divorce papers, dutifully signed by Kate and returned to him the following year, were consigned, like Percy Hazlitt, to the grave. Jessie herself had failed to offer, one supposes, a sufficient cause for the humiliating and difficult procedure involved; nor did their relationship long survive this impasse.

As always, or so it seemed to Horne, it was he, not Kate, who suffered most. Secure in her job as assistant to the London photographer G. S. Nottage, she continued feministically to support herself with the friendly help of the Dickens family. Dickens, in recommending her to her employer, had glowingly described her as 'of remarkably good appearance, a good manner, great perseverance and strength of character, no fine notions of any kind whatsoever', and as one who 'seeks to live by her own industry'. So Kate grew strong as Horne declined; and her independent femininity began to dominate his mind. Those strains in his nature which found fascination in the fatal, frigid woman, punishing, pursuing – the Artemis of *Orion* – suddenly found an actual justification in his wife. In law she was still his wife; in imagination she was fast becoming his chief persecutor.

To one already so adrift, the shock of Percy Hazlitt's death could have only one effect. Automatically it returned his thoughts to the Poet. In the theory of the Poet such sufferings alone had meaning. Even before the child's death his thoughts, disenchanted with the active life, had been slowly returning to the mission. Already he had taken out his manuscripts of *Ancient Idols*, wondering if he ought not still to attempt to salvage something of his message to humanity by preparing the work for publication. With Percy's death the project gained rapid emotional pace, and the struggles of persecutors with the persecuted became once more absorbing subjects. But inevitably the work was put aside as more pressing practical issues demanded his mind, and fears of exposure played upon his conscience. He was not yet ready for the poet's resurrection, and not even the assurances of Mary that 'no time and labour must be spared' (to which, curiously, were added similar assurances from Kate herself) could prevent its abandonment. He began once more to doubt if the message were worth the cost:

> *I have sometimes a dreadful thought*
> *Forcing itself upon my brain,*
> *That all the good by genius wrought*
> *For man's advance may be in vain.*
> *And every noble battle fought*
> *The world will have to fight again.*

The poet on this occasion had flickered only briefly, but nevertheless showed unmistakable signs of reassertion. And it was that same poet, wearing the guise which it had worn long ago in *False Medium*, that inspired his next literary undertaking. At the start of 1859, taking up a book by a former London journalist, Frank Fowler, a racy account written on the author's voyage home of his experiences during three years in New South Wales, Horne felt deep, half-forgotten indignations stirring. Fowler had claimed that the artistic and educated man was well received in Australia. Horne could not let such a statement pass. Moreover Fowler's other remarks – not so favourable – on Australian situations and habits roused in Horne a love for this country that was in so many ways his prison – a love that he had scarcely before expected or revealed. Writing in that attractive disinterested style he had used successfully for Charles Dickens, he produced a book entitled *Australian Facts and Prospects* which Smith Elder published that same year in London. His intention had been threefold: to correct wrong impressions detrimental to Australia, to correct at the dictates of his own sense of persecution the idea that a man of sensitivity and education might materially prosper in Austra-

lia, and to present to the world a glamorized picture of the author of
Orion in the colonies. And on all counts he succeeded: his book was
labelled 'reliable', 'sober', and 'agreeable' – as indeed it was, except for
the autobiography of his Australian career which prefaced it.

That autobiography provoked justifiable jeers in Melbourne from
those who knew him, but it was a personal triumph in England. For
seven years the name of 'Orion' had been lost to the English public;
and now here was he, the self-styled cool adventurer, galloping with
drawn sword across the Australian bush, resting in his lone tent in the
primeval forests, or being harmlessly and engagingly duped by brash
materialist colonials. Scarcely an English critic was unconvinced. He
had turned, enthused the *Athenaeum* reviewer, from dreaming to working, proving the adaptability of true genius. If in Australia Horne's
career was in chaos, it seemed to bandaged English eyes triumphant.

Australian Facts and Prospects ran into a second edition in 1860.
Though his friend Archibald Michie, commenting on the author's
boast that he would achieve his fortune by 'horsemanship in the
Australian bush', could quip that Horne must intend riding horses in a
circus, there poured in a gratifying stream of letters from Robert Bell,
Edmund Ollier and numerous half-forgotten friends. In writing the
book he had realized how closely he identified himself with Australia;
the letters now showed him the opposite side, how keen was his isolation from England and his old life. These letters, too, in renewing his
ties with England, reminded him how many of those he once had loved
were dead; Leigh Hunt's death in 1859 recalled intensest feelings. He
was afraid, he confessed, to read the death notices in the English mail,
for fear what fresh names they might contain.

With the success of *Australian Facts and Prospects*, his jaded desires
to succeed in Australia received fresh life. Suddenly and unexpectedly
his assumed self-confidence had found a legitimate basis. But elation
over its success was countered by what seemed the inevitable spite of
Fate – another defeat. At the end of 1859 in an economic depression the
Water Commission was abolished. Left, as he succinctly put it, 'high
and dry', with no job and insufficient reputation to attract one, he was
once more hurtled into a familiar position: fighting not only anxiety
about his future but also malicious rumours that he was incompetent
and even downright dishonest. He was the popular scapegoat; he was
accused of voting himself a year's salary, and signing the cheque himself, the moment he heard of the intended abolition of his position;
and he was accused of being alone responsible for losing £45,000 in
uncollected rates. These rumours magnified his own feelings of per-

secution, and his feelings did not completely recede when to his surprise the press took his part.

Even worse than immediate persecution was the dispiriting prospect
of starting once more on the search for work. The months stretched
before him wretchedly. Sensibly he threw himself into theatrical
activities, and esoteric schemes for Australian development – into
anything that would take his mind from present problems. He had
already begun an enterprise with an old friend of Waranga days, the
young Burgundian, Ludovic Marie, a storekeeper now turned vig-
neron and surveyor. Along with other less practical schemes for
cochineal-cultivation and kangaroo-farming, he and Marie set about
floating the Goulburn Vineyard Proprietary, a public company of which
Horne was to be honorary secretary and Marie manager. Some incentive had come from a foolhardy business transaction of Horne's in
1854 when on impulse he had bought small blocks of land on the
Goulburn river at Murchison, picturing that village as one day the
St Louis of Australia. Since the village grew slowly he was eager to
promote any venture which might bring prosperity to the district in
which his land speculations depended.

Plans for the vineyard were far from blessed. When a third partner
died mysteriously in the Melbourne scrub, the embryonic company,
already floundering, crashed. With effort Horne managed to gather
supporters, bought more land along the river, and in 1860, among the
lily-sprinkled lagoons and verdant meadows of Tabilk, laid with
success the first of the olive groves, mulberry plantations and rows of
vines. Tabilk still flourishes; and Horne's later claims that he was father
of the Australian wine industry – though his claim ignored long-
planted vineyards in other colonies – had slightly more truth than some
of his other boasts. The vineyard's ultimate success, however, did not
compensate Horne for the money he had lost in his attempt to float
the company.

The promoter of vineyards meanwhile had time to promote his own
plays. In July 1860, hastening down Melbourne's broad, rough streets
to rehearsals at the theatre, Horne had the new and curious experience
of anticipating the performance of one of his own plays. Apart from
those Jacobean reconstructions acted at Sadler's Wells, he had never
seen his work on a stage. Now at Melbourne's Theatre Royal he watched
The Death of Marlowe give 'unqualified satisfaction to many', and he
read next day that the play was a 'masterpiece', lacking only the superior
acting that would have done full justice to its beauty. A few weeks
later, his emotions were the reverse as he read in *The Argus* the most

belittling review of the opening night of *A Spec in China*, a comedy he
had written for the booming Australian stage. His season of fame as a
writer of 'acted' plays lasted only a few weeks.

He was looking his age; and he was probably feeling more than
his fifty-eight years. Noticeably thinner – his weight down to eleven
stone – his hair and moustache almost white, and the pouchy flesh
around his eyes much flabbier, that melancholy that was always in his
face was now much more pronounced. The eyes looking from photographs of that time were tired and sad. And with good reason, for life
now seemed merely a struggle to make a little money and to preserve a
little fame. Mask it as he might by play-acting, the mask did not even
quite convince himself. Bereft of his mission, he was bereft of his
proper self.

From Carlton he had moved four miles away to the seaside settlement of St Kilda, to the Star and Garter, a hotel in Robe Street within
sight and sound of the sea where he swam most days. Soon, fortunately,
the affairs of the small community began to absorb him. He lectured on
the English poets to appreciative audiences in the hotel dining-room,
and resurrected his old lectures on Italy and Ireland at the local
Mechanics Institute. But the sea was his greatest solace. Attracted
always, like his hero Shelley, to that symbol of peace, immortality and
destruction, Horne found both satisfaction and forgetfulness in daily
swims at Captain Kenney's bathing ship – an old brig that was
anchored in a fenced enclosure by the sandy beach at the end of his
street. With those skills he had acquired in Edmonton streams and
Mexico, Horne was a star performer amongst the leading athletes and
professional men who met at Kenney's, winning gold and silver medal-
lions and cups and a claret jug. At the competitions which the bluff,
befreckled captain held for his clientele, bands would play and onlookers would crowd the narrow bridge connecting ship and shore to
watch, for the sum of two and six a head, the sight of Horne cavorting
naked in the water or swimming bound hand-and-foot. The Melbourne
Punch, like Dickens more than a decade earlier, found this view of
Horne not the most palatable. 'Horn, the lusty Horn,' quipped one
reporter describing a contest, also possibly implying that Horne's
amatory life was common knowledge in journalistic circles. But no
amount of criticism – and Horne did not altogether dislike the image of
buffoon – could destroy the delight and elation he felt in the water:

Smile at the storm, exult amidst the foam
The rolling squadron and the sparkling spray:

Feel that the ocean is thy natural home,
Though briefly, yet with soul that knows no clay:
Thou hast no weight of body, heart, or mind –
A charmed life, for none but ye designed.

Yet even that elation had undertones. His feats at Kenney's were part of an uneasy pattern. He resented and fought against the diminution of his physical powers as intensely as twenty years before he had fought against the waning of his poetic faculty. And just as that had produced in him a vigorous intellectual Indian summer, now it produced the same in physical terms, heightened perhaps by an environment which set such store on physical prowess. He frequently frolicked at Kenney's; he took part in an impromptu race at the Zoological Gardens carrying a man of six foot four on his shoulders, giving his opponent in addition fifty yards start, and was disappointed when he lost. In Robe Street, in a vacant garden, he set up parallel bars and exercised daily like 'a pair of Kilkenny cats'. He could not bear the idea of physical disintegration that age must eventually bring.

No amount of vigour, however, could disguise his poverty late in 1860. Nor could it disguise the ineffectiveness of his schemes to counter it. From the comfort of the Star and Garter (closed when the landlord, who boasted his abilities to fulfil the most recherché of requirements, became presumably so obliging that the police condemned his house as a haunt of prostitutes) Horne moved to a cheaper cottage down the street, one of a terraced pair owned by a garrulous Irishwoman named Mother McGuirk. Into those damp tiny rooms he crowded his personal effects – cooking pots alongside Piranesi engravings, fine guitars and rare editions. In his isolation those solaces, sent out presumably by faithful Mary, rubbed against his guns and saddles and exercising dumb-bells: the poet rubbing shoulders with the man. He was now desperately poor. The vineyard scheme had taken his savings, and nothing came in. Those fears which had haunted him since his decision to write had come to pass, not as he had imagined in a garret in Grub Street, but in a degraded colonial cottage. Moreover, troubles with Kate once more inflicted themselves upon him. Never happy with his promise to pay Kate a yearly allowance, he had, in 1859, sent only part of that allowance, excusing himself by pretending that Victoria was commercially sick, and enclosing in lieu a revised but quite unmarketable old play which he insisted Charles Dickens should help Kate to sell. Understandably the Foggos and Dickens alike were indignant. Now, in 1860, Horne was like the child who cried fire. Victoria was suffering from a genuine commercial depression, and Horne was one of its victims. When the promised allowance once more failed to arrive the Foggo brothers sent threats. Shielded by distance but fearful of what his brothers-in-law might do to his English reputation, he found no alternative but to pay them off with what he could.

In such a predicament any work was welcome. At the start of 1861 he began a lecture tour, for lecturing was one of his few remaining marketable skills. Like a 'wandering minstrel' he travelled through Victorian provincial centres repeating his old lectures on Italy and Ireland and adding to his repertoire three new lectures: *Songs of Seven Nations* which he illustrated with his own voice and guitar; *Insane Kings* (insanity in historical figures having long attracted him); and *The Causes of Success in Life*, presumably modelled on Hazlitt's similarly-named lecture. This last lecture, when reports filtered back to England, understandably caused mirth among his former friends, particularly Dickens. His few remaining friends only wished Horne himself could have followed his own sensible advice.

The tours were strenuous. Bad roads, draughty halls, draughtier hotel rooms, damp beds, and above all his advancing years made him complain of the physical misery. He caught bronchitis in one town and lost his voice; he returned with a 'villainous "something" at the hip joint'. Though his tours may have placated his restlessness and satisfied his urge to be busy and self-reliant, financially they were a fiasco. The public response was far from gratifying; the lectures were undeniably tedious. The towns, moreover, were often small and rough: at the mining town of Talbot, he complained, he was unable even to find a boy to snuff his stage candle and bring him a glass of water. After five months of intermittent touring he calculated both his profits and expenses at £12: the net result was a very bad cold.

It was much the same when, at the end of 1861, he clutched at an invitation to stand again for Parliament. He had sworn never again to be so foolhardy, but he was now prepared to try anything; he had been disappointed when nothing came of an earlier invitation a year or so before. This time a government association was to sponsor him, paying all expenses. They promised him, moreover, the hope of victory in the electorate centred on Belfast, a small sea port in Victoria's Western District.

Horne had misgivings, both intellectual and material. The Government policy was protectionist, which he felt was unfitting for a disciple of W. J. Fox. Financially, too, he felt doubtful whether the venture would be profitable, though the association soothed his fears and promised to pay. His opponents at least were intelligent and experienced: and amongst those who travelled with the candidates was the influential Charles Gavan Duffy. It was thus a formidable political company abrim with intrigue that assembled in Melbourne in the ship that was to sail west to Belfast. Duffy, misquoting Tennyson aptly and wittily, quipped that surely he did not see great Orion sloping slyly to the West, at which Horne laughed uneasily.

When he reached Belfast, Horne realized his apprehensions were not ill founded. At the port – austere basalt buildings huddled on a windswept plain – he confessed he felt like a 'winter robin' alone in its feathers. His opponents were, he discovered, rather unscrupulous, and public feeling was not in his favour. On a show of hands he was well defeated, but he called, as before, for a poll. At the polls he was equally well defeated. Cruellest of all, he was left with the inevitable and confusing debts for carts, placards, candles, a clarinet player, a bell man; and not half of these debts he now found were covered by the association. And over his contest hung a personal shadow. As he went one day to the bleak sea shore, pounded by violent surf and littered with dark boulders – so impressive a sight that he would later feelingly record it – his thoughts strayed from the immediate election issues to the past: to memories of Elizabeth Barrett. The latest mail from England contained another of those dreaded announcements – she, too, was dead.

Once again he had failed, wasting his talents and energies. Once again he was sensible of his mental and physical isolation –

> *See'st thou that shipwreck'd sailor in his cave?*
> *That anchorite in his secluded grot?*
> *That man who lives alone in a dark hut,*
> *Whose patch of garden with the heavens above*
> *Seems all his world? . . .*
> *Each of these men perhaps has had, and still*
> *Endures, a thrilling tenderness of heart –*
> *Memories of trustful sensibilities,*
> *Wasted on objects all insensible,*
> *Unworthy, or ungrateful, yet even now*
> *Felt as of old in that sore-wounded breast,*
> *Of all affections capable, and thoughts*
> *Of deepest, sweetest love, and generous aims –*
> *But having found no spot wherein to root*
> *The fibres of his nature's truest strength,*

Retires to moulder out – unseen – unknown –
Unweeping, and unwept. Oh heart, be still!

He needed renewal; and he sought it as before through sexual love.
Jessie Taylor had left him some time previously, but it was not so
difficult to find a fit successor: he was now past worrying over lack of
mental sympathy or moral implications. All that he was aware of with
M. J. H., as he referred to her constantly in his diaries (her full name is
never given), was his need of her. At fifty-nine, conscious of his waning
physical powers, wretchedly alone, he was a waiting victim for her
predatory femaleness.

By the start of 1862 she was living in his Robe Street cottage,
reduced now to a few barely furnished rooms. In those jumbled
quarters, alive with lizards after rain and damp with mould, his etchings
and library and guitars still stubbornly clung to, he and M. J. H. co-
existed uneasily. She was a milliner and dressmaker with no time for his
intellectual pretensions. There can be little doubt that her main
interest lay in what she could wring from him. And Horne for his
part depended so on her and was so infatuated that he denied her nothing. Aware of her dishonesties, her schemes, her caprices, he was a
willing dupe, and as he set out on another lecture tour to support them
both (once more to Belfast and surrounding towns to lecture for the
Separation League, dedicated to converting the district into a separate
Australian colony) he fretted and agonized, at the same time recog-
nizing his folly. When the mail coach drew into those dusty Victorian
towns he rushed to the post for her letters, invariably to find she had
not written. 'Enraged,' he admitted to his diary, 'at no letters from her
by overland post.' Invariably too, returning to Melbourne, he found
his money squandered on her personal trifles and the rent unpaid.
Though he protested he always forgave her. In a community where
men so outnumbered women she could too easily have found a richer,
younger lover: he was entirely at her mercy.

Yet these degrading, agonizing months were producing a gradual
change, impossible perhaps in other circumstances. His drifting at last
began to take direction. The man in his nature was finished: an undoubted failure. The poet alone remained to restore him: it clamoured
for reassertion. And so it was that he now moved back to the comforting arms of the poetic mission. He began once more to write: an epic
based on his Australian experiences and two poetic dramas – probably
the first genuine poetry he had written for fifteen years.

With relief he felt his loyalties to the mission returning; and with

similar feelings of relief he allowed his claims on the mission to reassert themselves also. The Royal Literary Fund helped certain in-
digent literary men, might it not now help him? Certainly, of any man
alive he felt he had a claim: moreover, had he not advocated aid for
impoverished writers from his earliest literary years, and had not he
personally helped poor Leigh Hunt? With this in mind he considered
writing to Robert Bell, who had shown himself a true friend by praising his *Australian Facts and Prospects* and who was known to have
some influence with the Literary Fund.

When at the end of 1861 Horne wrote to Bell he was intent on
showing how far colonial insensitivity had reduced him, and thus
strengthening his claim for public assistance. It was a curious letter
with a contrivedly pathetic tone and full of barefaced lies – amusing in
the light of the true facts – and it was also a tragic letter in that Horne
had largely convinced himself that it was true. Always, on his own
admission, he had been at the mercy of his imagination; his trouble on
his return from Mexico in distinguishing fact from fantasy would seem
to have been an intensified symptom of a common condition. Now with
advancing age, and an advancing sense of futility, that dividing line
between imagination and reality seemed to have become mercifully
hazier.

He was living, he told Bell, in abject poverty at St Kilda, supping
an oatmeal and water, quite alone without even the comfort of a dog
(ignoring the unignorable M. J. H.). He was unable to fulfil financial
obligations to anyone, even to Mrs Horne, whom he felt did not expect
help (ignoring the incessant threats of the Foggo brothers). Bell, he
continued, must not be fooled by the tone of his other writings –
presumably the boasts of his colonial success which had appeared in
Australian Facts and Prospects. A blessed and characteristic 'elasticity',
he confessed, gripped him when he gripped his pen; and in fact he had
far from made his fortune in the colonies. The reasons for his failure
he did not really understand. But then really he knew – had always
known – the answer: genius was despised. Surely if any author ever
deserved help, he did: 'Can I find no friend to put forth a hand for me
in this far-off country?'

Undoubtedly Bell had heard it all before. Nor was he likely to be
deluded into thinking that philistine Australia or the implied poetic
destiny was the cause of all Horne's troubles. But past affection was still
sufficient to override objections and he rose magnificently to the
occasion. Within a month he had rounded up the necessary referees:
G. H. Lewes, Charles Knight, and ironically, Charles Dickens, who

very fairly attested to Horne's 'perseverance, zeal, good faith, steadiness and integrity'. Bell made the necessary application on Horne's behalf to the Royal Literary Fund, and by 1862 – five months after Horne's first request – the sum of £80 had come to his aid. Horne, rather unwisely, forgot his past assertions of poverty in thanking the Literary Fund's governors, and admitted to owning rare books and pictures.

To the improvident couple £80 was only pocket money and soon disappeared. M. J. H. became ill and could not work. Once more Horne was urgently forced to find work or money, and in July and August 1862, apparently confident after his success with Bell, he plucked two more names from the past, Monckton Milnes and Bulwer Lytton. To these eminent men, along with Knight and Bell and Dickens, he submitted another scheme. The unrealities of this, along with the unrealities contained in the letters, form a startling combination: at no earlier time in his life had his lack of contact with reality been more apparent. His scheme was that he should fill the chair of English Literature at the small University of Melbourne, an optimistic scheme in so far as no formal move to create such a chair was to be made until nearly two decades later.

Neither Lytton nor Milnes, Bell, Dickens nor Knight, responded with enthusiasm; even if they had, it was unlikely that their pens would have cut much academic ice. In vain Horne waited until the last day of January 1863. The Chancellor of the University of Melbourne, Mr Justice Redmond Barry, was then in London, and if Horne's hopes were to succeed, Barry must be persuaded at once by Horne's old London friends. Desperately, Horne tried another avenue. He had heard recently from the retired proprietor of the Melbourne *Argus*, Edward Wilson, of a visit to the Brownings in Florence shortly before Elizabeth's death, during which Wilson's mention of Horne's name had evoked exclamations of affection. Horne was both touched and grateful when he heard the story; he also knew his chance. The widowed Robert Browning was now back in London, and it was to him that Horne now wrote, breaking a silence of twelve years. It, too, was a curious letter: supplicating, demanding, affectionate, in places barely making sense. Browning, at Horne's request, was to approach Barry on his behalf. Browning was not unfriendly, but he presumably ignored the request. A few months later Horne complained that the chair of English had vanished into 'thin air'.

At the same time it appeared that M. J. H. was also about to vanish into the sea air. At the end of January she left him, to take 'rooms for herself' and commission 'some millinery and dressmaking business'. She was only gone, he tried to reassure himself, beyond his *immediate* protection, but in fact, as he possibly knew at heart, she was going troublesomely out of his life. 'I represented to her, at any rate, to remain at least till her health was thoroughly restored, but she insisted that her future interests were best consulted by leaving me.' As for the money she had squandered during his absence on another lecture tour – some £30 in three weeks – 'I made no reproaches but I felt she had broken faith with me.' Yet still he clung to her, unable to deny her anything, and gave her more money and the parting promise of another £20 when he could raise it. She also took furniture and linen by his 'tacit consent' from the cottage. It was indeed a day of reckoning, and one of the most pitiable in his life.

Through February, March and April she continued to visit him, her visits coinciding with the instalments of her £20. At the start of May, after an evening out, Horne returned to Robe Street to find his rooms broken into and articles gone. He suspected her but he called the police. His suspicions had been right, and the articles were recovered. Five days later he met her at the St Kilda post office, in an embarrassed encounter. Tentatively he offered his hand which she accepted. The incident left him shaken and he recounted in his diary: 'Reconciliation – we shook hands. Hope it is a success on her part.' He knew by now every facet of her mercenary nature and yet it made no difference. She could no more help her shallowness than he his irrational emotions: it was a situation in which both were powerless, and his only satisfaction lay in continuing to love her whatever pain she inflicted on him. 'In after life,' he remarked sadly, one mourns chiefly over those 'whose natures were not capable of continuity. But they could no more help that, than the others could help their infatuation.'

He felt so ill, poor and despondent: his sense of perspective had receded badly. He must, he decided, publish a last volume of poems before it was too late, for his despair convinced him that his life was almost over. Accordingly he wrote again to Bulwer Lytton for £50 to publish such a book. He received no reply. Even Horne, in later and saner moments, had to admit that the silence was not surprising.

By May 1863 M. J. H. had so far exhausted his funds that he begged Mrs McGuirk to reduce his rent to ten shillings a week. Yet still he sent her money. At the end of May he was clearly approaching destitution. There was no alternative but to write once again to Robert Bell. 'I live', he wrote, 'quite alone' in an existence from 'hand to mouth . . . every week the last guinea goes, there is no certainty about the next'.

On concluding his last lecture tour (the one, in fact, when M. J. H. had overspent) he had returned with just enough to pay 'my small arrears of Christmas and other bills'; life since then had been incessant struggling. There was nothing for it, however much it grieved him, but to beg the generous help of Bell and the Literary Fund.

Yet towards the end of that letter there were moments of truth. He had abandoned clearly the lost cause of 'horsemanship' and all the jingling pretences that went with it. He had returned to his true vocation of literature, though he admitted 'an utter absence of a field' for literature in Australia. Truest of all, he recognized his isolation. At 'this great distance' it was impossible to communicate successfully with friends or public in England; in Australia genius and poverty equally made for a different type of isolation. He was the outcast, the 'shipwreck'd sailor', no longer adrift but – scarcely bearable – mentally alone. Compared with that fate, poverty and discomfort were negligible: 'To me these trivial objectionables would be no hardship, were it not for their effect upon my mind, when contemplating the *future* of my present isolation.' 'I cannot help but feel,' he told Bell '. . . that the shadows are slowly but certainly *closing* in upon me . . .'

Before the Literary Fund could reply with another £60, Horne's future had been settled. Heeding at last his persistent requests for work, the Victorian Government had magnanimously made him the Registrar of Mines at the Blue Mountain, probably the most lawless and primitive of all Victorian gold fields, a place 'removed from all civilized nicety' and the ultimate in Horne's colonial isolation.

Chapter 19

The Blue Mountain

It was cold and tempestuous, swept by 'hail-storms and hurricanes, with a burning sun next day – barren and almost inaccessible . . . owing to bogs and swamps'. Horne went on to describe Blue Mountain, sixty miles north-west of Melbourne, as 'the Siberia of all the goldfields'. Spending £60 which had just arrived from the Royal Literary Fund on a 'bog-and-bush horse' and surveying instruments, he had set off for Blue Mountain at the end of June 1863 with a mixture of relief and despair, a mood not lightened when he saw his home. A dismal hut made of planks and logs and measuring a bare fifteen by ten, it made Mother McGuirk's a palace by comparison. The settlement itself of tents and huts was as rough as any he had encountered: the most degraded, it was said by the Melbourne papers, of any in the colony. In the next few months Horne would see many a colourful lawless character who would long remain in his memory – Gentle Annie, a miner's wife who declaring herself wronged drew a cleaver on the crowd in the butcher's shop; Mountain Mag, convicted on her eighth charge of drunkenness in a few months; and 'Homeric' fighting miners who sank to their waists in mud in the main street. In its primitive vigour Blue Mountain reached heroic heights.

His pitying Melbourne acquaintances had done their best to extricate him from the post and arrange something better. Even the newspapers had shown sympathy though a few correspondents had pointed out that his past government service did not qualify him for anything exalted. *The Argus* unkindly quipped that though he might have scaled Parnassus, Blue Mountain would not prove so easy; with 'true poetic spirit he must learn to find good in everything – even in disparate diggers, grog shanties, all the riot and romance of a new rush'. And it was advice that Horne appeared to follow. Possessing such unpredictable powers of adaptation and that zest since childhood for an atmosphere of vigour and violence, he began to make a surprising best of it. His days he spent in clerical matters and deciding petty mining disputes – work fortunately that was neither as demanding nor responsible as that at Waranga. His nights he often spent hunting by lantern-light the possum and the wallaby, or alone in his hut playing his guitar, sending through the dense eucalypt forests the strains of Beethoven and Mendelssohn. From St Kilda he had also brought the manuscripts of lyrical dramas; one entitled *Og* following the themes of *Ancient Idols*, showed to what extent he had reassumed the Romantic Poet's mantle. Gone from his work were those notions of the progressive poetry he had struggled with in 1852.

Into his daily life was implanted, by the rigours and loneliness of Blue Mountain, a sense of the nobility of the merest human existence and a sense of the precariousness and preciousness of all human life. Close to death, close to pain and violence and elemental nature, that part of his Romantic temperament that had been so long dormant in the sordidness of Melbourne suddenly flowered. Though there were undoubtedly many times when he bewailed his other isolation – sometimes he even saw Blue Mountain as a grave in which he would be 'buried alive' for the rest of his days – those 'savage solitudes' were working in Horne a miracle. He felt exalted and inspired. The return to the mission was complete. He began to write as he had not written since he arrived in Australia.

The fruit of this renewal was a lyrical drama, *Prometheus, The Fire-bringer*. Drafted as *Orion* had been in England with Leonhard Schmitz, rewritten in the dismal log hut, the subject of the drama was central to his loyalties and temperament: the suffering, mutilated hero, punished eternally for lighting the divine fire of wisdom in men's hearts. Just as in London he had once lived himself in *Orion*, now in the Australian wilderness he was Prometheus, Victoria was the wild Greek shore, and the wooded rise of Blue Mountain his Mount Aetna; he was the hero 'doomed' by Fate, denied by men, but dedicated still to imparting truth and love to an ungrateful universe. Writing far into the night 'without books – without any society – impressed at times with the precariousness of human life', he finished the play early in 1864, only to lose the first manuscript. Like Carlyle with the *French Revolution* he was forced to sit down and rewrite from memory. This second draft, finished by April 1864, he sent to Edinburgh to Leonhard Schmitz himself for correction and publication. The additional work, however, was not wasted. At the age of sixty-one, after almost two decades of poetic silence, Horne had written a play equal to any he had ever written. Nor were the critics slow to recognize it. In both hemispheres the critical notices showed surprise and even downright amazement that so uncivilized a setting could have produced so excellent a work, containing, as one critic perceptively remarked, both 'the earnest sympathies of the poet, and the personal experiences of the man'. Horne had become the unofficial Laureate of Victoria. It was a doubtful victory, however, when poets ranked lower in the average colonial mind than publicans. Moreover not many copies of the play were sold, although an Australian edition appeared the following year, dedicated like its Scottish predecessor to Schmitz.

Though Horne continued to write, it would seem that *Prometheus* had exhausted him. And the mood of exaltation, though it would recur throughout his time at Blue Mountain, had grown less satisfying. Of the sincerity of those feelings, however, there can be no doubt. To Dickens he sent a poem for inclusion in *All the Year Round*, revealing both his fading poetic power and how profound was the faith that Blue Mountain had engendered in him.

From his hut he strays forth, to gaze on the night,
The old starry story, with mists round the dome;
And, below, 'tis a squalid and desolate sight;
A hideous monotony – mud-gleams and gloom.

Beyond, sleeps the forest, all dark; and, between,
Gold-diggings, deserted, like huge graveyards yawn
(The Last Day long pass'd from poor earth's work'd-out scene),
From whose gaps both the soul and the body are gone.

Back-gazing, he broods on his lonely retreat;
The blue-curtain'd lattice gleams faint o'er the swamp;
No living thing waits there his footsteps to greet,
He will find a void cell, and his time-waning lamp.

His arms are grown hard by the swing of the axe;
His palms dry and grain'd by the sap of the wood;
His hair, once all waves, now wind-hackled flax,
But he feeleth no change in his blood.

The Winds are gone down, and the night-hours are dead,
Yet silence so sad that it hints of no dawn;

The Blue Mountain hurricanes rang round his head,
Then left him in statue-trance, firm though forlorn.

In this Hades of hopelessness, think not he grieves,
Or feels his strong soul-life one moment despond
He believes in himself, because he believes
In the Voice of a Spirit beyond!

He was back with the mission; he had refound himself. And yet within him ran as ever that stream of feeling that drove him away from the rarified romantic isolation of Blue Mountain to the conviviality of Melbourne. Those journeys to Melbourne had at first been infrequent: undertaken on horseback, often taking days and ending with Horne losing his way and spending bleak nights in the dark gum-forests. With the dwindling of mining activity, however, his presence was, he felt, expendable; and leaving instead a *locum*, he would ride or take a coach to the train which now extended to nearby Kyneton, and within three hours find himself back at those tiny rooms he had continued to rent from Mother McGuirk. His absences indeed became so frequent that they irked his superior, the Secretary for Mines, Robert Brough Smyth, a brilliant geologist and anthropologist who was prey to persecutory fears that were possibly even greater than Horne's own. It was unfortunate that Horne should be serving under such a man, for their mutual personalities, in some ways so similar, inevitably conflicted. Sitting, Horne reported sadly, in his St Kilda 'hermitage', contemplating his 'grape-vine, and Virginia creeper, and passion flowers – and taking a breath for a new lease of a few days', his leisure was interrupted by messages, reprimands or trivial reports sent over by that 'damned Jack-in-Office' and 'half-mad Bureaucrat', Brough Smyth. Yet despite the reproofs and interference, he managed to cram into those 'few days' in Melbourne – which more often ran into a few weeks and even months – a vast number of activities.

Since *Prometheus* he had become indisputably the literary celebrity of Melbourne. Those cultural stirrings evident in the early eighteen-fifties had become more pronounced in Melbourne's eighteen-sixties and the periodicals were more numerous and less imitative of their English counterparts. The most notable writers gathered then at a low-roofed bookshop in Bourke Street owned by Henry Tolman Dwight, Horne's colonial publisher and a man of education and intelligence, whose back parlour nourished a literary salon long after remembered as 'the only confraternity of literary men of any importance known to Australia'. Its members were mostly young, with few exceptions under forty; boisterous, riotous men whose feverish talk, hard drinking, and practical jokes hid the unstable inner melancholy that – again with few exceptions – disturbed them all. In this salon Horne was said to be the leader: a living symbol of the Old World's Romantic Literature who inspired budding exponents of the New Literature with dedication to the mission: a man much lionised by those who hung around the literary fringes and won vicarious notoriety by recalling later the figure in the cloak and corkscrew curls.

How far Horne influenced this earliest Australian literary movement is doubtful. Of the four major figures of the movement, to only one can any definite evidence of Horne's influence be traced. It seems unlikely that Horne knew the Australian poet Henry Kendall, then a civil servant living in New South Wales, though he awarded him first prize in a literary competition. It seems equally unlikely that he knew well the depressive horseman-poet Adam Lindsay Gordon. Certainly he knew the choleric former bank clerk Marcus Clarke, in the earlier drafts of whose novel *For the Term of His Natural Life* Horne is said himself to figure. For the fourth alone is there sufficient proof of Horne's influence. Without doubt Horne did befriend the least-famous member of the quartette, the young artist and poet George Gordon Macrae, with whom he corresponded for over ten years. His letters to Macrae, so revealing of the commanding self-image he hoped to project, and equally revealing of the unrealistic figure he hoped to conceal, are some of the most interesting of his Australian career.

On the whole, Melbourne was more tolerant of the caperings and antics of 'Orion', now that their bitterer edge had been blunted at Blue Mountain. He was even fêted occasionally, to his intense delight; the visiting actor Walter Montgomery gave a dinner in his honour at a St Kilda hotel, with 'all sorts of unexpected honours', at which (Horne admitted coyly to friends) he became very drunk and sang and played the guitar with less than his usual perfection. He was now recognized as Melbourne's official literary spokesman, and relishing and obedient to this role he was ready with his play or poem whenever the occasion emerged. When in 1866 G.V. Brooke, the tragedian, was drowned in the Bay of Biscay on his return voyage to Australia, his friends were stunned, charitably forgetting the scandal that he had left Melbourne in company with an actress not his wife; and it was Horne who supplied the words for the *Threnodia*, 'sung very sweetly' at the Brooke Memorial Concert given by the Garrick Club. Horne, worried that insufficient time would be allowed for the encores to his item, was moved to remind the committee that he had had '*bouquets* thrown to me on the stage by ladies – the lead being taken by Lola Montez and Miss Catherine Hayes'; the Garrick Club must be prepared for similar demonstrations. Similarly it was his lyric masque *The South Sea Sisters*, sung to music written by a Melbourne musician C. E. Horsely, which delighted audiences in October 1866 at the opening of Melbourne's Intercolonial Exhibition. Its aboriginal choruses, rhythmically designed to suggest a corroboree, brought the audience to its feet, a triumph that no bewailing of critics next day could destroy. Though he grumbled that his only reward was 'a jolly supper party', his true feelings were otherwise. In Melbourne, as a poet, he at last had recognition.

As usual there was another side to the picture. Those frequent leaves in Melbourne had produced one dramatic result. On September 9, 1866, having requested a month's leave of absence, he had hurried to Melbourne for the birth of a child which he recorded in his diary: 'Bella Isolda, born Jeffcott St, Flagstaff Hill'. Of the identity of Bella's mother – or even of her father though one assumes it was Horne – there can now be no means of knowing. In the following month, under his direction, the baby was brought to St Kilda in the care of a nurse for whose payment Horne made himself responsible. For seven months the child remained there, visited, one assumes, by Horne on his frequent trips to Melbourne. Certainly his memory of Percy Hazlitt was brought home to him in those months, and in February 1867 he noted in the diary to which he confided such feelings: 'Percy Hazlitt Horne would have been ten years old this day, had he lived.' But the fate that had befallen Percy Hazlitt pursued Bella; at seven months she sickened and on April 17, 1867, 'Poor little Bella Isolda died.' Receiving the news at Blue Mountain, Horne rushed to Melbourne the following day; it was Easter, and sorrowfully he stayed on for the rest of the week. With Bella's death another tie with Australia had gone and another pain added to what was already an insupportable burden.

His thoughts turned increasingly to London: 'black-faced London'. There were times when standing alone at night in the forest at Blue Mountain, watching the night sky through the ragged waving tree-tops, he questioned his senses, wondering might this not really be a midnight wood in England, and tomorrow morning might he not see again his old dear friends? It was a fantasy he found both thrilling and harrowing; the thought of going back had an unreality he could not cope with. Nevertheless in July 1867, three months after Bella's death,

234

he had gone so far as tentatively to book a passage in the *Great Britain* to London. No personal tie, no still lingering hope of that fortune by 'horsemanship', remained to keep him. With the return to the mission, a return to London followed almost automatically, for he could only fulfil his mission there. He had now no need to escape from his destiny.

The one delaying factor was the hope of some sort of Government testimonial to compensate him for services rendered and for his dismissal from the Water Commission. How far he had a legitimate claim to compensation is difficult now to assess, but certainly Michie and Gavan Duffy – who despite past differences were still his friends – did their best on his behalf. Also, governmental troubles had halted his salary; it was not the best time to leave. He therefore cancelled his passage, and at the end of the year was still at Blue Mountain.

With the decline of gold-mining in the forest he was able to move from the rough log hut at Newbury, at the foot of the Blue Mountain, to comparative civilization four miles away. He took rooms in a boarding house in the wooden village of Trentham, becoming a member of the local dramatic group and the equally dramatic Oddfellows' lodge. Here too he made the curious decision, between the months of September and November 1867, to change his second Christian name from humdrum Henry to exotic Hengist. It was true that he had never liked the name of Henry; nevertheless this scarcely seems a sufficient reason for changing it, even when allied to his own explanation that he had out of gratitude taken the name of a Mr Hengist who had saved his life. Of the alleged Mr Hengist nothing is known; it is not even certain that he existed. All that is certain is that in November 1867 Horne came to Melbourne to join in celebrations on the arrival of Queen Victoria's son, the Duke of Edinburgh, and was styled as Richard Henry Hengist Horne, shortened soon after to Richard Hengist Horne. For a man of Horne's devious and troubled mental makeup, such an explanation for changing his name is unconvincing. The deeper reasons, at this distance, however, are impossible to probe.

As Richard Hengist he therefore came to Melbourne at the end of the year to join the festivities for the Royal Duke. He had two fingers in this Melbourne pie: his old friend Leonhard Schmitz had been the prince's tutor and therefore provided Horne with necessary letters of introduction; and Horne in his role of unofficial laureate had been commissioned to write verses for the royal welcome. A new 'odaic cantata', *Galatea Secunda*, its music by Joseph Summers, was Horne's offering and was received by critics lukewarmly and by the public with enthusiasm and by the Duke not at all, for he did not attend the performance. Horne himself, despite the letters from Schmitz, swam only on the edges of the royal party, and instead was forced to court the more accessible Oswald Brierly, the marine artist who accompanied the royal steam yacht *Galatea*. It was no doubt this, in part at least, that prompted Horne's claim that the Duke had personally expressed regret at not being able to take Horne back to England in the royal yacht. 'You see,' Horne wrote to a former Melbourne friend, the actor Harry Edwards now living in San Francisco, 'you see it is a man-of-war, and not his pleasure yacht. H.R.H. had previously requested that I should be presented to him, and I left my wilderness here and went to Toorak expressly for the purpose. I dare say I might have turned all this sort of thing to personal account but you know I have no touch of the snob . . .' Apparently there was no basis for Horne's story. Hearing it or reading it in the papers – for Horne gave the statement to the press – Melbourne society was abuzz with laughter, much of it malicious. In England Anna Mary Howitt, to whom the episode was reported from Australia by her brother Alfred, wrote in reply: 'Who would have put that in but the author of "Orion" and what but blindness or vanity could prevent anyone seeing the true meaning.' But it was less vanity than disorder. Increasingly he was believing only what it was kind to believe; reality was varnished by a pleasing fantasy.

Such tendencies were discernible in his latest literary project. He was writing now in earnest an epic based on his Australian experiences, begun fitfully during the years of misery at St Kilda. To be called *John Ferncliff* and illustrating his experiences 'not only in Melbourne, Ballarat, Castlemaine and the great cities of our present civilization, but also in the wilds and scenery of the bush, among remote goldfields, and isolated settlers, and among the aborigines in the primeval forests', it was to be a legacy to the colony that had sheltered him. Through the last half of 1867 he agonized over its composition and its publication, carrying on a double correspondence with Henry Tolman Dwight, its projected publisher, and George Gordon Macrae, its projected artist, that betrayed his impatience, self-deceptions and frustration. '*Haste*' he scrawled across his letters to Dwight, or '*Immediate*', overloading his meaning with reproofs, demands, imperious orders. To Dwight he was in a fever over lack of advance orders for the book and in agonies over the slowness of the completed proofs, though now and again he lightened the tone of his letters with a touch of affection or endearing vanity: 'P.S. I send you an itinerant bush photographer's picture of me as an axe man. He took me, or caught me.' To Macrae he was rather more paternal but often just as peremptory: 'What am I to think or believe, or imagine of your prolonged silence.' Even on the details of the artist's illustrations, he was full of fuss:

I allude to corroboree scene [he wrote fractiously] at the great fire, where they are baking a *man* enveloped in clay (let us hope a black-fellow, taken in battle). An emu striding around the blaze! An Aurora Australis overhead, above and beyond the volumes of smoke. Make preliminary sketches of this, and etch it last of all. It is a great opportunity for you to show *London* Artists what real bush-knowledge is, as well as Australian Art.

Through 1868 he continued to thunder from Blue Mountain at *John Ferncliff's* delays: a game part in fun, part in earnest, from which he obviously drew much satisfaction; yet despite his demands and cajolery only the prospectus of the book managed to appear. Meanwhile he kept to himself another manuscript that was equally indicative of his state of mind. He had returned, heavily, to religious preoccupations. Into a notebook marked 'for private circulation' he had pasted a manuscript expressing views more personal than any he had made since *Ancient Idols*, many of them views confirmed by his recent reading of Ernest Renan's conroversial *Life of Christ*. Those findings in *Unknown Seas or Thoughts on the Future Life*, by which he called his manuscript, betrayed transformations in his most ingrained thinking. How much those recent years had exhausted him – how weary he was, how disillusioned – was never reflected more clearly than in these arguments. Even death, that old and terrifying obsession, had lost its sting in comparison with the sufferings of life. Deliberate martyrdom was no more a noble and glamorous necessity. Man's reason was a lost cause. His weary phrases altered so much that he had once believed; and he now saw Christ's crucifixion as an 'exalted form of monomania', mankind swayed solely by 'passions and instincts', and death a possible annihilation of the self that was profoundly to be wished.

Only on the question of sex did the old fire reappear, as, attacking the 'misery and immorality of continuing a revolting union', he let loose his fury over his marriage. The same fury took control in a play he was writing on biblical themes, *John the Baptist*. Once more to the fore came the old mutilation motif and a motif that was growing more prominent – the fatal frigid woman. In *John the Baptist* (artistically in no way a worthy successor to *Prometheus*) the persecuting female was divided into two: Salome, the cold and unmoved innocent, the unconscious rouser of men's passions, and Herodias, the calculating persecutor and manipulator. In Horne's mind Kate was assuming both roles: formerly the innocent, she was fast becoming the manipulator. When, thirteen years later, *John the Baptist* finally appeared in print, Salome and Herodias would have even greater personal meaning.

Exhaustion and disillusion gripped him, England beckoned, and at Blue Mountain his work virtually ceased. Now it was only *John Ferncliff* that seemed to keep him, for subscribers still evaded his peremptory searchings. Melbourne, it seemed, lacked sufficient gratitude to the author of *Orion* to buy his farewell epic and thus speed his parting. Perhaps the United States would welcome him, and during 1868 his spirits briefly soared as a scheme occurred to him to tour America on his way home with his tired repertoire of lectures: *Insane Kings, The Causes of Success, Songs of Seven Nations*, and a new and assertive lecture, *Celebrities I have Known*. Into his letters to Harry Edwards, his friend in San Francisco whom he hoped would organize his lecture tour, he infused his old exuberance and disarming egotism, and for ten pages he 'blew the drum and beat the trumpet' of his achievements and qualifications. Only here and there emerged the truth: 'Ages,' he wrote, 'my dear fellow, have slipped over us, though now as then, no doubt, too roughly to merit so soft a term.' The frantic ebullience subsided as Edwards failed to reply to Horne's enthusiastic proposals for the tour. When finally he did reply with gentle discouragement, Horne was quick to realize the letter's tone and hastily saved face by replying that the voyage home through North America would be too long and exacting. His hurt can only be guessed at.

One final indignity awaited him. He intended to resign from his sinecure at Blue Mountain at the end of the year 1868; before he could resign, however, the Government apparently dismissed him with the excuse that the waning goldfield no longer required a mining registrar. Writing to Macrae, Horne announced his intention of leaving his '*billet* in these wild forests' on the last day of December 1868. From there he proposed to drive to St Kilda, and 'thence as early as possible ... "to the place from which he came", and then hang out his banners on the London wall'. Free, for the most part, of Australian anxieties and hurts he was exquisitely free and almost happy.

Back at St Kilda he arranged to sell his treasures, to which all through his poverty he had so stubbornly clung, seeing them as his only link with a finer past. He was going back: he had no more need of them. Also, thanks to governmental squabbles, his salary was still some months in arrears and he needed money immediately. At Mother

McGuirk's he sorted his possessions, made last excursions into Melbourne's cultural life – performing in a seventeenth-century cantata 'exceedingly well' – and made his last futile attempt to publish *John Ferncliff*. His parting legacy never saw the light of printed day; not even the polished manuscript remains today, beyond a very rough copy in the Mitchell Library in Sydney.

Young George Macrae, invited to visit Horne for the last time, went down to St Kilda one afternoon in March 1869. It was so memorable a visit that he afterwards recorded it in nostalgic detail. On Mrs McGuirk's aggressive directions he had gone into the garden that ran behind the terrace houses to find Horne in his shirtsleeves, a broad-brimmed hat on his head, sitting beneath an enormous fig tree eating the fruit. On seeing Macrae he had given an elaborate start – he had forgotten he had made the invitation. Then with great show he had begun to pull himself together and organize their entertainment. He would give him home-grown roast potatoes, done to perfection by Mother McGuirk, and a tin of pheasant fetched by Horne with the aid of his library steps from among the confusion of the top bookshelves, and a glass of sparkling Moselle in Bohemian crystal glasses, produced from further confusion with numerous flourishes. Talking continuously, Horne arranged the meal. Their 'feast of Reason' concluded, he took up his guitar for the 'flow of the Soul'. Slipping the blue riband over his shoulder, throwing himself on the sofa with crossed legs, he 'poured out Spanish and Mexican songs with the greatest energy and enthusiasm, plenty of volume and all in excellent harmony'. That done, he produced his portfolio of line engravings – the celebrated Piranesi's of Ancient Rome among them – for Macrae's practised admiration, and finally a black quarto-sized case which he sprung open to show a magnificent miniature on ivory of a beautiful dark-haired girl. To Macrae's cries of 'Magnificent woman', he simply replied, 'My wife'. He snapped the case shut; the visit was over.

After wranglings over his treasures Horne finally sold them for £60 6s. 3d. at public auction. Probably the most extraordinary literary collection offered in Australia, it included first editions of Shelley, Keats, Hazlitt, the rare first edition of *Queen Mab*, presentation copies of Browning, Talfourd, Hunt, bound periodicals and lexicons, rare copies of Donne, the Decameron and the Koran: the artifacts of his mental life, along with guitars, trumpets, and violas. Meanwhile he had one last attempt at Government compensation. In March he had written a long letter to the Chief Secretary setting out his career and claims, Brough Smyth adding a note that he believed Horne entitled to compensation. At the start of April he still had no reply and wrote less tactfully from Robe Street demanding answer: 'Nor, I venture to add, can you, Sir, think that, in any case, my services in this Colony merit the neglect I have experienced.' When the reply came it was merely to tell him to send his requests to the Minister for Mines. Horne was downcast. He had hoped the Chief Secretary and Premier would declare in Parliament that his was an exceptional case from which no precedent could be drawn, and leave the House to decide the compensation. Gavan Duffy had promised to 'bring forward a motion for . . . compensation, which would be seconded and supported by influential members on both sides'. The motion did not appear.

He left St Kilda. From Melbourne's Athenaeum Club he sent out a parting message to the colony for which his feelings were so equivocal. Published in the *Ballarat Star* his last statement was, like so many others, a chronicle of achievements and unmerited disappointments and bitterness. He packed his crates of Australian wines, bundled his wallaby skins and the few books and manuscripts he was taking with him, and booked his first-class passage on the clipper *Lady Jocelyn*. She sailed from Melbourne on June 12, 1869. On that Saturday afternoon a 'large gathering of friends and admirers' congregated in the ship to see him off – though some arrived so late that they could only wave to him from the wharf. He had already startled spectators by braving the winter cold and plunging from the ship's side into the Port Melbourne waters for a farewell swim. James Hingston, so often there at moments of crisis in Horne's career, spoke with him briefly. 'I am to have my good things in heaven – when I get there,' Hingston remembered him saying. And so Horne stood on the deck and watched through the winter afternoon the outlines of Melbourne disappear: the last outlines of that sunny and too-seductive shore that had been at first his refuge and then his prison and finally, in a sense, his salvation.

Chapter 20

The Mission Triumphant

Horne's arrival in England in 1869 was not unlike his Mexico homecoming; his life, it seemed, was forever a making of adjustments, and
at sixty-seven he was too old to adjust easily. The voyage itself was a
welcome interlude of emotional security, with at the end the prospect
of a triumphant homecoming. To the captive shipboard audience he
spent much of his time playing the guitar or lecturing on the *Causes
of Success in Life*; he gave a champagne dinner on rounding his 'rocky
namesake', Cape Horn, and with a former editor of the *Ceylon Observer*
he entertained the passengers with a weekly journal called *Lady
Jocelyn's Weekly Mail*. Altogether it was a satisfactory trip. And when
on September 25, in sunshine worthy of Australia, they sighted England,
his joy was uncontainable. He was returning, he had come to believe,
with that 'fortune' for which he had set out; he had deluded himself into
thinking that his savings were sufficient to support him without anxiety
for the rest of his days. The sojourn in Australia had not been, after all,
a waste of time.

With this in mind he rushed below and dashed off hasty, excited
letters to former friends, including Charles Dickens, confidently
expecting them to share his own exhilaration. Disembarking at
Gravesend, however, brought home to him the inevitable legacy of
bewilderment of seventeen years' absence, leaving him with doubts,
he confessed, as to his 'own identity'. He was 'Rip Van Winkle'.

And so it was to be for some time. The appearance of his homeland
astounded him; his own appearance, he was aware, was alien. And
Australia, once despised, became once more the sunny and seductive
shore. Faced with unending lines of grimy tenements he longed for the
clean, familiar gum-trees. In the daily papers and the bookstalls he
devoured any news of his former home. Perhaps, as Dickens had said

to a mutual friend, he had been a fool to come back. For apart from
Mary Gillies, in those early months, all that seemed to await him was
death and estrangement. 'The terrible finality of death' was forever
before him, as he pronounced the names of his friends: Talfourd, Jerrold,
Fox, Hunt, Elizabeth Barrett, Miss Mitford, Southwood Smith: they
were all gone. A short time after his arrival he had gone to an unveiling
by Monckton Milnes of a memorial to Leigh Hunt at Kensal Green
cemetery, where in a room adjoining the chapel he was able to look
around the dwindling ranks of the Hunts' – and his – friends. And what
perhaps was worse, of those who did survive, so many had turned
against him. A thousand stories seemed to circulate about himself and
Kate – many of them admittedly amusing, most without foundation
and all against him. Jerrold was said to have coined the phrase that
Horne had shown his wife 'unremitting kindness'; the Howitts were
responsible for the tale that his only gift to Kate from Australia was a
squashed flea on a visiting card. The funniest of all was told by Browning at dinner parties, its original source unknown. Horne, went the
tale, had sent Kate an enormous box from Australia which she had
refused to open except in the presence of Charles Dickens. He had
therefore been summoned and the box opened, the two of them waiting
breathlessly in expectation of a nugget of gold at least. What had
emerged, however, were photographs of Horne in countless poses
(here Browning, to the mirth of fellow guests, would assume the
various poses). Literary London roared with laughter; and even those
men, fumed Horne, like Bulwer Lytton and Charles Dickens who had
abandoned their own wives, were self-righteous in their indignation;
Dickens even snubbed Horne when they chanced to meet in the
Athenaeum Club. Horne's frequent protests that Kate had separated
herself from *him*, and that he had indeed sent her what remittances he
could, failed to bridle the rumours.

He could not bring himself yet to blame Kate. Rather he blamed her
brothers – and Dickens. Dickens seemed genuinely to believe the
charges and to have roused a faction against him: wracked by his own
broken marriage and illicit love for the actress Ellen Ternan, Dickens
seemed to be projecting his own self-disgust into his hatred for Horne.
And unsuspectingly Horne had thus earned the enmity of probably the
most powerful literary man in England; not even Dickens's death less
than a year after Horne's return could quieten the storm of hate that
was blowing.

In this unhappy situation the one saving grace was Mary, who did
her best to soothe his feelings of persecution and to reconcile him with

Kate. But neither her goodwill nor her soothings were sufficient to persuade Kate, now living with her mother, to set eyes once again on her husband. When Kate refused to see him he recalled an earlier statement by Southwood Smith, who had certified that a relative of Kate's was mentally disturbed, and who observed that such things ran in families and that Kate herself might have the seeds. Horne began to wonder if that might not be the explanation. She had, he decided, a physical indisposition to marriage, though he admitted that this did not explain her erratic behaviour. Kate was an enigma, and in his eyes a dangerous one.

Of those who changed appearance caused him a shock, Mary Gillies must have produced the most severe shock. Well over seventy, she was, he was painfully forced to realize, an old woman. In July 1870 came a shattering blow: Mary died. Numb with shock he came home from the funeral, his head aching, and sat down to write to Robert Browning, who like himself remembered Mary in the glory of the Craven Hill days. 'My oldest and truest friend,' he wrote, 'is just dead – the funeral flowers but now in my hands. True, she was very old – Mary, the elder Miss Gillies – over seventy – but when an angelic nature leaves the earth, all thoughts of time seem to melt into one . . . As you must well feel.'

From his old friends he was estranged, by the English public he was forgotten; his time spent furthering the man under the Southern Cross was so much 'a waste . . . of my alloted [sic.] span'. Those who had once 'been at my feet' were 'grown to giants' – hostile giants who would do 'anything rather than help me rehabilitate myself and regain my position in literature'. Rehabilitation was now his ruling hope, a necessity both mentally and materially. That 'fortune' brought from Australia he now found less than a year after his arrival was meagre for his simple needs. Already he saw the familiar demon of poverty coming to claim him.

Anxiously he worked to regain his old literary place. He gave the inevitable public lectures. He turned to old friends. He recalled the more profitable of past memories, sending to the newspapers letters and articles on anything from recollections of Jeremy Bentham to notes on swimming; the clippings were then sent to a variety of past acquaintances from Monckton Milnes and Lytton to Disraeli and Carlyle. His methods were not subtle, but this was a time for drastic measures. To periodicals he sent memoirs of past celebrities, adapting or snipping them from his lectures on *Celebrities I have Known*; but this simple plan met saboteurs. Publishing some of his memoirs in

Macmillan's Magazine, Horne received a notice from the editor, demanding permission in writing from all those mentioned or from their relatives. John Forster, on hearing of the proposed articles, had warned the editor that his own and Dickens's names must be mentioned only with discretion. Writing to Browning for permission to use Elizabeth's now fading and fragile letters – a permission gladly granted, though Browning had denied it to others – Horne unleashed his dismay and bitterness: he could forgive some taking sides against him, particularly when the true facts were not known, but 'one can't *go on* forgiving bolts and bars and checks at a front door, with a wolf smiling at the back kitchen window! If any more equally cruel and gratuitous interferences occur, I shall undoubtedly shake my quills over a pretty wide field of memory.' In fact, Forster's threat had blunted Horne's drawn sword. Apart from a damaging obituary of Forster in 1876 – drastically cut by a prudent publisher – his articles on past acquaintances were sadly tame and insecure.

He was bitter, and he was tired. Nothing was as he had expected it. Nevertheless he knew what he must do, and it was now that his courage and those powers of adaptation which never ceased to amaze observers came to his aid. While reprints of his past books – *The Death of Marlowe* which he dedicated to the 'dear memory' of Leigh Hunt, *The Poor Artist, Orion*, and his children's stories – came from the presses of trusting publishers, Horne, not content with living in the past, threw himself into new circles and new movements in English poetry.

He had taken rooms in Northumberland Street, now Luxborough Street, a 'double row of houses, all alike, with two-storeyed fronts of smoked brick and four steps that led to a dark door on each side of which hung a ponderous wrought-iron knocker'. Nearby the clock of St Marylebone Church – where his beloved Elizabeth Barrett had been married – measured out his day with its chimes, and Horne was close to Regent's Park, which he had admired as a child, and in whose tranquil gardens he now often sat and walked. In his 'chaotic' second-storey chambers, where the magpie squalor of St Kilda was translated to London and the surviving Piranesi etchings stood once more with his cooking pots, guitars, a grand piano, Horne entertained a coterie of new friends. Nearby lived Westland Marston, the dramatist, remembered from old 'Syncretic' days. At his Sunday evening parties Horne met that new literary group that had flourished so exotically while he had been away, the Pre-Raphaelite Brotherhood, whose aesthetic ideals, with their premium on beauty and feeling, carried on, in a time when generally their validity was doubted, so many of the ideas of the Spasmodic Movement. Its writers were congenial to him, mentally and emotionally: at Marston's he met its talented and demented leader, the painter and poet Dante Gabriel Rossetti, who had been so impressed in youth with Horne's own *False Medium*. He met Algernon Charles Swinburne, the wild, red-haired, and brilliant poet, as yet untamed into respectability by life on Putney Hill with his literary guardian Watts-Dunton; Swinburne had greeted Horne with an ecstatic burst of recognition as the author of *Orion*, a poem that had delighted his adolescence. At Marston's house Horne may have also first met Mortimer Collins, a journalist and aspiring poet, six feet tall, immensely strong, and a deeply religious man. Their friendship flourished until Collins's much mourned death in 1876, after which Horne continued to visit his widow and children.

At Marston's Horne certainly met a crowd of poetic hangers-on: young men agreeably ready to court an older once-famous poet. Chief of these was a twenty-eight-year-old post office clerk with literary interests, Harry Buxton Forman. The son of a naval surgeon, he had published the previous year articles on poetry in *Tinsley's Magazine*, and had recently become the acquaintance of Rossetti; like Horne he was devoted to the work and lives of Keats and Shelley. It was a fertile friendship that grew that year between the young literary clerk and the aged poet, and it would develop into the most considerable of Horne's remaining years. Forman's value for Horne lay largely in his respectful companionship, but he also possessed practical literary abilities which won him a professional respect that Horne did not often give to his younger literary friends. Few better editors and annotators of texts, particularly those of Keats and Shelley, were to be found in the late nineteenth century, though modern bibliographers might consider some of Forman's notes too trivial. By 1873 Horne had already come to rely on Buxton Forman. He saw Horne's books through the press, correcting proofs, and selecting manuscripts from the piles of scribblings which Horne proudly called 'my Hornucopias'. Longevity had become Horne's most practical asset.

It was at Marston's, too, that he met another young man who would entwine his remaining years: Edmund Gosse, son of the celebrated zoologist whose strict Plymouth Brethren ways cast so inhibiting a pall over father and son alike, forcing the one to reject ideas of evolution and forcing on the other an austere and troubled childhood. Gosse in his early twenties was bullied unmercifully by Horne in his role of imperious doyen, but he had the sharpness and wit to record most faithfully and illuminatingly Horne's old age. Assistant in the depart-

ment of printed books at the British Museum, he had come enthusiastically to the outskirts of Pre-Raphaelite society in the early 'seventies,
and first set eyes on Horne at a wedding breakfast when Marston's
daughter married the minor poet Arthur O'Shaughnessy. Gosse's
description of that first meeting has become the classic portrait of
Horne:

> Then entered 'Orion' Horne, a tiny old gentleman, who all un-
> invited, began to sit upon the floor and sing, in a funny little
> cracked voice, Spanish songs to his own accompaniment on the
> guitar. The guests grew restless and impatient, but Browning,
> throwing a protecting arm over the guitarist, exclaimed, 'That was
> charming, Horne! It quite took us back to the sunny warm South,'
> and tactfully put an end to the incident.

Fortunately, on the back of that charming portrait, one can paint
Horne's own description of the wedding breakfast, which he related
coyly to his friend Harry Edwards in San Francisco: 'A young gentleman by particular desire played a "Bolero" on the guitar, with a song to
match and was nearly overcome by three or four successive storms of
applause.' It was typical of the way Horne could now construe a
situation.

Gosse saw Horne as a succession of contradictions. He met him, he
wrote, at afternoon parties carrying his guitar under his arm which he
'used ceremoniously to introduce as Miss Horne' – his daughter. He
monopolized the prettiest women, he had incredible physical strength,
and he thirsted for publicity of any sort – he would box, swim, or sing
in public at the slightest provocation. 'A wonderful little ringleted
athlete, no doubt!' He noted also Horne's courage and 'cheerfulness',
with admiration but with less surprise than those who had known
Horne twenty years before. In those first years of the eighteen-seven-
ties, Horne, the chronic depressive and introvert, seemed at last to have
come to terms with his nature. Partly it was because so much was now
passed in semi-fantasy; his contact with reality grew hazier, his communications with those around him were increasingly on his terms, not
theirs. It was noticeable in his play-acting, the effects of which he no
longer at all discerned. In 1872 he had gone on a lecture tour of
Scotland, promoted by his old acquaintance, W. B. Hodgson, and had
been entertained on the strength of his past poetic reputation at prominent Edinburgh homes. The results had been a pantomime. Young
David Masson, later Professor of Chemistry in Melbourne, and son of

the Professor of English at Edinburgh University, would never forget the frosty bewilderment of Edinburgh matrons when Horne's 'queer little figure' with its 'abundant white hair and his guitar' gave a Maori war song (studied authentically during his call at New Zealand on his homeward passage) and ended 'by flinging himself full length of the drawing room carpet in fatigue – or assumed fatigue'. Matronly Edinburgh society had been 'shocked'.

His insensitivity was noticeable equally in his letters. He now spoke at, and not to, his correspondents, with accounts – most often boastful – of his activities and woes, interspersed with commands and orders to his younger correspondents. His judgment on submitting articles to magazines was frequently as dismaying. Townshend Mayer, a recent friend and editor of *St James's Review*, who would later edit more than one of Horne's books, begged him not to offer *Te Aie Ya*, a Maori tragedy in verse, to 'Fraser, Macmillan, Temple Bar or Cornhill. It is not suitable for any of them and the offer would only bring upon you disappointing and unpleasant refusals.' Horne's judgment of the merit of his work had almost entirely vanished.

Fantasy undoubtedly was largely responsible for lightening these years. Resignation was also responsible. At Blue Mountain Horne had acquired a fatalism with which to fight anxiety. He had come back to the mission and with it to his true identity. He had ceased to fight an inevitable fate: he had accepted what always he had known to be his destiny. In such a submission he had found a contentment, and it was that contentment that sustained him now in London. At last, after seventy years of struggle, he had learned to live only for the day.

Yet it was not all resigned fantasy. Inevitably those old pursuers were able at intervals to pierce the mental shield. His poverty forced him to apply for a pension to the Government, and on his behalf and at his request a formidable list of names signed his petition to William Gladstone, First Lord of the Treasury; among the signatories were Browning, Tennyson, Carlyle, Harriet Martineau, Rossetti, Matthew Arnold, William Morris, John Ruskin and Bulwer Lytton, and Horne's main regret was that he was unable to persuade Shelley's son also to sign. But Gladstone refused it. And to Horne's ears came the rumour – not unfounded – that the refusal was based on Horne's supposed treatment of Kate. The persecutors were unleashed; and once out there was no restraining them. Horne's letter, which had ordinarily held a moderate number of allusions to the unfair rumours over Kate, became tirades of indignation. He poured his feelings indiscriminately and even resurrected acquaintances of the past in order to unburden his fears. Professor Owen – to whom Horne had dedicated the *Poor Artist* twenty years before – confronted by these miseries, smiled Horne firmly into silence; George Meredith, a deserted husband from whom Horne had automatically expected sympathy, was embarrassed by Horne's story and by sudden contact with a past that he wanted to forget; he replied politely but discouragingly.

It was on Browning, patient and compassionate, that he released most of his distress, writing with a frankness (though he was apt also to display this frankness to those he scarcely knew) and a sense of child-like dependence that was quite disarming. Everything worried him. He was terrified of what Forster might do against him: terrified that that 'joyous returning note', dashed off to Dickens in 1869, exaggerating his Australian fortune so that Dickens might not feel he was arriving as a liability, would be used maliciously against him. To all this Browning was expected to reply with the soothing reassurance he might normally give to a frightened child. Horne drew up, moreover, a short history of his marriage, discussing Kate's 'physical indisposition' with total lack of reticence, and despatching the document to Gladstone. The effect of so surprising a document was easy to foresee. Gladstone remained unmoved despite the renewed requests of Browning whose reputation was now as eminent in society as poetry. It remained aptly for the son of the first prophet of the Professional Authors, Benjamin Disraeli, an author himself and undoubtedly sympathetic to the ageing author of *Orion* and *False Medium*, to show practical compassion. Disraeli's succession to power was also Horne's, and in June 1874, after renewed applications, he was granted his longed-for pension of £50 a year. Browning, with psychological insight, wrote to Horne soothingly, 'Gladstone ought not to have let slip this piece of grateful justice, but the gods are against him now.'

The pension had removed pressing financial burdens, though it was insufficient to remove completely, as he had hoped, the tiring need to write articles for magazines. At the same time it was true that no matter how large the pension, Horne would continue to write: not only the 'great works' on which he hoped to spend his remaining years, but the humbler articles. He wanted public recognition as much as money. He continued to publicize his past, whether his correspondence with Elizabeth Barrett, which began to appear together with his commentary in the *Contemporary Review* in 1874, or some ephemeral link with a famous author or man of affairs. Publicity was the sauce that spiced his daily loaf.

Regrettably, at the end of 1874, that sauce of publicity curdled. He had been in the habit of taking his holidays at the sea, particularly Eastbourne, in the cheap off-season of winter, and had taken lodgings with a Mrs Lennox, the mother of several daughters, the youngest, Ellen, less than thirteen years of age, a girl precocious for her years. Into this household Horne had been welcomed, his learning and education a cause for wonder, his offer to help young Ellen Lennox readily accepted. Through the autumn of 1874 he instructed her how to play the guitar and how to read and do her arithmetic, until in November came castrophe. In a terrible scene the parents accused him of indecent assault on their daughter, the distraught girl herself supporting their claims. The police and the surgeons were sent for; Horne, so it was later claimed by the Lennox family, equally distraught, confessed his guilt and begged to make amends. He was arrested, and in panic, amidst only too-real persecutors, wrote frantic letters to his friends, describing the accusations in varying degrees, admitting to Browning that he was accused of 'acts of which I am incapable', and hoping throughout that the scandal would not reach the London newspapers. Removing himself to Brighton, he waited in agony through December for the case to come before the grand jury, knowing that such an offence, if proved, could be punished by two years' hard labour.

His main consoler was his younger brother James, a relationship suddenly intensified in his misery, after years of silence and casualness. James proved his loyalty; staying at Eastbourne he kept his brother informed on local feeling, and begged him unconvincingly not to bother about the publicity, since 'most people seem to know of the affair'. The case was at last heard in January 1875, and Horne's defence was strong; for a petition had been circulated by Horne's solictor to his friends for signatures testifying to his impeccable moral character and it had been readily signed by many of those who had so recently signed the petition for his pension – Forman, Carlyle, Octavia Hill, George Eliot, G. H. Lewes, Leonhard Schmitz, and his old Australian friend Archibald Michie. The jury decided for Horne, a few days after his seventy-second birthday. Paying £52 in legal expenses which he could ill-afford, but indescribably grateful for his escape, he now had the disagreeable task of writing letters to his friends. The 'wretches who were seeking to persecute me with lies and perjuries have been blown up to the moon . . . such things may happen to almost anybody! Pray forget it.' Of his true guilt or innocence at this distance it is impossible to judge. One wonders, however, if there was not, as in most charges against Horne, a grain of truth, even if not a grain so fertile.

For certainly his writings of that period testify that his mind was deeply troubled. The motifs of mutilation and the fatal, pursuing, frigid woman, already an integral part of his creative scheme, had intensified. Religion, particularly the Old Testament theme of the punitive, oppressing God, had come swamping into his poetry. His play, *Sithron the Star-Stricken* (published in 1883 but most likely drafted now), artistically rubbish, and reiterating frighteningly and tiresomely the wickedness of circumcision inflicted on man by a tyrannical Jehovah, was the product of no ordered mind. While at times, as in the lines he wrote on the death of George Sand in 1876, he could achieve a semblance of his old mastery, his private, deep-felt writings were often disordered and strange.

His thoughts often reclaimed his childhood; his magazine articles, recalling often his most distant memories, stimulated his natural recall. He relived, in a disjointed novel, the pain of A's rejection of him with an immediacy and poignancy that was probably in part the result of an old man's nostalgia but was nevertheless convincing and charming. Among his most serious projects was that selected anthology and biographical study of his poems which he had planned as long as twenty-five years before but was now a driving ambition; he had hopes that, if he died before the task was completed, Buxton Forman might complete the editing. With this seemingly in mind he made elaborate plans and notes; and the biographer now, searching his papers in the Mitchell Library in Sydney, is apt to have the unnerving experience of finding a note in Horne's handwriting for Horne's future biographer. But chiefly and inevitably his thoughts returned to *Ancient Idols* and to that duty that he could not neglect but could never fulfil. In 1876 he began the last, most inexpert, and most pathetic revisions, prefacing it with another long effusion entitled *Sacred Symbols* and full of fantasies from which the links of reality had largely gone. Rationally and creatively, except for odd and infrequent flashes, the substance had gone from his work; tragically, he had never written so prolifically.

Socially he was restless; gregarious, yet in a way untouchable: little changed by outside happenings, more secure than he had ever been in the role he was now playing. He was becoming a type of literary tourist attraction; people came to look at him, and he enjoyed it. From the United States came a young man named Stoddart, a respectful novice whom Horne had already addressed by letter at domineering length, including a photograph which seemed to Stoddart to be 'as grave-looking as Confucius, with its thin fringe of hair coiled in ringlets like those of a Polish Jew'.

Stoddart was a ready-made audience, absorbent as blotting paper, and author of one of the sharpest visual descriptions of Horne. The small rooms at the top of the hall stairs at number seven Northumberland Street were in confusion when the young poet paid his call, for Horne had just moved along the street from number thirty-two. (Two years later, however, another observer would record the same dirt and confusion.) Greeting Stoddart, Horne had offered him a glass of claret which he 'rinsed in a little cupboard at the side of the chimney, standing with his head deep in the cupboard and talking all the time'; he had drawn the cork of the bottle 'with great ease' and sat down in the contrived setting of an enormous chair draped with wallaby skin (which to Stoddart's American eyes became a buffalo skin) with three plumes of pampas grass towering behind. 'The ribbon-like leaves,' Stoddart recalled, 'fell over his face. He looked highly-Druidical, with his snow-white ringlets and the slant-wise droop of the eyelids.' The room in which he sat was like a workshop, the table littered with papers, few books in sight, the walls crowded with eighteenth-century French oils of flowers, a copy of Raphael's head of Homer, the Piranesi engravings, and a marble medallion depicting Horne's head, made by an Australian sculptor. In the bedroom next door Stoddart was taken to the window to see a grape vine Horne had reared and a Virginia creeper he had trained into shape by spending seven hours on a step ladder the day before. Proud of his fitness, he assured his young friend that he spent many hours at the neighbouring baths, that he ate and drank sparingly to keep down his weight. He idealized everything, Stoddart recorded, with a 'sunny affection for life', discoursed at length of the recent republication of his play *Cosmo de' Medici*, on which he had received congratulations from such notable personages as Princess Louise and the 'chief proprietor of *The Times*'. He had hopes, he confided, of settling in France and intended soon to go there as guest of a branch of the Bonaparte family: a reference presumably to Bonaparte Wyse, a minor minor Franco-Irish poet with whom Horne corresponded, and who was descended from one of Napoleon's nieces.

He was still restless and eager to travel – whether to France or the United States or any country that offered him hospitality and respect. At the end of 1875 he abruptly revived the idea of a lecture tour of the United States, and even went so far as to inform the literary magazines that Mr Horne proposed to leave in the following March for America in the company of Mr Townshend Mayer. In fact the lecture tour appealed more to Horne than to any American promoter, and March saw him still in England. The announcement did, however, revive one friendship that would bring him satisfaction. At his home in New Haven, Connecticut, W. J. Linton, the poet and wood engraver whom Horne had first met at Craven Hill and known so well in the Chartist eighteen-forties, had read of Horne's proposed lecture tour and wrote his delight at the prospect of seeing Horne again, and though Horne was forced to reply that the chances of his visit diminished monthly, their correspondence, once revived, did not languish.

Much of his energy now went into his letters – to Harry Edwards in San Francisco and to Robert Browning and Algernon Charles Swinburne. He had defended Swinburne in the preface of his republished *Orion* from attacks on the so-called 'Fleshly School of Poetry', and the self-conscious, rather effusive letters he wrote to Swinburne revealed his respect for the younger poet's work, and possibly a slight uneasiness for him as a man. In turn, Swinburne's attitude to Horne was almost the reverse, admiring him as a man, regretting that as a writer he had long outlived his merit.

Age, Horne proudly insisted, had not diminished his physical powers, and the doctor's prediction that he might die suddenly seemed unfounded. His chest, he claimed, still measured forty-two inches, his weight was not over twelve stone and on seaside visits he swam each morning. Old 'Orion' would see a hundred. Yet there were signs of failing strength. Each winter brought bronchitis; on winters' evenings he feared to venture out. 'I will dine with you,' he wrote to a friend, 'in imagination – by my lonely fire, and drink a deep basin of old man's mutton broth to you.' Heavy exertion was likely to leave him with pains in his chest which he uneasily dismissed as 'indigestion'. Worst of all for a writer, his eyesight was failing; and in the street he wore blue-tinted goggles. Writing for magazines became increasingly tiring, not least for the editor and compositors who had to read his scrawled script, and it was with relief that he heard in 1880 that Disraeli had doubled his pension. Too blind to go out alone at night through London's 'populous thoroughfares', he sat at home; when each winter he spent several months at Margate – he prudently avoided Eastbourne – he often spent the evenings dozing in his chair until bedtime for lack of anything else to do. Despite the pension his life was parsimonious. In London he spent no more than a guinea a week on food and nothing on wine, which came to him regularly as a gift from Australian friends; at Margate his lodgings cost a bare three shillings a day.

Yet there were visits to friends. He stayed often with Frances Collins, the impoverished widow of his friend Mortimer Collins, and insisted on giving her money and providing her household with a leg of Welsh mutton and two or three bottles during his visits; and she in turn gave him that motherly concern that he craved. There were visits, too, to Margaret Gillies who survived her sister, to Caroline Hill, and to a new friend, Pakenham Beatty, an aspiring poetic dramatist to whom Horne gave affection, reminiscence and the usual domineering advice in a series of lively letters. At Beatty's home he was welcomed as a close family friend, was affectionately mothered by Mrs Beatty, and was chosen as godfather to small Pakenham William Albert Hengist Mazzini Beatty, to whom as a christening present he brought a pair of baby boxing-gloves.

His strength was perceptively failing and yet he was normally full of mental vigour. He would stand no nonsense, an attitude he made clear to reviewers in 1880 when his play *Laura Dibalzo* appeared. Mostly written twenty years before, during his interest in the Italian uprisings (written, he claimed, out of conversations with Mazzini), it was as poor as all his later offerings. Critics therefore faced the dilemma of whether to dismiss the play or, out of pity, prevaricate. *The Athenaeum* charitably did the latter, to be rewarded with pages of Horne's opinion of the dishonesty of modern criticism; *The Daily News* did the former, and promptly received from Horne a rambling and largely irrelevant tirade on their 'baseless and senseless display of ribaldry'. Nor did he consider himself in that year too old for another attempt at that lecture tour of the United States. He had hopes that the noted catering firm who were also well-known promoters of entertainers, Spiers and Pond (it had been Major Pond he had carried on his back in the race in Melbourne in 1861 at the Zoological Gardens), would sponsor him. He wrote to Harry Edwards in tearing spirits and brushed aside Edwards' hasty objections. As usual he was eager with tortuous business arrangements and superbly confident. As usual he was downcast when the tour did not eventuate.

He went instead to Margate, and to speculations on death –

If when I'm dead, I know not I am dead,
And have no thought at all,
It is but sleeping dreamless in my bed,
Without a matin call.

He called the poem *Smile at Annihilation*. It was probably at Margate, too, that he wrote *The Last Words of Cleanthes*, a prayer with related thoughts of an old man with sea around his feet –

O Zeus! no claim have we to aught beyond!
We bless thee for the life we have enjoyed;
We hope our spirit shall not be destroyed:
Thy waters to my dying hymn respond
In harmonies that change, ere rapture-cloyed.
O Zeus! I hear the broad waves gently flowing
Over my feet, and nestling round my knees!
My senses melt away by soft degrees!
My thoughts, like seeds, thy hand afar is sowing!
Sweet songs are in my brain – sweet birds in trees!

Now he feared death in life: long, painful illness with the human spirit broken, the human dignity gone. Better like Cleanthes to end one's life oneself in the sea; or preferably in an opiate sleep 'So that no pangs the sense invest':

Physician! strong of mind as tender-hearted,
Let not the body, whose last hold hath parted,
Linger in agony, and at Death's porches
Swing blind, with frantic arms . . .

His extraordinary bursts of mental and physical vigour became less frequent, but he amazed the citizens of Margate by plunging into the grey January sea on his eightieth birthday. His eyesight had so deteriorated – one eye being almost totally blind and the other filmed by mist – that he had difficulty in groping his pen into the inkwell and now wrote mostly with a pencil. Much of what he wrote was rejected by the patient editors of literary magazines, and he must have been galled to receive back from *The Contemporary Review* his last fervent credo; entitled *Two Last Canons of Poetic Criticism*, it reiterated his Romantic distaste for the disciples of Matthew Arnold and recalled the magnificence of *Queen Mab* and the splendid sight of young Shelley fighting to set right the wrongs of the world. Despite these worries, he remained reasonably cheerful; indeed W. J. Linton who came to London and visited Horne through 1883 found him surprisingly so as he pottered over his cooking pots and chattered about life in Australia. To Linton, too, he confided his thoughts about the future of his revered manuscript, *Ancient Idols*. Of all men now living, only himself and Leonhard Schmitz and Buxton Forman knew its contents; anticipating his death he was haunted by the thought that it must be printed. But it must be privately printed – say, thirty copies, of which he would present five each to Schmitz, Forman, and Linton. Would Linton, who was a fine engraver, undertake it? What reply Linton made is not known.

The summer of 1883 brought illness – a severe gastric fever – and shortly after an accident with a van in Lisson Grove, near his lodgings. Visiting him, both Gosse and Forman saw that his vigour was fast leaving him. He complained of perpetual dryness at the back of his throat. Nevertheless with the coming of winter he left for Margate, and settled down in his usual room in one of the old grey terrace houses that curved crookedly up Trinity Hill. Life there was peaceful and predictable and the sight of the ocean soothed him. He would have his breakfast at nine o'clock, spend the rest of the day in his room among his papers, and dine at six on curry and macaroni. If it were fine, he would walk to Fort Green and sit on the covered seat, a pencil and paper on his lap to record any thoughts that came to mind. If he fell asleep there his gnarled old landlady, Mrs Horn, would fetch him. If it rained he would sit on the landing outside his room and play the guitar. The Horns were kind to him; indeed he came increasingly to depend on Mrs Horn and prefer her illiterate company to that of anyone else. He called her 'Mrs Goody'; as he grew weaker and took to his bed she nursed him.

By February 1884 he was seriously ill, with what the Margate physician diagnosed as general inflammation of the mucous membrane of the stomach, chest and throat. He could tolerate little food, and lived mainly on ice. On February 4 he sent for a solicitor to make a new will leaving to James Horne, with whom, since the Lennox case, he had had a closer relationship, the miniatures of their parents; to Harry Buxton Forman, his desks, books, manuscripts and papers; to his London doctor, George Bird – a noted literary physician – the paintings and engravings on his walls; and to W. J. Linton, his portfolios of prints. Buxton Forman was to be his literary executor. To his niece Georgina Sabine, to Buxton Forman's daughter Gwendolen, and to a mysterious Mrs Fanny Chinery and her daughter Amy Bella-Isolda Williams (bringing to mind that other dead Bella Isolda) he left that land lying beside what the solicitor's clerk ironically recorded as 'the Golden River' in Australia (land long since, though he did not know it, repossessed by the crown for unpaid rates), along with all profits present and future from his estate and sales of literary works. For Kate he had one last taunt. She – his 'sometime Wife' – should have, if she accepted, his chest of drawers, linen, blankets – and bed. His last request was that if possible he should lie in Edmonton Churchyard near

Charles and Mary Lamb; that there should be a post-mortem examination of his body (was it, one wonders another aspect of the old mutilation motif?); and in defiance of the thunderings of the hated Jehovah no orthodox burial service be said at his grave. He wanted, he said, a selection of passages from Thomas Browne's *Urn Burial* to be recited or read over his body. Weakly holding the pen he traced a straggling, almost unrecognizable signature across the page.

The start of March saw his condition worsening. Ulceration was said to have set in. *The Athenaeum* bore bulletins of his progress. Horne refused to be moved to London; he wanted to die in Margate. He refused also to call his friends from London, even his brother James. He clung to Mrs Horn. 'Scarcely any hope,' wrote *The Athenaeum*, 'is now held out for his life.' And even as those words went to press the struggle was over. Quietly, in his opiate sleep, on Thursday evening, March 13, 1884, he died.

James Horne rushed to Margate, important and angry that he had not been summoned earlier. 'Everybody,' he wrote, 'seems to have known more about him than either I or my Wife or Daughters.' He was not, he added, 'too unwell to do what is required'. Horne nevertheless was not, as he had wished, taken to Edmonton; instead he was buried, in orthodox manner, at the Margate cemetery, the stone lying over his grave recording that he was 'Poet, Dramatist and Critic, Author of Orion, Cosmo de' Medici, The Death of Marlowe, Gregory VII, Judas Iscariot, etc.' The London literary papers carried long and affectionate obituaries. In Melbourne on March 17 the overseas intelligence bore announcement of his death along with news of the expulsion from Vienna of the Anarchists; and in the following days Australian papers printed detailed reminiscences, so that he was remembered, as he would have wished, in both hemispheres.

But Richard Hengist Horne had already composed his own secret obituary. In May 1882, revising yet again the fantastic preface to *Ancient Idols*, he describes a symbolic Forest sheltering those spirits who had awakened the Soul of Humanity: Homer, Aeschylus, Dante, Michelangelo, Shakespeare, Milton, and that champion of humanity, Shelley. Next to Shelley is a veiled figure: about its head are the leaves of laurels and the Australian eucalypt, above it shine Orion's three immortal stars. . . .

Acknowledgements

I became interested in Richard Hengist Horne while a final-year student in the University of Melbourne in 1956. At first I was mainly interested in his seventeen years in Australia but then realized that this was only one episode, and far from the most revealing, in his long life. The search for his private correspondence and voluminous published works, some of them rare, was a long task, and would have been impossible but for the many people who guided me to information and the libraries which allowed me access to their collections and gave me permission to quote manuscripts. I am grateful to the trustees and staff of the Mitchell Library in Sydney, the State Library of Victoria and the Baillieu Library of the University of Melbourne, the Alexander Turnbull Library in Wellington, New Zealand, the British Museum, and the following United States libraries: Cornell University, Yale University, Harvard College, State University of Iowa, Columbia University, Ohio State University, Henry E. Huntington Library and Art Gallery, Historical Society of Pennsylvania, New York Public Library, Pierpont Morgan Library, and Folger Shakespeare Library (Washington, D.C.). I am grateful also to the government record repositories in Australia and England which supplied birth, death, and marriage certificates and other civil documents, and particularly the Archives of the State Library of Victoria which holds much correspondence on Horne's colonial career.

I must also express my debt to Professor Ronald Freeman of the University of Southern California and the trustees of the Pierpont Morgan Library for allowing me to read the valuable Horne–Barrett correspondence which Professor Freeman is preparing for publication.

Mrs Mary Walker, of Lakes Entrance, Victoria, Australia, generously allowed me to see the private correspondence of William Howitt and his family. The late Dr Eri J. Shumaker, of Denison University, Granville, Ohio, gave me much information unattainable elsewhere, from his own Horne records collected in the early 1830s; these included letters from people who remembered Horne, some of Horne's own annotated works, and copies of several Horne manuscripts which are now in unknown hands. Indeed Dr Shumaker pioneered research into Horne's life, writing a short dissertation on Horne as a thesis for Ohio State University in 1934, and publishing at his own expense in 1943 a concise bibliography of Horne's writings. After his death his

257

daughter, Mrs Eleanor Oatman, sharing his enthusiasm, painstakingly sorted his papers in search of letters that could be useful to me; she also entertained me most generously when I visited Chicago.

I am particularly indebted to Professor J. A. La Nauze, Mr W. A. P. Phillips, Dr D. E. Kennedy, Professor Alan Davies, and to my husband for discussing my work and reading my manuscript. My work was also aided by a research grant from Melbourne University.

Melbourne   ANN BLAINEY
May 1967

Notes and Bibliography

The punctuation in some of the verbatim quotations in this book has been slightly altered. In some letters and draft poems, for example, Horne so spattered the pages with commas and dashes that, on first reading, his meaning was often submerged; I did this reluctantly in the interests of coherence.

The following abbreviations are used in the notes; they refer to collections of published and unpublished correspondence which I frequently cite.

B-H   *Letters of Elizabeth Barrett Browning Addressed to Richard Hengist Horne*, ed. S. R. Townshend Mayer (London, 1877), two volumes.

B-M   *Elizabeth Barrett to Miss Mitford*, ed. Betty Miller (London, 1945); the letters were written between the years 1836 and 1846.

False Medium   R. H. Horne (anon.), *Exposition of the False Medium and Barriers Excluding Men of Genius from the Public* (London, 1833).

H-B   Collection of manuscript letters from R. H. Horne to Robert Browning, 1863–83, in Alexander Turnbull Library, Wellington, New Zealand.

H-F   Collection of manuscript letters from R. H. Horne to W. J. Fox and family, 1833–47, in Alexander Turnbull Library, Wellington, New Zealand.

Miscell.   R. H. Horne, 'Miscellaneous Thoughts', 1829, unpublished ms, pages unnumbered, Mitchell Library, Sydney, Australia.

ML   The Mitchell Library, Public Library of New South Wales, Sydney. It has the largest single collection of Horne material, but the collection was uncatalogued at the time I used it. The library bought this valuable collection from a descendant of Horne's literary executor, H. Buxton Forman.

RH   Richard Henry Horne, known after 1867 as Richard Hengist Horne.

CHAPTER I: BLOOD OF YOUTH

The chapter title, 'the blood of youth', is taken from Horne's ms notes for a proposed book on 'Education of Deformed Children', Iowa State University Library.

CHILDHOOD: Edmund Gosse, *Portraits and Sketches* (London, 1912) 99–101; obituary of Horne in *The Saturday Review*, March 22, 1884, p. 369; B-M, p. 151; RH, 'Recollections of Childhood', an unpublished memoir (my copy was given to me by Dr E. J. Shumaker who in turn had acquired it from M. Buxton Forman, who held the original ms in 1930; the present whereabouts of the original is unknown); RH, 'Miscellaneous Thoughts', unpublished ms, pages unnumbered, 1829, ML (henceforth cited as *Miscell.*); details of James Horne's military appointments from Public Record Office, London; RH, 'Philosophical Poem with Notes', ms, ML; RH to Henry Maule, ms letter, July 18, 1832, ML; RH, 'Fairs and Markets of Europe', *Harper's Magazine*, *46* (1873), 379–81; RH, 'A Witch in the Nursery', *Household Words*, *3* (1851), 608; RH, 'Bygone Celebrities', *Gentleman's Magazine*, *7* (1871), 88–101.

ROMANTIC LITERARY MOVEMENT: for a discussion of chief traits, see Mario Praz, *The Romantic Agony* trans. by A. Davidson (London, 1933); and Jacques Barzun, *Romanticism and the Modern Ego* (Boston, 1944).

SCHOOL: The well-known versions of Horne's life seem to be confused about many landmarks, for instance when he was born, the names of his grandparents, and the name of his wife. While most of these errors are easily resolved, the question of where he went to school is still slightly puzzling. Horne himself said (*The London Academy*, April 19, 1879, ms 'Recollections of Childhood', and B-M, p. 93) that he attended the same school as Charles Wells and John Keats; and clearly they attended John Clarke's school at Enfield (R. D. Altick, *The Cowden Clarkes* (London, 1948), p. 16. On the other hand, Horne's close friend and literary executor, Harry Buxton Forman, wrote (W. Robertson Nicoll and Thomas J. Wise ed., *Literary Anecdotes of the Nineteenth Century* (London, 1905, p. 238)) that Horne went to a grammar school at Edmonton. The most likely explanation is that he attended each school for a time.

SANDHURST: RH, 'Confessions of a Nervous Soldier', *Fraser's Magazine*, *38* (1848), 79; the reference to the East India Company appears in obituaries but I have been unable to trace the original source; RH, ms poem, 'Sandhurst', ML; RH, 'A Soldier's Skull, or, The Murders of Discipline', *Howitt's Journal*, *3* (1848), 139–40; RH, 'By-Gone Celebrities of Bond Street', *Harper's Magazine*, *43* (1871), 757–9; RH, 'Eyes and Eye-Glasses', ms, ML; RH to Harry Edwards, May 15, 1868, February 1, 1881, Alexander Turnbull Library, Wellington, New Zealand; RH, *Exposition of the False Medium and Barriers Excluding Men of Genius from the Public* (London, 1833), fn. 241, 242, henceforth cited as *False Medium*.

AFTER SANDHURST: RH to Pakenham Beatty, June 15, 1883, ML; RH, 'Education of Deformed Children', ms, Iowa State University Library; RH, 'Metaphysical Meditations', unpublished journal, 1823, typescript in my possession copied by E. J. Shumaker from the original in Union Book Shop, New York City, *c.* 1930.

SWIMMING PROWESS: RH (pseudonym), 'The Fine and Froggy Art of Swimming', *Fraser's Magazine*, *26* (1842), 477–86.

THE BYRONIC LEGEND: Peter Quennell, *Byron: The Years of Fame* (Penguin edn, 1954), pp. 193–4.

THE STUDENT: RH, 'Lines to a Dead Linnet by a Solitary Student', *Household Words*, *1* (1850), 447 (according to ms notes in ML the poem was written in late adolescence); RH to his mother, June 24 and August 8, 1826, Iowa State University Library; RH to Elizabeth Barrett, August 27, 1843, Pierpont Morgan Library, NY; RH, 'By-Gone Celebrities of Bond Street', *Harper's Magazine*, *43* (1871), 759–60.

CHARLES WELLS AND HIS CIRCLE: RH, 'Charles Wells', *The London Academy*, April 19, 1879; T. Watts-Dunton, 'Rossetti and Charles Wells, A Reminiscence of Kelmscott Manor', an essay prefacing Charles Wells, *Joseph and his Brethren* (OUP World Classics edn, 1908), pp. xliii–xlix; H-B, February 10, 1873; RH, *False Medium*, pp. 249–50; Robert Gittings, *John Keats: The Living Year* (London, 1954), pp. 120–2; RH (anon.), 'Retrospective Glances', *Monthly Repository*, *9* (1835), 330 (Horne's anonymous and pseudonymous articles are acknowledged in his own copies of the magazine in the State Library of Victoria, Australia); P. P. Howe, *The Life of William Hazlitt* (Penguin edn, 1949), pp. 272–4, 305–12, for discussion on Cockney School; Peter Quennell, *Byron in Italy* (Penguin edn, 1955), pp. 224–5, for discussion of Keats's last years.

CHAPTER 2: THE MISSION REVEALED

SHELLEY'S FUNERAL PYRE: Peter Quennell, *Byron in Italy*, op. cit., p. 204.

HORNE'S SELF-IDENTIFICATION WITH SHELLEY: RH, 'Two Last Canons of Poetic Criticism', p. 25, unpublished ms, ML; Edmund Blunden, *Shelley: A Life Story* (London, 1948), *passim*; RH, 'Ancient Idols', unfinished poem, 1882, ML (the poem's vision of Horne, immortalized beside Shelley, seems to indicate that his worship of Shelley was lifelong).

ATTRACTION TO THE POETIC NATURE: RH, 'The Dreamer and The Worker', *Douglas Jerrold's Shilling Magazine*, *5*, 389–90, and *6*, 498; RH, *False Medium*, has many references to poets of genius and reflects Horne's veneration for them.

AWARENESS OF HIS POETIC NATURE: Percy Shelley, 'A Defence of Poetry', in H. Buxton Forman ed., *Shelley's Works in Verse and Prose* (London, 1880), vol. 7, p. 138; RH, *Miscell.*, op. cit., for Horne's intensive self-examination, particularly of poetic qualities; RH, 'Disquisition on the Genius, Writings, and Character of William Hazlitt', *Monthly Repository*, *9* (1835), 163; RH, 'Sebastiano del Guaradi', unpublished novel, ML, for fictionalized self-examination; RH, Rough Notes on a Projected Biography, ms, ML.

NECESSITY FOR SUFFERING: RH, *Miscell.*; RH, 'Philosophical Poem with Notes', March 1823, ms, ML.

HORNE'S HOPES OF WEALTH: RH to Henry Maule, draft letter, July 18, 1832, ML.

CHAPTER 3: MIDSHIPMAN IN MEXICO

SELF EDUCATION: RH, 'Sebastiano del Guaradi', completed 1826 but begun several years earlier, ms, ML.

MEXICAN EXPEDITION: RH, 'By-Gone Celebrities of Bond Street', *Harper's Magazine*, *43* (1871), 763; RH, 'Extraordinary Sea-Story of a Midshipman', ms, ML; RH (pseud.), 'Mexican Sketches', *Monthly Repository*, *10* (1836), 608–14, 675–80, and *11* (1837), 22–8; C. K. Webster ed., *Britain and the Independence of Latin America*, 1812–30 (London, 1938), vol. 1, 443, and vol. 2, 190, 515; RH, sketchbook, begun at Sandhurst and carried to Mexico and the United States, ML; RH, 'Reflections in a Foreign Country', *The Edinburgh Spectator*, 1832, 2, 30; RH, *Miscell.*, for frequent descriptions of incidents in Mexico and North America, especially his preoccupation with death; RH, 'Scenes from Foreign Lands', ms, ML; RH (anon.), 'Madrid in 1835', *Monthly Repository*, *10* (1836), 538.

TRAVELS THROUGH AMERICA: RH to Harry Edwards, May 15, 1868, Alexander Turnbull Library, N.Z.; RH to his mother, June 24 and August 8, 1826, Iowa State Univesrity Library; RH, poem 'Genius', in *Cosmo de' Medici and Other Poems* (London, 1879), p. 123; RH, *False Medium*, pp. 325–7; RH, *Miscell.*, for Niagara swimming and the fight with the Indian.

CHAPTER 4: FALLEN FRUIT

The basis for much of this chapter is the manuscript of self-probings entitled 'Miscellaneous Thoughts' (abbrev. as *Miscell.*), written in 1829 and preserved in the Mitchell Library.

RETURN VOYAGE: *False Medium*, 327.

STATE OF MIND ON RETURN: *Miscell.*; RH, 'Orpheus', a poem written in 1827 and published in *Monthly Chronicle*, March 1841, together with autobiographical note; RH, 'Homer's Soliloquy', ms poem, ML; RH, 'Hecatompylos' in *Athenaeum*, *1* (1829), 360; RH, 'Erurus or the Wrestling of the Winds' in *Oriental Herald*, *17* (June 1828), (ms in ML).

RELATIONSHIP WITH 'A.': *Miscell.*; RH, unfinished novel, 'In Search of a Wife by a Bachelor of the Inner Temple', 1876, pp. 12–36, ML; RH 'Forget me Not', unpublished poem, ML; William Hazlitt, *Liber Amoris* in vol. 9 of *The Complete Works of William Hazlitt*, ed. P. P. Howe (London 1932).

AFTERMATH OF LOVE AFFAIR: RH, 'Albert Westley' and 'Guardia', unpublished novels, ML; *Miscell.*; William Hazlitt, *Characteristics in the Manner of Rochefoucauld's Maxims*, vol. 9 in Howe edn. of *The Complete Works*.

ROMANTIC VIEW OF POET: I am indebted to the discussions of the Romantic view of art and of the artist in Peter Quennell's biographies, *Byron: The Years of Fame* (Penguin, 1954) and *Byron in Italy* (Penguin, 1955), in M. H. Abrams's *The Mirror and the Lamp: Romantic Theory and the Critical Tradition* (New York, 1953), in J. H. Buckley's *The Victorian Temper: A Study in Literary Culture* (Harvard, 1952), in Mario Praz's *The Romantic Agony* (London, 1933) and in Jacques Barzun's *Romanticism and the Modern Ego* (Boston, 1944).

CHAPTER 5: THE FALSE MEDIUM

HORNE'S INABILITY TO PUBLISH: *Miscell.*

SELF EDUCATION: *False Medium* is virtually a testament of how he educated himself.

VISIT TO HAZLITT'S DEATHBED: RH, obituary of 'Charles Wells', *The London Academy*, April 19, 1879; RH, ms poem 'Scene in a London Lodging House, Homely Epistle sent to the late Thomas Carlyle, on the death of a Man of Letters', ML.

NEGLECT OF GENIUS: RH, 'Elegaic Ode', *Monthly Chronicle*, 1839, *4*, 134–8 (written in 1830); *Miscell.*

IRELAND THE FORGER: RH, 'Dies Sub Coelo', *Monthly Repository*, *9* (1835), 365–92; RH, 'Bygone Celebrities', *The Gentleman's Magazine*, *7* (1871), 468–77.

THE 'TRUE SUN': RH, 'John Forster, His Early Life and Friendships', *Temple Bar*, April 1876, pp. 492–3.

QUARREL WITH MAULE: draft of letter, RH to Henry Maule, July 18, 1832, ML.

INTEREST IN D'ISRAELI: *False Medium*, pp. 20ff.

OBSERVATIONS ON SHELLEY'S LIFE: *False Medium*, esp. pp. 128, 241.

THE PROFESSIONAL AUTHORS: K. J. Fielding, 'Thackeray and the "Dignity of Literature" ', *Times Literary Supplement*, September 19 and 26, 1958. Fielding believes that Bulwer's article in the *New Monthly* in March 1833 inspired *False Medium*, but it should be noted that Horne claims that he had substantially written much of the book before he read Bulwer (p. 288n).

REVIEWS OF 'FALSE MEDIUM': Christopher North, 'Morning Monologues – by An Early Riser', *Blackwood's Magazine*, *34* (1833), 429; W. J. Fox, *Monthly Repository*, new series, *7* (1833), 584n.

CHAPTER 6: CRAVEN HILL

CRAVEN HILL AND ITS PEOPLE: Margaret Howitt ed., *Mary Howitt: An Autobiography* (London, 1889) p. 183; RH, 'Lectures on London Celebrities', ms, ML (for excellent descriptions of Fox and Southwood Smith); Betty

Miller, *Robert Browning: A Portrait* (Penguin edn, 1958), pp. 50ff.; Mary and Charles Cowden Clarke, *Recollections of Writers* (London, 1878); F. A. Hayek, *John Stuart Mill and Harriet Taylor: their correspondence and subsequent marriage* (London and Chicago, 1951); Richard Garnett, *The Life of W. J. Fox* (London, 1910); Horne–Fox ms letters in the Alexander Turnbull Library, Wellington, New Zealand, enable a detailed reconstruction of Horne's relationship to the circle at Craven Hill; RH, 'Alsargis', ms play, ML; RH (anon.), *Spirit of Peers and People: a National Tragi-Comedy, Allegory, and Satire* (London, 1834).

MARY AND MARGARET GILLIES: Lady Lindsay, 'Some Recollections of Miss Margaret Gillies', *Temple Bar, 81* (1887), 265–73; *Notes and Queries*, 12th series, 196 (1923); *The Dictionary of National Biography*, vol. 7, 1247 (it refers to Margaret as the elder sister, but H-B, July 25, 1870, calls Mary the elder Miss Gillies, as does Lady Lindsay, op. cit.); Hayek, op. cit., p. iii; Mary Howitt, 'Reminiscences of My Early Life', *Good Words*, 1886 (cited by Lady Lindsay); ms letters and fragments of letters from Mary Gillies to RH, undated or inadequately dated, ML; ms letter Mary Gillies to RH, February 1838, in my possession; ms commentary on *Cosmo de' Medici*, ML, signed 'P. Y.' ('P. Y.' was Mary Gillies' pet-name; RH marked the envelopes of several of her letters to him by these initials; Leigh Hunt also refers to Mary as 'P-, "Mary I mean" ', B-H, vol. 2, 286.

THE 'MONTHLY REPOSITORY': F. E. Mineka, *The Dissidence of Dissent: The Monthly Repository 1806–38* (University of North Carolina, 1944); Garnett, op. cit.; RH, 'Our Representatives', *Monthly Repository*, new series *11* (1837), 1; H-F, esp. April 25, 1835, February 10, 1836, July 10, 1836, November 1, 1836, April 12, 1837.

LEIGH HUNT AND THE 'REPOSITORY': B-H, vol. 2, 280–96; Hunt to Talfourd, December 9, 1837, ms letter, Harvard College Library; Edmund Blunden, *Leigh Hunt: a biography* (London, 1930), pp. 269ff.

CHAPTER 7: AN UNACTED DRAMATIST

LOSS OF INCOME: H-F, April 12, 1837.

LEIGH HUNT: E. Blunden, *Leigh Hunt*, op. cit., *passim*; B-H, vol. 1, 184–8, vol. 2, 57; P. Quennell, *Byron in Italy*, op. cit., pp. 195ff., *Byron: The Years of Fame*, op. cit., pp. 129–30; RH ed., *A New Spirit of the Age* (London, 1844), vol. 1, ch. 2; RH, 'Leigh Hunt. In Memoriam', *The Southern Cross* (Sydney), December 3 and 10, 1859; Leigh Hunt, *Autobiography* (London, 1850), vol. 2, 269ff (Horne's copy with marginal comments is in Baillieu Library, University of Melbourne); Hunt to RH, August 2 and 5, 1837, State University of Iowa Library.

'COSMO DE' MEDICI': RH, *Cosmo de Medici. An Historical Tragedy* (London, 1837); RH to Forster, March 9, 1844, ML; *The Literary Gazette*, March 25, 1837; *Monthly Repository*, new series, *11* (1837), 191, 250.

HORNE'S THEORIES OF DRAMA: RH, 'An Essay on Tragic Influence' in
Gregory VII. A Tragedy (London, 1840).

MACREADY AND THE STATE OF ENGLISH DRAMA: RH ed., *A New Spirit
of the Age*, op. cit., vol. 2, ch. 5; Allardyce Nicoll, 'The Theatre', in G. M.
Young ed. *Early Victorian England* (London, 1951), vol. 2, 267ff.; Allardyce
Nicoll, *A History of Early Nineteenth Century Drama*, 1800–50 (London,
1930), vol. 1, 171, 205–7; J. C. Trewin, *Mr Macready: a nineteenth-century
tragedian and his theatre* (London, 1955), *passim*; RH, 'John Forster. His
Early Life and Friendships', *Temple Bar*, April 1876.

MACREADY AND 'COSMO': William Toynbee ed., *The Diaries of W. C.
Macready* (London, 1912), entry for March 24, 1839; H-F, undated letter,
beginning 'Accept my best acknowledgements'; RH to Forster, March 9,
1844, ML; RH (anon. pamphlet), *Russian Catechism* (London, 1837), copy in
ML.

BIOGRAPHY OF HAZLITT: RH, introduction to William Hazlitt's *Characteristics: In the Manner of Rochefoucauld's Maxims* (London, 1837); RH,
'Disquisition on the Genius, Writings and Character of William Hazlitt',
Monthly Repository, new series, *9* (1835), 629–36, 742–8; H-F, undated
letter beginning 'God help the young man', and also April 25, 1835; note,
'The late William Hazlitt and R. H. Horne', *Notes and Queries*, *20* (1873),
337.

CHAPTER 8: THE PIT OF TALENT

HORNE'S ATHLETICISM: RH, 'Lectures on London Celebrities', ms, ML.

'DEATH OF MARLOWE': first published in *Monthly Repository*, new series,
9, (1837), 128ff, and then as *The Death of Marlowe. A Tragedy, in One Act*
(London, 1837); Leigh Hunt's review, *Monthly Repository*, new series, *9*
(1837), 365; Landor's comment cited in RH, 'Syllabus of Lectures', pamphlet, 1875, in author's possession; RH to Thomas Talfourd, December 24,
1837, Henry E. Huntington Library.

THOMAS CARLYLE: RH ed., *A New Spirit of the Age*, op. cit., vol. 2, 253ff;
RH, preface to a projected volume of poems, March 1852, ms, ML; Thomas
Carlyle, 'On Heroes, Hero-Worship, and the Heroic in History', published
with *Sartor Resartus* (Everyman edn., 1948), pp. 383ff.

HORNE MEETS CARLYLE: Leigh Hunt to RH, December 8, 1837, Iowa
State University Library; RH to Hunt, December 12, 1837, Hunt mss,
British Museum; RH, 'Thought for Michael Angelo', *Monthly Repository*,
new series, *11* (1837), 422; David Masson, *Memories of London in the Forties*
(Edinburgh, London, 1908), 491; Harriet Martineau, *Autobiography* (London,
1877), vol. 1, 381.

CARLYLE AND HUNT CONTRASTED: RH ed., *A New Spirit of the Age*, op.
cit., vol 2, 278–80.

CARLYLE ADVISES HORNE: Carlyle to RH, February 26, 1838, Yale University Library; Mary Gillies to RH, envelope post-marked February 1838, ms letter in author's possession.

HUNT'S POVERTY: RH, 'Leigh Hunt. In Memoriam', *Southern Cross* (Sydney), December 3, 1859; P. Quennell, *Byron in Italy*, op. cit., p. 212.

TALFOURD: RH ed., *A New Spirit of the Age*, vol. 1, ch. 8; Sylva Norman, *Flight of the Skylark: The Development of Shelley's Reputation* (Oklahoma University Press, 1954), p. 151n.

JOHN FORSTER: RH, 'John Forster. His early life and friendships', *Temple Bar*, April 1876. (An unedited version of the article appeared under the same title in *Appleton's Journal*, *8*, April 1876, 15.) Malcolm Elwin, *Savage Landor* (New York, 1941), p. 301.

CAUSE OF AUTHORS BY PROFESSION: K. J. Fielding, 'Thackeray and the "Dignity of Literature" ', *Times Literary Supplement*, September 19 and 26, 1958.

HUNT PRIVATE LIST: letters between RH and Mrs Hunt 1838–40, Hunt mss, British Museum; RH to Talfourd, July 29, 1839, Harvard College Library; RH to Mrs Hunt, dated November 2, Iowa State University Library; list of subscribers to Leigh Hunt Private List, ML.

HORNE AND THE THEATRE: RH, 'The Burlesque and the Beautiful', *Contemporary Review*, *18* (1871), 394; J. C. Trewin, *Mr Macready*, op. cit., 161; RH (pseud., identifiable at ML), Ephraim Watts, *The Life of Van Amburgh: The Brute Tamer. With Anecdotes of His Extraordinary Pupils* (London, undated); review of *Van Amburgh* in *Monthly Chronicle*, August 1838, p. 84.

GREGORY THE SEVENTH: H-F, September 5 and 12, 1838, April 24, 1840; RH to John Forster, draft letter March 9, 1844, ML; RH, *Gregory VII: A Tragedy* (London, 1840).

HORNE'S VIEWS ON BIOGRAPHY: RH, review of Forster's *Eminent British Statesmen* in *Monthly Repository*, *10* (1836), 461.

BIOGRAPHY OF NAPOLEON: William Hazlitt to RH, December 19, 1838, Baillieu Library, University of Melbourne; Carlyle to RH, December 19, 1838, Baillieu Library, University of Melbourne; RH, 'Napoleon's Remains', poem in *The Monthly Magazine*, third series, *5* (1841), 103; RH ed., *The History of Napoleon* (London, 1841), two vols.

CHAPTER 9: THE CRY WITHIN

GILLIES' CRISIS: RH to Mrs Hunt, July 7, 1839, Hunt mss, British Museum.

VISITS TO FOX AND HUNT: R. Garnett, *The Life of W. J. Fox*, op. cit., 201; Edmund Gosse, *Leaves and Fruit* (London, 1927).

BELL AND 'MONTHLY CHRONICLE': B-H, vol. 1, 36, 124–7; Horne's articles in *Monthly Chronicle* are collected in ML.

MEETING THACKERAY: B-H, vol. 2, 274.

LEIGH HUNT'S AFFAIRS: RH to Hunt, November 1, 1839, Hunt mss, British Museum; RH to Talfourd, July 29, 1839, Harvard College Library.

HORNE'S FINANCES: Hunt to RH, *c.* April 3, 1840, Iowa State University Library.

AT GRAY'S INN: RH, 'John Forster, His Early Life and Friendships', *Temple Bar*, April 1876, p. 496ff; RH, 'Lectures on London Celebrities', ms, ML; D. A. Wilson, *Carlyle on Cromwell and Others, 1837–48* (London, 1925), *passim*, for sharp descriptions of members of Horne's circle.

HORNE AND CARLYLE: RH, introduction to A. W. von Schlegel, *Lectures on Dramatic Art and Literature*, trans. J. Black (London, 1839); Horne-Carlyle correspondence, November 23 and 30, 1839, Yale University Library.

HORNE'S STATE OF MIND: RH to John Forster, March 9, 1844, ML; Thomas Powell, *Living Authors of England* (New York, 1849), p. 221.

THE SYNCRETICS: *Westminster Review*, *41* (1844), 360; B-H, vol. 1, 41ff; RH to Hunt, undated, Hunt mss, British Museum; RH to James Planche, October 29, 1841, Henry E. Huntington Library, California.

CHRISTOPHER NORTH: RH, 'Essay on Tragic Influence Addressed to John Wilson', galley proofs and introductory note in ML; Hunt to RH, February 21, 1840, Iowa State University Library.

HENRY CHORLEY AND 'ATHENAEUM': H. Hewlett ed., *Autobiography, Memoirs and Letters of H. F. Chorley* (London, 1873); B-H, vol. 1, 238; *Athenaeum*, September 5, 1840.

CHAPTER 10: SMOKY SYMBOLS

FACTS VERSUS POETRY: G. M. Young, *Victorian England: Portrait of an Age* (Oxford Paperback, 1960), pp. 33, 47; J. H. Buckley, *The Victorian Temper: A Study in Literary Culture* (Harvard, 1952), chs. 2 and 3; RH ed., *A New Spirit of the Age*, op. cit., vol. 2, 14.

SHELLEY'S INFLUENCE: S. Norman, *Flight of the Skylark*, op. cit., pp. 144ff; H. Buxton Forman ed., *Shelley's Works in Verse and Prose* (London, 1880), vol. 2, 99, for 'A Defence of Poetry'; Mary Gillies to RH, undated ms letter, ML.

CHILDREN IN FACTORIES: RH to Talfourd, undated ms letter, Harvard College Library: RH ed., *A New Spirit of the Age*, vol. 1, ch. 2, for Southwood Smith and Lord Ashley; RH, 'Lectures on London Celebrities', ms, ML, for description of Southwood Smith; RH, 'The Children's Employment Commission', *Douglas Jerrold's Illuminated Magazine*, *1* (1843), 45; 'Reports and Evidence of sub-Commissioners on Children's Employment Commission in

Trade and Manufactures', *Sessional Papers, House of Commons, 30* (1843); B-H, vol. 1, 21.

RECEPTION OF REPORT: RH to Lord Ashley, draft letter, undated, ML; George Gilfillan, *Galleries of Literary Portraits* (Edinburgh, 1856), vol. 1, 193.

CHAUCER MODERNIZED: B-H, vol. 1, 95–127; RH to Hunt, headed 'Loughton Friday', undated, Hunt mss, British Museum; RH to Hunt, three letters (two undated and one October 19, 1840), Iowa State University Library; RH to Thomas Powell, January 9, 1840, Yale University Library.

THOMAS POWELL: T. L. Hood ed., *Letters of Robert Browning, Collected by Thomas J. Wise* (London, 1933), p. 257; RH, ms letter to editor *Daily News*, February 1880, ML, for a long account of his experiences with Powell.

PUBLICATION OF CHAUCER: RH ed., *The Poems of Geoffrey Chaucer, Modernized* (London, 1841); anon. review, *Athenaeum*, February 6, 1841.

THE SYNCRETICS: *Athenaeum*, August 21 and 28, 1841; B-M, pp. 90–1; RH to James Planche, October 29, 1841, Henry E. Huntington Library, San Marino, California; RH to James Planche, copy of ms letter, May 3, 1842, sent to me by E. J. Shumaker (whereabouts of original unknown).

CHAPTER 11: FLOWERS IN A GREENHOUSE

Many parts of chapters 11 to 13 were reconstructed substantially from Elizabeth Barrett's letters to Horne (cited as B-H), to Mary Russell Mitford (cited as B-M), and from the invaluable manuscript collection of Barrett-Horne letters covering the period of their friendship 1839–47 and owned now by the Pierpont Morgan Library, New York. In deference to the wishes of the trustees of that library no direct quotation has been made from the manuscript collection; letters from the collection published in 1877 (B-H) are naturally not included in this prohibition.

EARLY FRIENDSHIP WITH ELIZABETH BARRETT: Betty Miller, *Robert Browning: A Portrait*, op. cit., ch. 2; H-F, April 6, 1840; RH, 'To the Greek Valerian', *Monthly Chronicle, 6* (1840), 141–4.

ELIZABETH'S SELF-ABSORPTION: B-H, vol. 2, 82–3.

HER GRIEF AT BROTHER'S DEATH: B-H, vol. 1, 14.

HORNE'S NERVOUS MOTHER: RH to Elizabeth Barrett, August 27, 1843, Pierpont Morgan Library.

THEME OF 'PSYCHE APOCALYPTE': B-H, vol. 2, ch. 4; B-H, vol. 2, 106.

ELIZABETH'S PRESENTS TO HORNE: B-H, vol. 1, 18, 33, and vol. 2, 83.

HORNE'S AGEING APPEARANCE: Two portraits of Horne, both by Margaret Gillies, were exhibited at the Royal Academy in 1837 and 1846; the latter is in the National Portrait Gallery, London. A copy of what presumably is the 1837 portrait (a miniature) is in Harvard College Library. The miniature corresponds closely with Elizabeth Barrett's description of it on December 6, 1842 (B-M, p. 151), and shows Horne's whiskers which he removed in 1841. This evidence seems to refute Horne's own note on the back of the Harvard copy, saying that it was painted at the time of *Orion* (1843); Horne had written that note in July 1882, when presumably his memory was fading.

'ANCIENT IDOLS': RH, 'Ancient Idols; or The Fall of The Gods', ms epic poem, heavily revised from time to time, versions in ML and Ohio State University Library; RH, 'Lectures on London Celebrities', ms, ML, for description of Schmitz.

SOURCES OF 'ANCIENT IDOLS': A. Humphry House, 'Qualities of George Eliot's Unbelief' in British Broadcasting Corporation's *Ideas and Beliefs of the Victorians* (London, 1949), pp. 151ff; Mary Gillies to RH, letter dated 'Sunday ½ past 3', ML.

MARY GILLIES' OPINION: ms notes by Mary Gillies on version of 'Ancient Idols' in ML.

PROSECUTION OF 'QUEEN MAB': S. Norman, *The Flight of the Skylark*, op. cit., pp. 151–3.

CHAPTER 12: THE FARTHING EPIC

GENESIS OF 'ORION': The most stimulating discussion of *Orion* and the Spasmodics is Jack Lindsay, *George Meredith* (London, 1956), pp. 43ff; RH article discussing conversations with the Hunts and Lewes, in Thornton Hunt's journal *The Leader*, September 1850, cited by E. J. Shumaker's thesis, Ohio State University; Ian Jack, 'The Realm of Flora in Keats and Poussin', *Times Literary Supplement*, April 10, 1959; RH, 'Disquisition on Genius, Writings and Character of William Hazlitt', *Monthly Repository*, new series, *9* (1835), 629.

INTERPRETATION OF 'ORION': RH, 'Brief Commentary', prefacing *Orion: An Epic Poem in Three Books* (London, 1874); RH, 'Preface' to projected volume of poems, 1852, ML (the preface, never published, gives his clearest explanation of *Orion* and of his preoccupation with the struggle between the intellectual and practical).

BRIGHTON INTERLUDE: RH to Hunt, letter May 8, 1843, Hunt mss, British Museum; RH to Elizabeth Barrett, letter May 26, 1843, Pierpont Morgan Library.

CHOICE OF A FARTHING: RH, letter in *Home News*, May 20, 1870, p. 5; RH to Hunt, letter June 3, 1843, Hunt mss, British Museum; RH, 'The Dreamer and The Worker', *Douglas Jerrold's Shilling Magazine*, *6* (1847), 492, for his advice to unpopular poets.

THE FURORE: this is graphically described in letters from Horne to Elizabeth

Barrett, Pierpont Morgan Library, esp. June 9, 15, 22, July 3, 1843; J. H. (James Hingston) in *Once a Month* (Melbourne), *1* (June 15, 1884), 177; Richard Garnett, *The Life of W. J. Fox* (London, 1910), p. 198, for story of 'penn'orth of epics'.

HIS FRIENDS' OPINION OF 'ORION': RH to Elizabeth Barrett, June 15 and 19, 1843, Pierpont Morgan Library; B-H, vol. 1, 57–63; Hunt to RH, June 1, 1843, Leigh Hunt Collection, Iowa State University Library; Mary Gillies, 'Things Present and Things Unseen', *Howitt's Journal*, *3* (1848), 88; Thomas Carlyle's opinion quoted in R. Owen, *The Life of Richard Owen*, vol. 1 (London, 1895), 283.

REVIEWS OF 'ORION': *Westminster Review*, June 1843, cited Eric Partridge, *Orion* (Scholartis Press edn, London, 1928), p. xxix; *Athenaeum* (anon., in fact Elizabeth Barrett), June 24, 1843, p. 583; *Douglas Jerrold's Illuminated Magazine*, *1* (1843), 119–21; *Graham's Magazine* (E. A. Poe), *24* (March 1844), 136–41; RH, 'Preface' to projected volume of peoms, ms, ML, for his dissatisfaction with *Athenaeum* review.

ILLNESS AND FINANCIAL TROUBLE: RH to Elizabeth Barrett, June 19, August 2, 1843, Pierpont Morgan Library.

VISIT TO MISS MITFORD: B-H, vol. 1, 71–9; B-M, vii-xv, 188, 190–1, 193–6; RH to Elizabeth Barrett, August 27, 1843, Pierpont Morgan Library.

CHAPTER 13: THE DISASTROUS MENAGERIE

'NEW SPIRIT OF THE AGE': RH to Elizabeth Barrett, August 2 and 4, 1843, Pierpont Morgan Library; RH to Talfourd, October 5, 1843, Harvard College Library.

HORNE'S CO-AUTHORS: B-H, vol. 1, 132ff; the late Dr E. Shumaker kindly sent me evidence of Powell's assertions on authorship of the various essays, taken apparently from Powell's own annotated copy of *New Spirit*, inscribed 'Thomas Powell, New York, June 1, 1849', present whereabouts unknown. Powell's assertions are denied by Horne in an undated letter to Elizabeth Barrett (letter referring also to meeting with Chorley), Pierpont Morgan Library.

ELIZABETH BARRETT'S FEARS OF DETECTION: RH to Barrett, November 1 and 3, 1843, Pierpont Morgan Library.

HORNE'S ATTACK ON INGOLDSBY LEGENDS: RH ed., *A New Spirit of the Age* (London, 1844), vol. 1, ch. 3; review by W. M. Thackeray (pseud., Michael Angelo Titmarsh), *The Morning Chronicle*, April 2, 1844; Leigh Hunt's comment in margin of his copy of *New Spirit* in Harvard College Library.

HORNE AND ELIZABETH: Horne's confidings about the book, and its essay on Elizabeth, are in the Pierpont Morgan Library Collection, esp. letters, March 15, 21, 1843, February 5, 1844, March 4, 1844.

REVIEWS AND REACTIONS TO 'NEW SPIRIT': R. H. Super, *Walter Savage Landor* (London, 1957), p. 356; D. A. Wilson, *Carlyle on Cromwell and Others*, op. cit., p. 212; G. H. Ford, *Dickens and his Readers* (Princeton, 1955), 265; review (according to Horne, by Harrison Ainsworth) in *Ainsworth's Magazine*, 1844, pp. 317ff; review (according to Horne, by H. Chorley) in *Athenaeum*, 1844, pp. 263, 291ff; anon. review in *Westminster Review*, *41* (1844), 375ff; Thackeray's review in *The Morning Chronicle*, April 2, 1844.

HORNE FEARS MALICIOUS FACTION: RH to Elizabeth Barrett, April 4, 1844, and undated letter headed 'Thursday', Pierpont Morgan Library.

ELIZABETH AND REVIEWS: B-H, vol. 1, 260ff and vol. 2, 17–25;

HORNE MEETS VICTIMS: B-H, vol. 1, 235–6, 259 and vol. 2, 276–9.

INABILITY TO PUBLISH: anon., *The Letters of Robert Browning and Elizabeth Barrett Barrett* (London, 1899), vol. 1, 120; George E. Woodberry, *The Life of Edgar Allan Poe* (New York, 1909), vol. 2, 50–2.

PROPOSED VISIT TO ELIZABETH BARRETT: Horne-Barrett correspondence in Pierpont Morgan Library, esp. postscripts to two consecutive letters by RH, neither dated, but the first referring to meeting with Chorley and therefore possibly June 1844, and also the letters dated July 23 and 27, 1844; the reference to portraits of Elizabeth and Miss Mitford are in the same collection of RH letters, October 17 and 20, 1843; G. H. Taplin, *The Life of Elizabeth Barrett Browning* (Yale, 1957), p. 149; *The Letters of Robert Browning and Elizabeth Barrett Barrett*, op. cit., vol. 1, 315.

CHAPTER 14: MAN AS MAN

IN COLOGNE: RH, 'The Great Fairs and Markers of Europe', *Harper's Magazine*, *46* (1873), 376.

ELIZABETH'S LETTER: E. Barrett to RH, November 7, 1844, Pierpont Morgan Library.

MEETING KINKEL: RH (anon.), 'Gottfried Kinkel', *Household Words*, *2* (1850), 121–5.

CLIMBING ACCIDENT: *The Letters of Robert Browning and Elizabeth Barrett Barrett*, op. cit., vol. 1, 7.

CHILDREN'S LITERATURE: RH (anon.), 'A Witch in the Nursery', *Household Words*, *3* (1851), 601; RH to Joseph Crundall, December 19, 1844, February 10, 17 and 22, 1845, March 2 and 20, 1845, April 18, 1845, May 10 and 28, 1845, July 15 and October 20, 1845, January 26 and May 26, 1846, and several undated letters, Henry E. Huntington Library, San Marino, California.

THE GILLIES CIRCLE: Carl R. Woodring, *Victorian Samplers: William and Mary Howitt* (University of Kansas Press, 1952), pp. 119ff; C. Edmund

Maurice ed., *The Life of Octavia Hill, As Told In Her Letters* (London, 1913), vol. 6, 32; Colbeck Radford and Co., pub., *The Ingatherer* (London), *33* (November 1933), 9, a catalogue of autographed letters and manuscripts.

PUBLICATION OF 'BALLAD ROMANCES' AND 'ORION' EDITION: RH to Charles Ollier, June 30, 1845, Pierpont Morgan Library; RH, *Ballad Romances* (London, 1846); RH, 'A Literary Publisher', *Temple Bar* (February 1880), 243.

THE BROWNINGS AND MISS MITFORD: anon., *The Letters of Robert Browning and Elizabeth Barrett Barrett*, op. cit., vol. 1, 61, 65, 369, 372, 380, 465, 468–9; Thurman L. Hood ed., *Letters of Robert Browning, Collected by Thomas J. Wise*, op. cit., p. 11.

HORNE ON THE 'DAILY NEWS': Edgar Johnson, *Charles Dickens: His Tragedy and Triumph* (London, 1953), vol. 1, 565ff; Dickens to RH, December 5, 1845, British Museum; RH to A. Ireland, November 25, 1845, Folger Shakespeare Library, Washington, D.C.

HORNE IN IRELAND: RH to *Daily News*, ms letters, February 1880, ML; RH, 'Lectures on Ireland', ms, ML; RH (anon.), 'Confessions of a Nervous Soldier; or the Adventures of a Night in County Clare', *Fraser's Magazine*, *38* (1848), 79–90; B-H, vol. 2, 184–5n; H-F, April 9, 1846; RH, 'An Irish Funeral', *Howitt's Journal of Literature and Popular Progress*, *1* (1847), 147; anon., *The Letters of Robert Browning and Elizabeth Barrett Barrett*, op. cit., vol. 1, 364 (see also vol. 2, 301, for RH, 'To the Memory of B. R. Haydon', a poem first published in *Daily News*).

CHAPTER 15: MARRIAGE

HORNE'S LANCASHIRE LECTURES: RH, 'Recollections of the Late W. B. Hodgson, LL.D.', undated ms, ML.

THE HOWITT CIRCLE: C. R. Woodring, *Victorian Samplers: William and Mary Howitt*, op. cit., 115ff; D. F. Mackay, 'The Influence of the Italian Risorgimento on British Public Opinion with Special Reference to the Period 1859–61', thesis, 1958, Oxford University, 89–107.

ELIZABETH'S MARRIAGE: *The Letters of Robert Browning and Elizabeth Barrett Barrett*, op. cit., vol. 2, 394–5, 403; B-H, pp. 182–8.

HORNE'S MARRIAGE: Certified Entry of Marriage, June 17, 1847, General Register Office, Somerset House, London; Death Certificate of Maria Horne, June 5, 1847, Somerset House; RH, 'The Balance of Life', *Howitt's Journal*, *1* (1847), 66; F. G. Kenyon ed., *The Letters of Elizabeth Barrett Browning* (London, 1898), vol. 2, 31–2; RH, 'The Dreamer and The Worker', published as a novel in London in 1851 but originally a serial in *Douglas Jerrold's Shilling Magazine in* 1847 – for specific references see *5*, 389–90 and *6*, 491, 497; RH, 'The Closed Door', ms poem, ML; RH, unfinished draft of letter to Melbourne *Argus*, headed 'The Mock Divorce-Bill', late 1850s but undated, ML; RH, private pocket diary for 1847, ML.

LIFE AT FINCHLEY: H-F (RH to Eliza Fox), November 4, 1847; Margaret Howitt ed., *Mary Howitt, An Autobiography*, op. cit., p. 183; RH, 'King Penguin, A Legend of the South Sea Isles', *Howitt's Journal, 3* (1847), 52–4, 73–6; RH, 'My Second Election Contest', unpublished article, p. 35, ML; B-H, vol. 2, 262–6; printed letter from Currer Bell to RH, December 15, 1847, ML; RH, 'Lectures on Ireland', ms, ML; Walter Dexter ed., *The Nonesuch Dickens: The Letters of Charles Dickens* (Bloomsbury, 1938) vol. 2, 70; RH, 'The Dreamer and The Worker', *Shilling Magazine, 6*, 493; RH, preface to a projected volume of poems, unpublished, 36ff, ML.

HORNE'S POVERTY: W. B. Jerrold, *The Life of Douglas Jerrold* (London, n.d., second edn), pp. 263–4; RH to Leigh Hunt, October 27, 1848, British Museum; Hunt to RH, dated 'Tuesday, ¼ to 4', British Museum; T. L. Hood ed., *Letters of Robert Browning, Collected by Thomas J. Wise*, op. cit., 19–21; B-H, vol 2, 188–94 (this letter by Elizabeth was actually written from Florence, not from Pisa, and was written two years after the 1846 date assigned by the editor of the volume).

MARITAL TROUBLES: RH, 'The Closed Door', unpublished poem, ML; RH, 'Copy of a letter to the First Lord of the Treasury', in H-B, February 1, 1873; RH, 'Lines Addressed to Mary Howitt', *Howitt's Journal, 3* (1848), 400; RH to Leigh Hunt, June 15, 1850, British Museum.

CHAPTER 16: 'FOR I AM FREE'

'JUDAS ISCARIOT': RH, *Judas Iscariot, a Miracle Play in Two Acts* (London, 1848); reviewed in *Athenaeum*, April 20, 1848, and *Howitt's Journal*, May 13, 1848.

PERFORMANCES AT SADLER'S WELLS: RH (written with Charles Dickens), 'Shakespeare and Newgate', *Household Words, 4* (1851), 25–7; RH to Leigh Hunt, February 26 and March 9, 1849, British Museum.

THE POOR ARTIST: RH (anon.), *The Poor Artist, Or, Seven Eye-Sights and One Object* (London, 1850), dedication to Professor Owen; reviewed in *Athenaeum*, January 19, 1850; RH to Leigh Hunt, October 27, 1848, British Museum; W. Dexter ed., *The Nonesuch Dickens: The Letters of Charles Dickens*, vol. 2, 167.

'HOUSEHOLD WORDS' AND DICKENS: Edgar Johnson, *Charles Dickens: His Tragedy and Triumph*, op. cit., vol. 2, 702ff; RH, 'The Dreamer and The Worker', *Douglas Jerrold's Shilling Magazine, 6* (1847), 491–2; B-H, vol. 2, 270–3; for RH contributions to *Household Words* (1850–3) see E. J. Shumaker, *A Concise Bibliography of the Complete Works of Richard Henry (Hengist) Horne (1802–84)*, (Granville, Ohio, 1943). I am also indebted to Mr K. J. Fielding for the same information, derived from the official contributor's register.

QUARREL WITH FORSTER: RH to John Forster, March 9, 1844, ML.
SOCIAL LIFE WITH DICKENS: B-H, vol. 2, 199–261; Edgar Johnson,
Charles Dickens: His Tragedy and Triumph, op. cit., vol. 2, 710, 721, 723ff.
HORNE AT SADLER'S WELLS: RH to William Hazlitt Jr., undated, Berg
Collection, New York Public Library; Gordon S. Haight ed., *The George
Eliot Letters, 1836–80* (Yale, 1955), 2, 487.
MARITAL TROUBLES: H-B, July 27, 1870; Edgar Johnson, op. cit., vol. 2,
748ff.
NEW POETIC SCHEMES: Jack Lindsay, *George Meredith: His Life and Work*
(London, 1956), pp. 31ff; RH to Pakenham Beatty, June 13, 1882, ML;
George Meredith to RH, March 8, 1849, in *Letters from George Meredith to
Richard Henry Horne* (Cape Town, 1919) privately published by M. Buxton
Forman; correspondence between RH and Edmund Ollier, 1850–2, Iowa
State University Library; RH, preface to projected volume of poems, ms,
ML; W. Dexter ed., *The Nonesuch Dickens: The Letters of Charles Dickens*,
op. cit.,vol. 2, 385–7 (see also vol. 2, 227, 229, 280 for Horne's differences with
Wills).
HORNE'S DEPARTURE: William Howitt, 'Notes for an Autobiography', ms
in possession of his descendant, Mrs Mary Walker, Lakes Entrance, Victoria,
Australia; Geoffrey Blainey, *The Rush That Never Ended: A History of
Australian Mining* (Melbourne, 1963), pp. 37–8; RH, 'Voyage to Australia',
ms poem, ML.

CHAPTER 17: THE SEDUCTIVE SHORE

FAREWELLS AND VOYAGE: W. Dexter ed., *The Nonesuch Dickens: The
Letters of Charles Dickens*, vol. 2, 395, 396; RH, 'A Digger's Diary', *Household Words, 6*, 457–62, 545–51, *7*, 125–9, *8*, 6–11 (this is a fictionalized
account of Horne's preparations, voyage, and arrival in Australia); William
and Alfred Howitt, ms letters to Mary Howitt, and notes written on voyage to
Australia, now in possession of Mrs Mary Walker; Eric Partridge, ed.,
introduction p. xii, *Orion* (Scholartis Press, 1928).
FIRST MONTHS IN AUSTRALIA: RH, *Australian Facts and Prospects:
to Which is prefixed the author's Australian autobiography* (London, 1859),
pp. 1–27; Margaret Kiddle, *Caroline Chisholm* (Melbourne, 1950), pp. 80–1;
reminiscences signed J. H., *Once A Month* (Melbourne), September 15, 1884;
William to Mary Howitt, April 1853, ms letter in possession of Mrs Mary
Walker; RH, personal diary for 1853, ML; RH, 'A Digger's Wedding' and
'Canvas Town', *Household Words, 7* (18—), 361–7, 511–12; W. Dexter ed.,
The Nonesuch Dickens: The Letters of Charles Dickens, op. cit., vol. 2, 438,
449–51; RH, *Orion: An Epic Poem in Three Books* (Melbourne, 1855), pp.
v–vii.
HORNE AT WARANGA: RH, *Australian Facts and Prospects*, op. cit., 27–44;

RH, 'Notes on the Report of the Commission of Enquiry on the Goldfields', *The Melbourne Monthly Magazine*, May 1855; RH, personal diary for 1854, ML; on Horne's relations with the Victorian Government there are many valuable files in the Chief Secretary's Archives, State Library of Victoria, Melbourne – esp. the file (Box 281) covering Horne's dismissal from Waranga.

HORNE AND KATE: RH, personal diary for 1854, ML; C. Edmund Maurice, ed., *The Life of Octavia Hill as Told in Her Letters* (London, 1913), pp. 13–21, 30–1, 34; H-B, February 1, 1873 (statement on his marriage, written on July 25, 1870, to First Lord of the Treasury, is enclosed in this letter to Browning).

CHAPTER 18: ADRIFT

SOCIAL LIFE: H. G. Turner, 'Representatives of Literature and Art in the 1850s', ms, State Library of Victoria, esp. 33–4; Geoffrey Serle, *The Golden Age: A History of the Colony of Victoria, 1851–61* (Melbourne, 1963), esp. pp. 353ff; James Blundell to RH, July 28 and August 11, 1854, ML; James Hingston, reminiscence in *Once A Month* (Melbourne), September 15, 1884; C. Gavan Duffy, *My Life In Two Hemispheres* (London, 1898), p. 139; C. Gavan Duffy to RH, November 16 (1856?), Baillieu Library, University of Melbourne; RH, personal diaries for 1855, 1856, 1857, ML; RH to Chief Secretary, July 11, 1856 (no. 56/X5770) Archives, State Library of Victoria.

GARRICK CLUB: *The Age*, October 30, 1855, p. 5; Melbourne *Punch*, 1 (1855), 153.

LOLA MONTEZ: RH, 'My Second Election Contest', ms, p. 34, ML; RH, 'The Fair Chameleon', ms 'burletta', 1855, ML; RH, 'Preliminary Essay to the Poor Artist', ms, 1871, ML.

HORNE'S ELECTION CONTEST: RH (anon.), 'An Election Contest in Australia', *Cornhill Magazine*, 5 (1862), 25–35; RH, *To The Electors of Rodney*, 1856, leaflet, ML; Alfred to Mary Howitt, October 1856, in possession of Mrs Mary Walker; *The Age*, October 8, 1856, p. 7, and October 25, 1856 (letter from 'Reefer').

RELATIONS WITH JESSIE TAYLOR AND KATE: RH, draft of letter to Melbourne *Argus* on 'Mock Divorce-Bill', undated, ML; W. Dexter ed., *The Nonesuch Dickens: The Letters of Charles Dickens*, op. cit., vol. 2, 579, 743, 808; birth certificate of 'Percy Hazlet', February 3, 1857, Government Statist, Melbourne; RH, personal diaries, 1856–8, ML; three receipts, signed RH, for 'nursing baby', August 29, September 12 and 26, 1857, ML; RH, 'Julius', ms poem, ML; H-B, February 1, 1873 (enclosures).

'ANCIENT IDOLS': RH, 'The Fatal Circle', ms poem, ML; Mary Gillies, notes on 'Ancient Idols', sent to RH, March 10, 1859, ML.

AUSTRALIAN FACTS AND PROSPECTS: Frank Fowler, *Southern Lights and Shadows* (London, 1859); Edmund Ollier to RH, February 6, 1860, Iowa State University Library; RH to editor, *The Age*, May 28, 1860; Michie's comment, *The Argus*, December 20, 1859, p. 5.

BOOK REVIEWED: *Athenaeum*, November 26, 1859, p. 701; *Literary Gazette*, February 4, 1860; *New Quarterly Review*, *8* (1859), 412–13.

WATER COMMISSION: *The Argus*, March 25, 1857 (RH letter), January 4, 1860; *The Herald*, March 2, 1861; Melbourne *Punch*, August 26 and September 2, 1858 (cartoon), March 15, 1860.

VINEYARD SCHEMES: documents on Goulburn Valley Vineyard Company, Horne papers, ML; *The Argus*, May 11 and August 4, 17, 1860, February 20, 1861.

THEATRICAL INTERESTS: reviews of *Death of Marlowe* and 'Spec in China', *The Argus*, July 13, 24 and August 4, 1860.

AT ST KILDA: Melbourne *Punch*, February 3, 1859; *The Argus*, January 31 and March 7, 1859, January 9, April 2 and December 3, 1860, January 28 and March 5, 1861; J. B. Cooper, *The History of St Kilda* (Melbourne, 1931), vol. 1, 164ff; RH, 'Parting Souvenir', ms poem, ML.

POVERTY AND WOMEN: RH, personal diaries, 1860–3, ML; H-B, February 1, 1873 (includes copies of RH correspondence with Foggos and his statement on his marriage); RH to Harry Edwards, February 8, 1860, May 15, 1868, Alexander Turnbull Library, NZ; W. Dexter ed., *The Nonesuch Dickens: The Letters of Charles Dickens*, op. cit., vol. 3, 66, 353; *Portland Guardian* (Victoria, Australia), January 30, February 6, February 11 and April 6, 1862, for lecture tours; RH to Robert Bell and to Royal Literary Fund Society, various letters 1861–4, quoted by K. J. Fielding, in *Meanjin Quarterly* (Melbourne) 1954, no. 57, pp. 247ff; K. J. Fielding, 'Charles Dickens and R. H. Horne', *English*, *9* (1952), 17ff; H-B, January 24, 1863, February 10, 1873; RH to Chief Secretary, Victoria, January 21 and 24, 1862, draft letters or ms copies, Iowa State University Library; RH, 'Isolation', ms poem, 1860, ML.

BELFAST ELECTION: RH, 'My Second Election Contest', unpublished ms, ML; C. Gavan Duffy, *My Life In Two Hemispheres*, op. cit., p. 216.

CHAPTER 19: THE BLUE MOUNTAIN

BLUE MOUNTAIN: RH to Royal Literary Fund, February 22, 1864, quoted by K. J. Fielding, *Meanjin Quarterly*, 1954, no. 57, p. 251; *The Argus*, June 23 and August 1, 1863; RH, 'Blue Mountain Goldfield', ms article, ML; RH, *Prometheus, The Fire-Bringer* (Edinburgh 1864, Melbourne 1866), especially 'dedication', v; RH, 'The Blue Mountain Exile', *All The Year Round*, 1865, *13*, 275; reviews of *Prometheus* in *Athenaeum*, July 8, 1865; *Bell's Life in Victoria*, November 4, 1865, and Melbourne *Australasian*, December 16, 1865.

MELBOURNE VISITS: RH to G. G. McCrae, dated 'May 14', ML; Brian Elliott, *Marcus Clarke* (Oxford, 1958), pp. 68, 85, 105; A. Patchett Martin, 'Orion Horne in Australia', *Academy*, March 29, 1884, p. 223; discussion of new aims in Australian literature in *The Colonial Monthly* (Melbourne), December 1868; RH to Harry Edwards, May 15, 1868, Alexander Turnbull Library, NZ; Alfred to Anna Mary Howitt, undated, in possession of Mrs Mary Walker; RH, personal diaries for 1863–9, ML.

HIS WORK PERFORMED: RH, *South Sea Sisters*, a lyric masque (Melbourne, 1866); *The Argus*, May 8 (p. 5) and October 25 (p. 7), 1866; *The Australian Monthly Magazine*, *3* (1866), 75, 234; RH, *Galatea Secunda*, an odaic cantata (Melbourne, 1867), and reviewed in *The Argus*, January 3, 1868.

HORNE'S DAUGHTER: RH, personal diaries for 1866–7, ML.

JOHN FERNCLIFF: RH to G. G. McCrae, ms letters, February 14, March 2, November 12 and 16, December 13, 1867, January 1 and 25, February 11 and 21, March 14 and 19, April 30, October 27 and 30, November 14, 1868, ML; RH to H. T. Dwight, ms letters, July 17, August 15, 19, 21, 24, 28 and 29, September 2, 14 and 19, October 3, November 12, 1867, February 7, 1868, Baillieu Library, University of Melbourne.

FURTHER WRITINGS: RH, 'Unknown Seas or Thoughts on the Future Life and Death of the Soul', ms dated 1866–7, ML; RH, 'John the Baptist', ms dated 1868, ML (published in *Bible Tragedies* (London, 1881)).

AMERICAN PLANS: RH to Harry Edwards, May 15 and November 21, 1868, Alexander Turnbull Library, NZ.

PREPARATIONS FOR DEPARTURE: RH to Chief Secretary, files T2041, T2786, 1869, Archives, State Library of Victoria; RH, 'Portraits and Memoirs', *Macmillan's Magazine*, 22 (1870), 359, for his sense of isolation; printed catalogue of Horne's library, 1869, ML; 'Sales by Auction' notice in *The Argus*, May 20, 1869; George Gordon McCrae, ' "Orion" Horne, 1869', *Southerly* (Sydney), *7* (1946), 14–17; RH to editor, *Ballarat Star* (Victoria), June 9, 1869; James Hingston in *Once A Month* (Melbourne), September 15, 1884.

CHAPTER 20: THE MISSION TRIUMPHANT

VOYAGE AND HOMECOMING: John Ferguson ed., *Lady Jocelyn's Weekly Mail* (London, Melbourne, 1869); RH (pseud.), 'New Arrivals' . . . By an Absentee of Seventeen Years, *Gentleman's Magazine*, *6* (1871), 119–35; RH, 'Portraits and Memoirs', *Macmillan's Magazine*, 22, (1870), 359–71; B-H, vol. 2, 50–2; 'The Journal of Benjamin Moran', entry for February 6, 1873, cited in *Modern Language Notes*, 1951, p. 323; H-B, July 25 and 27, December 7, 1870; K. J. Fielding, 'Charles Dickens and R. H. Horne', *English*, *9* (1952), 18–19.

LONDON SOCIAL LIFE: C. W. Stoddart, *Exits and Entrances* (Boston, 1903), 175–88; Edmund Gosse, 'Orion Horne' in *Portraits and Sketches* (London, 1912); H. Buxton Forman, 'Brief Account of R. H. Horne' in W. R. Nicoll and T. J. Wise ed., *Literary Anecdotes of Nineteenth Century*, op. cit., vol. 2; T. J. Wise pub., *Letters from Algernon Charles Swinburne to Richard Henry Horne* (London, 1920); F. Collins, *Mortimer Collins: his letters and friendships* (London, 1877); RH to Alexander Strahan, January 7, 1874, New York Public Library; RH to Harry Edwards, May 28 and June 28, 1873, Alexander Turnbull Library, NZ; M. Buxton Forman pub., *Letters from George Meredith to Richard Henry Horne* (Cape Town, 1919), letters 4 and 5.

SCOTTISH LECTURE TOUR: RH, 'Recollections of the late W. B. Hodgson', 18–27, ms, ML; Sir David Masson to Ernest Scott, August 19, 1928, in author's possession.

PENSION CLAIM AND SENSE OF PERSECUTION: printed petition, forwarded in 1872, *To The Right Honourable W. E. Gladstone, MP, First Lord of The Treasury*, ML; H-B, August 9, September 24, November 14 and 25, 1872, February 1, 8, 10 and 24, May 24, June 10, 1873 (these letters continue through 1873–4, touching sundry topics and particularly the publication of Elizabeth Barrett's letters to Horne); T. L. Hood ed., *Letters of Robert Browning, Collected by Thomas J. Wise*, op. cit., p. 164.

THE LENNOX CASE: collection of documents relating to the alleged assault, including RH to James Horne, November 18, 1874, James Horne to RH, January 9, 1875, newspaper clippings of January 1875 *Eastbourne Chronicle*, and copy of memorial signed by Horne's friends, ML; H-B, November 21 and 27, 1874, January 6, 1875; RH (pseud., identifiable at ML), *Sithron, The Star-Stricken* (London, 1883).

PROPOSED LECTURE TOUR OF USA: tour announced, *The London Academy*, January 15, 1876; W. J. Linton to RH, February 8, 1876, RH to W. J. Linton, June 10, 1876, Yale University Library; RH to Harry Edwards, February 1, 1881, Alexander Turnbull Library, NZ.

POVERTY AND FAILING STRENGTH: RH to Mrs M. Collins, April 19 and November 28, 1881, ML; H-B, August 3, 1883; RH to Pakenham Beatty, ms letters, 1879–82, ML.

LAST LITERARY PROJECTS: RH to editor *Daily News*, draft letter, February 1880, ML; RH, 'Two Last Canons of Poetic Criticism', ms, ML; RH to W. J. Linton, June 21, 1882, Yale University Library; RH, 'Smile at Annihilation', ms poem, New York Public Library; RH, *The Last Words of Cleanthes* (London, 1883); RH, 'Euthanasia', typescript of poem copied by E. J. Shumaker, whereabouts of original unknown; RH, rough drafts and notes for volume of autobiographical poems, ML.

LAST DAYS AND DEATH: Mrs Spratling to E. J. Shumaker, September 23 and October 7, 1934 (written by the daughter of Horne's landlady and describing his last illness), in author's possession; James Horne to Mrs M. Collins, March 15, 1884, ML; Melbourne *Argus*, March 17, 1884; *Athenaeum*, March 15 and 22, 1884; RH, last will and testament, February 6, 1884, Somerset House.

SELF EPITAPH: RH, 'Ancient Idols', last draft, May and June 1882, ms, ML.

Index